A Devotional Study of
Luke and John

The Man
and
Your God

Warren Henderson

All Scripture quotations are from the New King James Version of the Bible, unless otherwise noted. Copyright © 1982 by Thomas Nelson, Inc. Nashville, TN

The Man and Your God – A Devotional Study of Luke and John

By Warren Henderson
Copyright © 2025

Cover Design: Ben Bredeweg
Editing/Proofreading: David Lindstrom, Dan Macy

Published by Warren A. Henderson
1025 Iron Cap Dr.
Stevensville, MT 59870

Perfect Bound ISBN: 978-1-939770-78-3
eBook ISBN: 978-1-939770-79-0

ORDERING INFORMATION:
Copies of *The Man and Your God* are available through various online retailers worldwide.

Table of Contents

LUKE   **1**

Luke	3
Luke Chapter 1	15
Luke Chapter 2	27
Luke Chapter 3	37
Luke Chapter 4	44
Luke Chapter 5	53
Luke Chapter 6	61
Luke Chapter 7	70
Luke Chapter 8	78
Luke Chapter 9	88
Luke Chapter 10	105
Luke Chapter 11	112
Luke Chapter 12	126
Luke Chapter 13	136
Luke Chapter 14	148
Luke Chapter 15	155
Luke Chapter 16	159
Luke Chapter 17	167
Luke Chapter 18	174
Luke Chapter 19	181
Luke Chapter 20	189
Luke Chapter 21	197
Luke Chapter 22	206
Luke Chapter 23	224
Luke Chapter 24	233

JOHN   **241**

John	243
John Chapter 1	259

JOHN CHAPTER 2	272
JOHN CHAPTER 3	277
JOHN CHAPTER 4	286
JOHN CHAPTER 5	294
JOHN CHAPTER 6	301
JOHN CHAPTER 7	315
JOHN CHAPTER 8	323
JOHN CHAPTER 9	330
JOHN CHAPTER 10	335
JOHN CHAPTER 11	344
JOHN CHAPTER 12	349
JOHN CHAPTER 13	359
JOHN CHAPTER 14	366
JOHN CHAPTER 15	375
JOHN CHAPTER 16	384
JOHN CHAPTER 17	389
JOHN CHAPTER 18	397
JOHN CHAPTER 19	406
JOHN CHAPTER 20	416
JOHN CHAPTER 21	424
ENDNOTES	**429**

The Cover

Angelic beings testify of God's greatness (Ps. 103:20-22). These include cherubim, seraphim, and the four living creatures in heaven who reflect various glories of Christ while concealing their own intrinsic beauty with their wings. For example, the faces of these powerful creatures depict Christ as exemplified in each of the four Gospels. The *lion* is the king of the beasts, which reflects Matthew's perspective of Christ as being the legitimate King to sit on David's throne. The *ox*, as a beast of burden, is harnessed for the rigors of serving, and pictures Mark's presentation of Christ as Jehovah's lowly Servant. The face of the *man* portrays Luke's theme of the Lord's humanity. Lastly, the *eagle* flies high above all the other creatures to declare Christ's deity, which is John's theme.

Luke

Luke

Introduction

One night on a lonely hillside, some 2000 years ago, shepherds were dazzled by the sudden appearance of an angel, and then a whole host of angels praising God. Their heralded message was profound: *"Fear not: for, behold, I bring you good tidings of great joy, which shall be* **to all people***. For unto you* **is born** *this day in the city of David* **a Savior, which is Christ the Lord***"* (2:10-11; KJV). Through birth, Jesus Christ became connected with all people as the Savior. Man could not make Him a Savior; He was born Savior of the world. Through His birth, Christ's humanity was established – a link *"to all people."* As a man, He would likewise experience all the pangs of living on a cursed planet and, before dying, feel the very condemnations He, Himself, had imputed to humanity in the Garden of Eden. Luke skillfully captures the anguish of these aspects of the Lord's life.

Luke, as Andrew Jukes puts it, is the writer who "sees Christ as the Son of Adam or the Son of Man, not so much connected with a kingdom, or the Servant of God, [but] as the One whose sympathies as a Man linked Him with Adam's fallen and ruined children."[1]

William Kelly beautifully describes the theme of Luke's Gospel:

> The Holy Ghost undertakes to show us Christ as the one who brought to light all the moral springs of the heart of man, and at the same time the perfect grace of God in dealing with man as he is; therein, too, the divine wisdom in Christ which made its way through the world, the lovely grace, too, which attracted man when utterly confounded and broken down enough to cast himself upon what God is.[2]

The Author

"The beloved physician," as Paul calls Luke, was Paul's companion on many missionary journeys. Luke handles detail meticulously. Besides his conversations with Paul and other apostles, his keen eye notes many details that are simply passed over in the other Gospels. He is the only

Gentile writer in all of Scripture and the only one to write a Gospel sequel, the book of Acts. His authorship is soundly confirmed through the information and style of Acts.

The Date

Luke accompanied Paul on various missionary journeys into Asia Minor and Europe and was with Paul during his conveyance to Rome as a prisoner in 60 A.D. (Acts chs. 27-28). Luke closes the book of Acts by reporting that Paul was under house arrest in Rome for two years (Acts 28:30). Luke's record of early Church history concludes in 62 A.D., just a few years prior to the burning of Rome, Paul's and Peter's executions, and then the destruction of Jerusalem and the temple in 70 A.D.

If Luke had been writing his gospel account or the book of Acts after these events, he would have certainly mentioned them. Additionally, Luke, being with Paul until the time of his death in 67 A.D. (2 Tim. 4:11), would have undoubtedly included information about Paul's final days. As the book of Luke preceded the writing of the book of Acts (Acts 1:1), and the book of Acts concluded in about 63 A.D., a date of 61 to 62 A.D. for the writing of Luke's Gospel is reasonable.

The Gentile Flavor

The Gospel of Luke was written by a Gentile and to a Gentile audience. Paul clearly distinguishes Luke from "those of the circumcision." Because Luke's Gospel has a non-Jewish flavor, there are certain details and narratives in *Luke* are not mentioned in *Matthew*, *Mark*, and *John*. We observe both that a Gentile character named Theophilus is mentioned in Luke's introduction and Luke's objective of delivering a full and accurate account of the life of the Lord Jesus Christ (1:1-4).

Twice in the opening sentence, Luke announces that he is declaring, in an "orderly" means, what he knows to be truth from the testimonies of multiple eyewitnesses. (He does not specifically refer to Matthew and Mark.) Luke's personal compulsion to proclaim what he knew to be true would then be guided, arranged, and constrained by the Holy Spirit to present an "orderly" account of the humanity of Christ *"from the beginning."* This focus is why Luke provides such an in-depth account of the conception and birth of Christ – his foundation of the humanity of Christ is like no other.

Orderly does not necessarily mean chronological, but it does mean that he has organized the pertinent historical, political, moral, and spiritual content in a way which best relates to the human aspects of Christ's life and teachings. Sometimes teachings and narratives will be grouped together to provide an orderly presentation of a spiritual theme or to highlight human emotions or motives rather than to maintain chronological completeness. For example, the genealogy of Christ in chapter 3 seems out of place. Matthew begins with pedigree to prove royal lineage, but Luke waits thirty years to note the genealogy of Christ. Why did Luke wait so long to address the lineage of Christ?

Christ entered into a season of prayer promptly after His baptism. At that time, the Holy Spirit descended upon Him in the form of a dove, and the Father Himself declared from heaven, *"You are My beloved Son; in You I am well pleased"* (3:22). Luke then injects the lineage of Christ to show that, though He came from a "seed of the woman," He was a representative of Adam on earth. The genealogy ends with *"the son of Adam, the son of God"* (3:38). Where the first Adam failed, the Second, rather the Last, Adam would not. Immediately after this divine proclamation, the evil tempter assaulted the Lord for forty days. The Last Adam, the Son of God, triumphed over Satan – His righteous and holy character had been thoroughly proven. Luke waits two chapters to introduce the genealogy of Christ so that He might introduce his audience to the Last Adam, who was not human in the same way we are but was proven to be sinless and perfect. Jesus Christ was God's replacement representative for the first Adam (Rom. 5:12-21).

Not only is Luke the only Gentile writer in Scripture, but he also addresses both of his written works, Acts being the other, to his Greek friend Theophilus. Luke's personalized salutation acquaints us immediately with a strong appeal to "human affection" which will characterize his Gospel. Theophilus means "beloved of God," and Luke's salutation serves as a testimony that the Gentiles are loved of God. Mark wrote to the Romans, but Luke is setting forth an appeal to the Greeks concerning Christ. The Greeks prided themselves on intellectual observations and sought to apply knowledge and improve themselves (1 Cor. 1:22). They would be very interested in Luke's presentation of the "perfect" man and in a writing style that was well ordered and full of detail.

Besides the introduction, mentioned above, the following portions of Luke's Gospel are distinctly Gentile in application:

Only Luke makes mention of the Gentile aspects of the ministries of Elijah and Elisha: *"Elijah was sent to Zarephath, in the **region of Sidon**, to a woman who was a widow. And many lepers were in Israel in the time of Elisha the prophet, and none of them was cleansed except **Naaman the Syrian**"* (4:26-27).

The parable of "**The Good Samaritan**" is only found in Luke (Luke 10). It is the story of a Gentile who loved his needy neighbor. The hard-hearted religious Jews of the day had no compassion for the injured man, but those whom the Jews considered "dogs" showed love.

On one occasion, the Lord healed ten lepers (nine Jews, and **one Samaritan**). The nine Jews thought their religion (the temple) was more important than thanking the One who had healed them. Not so for the Samaritan, he alone turned back to *"give glory to God."* Ten lepers were cleansed, but only one Gentile was saved that day (17:17-19).

On the Tuesday before He was crucified, the Lord Jesus led His disciples up the Mount of Olives to provide final instructions and to preview the details of the forthcoming Tribulation Period with them. During this discourse, the Lord declared that *"Jerusalem shall be trampled by **the Gentiles** until the times of the Gentiles be fulfilled"* (21:24). The other Gospels do not record this detail, though many of the prophets in the Old Testament, such as Ezekiel, Joel, and Zechariah, do.

During the same dissertation, the Lord also mentioned, *"Look at the fig tree, **and all the trees**"* (21:29). Matthew only mentions the fig tree, which represents religious Israel (Jer. 24) and is distinct from political Israel (represented by a vine – 20:10; Isa. 5:2), which became a reality in May 1948. The Lord stated that the generation who sees religious Israel come alive again (represented in leaves on the tree, but no fruit; 13:6-9), would see the coming of the Lord. An accompanying sign was the birth of many new nations (pictured in the appearance of many trees).

Luke provides a wide-angle snapshot of the **Gentile political system of the day**. The other Gospel writers mostly ignore these details. For example, Luke informs us that Augustus was Caesar and Quirinius was governor of Syria at the time of Christ's birth (2:1-2). When Christ began His ministry at thirty years of age, Tiberius was Caesar, and Pontius Pilate was governor of Judea (3:1). After disclosing the names and offices of Gentile authorities, he then documents those Jewish civil and religious leaders who served under Gentile rule: Herod, Philip and Lysanias were tetrarchs, and Annas and Caiaphas were high priests (3:1-2).

The Personal Element

In Matthew, a star guided the magi, and Joseph received divine direction through the impersonal medium of dreams. Not so in Luke's account. An angel appeared to Zacharias while he was performing his priestly duties in the holy place of the temple. The two of them engaged in a face-to-face discussion, and the angel provided prophetic revelation to Zacharias concerning John the Baptist and the coming Messiah. This communication was all done through normal speech. Because Zacharias sought a sign to validate the message, he was smitten mute by the angel until after John's birth. Apparently, there are both advantages and disadvantages to direct personal communication with God's angels.

In the same chapter, the angel Gabriel speaks with Mary in her own home concerning the conception and birth of the Messiah. The home setting, the personal greeting (from an angel who identifies himself by name), and the tender dialogue entreats human sentiment to fully identify with the scene. Whether it be through the voices of Zacharias, Anna, Simeon, individual angelic messengers, or an angelic host praising God on a hillside, divine announcements to mankind are much more personal and less aloof in Luke than they are in Matthew.

Luke often is more specific in identifying the humanness of key characters associated with Christ's miracles and teachings than the other Gospel writers. Two examples will suffice to demonstrate this tendency. In the account of the healing of the leper, Luke specifically notes that *"a man who was full of leprosy"* came to Christ (5:12). Matthew, however, describing the same incident wrote, *"a leper came"* (Matt. 8:2). In the healing of the demon-possessed man, Luke states, *"there met Him **a certain man** from the city who had demons for a long time"* (8:27), but

Matthew refers to this man by using the pronoun "he" instead of the more familiar and personal identification (Matt. 8:28).

Systematic and Meticulous Presentation

Luke's Gospel is less chronological than Mark's and John's, but perhaps more systematic in presentation than any of the Gospel accounts. Like Matthew, Luke contains a distinct shift in the Lord's ministry after His transfiguration. David Gooding highlights the natural twofold advance of Luke's presentation of Christ:

> Luke's inspired presentation of Christ is arranged in two great movements: first the "Coming" of the Lord from heaven to earth; and then His "Going" from earth to heaven. The turning point between them stands at chapter 9 verse 51. An unforgettable scene marks the beginning of the "Coming": when Mary and Joseph arrive in Bethlehem to have their names registered in the census-lists of the world-empire, there is no room in the inn for the world's Savior to be born. Nonetheless the "Coming" ends in glory: at the transfiguration Christ appears supreme and central in the coming universal kingdom of God. An equally unforgettable scene marks the beginning of the "Going" (see Luke 9:51-56): certain Samaritans refuse to receive Him into their village.... Appropriately, the climax of the "Going" shows the man, Jesus, rejected and crucified on the earth, but now risen and ascending, being received up into glory.[3]

Luke was also meticulous with recording the names of cities and geographic regions and their respective governors. Between the books of Luke and Acts, Luke names thirty-two countries, fifty-four cities, and nine islands without error. N. Sherwin White comments on this astounding fact: "For Acts the confirmation of historicity is overwhelming... Any attempt to reject its basic historicity must now appear absurd. Roman historians have long taken it for granted."[4]

Key Words

As mentioned previously, Luke stresses the title theme of "Son of Man" in his Gospel to distinctly focus his audience on the humanity of Christ and how He related to mankind in fulfilling His sacrificial mission. The Lord Jesus was born to suffer and die. For comparison,

Luke refers to this title twenty-five times, while John has twelve occurrences.

Another key phrase in Luke is "all the people." It is found twice in Matthew, thrice in Mark, and once in John, but eleven times in Luke. In His birth and in His baptism, He was identified with "all the people." Frequently in His preaching and in His miracles, He was identified with "all the people." The writer of Hebrews states that He *"tasted death for every man"* (Heb. 2:9; KJV). He was truly a man of the people and for "all the people."

Matthew wrote of the "kingdom of heaven" thirty-three times in his Gospel, while only referring to the "kingdom of God" five times. Luke is nearly opposite this representation with thirty-three occurrences of the "kingdom of God" and no mention of the "kingdom of heaven." Certainly, the hierarchical presentation of Christ as king, versus a man, cascades into the decision of submission. The "kingdom of heaven" presents a choice, whereas the "kingdom of God" more closely acknowledges man's dependence upon a sovereign God. The Lord told the Jews that the "kingdom of God" was in the midst of them, but they did not recognize it; therefore, it would not come visibly but would continue in its invisible, spiritual form until Christ's Second Advent to the earth (17:20-21).

Four key words in Luke clearly express the manifold purpose of the Father sending His Son to planet Earth. Through Christ, God would bless mankind with mercy, peace, and joy.

Term	Matthew	Mark	Luke	John
Blessed (Bless)	19	7	30	2
Peace	9	2	10	0
Mercy	6	8	19	6
Joy	6	0	11	8
Total	**40**	**17**	**70**	**16**

The Son of Man

Who better than a physician to speak of the humanity of Christ? Not only does Luke show us the moral beauty and perfection of Christ, but he also reveals to us the frailties of His humanness. Luke presents to us a touchable Savior, who desires to touch others with compassion and kindness.

"The Son of Man" is an Old Testament term to express human association and, thus, links Christ to earth as a man. As stated in the previous section, Luke applies the title to the Lord Jesus twenty-five times in his Gospel, while, in contrast, John, whose theme is the deity of Christ, only refers to the Lord as the Son of Man twelve times. The Lord Jesus spoke more often of Himself as "the Son of Man" than as "the Son of God," for the title identified His mission and not His essence. It is noted that only the Lord Jesus speaks of Himself as "the Son of Man" in the Gospels, some eighty-four times; yet, there are fourteen references to "others" identifying the Lord Jesus as the "Son of God," a title He applies to Himself only five times (all occurrences are rightly placed in John). The Lord normally spoke of His humble station and ministry, while others were privileged to acknowledge His divine rule and essence.

One of the early references in the Bible to the "Son of Man" is found in Psalm 8. This Psalm is then quoted in the epistle to the Hebrews and applied to speak of the incarnation of Christ. The title "Son of Man" is not found in any New Testament epistle, except for the one reference in Hebrews 2:6-9, which refers to Psalm 8. The epistles are books of wisdom given to the church to understand the great mysteries of God, which were before hidden in the recesses of God's mind. The Church, in Christ, has a heavenly, not an earthly, calling. The Lord Jesus will always be a man, but now He is highly exalted and at the right hand of God in heaven. Hence, it would be inappropriate to address Him personally as the "Son of Man." This is why the expression is not found in the epistles, save once in Hebrews as an explanation of Psalm 8. Christ finished that mission to earth, and consequently, at the pleasure of the Father, now has a name above all names.

The Unique Conception and Birth of Christ

What are miracles? Everything mankind has observed in creation he has sought to characterize by rules of order. Conservation of energy and motion, laws of gravity and thermodynamics and the like represent our knowledge of creation based on observation. Therefore, God has to cause some non-regularities in our ordered world in order to call our attention to the fact that there is an outside influence to be reckoned with – the Creator.

Such were the births of Isaac, John the Baptist, and Jesus Christ. Before each miracle (an irregularity in an ordered system) occurred, Scripture records that the people understood the natural order that was in place. These were not ignorant people. They knew how babies were made and when procreation could no longer happen. If they had not known these things, no miracle would have been recognized, and God would have received no glory in doing it. In the case of Sarah and Elizabeth, they both were past menopause and physically incapable of bearing children (1:18, 36; Gen. 18:11). In the case of Mary, the mother of Jesus, she was a virgin (1:34). So, it is really thanks to science that we have the wherewithal to actually recognize the hand of God in our lives! Without the understanding of order, we would not be able to recognize a miracle when one occurs. Luke is very careful to document the "order" of things, so we might better recognize the divine miracle of the incarnation of Christ.

The conception and birth of the Lord Jesus was "unique." There is no patient confidentiality in this matter; Luke provides a full medical report for all to read:

1. The conception of Christ was through the power of the Holy Spirit (1:35).

2. The conception of Christ did not involve any man (1:34).

3. The conception of Christ took place in the womb; normally, conception occurs in the fallopian tubes and then the embryo later attaches to the womb (1:31).

4. The conception of Christ would never be repeated again, for the Lord Jesus, the Last Adam, need only suffer once for sin (Heb. 10:10-18), and He would rule over the house of Israel *forever* (1:33).

5. The conception of Christ resulted in a virgin giving birth to *"the Son of the Highest"* (1:27, 1:32, 1:34).

The first three humans to walk upon this planet entered the world in different ways: Adam became a living soul after God breathed a spirit into a heap of dust gathered from the earth. Eve was created from materials taken from Adam's side. Cain was a product of human procreation. The Lord Jesus entered the world by a fourth means, a virgin birth. The means by which one enters the world does not determine if one is human or not, for Adam, Eve, Cain and Jesus Christ were all human, but Christ was of a different spiritual nature than any other, for He did not come from Adam.

The Unique Humanity of Christ

Satan was defeated at Calvary (John 12:31) and further humiliated at the resurrection of Christ (Eph. 1:19-21). His only recourse since those triumphant events has been to cast doubt upon the work of Christ and to defame His person and character. Satan and his worldly domain hate the Lord Jesus and will go to any extreme to slander Him and to discourage and frustrate those who desire to live for Christ (John 15:18-19). Any teaching which undermines the divine person and the moral perfection of Christ is an attack at the very foundation of the Christian faith; if no flawless Christ, if no divine nature – then no salvation. The Lord Jesus said, *"if you do not believe that I am [He], you will die in your sins"* (John 8:24). Note: *He* in the "I am" statement is not in the Greek text.

There are various erroneous teachings concerning the person of Christ. Some say Christ is not fully God, nor fully man. Others teach that Christ became some hybrid creature, a created being, between God and man, but neither God nor man. This view, commonly held among many cults today, is one that Paul confronts in the book of Colossians. Yet, others see a schizophrenic Jesus, someone with a dual personality, who switches back and forth in personality and natures. Christ is not diminished deity added to a human personality; God literally and personally became a human, without emptying Himself of any divine attributes (John 1:14). This issue will be discussed more thoroughly in the study of John's Gospel.

"Great is the mystery of Godliness. God was manifest in the flesh" (1 Tim. 3:16). Christ was fully man, but He had a unique human nature, different from our nature. Because there is no definite article in the Greek before "flesh," this verse is better rendered, as John Darby translates it, *"God has been manifested in flesh."*[5] God was manifest "in flesh," not "in the flesh." The Lord Jesus was veiled in flesh (Heb. 10:20); He was made flesh (John 1:14) but was not in the flesh – the nature of His flesh did not rule Him; it served Him. His flesh had not been invaded by the corruption of sin.

Paul explains the difference: *"What the law could not do in that it was weak through **the flesh**, God sending His own Son **in the likeness of sinful flesh**"* (Rom. 8:3; KJV). The same Greek word *homoioma*, translated as "likeness" in this verse, is also applied in Philippians 2:7, which states that Christ *"was made in the likeness of men."* The word "likeness" in both verses means "resemblance" or "form." Humanly speaking, His form was that of a man, but He was more; He also possessed a divine nature. The Lord looked like everyone else, but He didn't act like everyone else. His life was unique, for *"in Him is no sin"* (1 Jn. 3:5); He *"knew no sin"* (2 Cor. 5:21); and He *"did no sin"* (1 Pet. 2:22).

Speaking of Christ, the writer of Hebrews declares the matter frankly, *"who **being the brightness of His [God's] glory**, and **the express image of His [God's] person**, and upholding all things by the word of His power, when He had by Himself purged our sins, sat down on the right hand of the Majesty on high"* (Heb. 1:3; KJV). It was needful for Christ to be veiled in flesh, or mankind would have been consumed by the direct presence of Almighty God. The veil of flesh allowed Christ to outshine the direct moral glory of God to the World. J. B. Phillips wrote: "Christ is the aperture through which the immensity and magnificence of God can be seen."[6] When you looked upon the Lord Jesus, you would see the form of a man, with the character of God shining through. Mark the words of Christ to Philip:

> *Philip said to Him, "Lord, show us the Father, and it is sufficient for us." Jesus said to him, "Have I been with you so long, and yet you have not known Me, Philip? He who has seen Me has seen the Father; so how can you say, 'Show us the Father'? Do you not believe that I am in the Father, and the Father in Me? The words that I speak to you I do not speak on My own authority; but the Father who dwells in Me does the works"* (John 14:8-10).

As stated previously, Christ was fully human but had a different spiritual nature than Adam. According to Ecclesiastes 7:29, Adam was made "upright" or "innocent." Until Adam sinned, he reflected the character of God, for he bore God's image and likeness (Gen. 1:26). Adam was God's representative of Himself in creation before the fall of man (Heb. 2:6-8). After Adam had sinned, he no longer bore the likeness of God, but his own likeness (Gen. 5:3). The Last Adam, Christ, was not just *innocent humanity,* as Adam was; He was *holy humanity* (1:35). *"For in Him dwells all the fullness of the Godhead bodily"* (Col. 2:9). Nowhere in scripture do we read of Adam being "holy." God was not in Adam, but *"God was in Christ, reconciling the world to Himself"* (2 Cor. 5:19).

When Adam sinned, he made a transition from *innocent humanity* to *condemned humanity* and was cursed by God. Everyone coming from Adam is condemned as well (Rom. 5:12-14). Through the obedience of Christ came the offer of grace, forgiveness and restoration (Rom. 5:15-21). Those who respond to the gospel of Christ become *redeemed humanity* and wait to become *glorified humanity* at Christ's return to the air (1 Thess. 4:13-18). The work that started with regeneration will be complete, and the believer will be instantly and fully conformed to moral excellencies of Christ (Rom. 8:29). What Adam lost is fully restored through the Last Adam, the Lord Jesus.

Outline
I. Preface: The Author's Purpose and Method: 1:1-4
II. Christ's Advent and His Forerunner: 1:5-2:52
III. Christ's Preparatory Development for Ministry: 3:1-4:15
IV. Christ's Ministry in Galilee: 4:16-9:17
V. Christ's Ministry in Decapolis: 9:18-56
VI. Christ's Ministry in Judea: 10:1-13:21
VII. Christ's Ministry in Perea: 13:22-19:27
VIII. Christ's Final Week of Ministry in Jerusalem: 19:28-23:56
IX. Christ's Resurrection and Ascension: 24:1-53

Luke Chapter 1

Introduction (vv. 1-4)

Besides being the longest testimony of the four Gospels, the book of Luke is also the longest book in the New Testament. Not only is Luke the only Gentile writer in Scripture, but he also addresses both of his written works, Acts being the other, to his Greek friend Theophilus.

Luke's personalized salutation acquaints us immediately with a strong appeal to "human affection" which will characterize his Gospel. Theophilus means "beloved of God" or "friend of God," and Luke's salutation serves as a testimony that the Gentiles are loved by God. Mark wrote to the Romans, but Luke is setting forth an appeal to the Greeks concerning Christ. The Greeks prided themselves on intellectual observations and sought to apply knowledge and improve themselves (1 Cor. 1:22). They would be very interested in Luke's orderly presentation of the "perfect" man, the Last Adam (1 Cor. 15:45).

Twice in the opening sentence, Luke announces that he is declaring, in an "orderly" means, what he knows to be truth from the oral and written testimonies of multiple eyewitnesses (vv. 1-2). (The historian does not specifically refer to Matthew and Mark, but certainly their testimonies would have been included in his work.) An orderly account does not mean that his gospel record is presented in chronological order, but rather it is organized thematically to declare spiritual lessons pertaining to the humanity of Christ.

Luke's personal compulsion to proclaim what he knew to be true would then be guided, arranged, and constrained by the Holy Spirit to present an "orderly" account of the humanity of Christ *"from the very first"* (v. 3). This focus is why Luke provides such an in-depth account of the conception and birth of Christ. Luke desired that his friend Theophilus would know *"the certainty of those things"* in which he had already been taught concerning the Lord Jesus Christ (v. 4).

Who better than a physician to speak of the humanity of Christ? Not only does Luke show us the moral beauty and perfection of Christ, but he also reveals to us the frailties of His humanness. Luke presents to us a touchable Savior, who desires to touch others with compassion and kindness. Hence, the theme of Luke's Gospel is expressed this way, *"For the Son of Man has come to seek and to save that which was lost"* (19:10). The Son of Man came from heaven to love and to die for lost sinners.

The Birth of John the Baptizer Is Predicted (vv. 5-25)

Luke commences his narrative by introducing the parents of John the baptizer, the foretold forerunner of Christ. John's father, Zacharias, was a priest of the division of Abijah; his name means, "the Lord remembers." John's mother was Elizabeth, who was also in Aaron's priestly lineage; her name means, "oath of God." John's parents lived in the days of Herod the Great, an Idumean (a descendant of Esau) who ruled over Judea.

Both Zacharias and Elizabeth were righteous in conduct and blameless in upholding the commandments and ordinances of the Law (v. 6). They were childless and advanced in years (v. 7). Elizabeth's barren state was a social reproach that grieved her heart greatly (v. 25).

Because of the growing number of priests, David divided the Levitical priests into twenty-four divisions, with each division serving in the tabernacle and then temple (1 Chron. 24:7-19). Each priestly division served from Sabbath to Sabbath twice a year. At the time that John was born, it was estimated that there were about 20,000 priests. This meant that lots had to be drawn by those in each division to determine who would enter the holy place of the temple to burn incense on the golden altar, trim the lamps on the golden lampstand, and replace the showbread on the table of showbread (v. 8). It was a special honor to be chosen by lot to minister in the holy place, as many priests would never receive this privilege, and others, only once in their lifetimes.

In the Old Testament, God used the casting of lots by the hands of a priest or prophet to direct His people. For example, Joshua and the High Priest Eleazar determined land disbursements for the various tribes by drawing lots (Josh. 14:1-2). This method of distribution had been previously commanded by Moses (Num. 26:55). It was understood that Jehovah was guiding the process to affirm His will, and the proceedings left nothing to chance (Prov. 16:33). On this day, the lot of the Lord was cast, and Zacharias was chosen to serve in the temple (v. 9).

Luke

The priests were not to enter the holy place of the temple without putting a sacrifice upon the Bronze Altar; to do so would have resulted in death (Ex. 29:38-46). God permitted the priests to enter the tabernacle twice per day after offering a lamb each morning and evening as a burnt sacrifice. Thus, the priests and the people would be reminded each morning and again at the end of each day that without sacrifice there was no acceptance with God.

Apparently, the Jews gathered at the temple to pray at the hour incense was being offered to the Lord on the golden altar in the holy place (v. 10). Centuries earlier, David wrote, *"Let my prayer be set before You as incense, the lifting up of hands as the evening sacrifice"* (Ps. 141:2). Later, John would describe the prayers of the saints as bowls of incense before the Lord in heaven (Rev. 5:8). William MacDonald observes the unique way that Luke both opens and closes his gospel account:

> It is inspiring to notice that the Gospel opens with people praying at the temple and it closes with people praising God at the temple (24:53). The intervening chapters tell how their prayers were answered in the Person and work of the Lord Jesus.[7]

While Zacharias was before the altar of incense, an angel of the Lord appeared and stood on the right side of the altar (v. 11). Angels were very involved in directing the affairs of men in association with Christ's first advent and Luke mentions them twenty-three times in his Gospel. Notice that Zacharias was busy faithfully serving and worshiping the Lord when he and his wife Elizabeth were informed of God's plan for their lives. This is a good example for all believers to follow – remain pure and faithful to God, while waiting to be summoned for new service.

The angel before Zacharias is later identified as Gabriel, who will also visit Mary in about six months' time to announce the conception of Israel's Messiah (v. 26). Zacharias, who was troubled by the angel's presence, was told not to be afraid, for God had heard his prayer concerning his wife and she would bear him a son whose name was to be John (vv. 12-13). John means "the favor of the Lord."

The angel announced that many would rejoice at John's birth, for he would be great in the sight of the Lord, he would not drink wine or strong drink, but would be filled with the Holy Spirit, even from his birth (vv. 14-15). This meant that John would be a Nazarite from his birth (see

Num. 6:1–21) and dedicated to God in a life of separation and service. This does not mean that John was saved from the womb, but rather the Holy Spirit would accompany and enable John's ministry as Christ's forerunner. Norman Crawford explains the meaning of the text as based on the contrast of being filled with (or controlled by) wine or by the Holy Spirit:

> Some have gone so far as to claim that John had a spiritual birth before he had a natural birth. All such human speculation is unnecessary. There is an obvious contrast being drawn between being filled with the Spirit and the words, he "shall drink neither wine nor strong drink." This is the contrast drawn by Paul in Ephesians 5:18. To be filled with the Spirit is to be under His control for service and is quite distinct from the NT truth of "indwelling," which was contingent on the resurrection and ascension of the Lord Jesus (John 14:12–17).[8]

In the Old Testament, the Holy Spirit often came on an individual to accomplish a divine purpose and then departed from him after God's work was achieved (e.g., Judg. 14:6, Ps. 51:11). As Christ's forerunner, the Holy Spirit would not depart from John until his divine ministry was finished; this occurred when Herod executed him.

Lastly, the angel informed Zacharias that his son's ministry of announcing the arrival of Israel's Messiah would turn many people back to God. His ministry was likened to that of Elijah, who centuries earlier confronted idolatrous Israel and labored to turn his countrymen back to the Lord (vv. 16-17). John's ministry would arouse careless parents to have a real spiritual concern for their children and to prompt rebel hearts to repent and to seek the Lord with the wisdom of the just. Through John's preaching, many in Israel would be spiritually prepared to meet God, when He, their Messiah, appeared. The deity of Christ is thus affirmed by the angel's announcement to Zacharias.

Unfortunately, Zacharias relied on human reasoning rather than trusting God's promise uttered by the angel, for he believed that he and his wife were too old to have a child of their own (v. 18). Zacharias expressed his doubt by asking the angel, *"How shall I know this?"* It is at this juncture that the angel identifies himself as Gabriel, an angel that waited before the Lord in heaven as God's specialized messenger. He had been divinely tasked to speak to Zacharias and convey God's promise to His righteous priest (v. 19). That Gabriel mentioned his name after Zacharias expressed doubt was a form of admonishment, for the angel's name means "God is Mighty." In other words, "God is able to do this, Zacharias!"

Although Zacharias had prayed to God for a son for many years, he doubted the validity of Gabriel's announcement and requested a confirming sign. Gabriel gave him one: he would be mute until John's birth (v. 20). The people waiting outside the temple marveled that Zacharias lingered so long in the holy place (v. 21). When he finally did exit the temple, he was mute and because he motioned with his hands, the people discerned that he had seen a vision while in the temple (v. 22).

After Zacharias finished the days of his priestly service, he returned to his home, and his wife Elizabeth conceived and hid her pregnancy five months (vv. 23-24). She praised God for hearing their prayers and taking away her reproach among the people (v. 25). Zacharias' name means "the Lord remembers" and Elizabeth's name means "the oath of God." God would demonstrate His sovereign awareness and control by remembering and honoring His word to this faithful couple. In their old age, they would have a son, John, whose name means "the favor of Jehovah."

The Unique Birth of Jesus Christ Is Foretold (vv. 26-38)

In the sixth month of Elizabeth's pregnancy, Gabriel was sent by God to the city of Nazareth in Galilee to deliver a message to a virgin named Mary (v. 26). Mary was betrothed to a man from Nazareth named Joseph, who was of the house of David (v. 27). Gabriel told her to rejoice, for she was highly favored, and because the Lord was with her, she would be called blessed among women – she would have the honor of giving birth to Israel's Messiah (v. 28). While Matthew records that God spoke to Joseph through dreams about his espoused wife's conception, the angel Gabriel personally visits Mary in the privacy of her home to explain God's plans for her.

Understandably, the appearance of an angel in one's home would be troubling, but Gabriel told Mary not to be afraid, for God had chosen her for a special role: she was to be the mother of Israel's Messiah (vv. 29-30). Gabriel informed Mary: *"Behold, you will conceive in your womb and bring forth a Son, and shall call His name Jesus. He will be great, and will be called the Son of the Highest"* (vv. 31-32). "Jesus" is translated from *Iesous* in the Greek, which is derived from two Hebrew words: *Yehovah* and *yasha`* which means "to deliver" or "to save."

Literally, *Jesus* means "Jehovah's salvation" or "Jehovah is the Savior." To utter the name "Jesus" is to refer to the sacred covenant name of God in the English language. It was by this name that God declared His gift to the World, His Son, who was born of a lowly maiden, swaddled in grave clothes and laid in a feeding trough. Mary's son would be *"the Son of the Highest,"* yet born in connection with fallen humanity, though not having a fallen nature, for Joseph was not his natural father. He would "be great" in respect to His personage and works. He would be the final and everlasting heir to David's throne and have universal rule over Israel and all peoples.

The conception of the Lord Jesus was "unique." There is no patient confidentiality in this matter; Luke, the physician, provides a full medical report for all to appreciate:

1. The conception of Christ was through the power of the Holy Spirit (v. 35).
2. The conception of Christ did not involve the agency of a man (v. 34).
3. The conception of Christ took place in the womb; an embryo normally attaches to the womb after conception (v. 31).
4. The conception of Christ would never be repeated again, for the Last Adam need only suffer once for sin (Heb. 10:10-18), and He, as David's heir, would rule over the house of Israel *forever* (v. 33).
5. The conception of Christ resulted in a virgin giving birth to *"the Son of the Highest"* (vv. 27, 32, 34).

After hearing Gabriel's declaration, Mary, likely a teenager, asked the angel how she could be pregnant because she had not had a sexual relationship with a man (v. 34). This was an understandable query of wonder, not one of doubt. Zacharias wanted a sign to believe Gabriel's message to him, but Mary merely asked the angel for an explanation. Mary was aware that previously God had miraculously granted barren couples with a child, such as a hundred-year-old Abraham and ninety-year-old Sarah being blessed with their son Isaac, but this was a different situation; she was a virgin.

Mary was not ignorant; she knew how babies were made and when procreation could no longer happen. If such things had not been known, then no miracle could have been recognized, and God would have received no glory in doing it. In the case of Sarah and Elizabeth, they both were post-menopause and physically incapable of bearing children (1:18, 36; Gen. 18:11). In the case of Mary, the mother of Jesus, she was a virgin (v. 34). Luke is very careful to document the "order" of things, so that we might better recognize the divine miracle of the incarnation of Christ.

Although betrothed (i.e., they were under a formal marriage covenant), Mary and Joseph had not yet consummated their marriage by marital relations. This time of purity normally lasted one year. Mary was a virgin and would become pregnant through the overshadowing power of the Holy Spirit (Matt. 1:18, 22). From conception to embryo development, to birth, the Holy Spirit would control cellular division and growth, such that nothing materially supplied by Mary (who had Adam's nature; Rom. 5:12) would mar Christ's impeccability. Hence, her son within her womb would be the "Holy One," the incarnate "Son of God" (v. 35). Norman Crawford explains how we must understand the use of the neuter adjective *hagion* to describe Christ's holy essence in this text:

> The statement, "that holy thing" (KJV), has been a problem to some. It has been suggested that this is the only time in Scripture that a neuter adjective is used for the Person of the Lord Jesus. This is not strictly true, for Acts 4:27 uses a neuter adjective for Christ who stood before Pilate. No one would suggest that it was not a true Man against whom Herod, Pilate, the Gentiles, and the people of Israel arrayed themselves. This statement in Luke 1:35 is best read as many have translated it, "Wherefore also the holy (One) which shall be born shall be called the Son of God."[9]

It must have been crushing news to Joseph to learn that his espoused wife was pregnant. He would have naturally thought that Mary had broken her marriage vow to him and been unfaithful. Under the Law, Joseph could have had Mary stoned for adultery, but being a just and kind man he rather thought to divorce her quietly and release her from the marital commitment (Matt. 1:19). However, an angel appeared to Joseph in a dream and said to him, *"Do not be afraid to take to you Mary your wife, for that which is conceived in her is of the Holy Spirit"* (Matt. 1:20). The angel also told Joseph that Mary would have a son, the prophesied Jewish Messiah, and that he should be named "Jesus" (Matt. 1:21).

Gabriel then informed Mary that nothing was impossible for God to accomplish and cited the pregnancy of her aged-relative Elizabeth as an example. Notice that Gabriel rejoices in God's faithfulness to bring about only what He can, rather than highlighting Zacharias' lack of faith in the matter of John's birth. May we also be encouraged by God's dependability rather than focusing on the failures of others. Elizabeth was in the sixth month of her pregnancy, but had kept the news private, so Mary was unaware of the miracle (vv. 36-37). In response to all that she had heard, Mary said, *"Behold the maidservant of the Lord! Let it be to me according to your word"* (v. 38). Mary willingly submitted to God's purpose for her, she was the Lord's property, a consecrated vessel in His divine hands to be used as He desires. Gabriel then departed.

Mary Visits Elizabeth and Exalts God (vv. 39-56)

Shortly afterwards, Mary journeyed south to a city in the hill country of Judah, to visit her aunt Elizabeth, who was six months pregnant with John (v. 39). The distance from Nazareth, through Samaria, to the hilly region just west of Jerusalem would be about ninety miles. This would have been a dangerous journey for a teenage woman by herself and required several days to accomplish. Mary likely traveled to this remote location and then remained there for three months to avoid the shame of what would certainly appear to be a scandalous situation if she remained in Nazareth. Gabriel had informed Mary of Elizabeth's miraculous pregnancy, so she was the one person that could understand what Mary was going through.

Mary entered the house of Zacharias and greeted Elizabeth (v. 40). As soon as Elizabeth heard Mary's voice the baby within her womb leaped with joy (vv. 41, 44). At this juncture, the Holy Spirit fills Elizabeth and she jubilantly speaks to Mary, *"Blessed are you among women, and blessed is the fruit of your womb!"* (v. 42). Elizabeth affirmed that Mary was pregnant with Israel's Messiah, whom she calls "my Lord" (v. 43). Elizabeth also commends Mary's faith for believing what the angel had previously told her and then states that all that Gabriel had said to her would come about (v. 45). Elizabeth's knowledge of this past conversation and what was said during Gabriel's visit with Mary could have only been revealed to her by the Holy Spirit. In fact, Elizabeth

Luke

is the only woman in Scripture who we read was "filled with the Holy Spirit."

Mary shared a song of rejoicing with Elizabeth (vv. 46-55). From this song, which refers to fifteen Old Testament passages, we gain some understanding as to why God chose Mary to be the mother of the Lord Jesus: She knew God's Word and was living purely before Him. She had God's Word hidden in her heart and the eternal Word hidden in her womb.

This is the opening line of her Magnificat: *"My soul magnifies the Lord, and my spirit has rejoiced in God my Savior"* (vv. 46-47). Mary knew that she would give birth to *Immanuel*, meaning "God with us," and that her son's name would be Jesus, meaning "Jehovah's Salvation." She therefore joyfully ascribed deity to her unborn child, who she declared was her own Savior also! Clearly, Mary was not sinless as some claim; she, like everyone else who descended from our first parents, needed a Savior.

There are many Old Testament passages which speak of the deity of the coming Redeemer and Savior of the World: *"For I am the Lord your God, the Holy One of Israel, your Savior"* (Isa. 43:3). *"I, even I, am the Lord, and besides Me there is no savior"* (Isa. 43:11). *"There is no other God besides Me, a just God and a Savior; there is none besides Me"* (Isa. 45:21). *"That I, the Lord, am your Savior, and your Redeemer, the Mighty One of Jacob"* (Isa. 49:26). God saw that there was no intercessor from among men, so *"His own arm"* brought salvation (Isa. 59:16). Clearly, God is the Holy One of Israel, and the only Intercessor and the only Savior for the nation of Israel. When we compare the above passages with the illumination of New Testament truth, there is only one inescapable conclusion – Jesus Christ is the Son of God, fully divine in essence and hence the only true Savior.

Mary states that *"all generations will call me blessed"* (v. 48). She would be held in esteem for giving birth to the Messiah, but she, herself, would not be imparting any blessings to anyone; rather she was the blessed one. Likewise, she speaks of the great things that God, whose name is holy, had done to her; she does not speak of herself as holy (v. 49).

The message of the gospel presented throughout Scripture is that God shows mercy to and honors those who fear Him, but He resists the proud and judges the wicked (vv. 50-53). Solomon informs us that, *"The fear of the Lord is the beginning of knowledge"* (Prov. 1:8). *"The fear of the*

Lord is to hate evil; pride and arrogance and the evil way" (Prov. 8:13), *"Pride goes before destruction, and a haughty spirit before a fall"* (Prov. 16:18), and *"A man's pride will bring him low, but the humble in spirit will retain honor"* (Prov. 29:23).

Mary concludes her song by mentioning that through her unborn Son, God will help His servant Israel (v. 54). Through Him, Israel's Messiah, all the promises that God made to Abraham, as pertaining to his descendants, would be fulfilled (v. 55). The Jews will ultimately have a land with large boundaries and be liberated from all Gentile oppression forever (Gen. 12:1-3, 15:18). The Jewish Messiah will rule the world with a rod of iron and all families of the earth will be blessed by Him.

Mary remained with Elizabeth for about three months, until the final weeks of her pregnancy. Afterwards she returned to Nazareth, where she would be viewed by many as a shameful fornicator. Even thirty years later, the Jewish leaders inferred that Jesus was the son of a fornicator, implying that He could not really know who His father was (John 8:41).

John Is Born and Named (vv. 57-66)

Even though Elizabeth was an older woman, and this was her first baby, she carried John full term and safely delivered him (v. 57). Her friends and neighbors realized the spectacular nature of John's birth and rejoiced with her, for God had shown Elizabeth great mercy (v. 58).

The Law required males to be circumcised on the eighth day after birth and it was customary to announce the baby's name at this time (v. 59). Often, boys were named after their fathers or grandfathers, but not in this situation; Gabriel had informed Zacharias nine months earlier that the child would be called "John" (v. 13). Elizabeth informed everyone gathering for this event that the boy's name would be "John" (v. 60). But this decision caused confusion, as there was no one in their extended family by that name (v. 61). Zacharias was then asked if the baby's name would be John (v. 62). It is interesting that Luke says that they made signs to Zacharias, but the priest was not deaf, just mute. Zacharias asked for a writing tablet and confirmed that the name of their son would be John (v. 63). The people were amazed that they would call their son by a name not known in their family.

Zacharias was slow to believe what Gabriel had foretold him would happen, but after nine months of muteness he had learned from his mistake. Now faith marked by obedience to God's will was paramount and as a result Zacharias's tongue was loosened and he began to praise God (v. 64). Many were astonished by what had happened and the news of John's miracle birth and the reversal of his father's muteness spread quickly through the Judean hill country (v. 65). The people discerned that the hand of God was on this child and wondered how God was going to use little John for His glory (v. 66).

Zacharias Prophesies (vv. 67-80)

There are those who teach that God is done with the nation of Israel, and that the Church has replaced the nation of Israel in God's plan of blessing. However, it should be emphasized that the New Covenant, sealed by Christ's own blood, was not confirmed with Gentiles, but with the houses of Israel and Judah (Heb. 8:8). God has sworn by His own name to complete what He promised Abraham He would do.

This truth was prophetically announced just prior to Christ's birth. First, Mary foretold that her Son would achieve the complete fulfillment of the Abrahamic Covenant (v. 55). Second, the priest Zechariah predicted that the Lord Jesus Christ would redeem His people, be a horn of salvation to Israel, deliver the Jews from all their enemies, and fulfill the covenant that God instituted with Abraham (vv. 67-80).

On the day of Christ's circumcision, while at the temple, two more prophetic announcements concerning what He would accomplish were stated. First, Simeon foretold that the infant Jesus would be the revelation of God's goodness to the Gentiles and the glory of Israel (2:32). Second, Anna proclaimed that Jesus Christ would bring redemption to Jerusalem (2:38). *"My covenant I will not break, nor alter the word that has gone out of My lips"* (Ps. 89:34). Our God is a covenant-keeping God! Who but God could have ever devised a plan to show so much grace to a rebellious people and a fallen race?

God had visited His people and raised up a horn of salvation for the house of David (vv. 68-69). A "horn" in Scripture represents power and rulership and this is how Jeremiah describes Israel's coming Messiah, *"Their Redeemer is strong; the Lord of hosts is His name. He will thoroughly plead their case"* (Jer. 50:34). Warren Wiersbe describes where Scripture states this strong Redeemer would come from:

> Where did the Redeemer come from? He came from the house of David (Luke 1:69), who himself was a great conqueror. God had promised that the Savior would be a Jew (Gen. 12:1–3), from the tribe of Judah

(Gen. 49:10), from the family of David (2 Sam. 7:12–16), born in David's city, Bethlehem (Micah 5:2). Both Mary (Luke 1:27) and Joseph (Matt. 1:20) belonged to David's line. The coming of the Redeemer was inherent in the covenants God made with His people (Luke 1:72), and it was promised by the prophets (Luke 1:70).[10]

Just as the prophets of old had foretold, the Jewish people would be delivered from all Gentile oppression forever through their promised Messiah (vv. 70-71). After God fulfilled all His promises to Abraham, his descendants would be able to serve God in holiness and righteousness, and without fear of retaliation (vv. 72-75).

Zacharias also confirmed the ministry of his son John, but only after he had given Israel's Messiah first place in His prophecy. John would be a prophet of the Highest that would *"go before the face of the Lord to prepare His ways, to give knowledge of salvation to His people by the remission of their sins"* (vv. 76-77). The word "remission" here means "to send away" and the context is "to dismiss a debt." None of us is without sin; we have all broken God's Law, which shows us that we cannot be accepted by a holy God, but rather we deserve His wrath (Rom. 3:20). There is only one way that our debt of sin can be forgiven (i.e., dismissed) and that is through receiving the One who came to pay the judicial penalty for our sin, Jesus Christ (Rom. 4:4-5).

John would inform his countrymen that the *"Dayspring from on high"* had visited them to illuminate the way of salvation (v. 78). The idea of "dayspring" is a new sunrise. The Gospels inform us that Zacharias's prophetic announcement concerning Christ (about six months before His birth) was being fulfilled – a new day of spiritual illumination had begun. Through Christ, God promised *"to give light to those who sit in darkness and the shadow of death, to guide our feet into the way of peace"* (v. 79). Years later, the Lord Jesus declared, *"I am the light of the world"* (John 8:12). He was *"the true Light which gives light to every man coming into the world"* (John 1:9). Through Christ, those locked in spiritual darkness and death could be led into the light to experience God's peace and eternal life.

John grew and became strong in spirit. Eventually, probably after his parents had died, John lived a self-denying life in the wilderness until he was summoned by God to commence his ministry. John was in his late twenties when God commissioned him to begin preaching the necessity of repentance to prepare the people to receive Christ's kingdom offer.

Luke Chapter 2

The prophet Micah, writing in the eighth century B.C., foretold the birth of Israel's future Deliverer and His work. The Messiah's birthplace would be the same as David's, Bethlehem, located just south of Jerusalem: *"But you, Bethlehem Ephrathah, though you are little among the thousands of Judah, yet out of you shall come forth to Me the one to be Ruler in Israel, whose goings forth are from of old, from everlasting"* (Micah 5:2). Israel's Messiah would be the eternal God incarnate – the One who literally stepped out of "the days of immeasurable time" into time! At that time, God's Son would take on flesh to become the world's Savior (John 1:14). Micah affirms the deity of Christ, who would be born of a virgin (Isa. 7:14) in the small town of Bethlehem of Judah.

The phrase *"little among the thousands"* literally means, "too small to be among." Each tribe was divided into its thousands of soldiers. Places too small to form a thousand by themselves were united with others to do so. So lowly was Bethlehem that it was not counted among the possessions of Judah when Joshua divided the land.

As there was a Bethlehem in Galilee, naming the region, Ephrathah, ensured that there would be no confusion as to which town Micah was speaking of. Luke records the story of Joseph and Mary venturing from Nazareth to Bethlehem for a census, and that Mary gave birth to the Lord Jesus in a stable in Bethlehem (vv. 4-7). Bethlehem means the "house of bread" and wonderfully represents the work of Christ to save sinners: *"For the bread of God is He who comes down from heaven and gives life to the world"* (John 6:33).

Little Bethlehem wonderfully foreshadows both of Christ's advents. In Genesis 35 and Micah 5, a **Son** is born. In Ruth 2, a **Savior** (i.e., a Kinsman Redeemer) and the Lord of the harvest appears. In 1 Samuel 16, a **Sovereign** is anointed (the Shepherd and King of Israel). While the Son, the Savior, has already come to seek and save the lost, the latter aspect of Christ's rule is yet future. May all humanity rejoice in God's life-giving message and Messenger from "little Bethlehem"!

Jesus Christ Is Born in Bethlehem (vv. 1-7)

Caesar Augustus (Gaius Octavius), who ruled as Rome's first "emperor" from 27 B.C. to 14 A.D., ordered a census (or registration) throughout the Roman Empire (v. 1). Rome took a census every fourteen years for both military and tax purposes, and each Jewish male had to return to the city of his fathers to record his name, occupation, property, and family.[11] Luke notes that this census required individuals to return to their place of origin to be registered (v. 3). But when was this census conducted?

We know that Herod the Great died in 4 B.C., approximately one to two years after the birth of Christ (Matt. 1:4, 16). Hence, the census Luke is referring must have occurred in 6 to 5 B.C. However, Luke stated, *"This census first took place while Quirinius was governing Syria"* (v. 2). But according to Josephus and other non-biblical sources, the census initiated by Publius Sulpicius Quirinius, the governor of Syria, did not occur until 6 A.D.[12] This census for taxation purposes triggered a revolt of Jewish extremists led by Judas of Galilee. So, either Luke is in error about this detail, or there is a legitimate explanation for what seems to be an inconsistency. There are at least two possible explanations that resolve this apparent discrepancy.

First, although Quirinius did not become the governor of Syria until about 6 A.D., he did lead Syria's military from 12 to 2 B.C. The Greek verb (a participle) rendered "was governing" in verse 2, is *hegemoneuo* and simply describes one who is leading; the word does not describe a particular office. This Greek verb could refer to Quirinius' military or political leadership. Another possibility is that Quirinius was in a position of authority in Syria on two separate occasions as affirmed by a Latin inscription discovered in 1764 A.D.[13] In summary, it is possible that there was an earlier census other than the widely accepted one in 6 A.D, which Quirinius was overseeing.

Second, the Greek word *protos* rendered "first" in verse 2 can also be translated "before." With this understanding, the intended meaning of Luke's statement would be: "This was the census taken *before* Quirinius was governor of Syria." Luke would have certainly been aware of the 6 A.D. census and subsequent Jewish uprising, so he is saying that the census that he is referring to occurred before those events.

Joseph, being from the tribe of Judah and a descendant of David, was required to register in Bethlehem (v. 4). Although her time of delivery

Luke

was near, Joseph took Mary with him to Bethlehem to be registered (v. 5). Notice that Luke refers to Mary as Joseph's "betrothed wife," which meant that though they were under a marriage covenant, Mary was still a virgin. Matthew tells us plainly that Joseph and Mary did not have marital relations until after the birth of Jesus (Matt. 1:18, 25).

Because of the census, there were many travelers arriving in Bethlehem, which created a housing shortage. As there was no available lodging for Mary and Joseph, they took shelter in a stable, where Mary delivered her firstborn son, Jesus (vv. 6-7). She wrapped her Son in swaddling clothes (grave wrappings) and laid Him in a manger (a feeding trough).

The events surrounding Christ's birth well picture the world's condescending attitude towards Him. He was born in a stable because there was *"no room in the inn."* He was *"wrapped in swaddling clothes"* which depicted the clear purpose of His birth – to suffer and to die. He was *"laid in a manger"* which declares His human poverty. Yet, the manger provided accessibility to all. If the Lord had been born in a palace, only the "well-to-do" and the nobility would have seen Him. Yes, access to Him would have been limited in a palace, but not so lying in the manger of a stable; any inquisitive soul who wanted to behold the Savior was welcome.

What time of the year was Jesus Christ likely born? William Ramsay suggests that the Romans typically conducted their censuses in the warmer months of the year, especially in August to October, to avoid the cold, winter rainy season which made traveling difficult.[14] Likewise, the Lord mentioned that the dead of winter would be the worst time for women and children to be journeying (Matt. 24:20). Luke tells us that in the surrounding hill country, there were shepherds living among their sheep and keeping watch over them at night. Shepherds did not live out on hillsides with their sheep during the winter months. This reasoning would indicate that the birth of Christ likely occurred in the late summer of the year, in either 5 or 6 B.C.

In the fourth century A.D., the Roman Catholic Church established the birthdate of Christ to align with the pagan festival that the Anglo Saxons had been celebrating for centuries during the winter solstice. Alexander Hislop clarifies the real reason that a holiday was created to celebrate Christ's birth and why it was affixed on December 25th:

> Long before the fourth century, and long before the Christian era itself, a festival was celebrated among the heathen, at that precise time of the year, in honor of the birth of the son of the Babylonian queen of heaven; and it may fairly be presumed that, in order to conciliate the heathen, and to swell the number of the nominal adherents of Christianity, the same festival was adopted by the Roman Church, giving it only the name of Christ. ... That Christmas was originally a Pagan festival is beyond all doubt. The time of the year, and the ceremonies with which it is still celebrated, prove its origin. In Egypt, the son of Isis, the Egyptian title for the queen of heaven, was born at this very time, "about the time of the winter solstice." The very name by which Christmas is popularly known among ourselves – Yule-day – proves at once its Pagan and Babylonian origin. "Yule" is the Chaldee name for an "infant" or "little child"; and as the 25th of December was called by our Pagan Anglo-Saxon ancestors, "Yule-day," or the "Child's day," and the night that preceded it, "Mother-night," long before they came in contact with Christianity.[15]

Sadly, the date which honored the Sun-god *Mithras* became the celebrated birthdate of Jesus Christ, the Son of God. The Roman Church also created the *Easter* holiday to align with the pagan holiday which honored *Eostre* the fertility goddess at the spring equinox (nine months earlier, which is the human gestational period). The Easter bunny and egg came from the pagan symbols of fertility honoring Eostre. The Roman Church hoped to lure many pagans into their sphere of influence by creating these two new holidays, which were similar to the pagan ones that they were already familiar with.

Returning to the text, an angel suddenly stood before the shepherds who were watching over their sheep near Bethlehem and the glory of the Lord illuminated the nighttime vista about them (v. 9). This sight caused the shepherds to be greatly afraid, but the angel told them not to be frightened, for he was heralding *"good tidings of great joy which will be to all people"* (v. 10). What were these good tidings? That a Savior, Christ the Lord, had been born to them that very day in Bethlehem, the city of David (v. 11). The shepherds were to seek for this babe, whom they would not find in a home, but in a stable, wrapped in swaddling clothes and lying in a manger (v. 12).

As soon as the angel finished describing the sign that would identify their infant Messiah, a multitude of angels suddenly appear to praise God in unison: *"Glory to God in the highest, and on earth peace, goodwill toward men"* (vv. 13-14). Through birth, Christ's humanity was established – a link *"to all people."* Man could not make Him a Savior; He was born Savior of the world. As a man, He would likewise experience all the pangs of living upon a cursed planet and, before dying, feel the very judgments He Himself had levied upon humanity in the Garden of Eden. More than any of the other Gospel writers, Luke skillfully captures the anguish of these aspects of the Lord's life.

As soon as the angels had departed, the shepherds agreed that they must immediately travel to Bethlehem to investigate what they had been informed of by the Lord (v. 15). How far the shepherds journeyed to arrive at Bethlehem we are not told, but it did not take them long to find Mary and Joseph and the baby Jesus lying in a manger (v. 16).

After seeing the babe, their Messiah, the shepherds widely publicized the events of that evening and many who heard their testimony marveled at their story (vv. 17-18). Although Mary had been told by Gabriel who her son was, she chose not to disclose the information to the shepherds, but rather to treasure in her heart what God had brought about through her and more importantly what He would achieve through her Son (v. 19). After seeing the baby Jesus and telling others of the angelic announcement that they had witnessed, the shepherds returned to their flock praising and glorifying God (v. 20). God had chosen to reveal the birth of His Son to lowly shepherds, and they counted themselves greatly blessed for the experience.

Christ Presented at the Temple (vv. 21-24)

As required by the Law, the Lord was taken to the temple to be circumcised eight days after His birth. Paul explains, *"When the fullness of the time had come, God sent forth His Son, born of a woman, born under the law"* (Gal. 4:3). Christ, as a Jew, was born under the Law and would keep every aspect of the Law to show that He was God's suitable Lamb of sacrifice. It was at the time of His circumcision that Jesus received His name, as previously declared by Gabriel before His conception (v. 21). This would be the first of three rituals that Mary and Joseph would observe under the Mosaic Law.

The second ritual related to returning to the temple to offer a sacrifice after Mary's days of post-delivery purification had been completed. Leviticus 12 provides the details that had to be followed. A new mother was considered to be initially unclean and then for additional days she was merely regarded as ceremonially unclean. She was considered contagiously unclean (i.e., was not to have direct contact with others) for seven days after the birth of a boy and fourteen days after the birth of a girl; this related to postnatal discharge. The limitations of this period of uncleanness were the same as experienced during her monthly menstruation cycle (Lev. 12:2).

If a mother gave birth to a boy, the flesh of his foreskin was to be circumcised on the eighth day. After the days of the new mother's separation were fulfilled, an additional period of thirty-three days for the birth of a boy and sixty-six days for that of a girl were to be added before she could be ceremonially purified (Lev. 12:4-5). During this time, she could not touch anything that had been consecrated in the service of God, nor could she enter the sanctuary. The total time of purification for a boy was then forty days, and for a girl, eighty days.

At the end of this time, she was to venture to the tabernacle/temple and offer a yearling lamb as a burnt offering and a pigeon or dove as a sin offering. If poor, as in the case of Mary, she could offer two birds: one as a sin offering and the other as a burnt offering (Lev. 12:6-8; Luke 2:22-24). The atonement was necessary for ritual purification only. The mother had not sinned in giving birth, but she had brought a child into the world having a fallen nature, a nature that adamantly opposes God and His interests. This reality was not true for Mary's Son, but she obeyed the Law as a faithful Jew regardless.

The third ritual pertained to the Law's requirement that whoever opened the womb for the first time (man or beast) had to be redeemed by the life of a lamb (Ex. 13:2, 12). Luke quotes the decree in verse 23. Initially, to avoid their deaths, God redeemed the firstborn of the Israelites in Egypt by the substitutional death of the Passover lambs (Ex. 12). Hence, the firstborn was God's portion among the Jewish nation. God later exchanged the firstborn Jews living at that time for the tribe of Levi, who would officiate worship to the Lord on behalf of the nation afterwards (Ex. 28:1-2). This meant that every firstborn male, not from the tribe of Levi, thereafter, had to be substitutionally purchased by a lamb or by paying five shekels of redemption money (Num. 18:15-16).

Being poor, Mary and Joseph were permitted to offer two doves for the purification ritual. They also paid five shekels to redeem their firstborn son as required by the Law. This price acknowledged that their firstborn Son was God's portion in Israel and that He was being set apart for God's honor. As a baby, the Lord Jesus was dedicated to God by Mary and Joseph.

Simeon's Prophecy (vv. 25-35)

Simeon was part of the godly remnant of Israel that was patiently waiting for "the Consolation of Israel" (i.e., that God would fulfill His covenant promises by sending His Messiah to the Jewish people; v. 25). The Holy Spirit was with Simeon and had revealed to him that He would not die until He saw the Lord's Christ (v. 26). While Mary and Joseph were at the temple to redeem their firstborn Son, the Holy Spirit led Simeon to the temple to meet his Savior (v. 27).

After arriving and seeing the babe, Simeon took Jesus up in his arms and blessed God saying, *"Lord, now You are letting Your servant depart in peace, according to Your word; for my eyes have seen Your salvation"* (vv. 29-30). Simeon, as prompted by the Holy Spirit, then prophesied that the very child that He was holding would be a light of revelation to the Gentiles (speaking of the Church Age occurring after Christ's first advent) and a glory to Israel (speaking of the Jewish remnant to be converted at His second advent). Clearly, the Messiah was not only sent to bless the Jews, He would also benefit all families of the earth, just as God had promised Abraham long ago (Gen. 12:3). This meant that Christ would be giving His life for a ransom for all men (1 Tim. 2:5; Heb. 2:9).

Notice how Luke protects the doctrine of Christ's incarnation by mentioning that "Joseph and His (Jesus') mother" marveled at Simeon's prophecy (v. 33). Joseph was not Jesus' natural father, but Mary was the natural mother of Christ, as Luke again affirms in verse 34.

After blessing the Child, Simeon uttered one final prophecy to Mary, *"Behold this Child is destined for the fall and rising of many in Israel, and for a sign which will be spoken against (yes, a sword will pierce through your own soul also), that the thoughts of many hearts may be revealed"* (vv. 34-35). Simeon's statement can be summed up by the questions the Lord Jesus later asked of His disciples, *"Who do you say that I am?"* (Matt. 16:15) and of the Pharisees: *"What do you think about the Christ?"* (Matt. 22:42). Peter responded to the first question, by declaring that Jesus was *"the Christ, the Son of the living God"* (Matt. 16:16). The Pharisees, however, declined to affirm that truth. Those agreeing with Peter will rise into God's favor and blessing, but those who reject that truth, or are indifferent to it, will remain in their sins and are destined for an eternal fall. How someone acts towards Christ reveals their inward motives and affections towards God. Those responding to Calvary with humility and repentance will be saved.

The sword that Simeon spoke of was the one that would pierce Mary's heart while she observed her firstborn Son suffering unto death while hanging on a cross (John 19:25). This propitiatory event is the centerpiece of God's redemptive plan for mankind; those receiving Christ as Savior will have eternal life in Him, and those who do not will suffer eternal death without Him.

Anna's Testimony (vv. 36-38)

Like Simeon, Anna, a prophetess, was also a member of the faithful remnant of Israel waiting for God's Messiah to come (v. 36). She was of the tribe of Asher and of a great age. She was married for seven years before her husband died and had not remarried. She had been a widow for eighty-four years (v. 37). Her age would likely have been between 105 and 110 years. Anna was a regular fixture at the temple, spending much time in prayer and fasting before the Lord, both day and night.

Apparently, just after Simeon had spoken to Mary and Joseph, Anna also appeared to confirm that their Son would bless all those looking for God's redemption in Jerusalem. Two faithful witnesses had affirmed the identity of the baby Jesus, Mary's firstborn Son, on the day that He was redeemed for five shekels of silver. He had now been ceremonially set aside and dedicated to the Lord per the edicts of the Law. Indeed, Christ would completely fulfill God's plan for His life.

Returning to Nazareth (vv. 39-40)

Luke does not record Joseph taking his young family to Egypt to escape Herod's wrath, but rather picks up his account after they returned to the city of Nazareth in Galilee (v. 39). Isaiah writes, *"There shall come forth a Rod from the stem [netzer] of Jesse, and a Branch shall grow out of his roots* (Isa. 11:1). The Hebrew word *netzer* in this prophecy more likely speaks of having disdain for another (e.g., John 1:46) than of being a "Nazarene," a person associated with Nazareth. In short, a Nazarene was someone to be despised. Like Christ, those who inhabited Nazareth bore this reproach in association with the name of their town.

The Lord Jesus grew and became strong in spirit; He was filled with wisdom, and the grace of God was upon Him (v. 40). The Lord developed in the same way you and I did: He learned to suckle, to eat, to walk, to talk, to work, to read, etc. Not being hindered by a fallen nature, His mental faculties excelled in learning, in understanding, in retaining information, and in rightly applying what He had learned (the idea of wisdom). During these early years, the Lord, as guided by the Holy Spirit, both learned and delighted in doing God's Word. The first twelve years of Christ's childhood pass without being mentioned in Scripture.

Jesus Visits His Father's House in Jerusalem (vv. 41-50)

Only in Luke do we get a glimpse of Christ's childhood. When the Lord was twelve years of age, He traveled with His parents and other families to Jerusalem to celebrate the Passover feast (vv. 41-42). After the eight-day feast of Passover and Unleavened Bread had concluded, the Lord's family, with others who had come down from Nazareth, began the long trek home. However, the Lord Jesus lingered in Jerusalem. Mary and Joseph thought their son was with relatives and friends, but His absence was detected after a day's journey (v. 43). Not finding Him in their company, they immediately returned to Jerusalem to seek for Him (vv. 44-45).

After three days of searching for their son, they found Him in the temple, among the religious teachers. Notice Luke's description of Christ's human exercise at this juncture: He was "**sitting** in the midst of the teachers, both **listening** to them and **asking** them questions" (v. 46). All that heard Him were astonished at His understanding and answers (v. 47). Joseph and Mary were also amazed at the scene (v. 48). Mary's expression, *"Look, Your father and I have sought You anxiously"* in verse 48, indicates that Joseph was accepted in the Jewish sense as the legal father of Jesus. The reference does not deny Christ's heavenly origin, but rather affirms who was legally responsible for His earthly care. Jesus *"was supposed the son of Joseph"* (3:23). From a human perspective, everyone would naturally view Joseph as the father of Jesus.

When His mother reproved Him for causing their anxiety-filled three-day search for Him, the Lord calmly replied, *"Why did you seek Me? Did you not know that I must be about My Father's business?"* (v. 49). Even at this early age the Lord was aware of and intent on doing His Father's will. However, Mary and Joseph did not understand His obscure statement to them; no doubt they were stunned by such a mysterious declaration coming from a twelve-year-old.

Jesus Increases in Wisdom, Stature, and Favor (vv. 51-52)

During His childhood, the Lord Jesus was in submission to parental authority. Luke informs us that *"He went down with them* [His parents], *and...was subject to them"* (v. 51). Until the Lord received new marching orders, He remained under the God-ordained authority He was placed under. This serves as a good example for all to follow. Godly authority is like a funnel; if we remain in proper relationship to it, God's blessings flow down to us through that funnel. If we rebel against it, we place ourselves under Satan's authority and lose the communion and blessings of God.

Christ experienced human growth and maturity: *"And Jesus increased in wisdom and stature, and in favor with God and men"* (v. 52). The Lord Jesus developed mentally (by increasing in wisdom), physically (by growing in stature), spiritually (by more fully displaying God's character) and socially (by increasingly demonstrating grace and patience towards others). The Lord was perfect in every stage of life that He advanced through, but it is understood that progressing in life requires steady growth.

The Lord learned to eat, crawl, walk, talk, etc. in the same way you and I did. Perhaps the angels gasped when the Lord stumbled while learning to walk or wondered when He jabbered as a baby. How could we fully identify with Him in our human frailty if He did not experience all these things and more, as we do? Although the Lord Jesus, as the Son of God, is all-knowing, there were certain things that He must learn through experience (Heb. 5:8). By this, we can be confident then that our Great High Priest in heaven can sympathize with all our infirmities and provide mercy in times of need (Heb. 4:15).

The Lord's home, until called to ministry, was Nazareth. Only Luke records that the Lord was "brought up" in Nazareth; Matthew merely states He returned there from Egypt. Despite growing up in a large family with limited financial means, with imperfect parents, in a despised town, and at a time of great spiritual despondency, yet eighteen years after this event, Jesus would emerge as One who well pleased God in all things (3:22). Most of us have little control of what happens to us during our earthly sojourn, but we can control what we do. May we follow Christ's example of being about the Father's will and pleasing Him in all that we do.

Luke Chapter 3

The Ministry of John the Baptizer (vv. 1-20)

Luke now informs us when John began his ministry and who were the political and religious leaders at that time. Tiberius Ceasar ruled over Rome from 14 to 37 A.D., thus the fifteenth year of his reign would be 28 A.D. (v. 1). John would have been in his early thirties. Pontius Pilate was the Roman governor of Judea from 26 to 36 A.D. Luke then names three tetrarchs in Palestine: Herod of Galilee, his brother Philip of Iturea and Trachonitis, and Lysanias of Abilene (only mentioned here in Scripture). He also states that Annas and Caiaphas were the Jewish high priests (v. 2).

Quirinius, the governor of Syria, appointed Annas as the Jewish high priest in 6 A.D. However, the Romans did not want a long-standing high priest. Limiting the high priest's tenure would reduce the priest's sway among the people. So Annas had been replaced in 15 A.D. by Valerius Gratus, the procurator of Judea, and then each of Annas' five sons were in turn appointed as the high priest and then Caiaphas, his son-in-law.[16] Luke confirms that both Annas and Caiaphas were high priests currently in verse 2, but this situation was contrary to God's Word and well pictures the religious disorder gripping Israel at this juncture. From the Jewish perspective, Annas was the true high priest, though Caiaphas was the acknowledged leader to pacify Roman rule.

John had been residing in the wilderness for some time, but now God had called him to the Jordan River region to commence his ministry of *"preaching a baptism of repentance for the remission of sins"* (v. 3). John informs us that his initial ministry took place in the most southern portion of the Jordan River at Bethabara (John 1:28).

Centuries earlier, the prophet Isaiah was a voice crying in the spiritual wilderness of Israel's apostasy, so God used him to speak of one that would come in a future day in the same spirit of ministry to announce the Lord's coming: *"Prepare the way of the Lord; make straight in the desert a highway for our God"* (v. 4; Isa. 40:3). All four of the Gospel writers apply this verse to John the baptizer (Matt. 3:1-4; Mark 1:1-4;

John 1:23). In ancient days, physical roads were smoothed out before visiting kings traveled over them. Although John would not be involved in any road construction projects, spiritually speaking, he was to prepare the people's hearts to receive the Messiah more readily when He arrived. William MacDonald describes the fourfold effect that Christ would have on Israel when He did arrive:

> **Every valley shall be filled** – those who are truly repentant and humble would be saved and satisfied.
>
> **Every mountain and hill** shall be **brought low** – people like the scribes and Pharisees, who were haughty and arrogant, would be humbled.
>
> **The crooked places shall be made straight** – those who were dishonest, like the tax collectors, would have their characters straightened out.
>
> **The rough ways** shall be made **smooth** – soldiers and others with rough, crude temperaments would be tamed and refined.[17]

In summary, those coming to Christ for salvation must rise from darkness into the light of truth, choose to humble themselves, and admit their sins to be spiritually revived and experience a change of heart and mind that is pleasing to God.

John was sent by God to be a witness to others of the Light that God was shining into the world through His Son, the living Word (John 1:6-8). Though John dwelt in the desert, his preaching formed a highway for the Lord Jesus through the spiritual wilderness of Israel, such that *"all flesh shall see the salvation of God"* (vv. 5-6). Ultimately, this declaration would be fulfilled in the Millennial Kingdom Age. "All flesh" means that in a coming day, the Jewish nation will be restored to the Lord and likewise Gentiles will enjoy the benefits of Calvary also. All humanity will be blessed by Christ when He reigns on the earth. At that time His glory will be evident everywhere.

Consequently, John announced that "the kingdom of heaven" was at hand and called the people to repentance to enter it (Matt. 3:5). Many came to hear John's message, and many repented of their sins and were baptized by John in the Jordan River to publicly affirm their new commitment to follow the Lord (v. 7). John did not invent this baptism of repentance. Rather, it was assigned by God to lead those repenting of their sins to trust in the One who was coming to save them from sin.

However, not everyone who came to hear John's message of repentance did so with an open ear. When John saw the Pharisees and Sadducees approaching him, he said to them, *"Brood of vipers! Who warned you to flee from the wrath to come? Therefore bear fruits worthy of repentance"* (v. 7; Matt. 3:7-8). The Pharisees and Sadducees, and indeed much of the Jewish nation, believed that being children of Abraham uniquely qualified them to receive God's blessing above any other people group (v. 8). But physical lineage did not mean that one was a spiritual child of Abraham and would receive God's blessing. Rather, those following Abraham's example of faith and obedience to God's Word would be blessed by God (Rom. 4:16-17).

Accordingly, John did not mince words with these self-righteous hypocrites, who in their own estimation did not need to repent of anything. They thought that because they were immersed in rabbinical tradition, that they were in good standing with God. John's message to these religious zealots was forthright: Your religiosity does not impress God; you need to experience spiritual transformation, which begins with repentance.

John warned them that there was only one way to avoid God's forthcoming wrath on the wicked: they must humble themselves and confess their sins to God. True repentance is more than lip service to God; it has tangible evidence of a changed heart. Repentance enables us to stand with God against ourselves and believes that God alone can make us right in His presence. Ultimately, forgiveness for their sins would come through Christ, the One of whom John was foretelling.

Just as a good tree bears good fruit, true repentance is shown by a changed life that seeks to honor God by engaging in righteous behavior (v. 9). Christ was coming to test their hearts and reveal who had truly repented. Those trees not bearing fruit worthy of repentance would be cut down and thrown in the fire. This announcement rattled the people, who asked John, *"What shall we do then?"* (v. 10). Although engaging in good deeds does not save anyone, John affirms that continuing in good works is evidence of true repentance; therefore, he describes the type of behavior that the people should cultivate if they were serious about following the Lord.

For example, it would be appropriate to share with those lacking proper clothing and food to eat (v. 11). Tax collectors were to no longer steal from the people, but to only collect what was lawful (vv. 12-13). Soldiers were not to abuse their authority by intimidating people or by falsely accusing people of wrongdoing; they were also to be content with their wages and not be given to complaining (v. 14).

John's modest demeanor and his powerful message excited the people as to whether he was the promised Messiah (v. 15). But John was not seeking fame, nor was he claiming to be the Messiah; rather, he was pointing people to the One that was to come, who was mightier than himself (v. 16). In fact, John proclaims that he was not worthy to untie the Messiah's sandal strap. He was only baptizing with water those who were publicly repenting of their sins, but when Christ came, He would baptize those in His audience with the Holy Spirit and with fire.

Some in Christendom have equated the baptism of the Holy Spirit and of fire mentioned in verse 16 as being the same thing and a desirable blessing from God. But careful examination of four pertinent passages will reveal quite a different understanding. First, when used metaphorically in Scripture, "fire" speaks of various forms of divine judgment (Gen. 19:24; Num. 16:35; Matt. 13:39-40). This means that God's fire is not desirable, with the only exception being that the Lord permits His people to pass through refining trials to better them (Job 23:10; Mal. 3:2-3). But this is obviously not Luke's meaning as he further clarifies that the baptism of fire is of an unquenchable nature that completely devours the chaff (unbelievers), in contrast to the wheat (true believers) which is gathered safely into God's barn (heaven; v 17).

Next, notice that in Luke's and Matthew's accounts John is speaking to a mixed audience of believers and rebels, so he mentions both baptisms (v. 7; Matt. 3:7). In a future day, believers would be baptized by the Holy Spirit, while those rejecting Christ would be cast into the eternal Lake of Fire. Yet, Mark records a different scene in which John is only speaking to those who had believed his message. To these he promises only the baptism of the Holy Spirit; there is no mention of fire (Mark 1:8).

Last, just before the Lord's ascension to heaven, He refers to John's promise: *"For John truly baptized with water, but you shall be baptized with the Holy Spirit not many days from now"* (Acts 1:5). The Lord is speaking to His disciples and there is no mention of fire. Dear believer, the Holy Spirit is not given in measure (John 3:34). If you have been born again, you have all of Him that you will ever get and all that you will ever need to achieve whatever God has for you to do.

John's spiritual forthright ministry exhorted the people to repent and live a life pleasing to God (v. 18). Many did repent and were baptized by

John, but others were offended by his preaching. For example, because John had publicly confronted Herod Antipas and Herodias' adultery and other evil deeds that Herod had done, the tetrarch was prompted to arrest John and put him in prison (vv. 19-20).

Herod the Great had at least fourteen children by eight different wives. Antipas and Philip were sons of Herod the Great, but were half-brothers. Herod Antipas apparently had an affair with his brother Herod Philip's wife, Herodias, after Philip settled permanently in Rome. Herodias left Philip and remained with Antipas in Palestine. Antipas divorced his wife (the daughter of Aretas, the king of Petra) to illegally marry his brother Philip's wife, and Herodias divorced her husband, which the Law did not permit. Herodias (the feminine form of Herod) was the granddaughter of Herod the Great, thus the niece to both her husbands, Philip and Antipas.

John rebuked their adultery publicly (Matt. 14:3-4). Although Herod esteemed John as a just and holy man (Mark 6:20), he considered putting John to death, to silence his public ridicule of his illicit relationship with Herodias. However, because he feared the people, who believed that John was a prophet, Herod chose to imprison John (Matt. 14:5). It is generally believed that John was imprisoned in Herod's royal palace/fortress at Machaerus, which faced Arabia on the southeast border of Herod's domain. Herod had several such residences.

The Baptism of Jesus Christ (vv. 21-22)

One day, the Lord Jesus came to John to be baptized (v. 21). Luke does not record John's reluctance to do so, nor Christ's conversation with John that caused him to baptize Him. Luke does inform us that immediately after His baptism, Christ began to pray. It was at this moment that heaven opened, and the Holy Spirit descended upon Him in the form of a dove. Then immediately, the Father Himself declared from heaven, *"You are My beloved Son; in You I am well pleased"* (v. 22). Hence, all three persons of the Godhead were involved with the commissioning and empowering of Christ's earthly ministry.

Genealogy of Christ Through Mary (vv. 23-38)

The Lord Jesus had now been anointed by God for the commencement of His ministry. Luke informs us that He was *about* thirty years of age at this juncture. As previously explained, the Lord

Jesus was likely born in 6 or 5 B.C., just before Herod the Great's death in 4 B.C. John's ministry began in 28 A.D.; thus the Lord would likely be 32 or 33 years old at this time.

Luke then injects the lineage of Christ into his record to show that, though He came from a "seed of the woman," He was a representative of Adam on earth. The genealogy ends with *"the son of Adam, the son of God."* Where the first Adam failed, the Last Adam would not.

Immediately after this divine proclamation from heaven, the evil tempter assaulted the Lord for forty days. The Last Adam, the Son of God, triumphed over Satan; thus, His righteous and holy character was thoroughly proven. Luke waits two chapters to introduce the genealogy of Christ so that He might introduce his audience to the Last Adam, who was not human in the same way we are, but was proven to be sinless and perfect. Jesus Christ was God's replacement representative for the first Adam (Rom. 5:12-21). Luke is writing to a Greek audience, and they would be very interested in Luke's orderly presentation of the "perfect" man, the Last Adam.

> Adam's righteousness was ours so long as he maintained it, and his sin was ours the moment that he committed it; and in the same manner, all that the [Last] Adam is or does, is ours as well as His, seeing that He is our representative. Here is the ... gracious system of representation and substitution.[18]
>
> — C. H. Spurgeon

The genealogies of Christ presented in Matthew 1 and Luke 3 are different from each other and serve distinct purposes. Matthew presents the genealogy of Christ through the royal line of David and Solomon from the tribe of Judah to Joseph (the husband of Mary), the legal earthly father of the Lord Jesus. The genealogy of Matthew 1 served as proof to the Jews that Jesus, through Joseph, was a direct descendant of David and, thus, the legal and rightful heir to David's throne. As to not distract from his theme of covenant fulfillment, Matthew begins with Abraham, not Adam, in rendering Christ's royal genealogy.

Luke's genealogy of Christ, however, is for a different purpose. Luke upholds Christ as the Son of Man, or more specifically, the Son of Adam. In so doing, Luke shows Christ to be the Last Adam, God's replacement representative of righteousness and the literal fulfillment of the prophesied Messiah being derived from the *"seed of a woman"* (Gen.

Luke

3:15-16). God wants mankind to understand that the Messiah would not be of the seed of fallen man, yet His royal lineage would be established through a man, Joseph, back to Solomon and David.

The two genealogies accomplish this: Luke focuses our attention upon the Lord's humanity derived from Mary through the power of the Holy Spirit, while Matthew demonstrates Christ's official authority, as a descendant of David, through Joseph. Hence, Matthew's wording is precise to indicate the human lineage of Christ through Mary: *"Joseph the husband of Mary, of whom was born Jesus who is called Christ"* (1:16). "Of whom" in the English is derived from *ek hos* in the Greek and the *hos* is a genitive, singular, feminine pronoun, meaning that the baby Jesus originated from Mary, but not Joseph. Luke's wording affirms this truth: *"Jesus ... being (as was supposed) the son of Joseph"* (v. 23). Mary (Heli being her father) was a descendant of David through Nathan (v. 31), while Joseph was a descendant of David through Solomon and later Jeconiah, who was cursed by God.

God had promised that one of David's descendants would sit on his throne forever (2 Sam. 7:13-16). However, God had removed wicked Jehoiachin (Jeconiah, a descendant of Solomon) from the throne and had pronounced a specific judgment upon him: none of his descendants would ever ascend to the throne of David (Jer. 22:30). This meant that the branch which sprouted from David would be the Messiah, but not directly in the line of Davidic kings because of this curse (Jer. 33:15-16).

This prophecy is used to magnify the incarnation of the Lord Jesus Christ as the Messiah. Joseph, the husband of Mary (the mother of the Lord Jesus), was a descendant of Shealtiel who was the son of Jehoiachin or Jeconiah (Matt. 1:12; 1 Chron. 3:17). Therefore, no son of Joseph could sit upon David's throne. Mary, however, was also a descendant of David through Nathan (Luke 3:24-38). Thus, the son of Mary could fulfill both prophecies, if she conceived supernaturally through the power of the Holy Spirit and not by Joseph her husband. Such a child would avoid the curse of Jeconiah, would not be corrupted by the fallen nature inherited from Adam, and would be the rightful heir to the throne of David.

God's cutting off the branch of David through Jeconiah would serve to assist the Jews in a future day to recognize the Righteous Branch of David through the genealogies recorded in 1 Chronicles and Matthew. Indeed, the One who would rule over them in righteousness forever was in the line of David, but not a descendant of Jeconiah.

Luke Chapter 4

The Testing of Jesus Christ by the Devil (vv. 1-13)
In chapter 2, the sinlessness of Christ was affirmed by the virgin birth. In chapter 3, we witnessed the absolute delight of the Father in His beloved Son. In this chapter, Christ's impeccability will be displayed.

Being filled with the Holy Spirit, Christ was led from the Jordan River and into the wilderness to be tempted (tested) by Satan (v. 1). While in the wilderness the Lord ate nothing (v. 2). Both Matthew and Luke inform us that the devil solicited Christ to do evil throughout the forty days, not just the final day, which is often believed.

Scripturally speaking, the word "temptation" has different meanings depending upon the context of the related passage. The word *peirasmos,* normally translated as "temptation," may also be rendered as "trial" or "testing." *Peirasmos* means "to demonstrate the proof of something," either by suffering through a holy trial or enduring an evil solicitation. Holy trials are those tests that originate with God for our edification and perfection. Unholy temptations, as in the text before us, though allowed by God, do not originate with Him, but rather these solicitations to do sin come from Satan and his domain of influence in the world.

But why was the Lord Jesus subjected to forty days of testing and not thirty or fifty? The number forty is used in Scripture to represent *probation* and *testing*, which explains its frequent occurrence. At times, God extended the nation of Israel forty-year probationary periods to test or prove them: the Israelites were tested in the wilderness forty years, delivered and had rest during the forty years that Othniel, Barak, and Gideon judged Israel and enjoyed dominion during the forty-year reigns of five kings: David, Solomon, Jeroboam, Jehoash, and Joash. Another example of forty as the number of probationary testing is found in God's dealings with Nineveh; Jonah preached that, unless the inhabitants repented, God's judgment would fall on them in forty days.

The Bible also records other occasions when individuals went forty days without food or drink through the supernatural care of God: Elijah during his wilderness experience (1 Kgs. 19:8) and Moses before

Luke

Jehovah on Mount Horeb (Ex. 34:28). How was this possible? Once, the disciples observed that the Lord Jesus had not eaten for an extended period of time, and they encouraged Him to eat something. He responded: *"'I have food to eat of which you do not know.' Therefore the disciples said to one another, 'Has anyone brought Him anything to eat?' Jesus said to them, 'My food is to do the will of Him who sent Me, and to finish His work'"* (John 4:32-34).

Clearly, there are times in which God supernaturally sustains an individual's body for the purpose of accomplishing His work. The Lord Jesus was led into the wilderness by the Holy Spirit; He was where God wanted Him, and God sustained the Lord's body during that time. The Lord teaches us that doing God's will should be the primary objective of one's life, and though the temporal facets of life, such as food and drink, are necessary, one should not be ruled by them.

We understand that Christ, as *holy humanity*, could not sin, for there was nothing in His members that would respond to sin; His very essence repulses sin and loathes its working. Some have suggested that Satan's forty days of external solicitations caused an internal moral struggle within Christ. This was not the case. How could the Father, looking down from heaven, declare, *"This is My beloved Son, in whom I am well pleased"* (Matt. 3:17), if the Lord was struggling internally with thoughts of sin? As John declared, the Lord Jesus **was**, not might be, *"the Lamb of God who takes away the sin of the world"* (John 1:29). The Father never questioned the impeccability of Christ – only Satan and men do that – He was blameless and perfect, the only acceptable substitutional sacrifice for man's sin.

The Lord Jesus knows all about being tested through sufferings; in fact, the writer of Hebrews states His full maturity was demonstrated in this manner (Heb. 2:10). He also is quite familiar with the latter form of testing, for this passage reveals that Satan externally solicited Him to do evil for forty days straight. But He did not respond to Satan's temptations or falter in character through life's difficulties.

Yet the Lord Jesus knows nothing about the second form of temptation (i.e., being drawn away by internal desires, Jas. 1:14)! This is the pragmatic lusting of our fallen members. John tells us that sin was an intruder into humanity; it was not inherent in Adam, but it entered in from the world and then passed down to the next generation. *"For all that is in the world – the lust of the flesh, the lust of the eyes, and the pride of life – is not of the Father but is of the world"* (1 Jn. 2:16). The ungodly lusting of our members originally came from the world.

The basis of lusting is dissatisfaction. Ever since Satan told Eve that she could be more than what God had created her to be and have more than what God had given her, humanity has been dissatisfied. Dissatisfaction advocates that "God is unfairly limiting me, and I desire more." Is it possible for Christ to have been dissatisfied? No, Christ, being God, is perfectly satisfied – He is self-sufficient. Lusting "in the flesh" is not of God, but of the world. Lucifer and Adam sinned because of dissatisfaction with being what God created them to be. But as the Creator, no such evil desire was a part of Christ's humanity. He only could and would do the will of God.

This was the aspiration of the Lord Jesus, when He quoted from Deuteronomy 8:3 to counter Satan's test: *"If You are the Son of God, command this stone to become bread"* (v. 3). Though hungry after forty days of fasting, the Lord did not think so little of God's food, His Word, that He would turn stones into loaves of bread to satisfy His hunger. Instead, He quoted Scripture to exhibit the power of God's Word to defeat Satan's attack: *"Man shall not live by bread alone, but by every word that proceeds from the mouth of God"* (v. 4). The outcome of this test was that the Lord was sustained in His hunger, God was glorified, and Satan was disgraced. We experience the same type of victory when we, by faith in God's Word, resist and ignore Satan's deception.

Next, Satan took Christ to a high mountain and showed Him the kingdoms of the world in a moment of time (v. 5). The devil then offered Christ rulership of these kingdoms if He would bow down before him (vv. 6-7). Since our first parents sinned, the world has been under the devil's authority, and will continue to be until Christ reestablishes God's kingdom on earth and restores what was lost in Eden. The Lord again defeats the attack of the enemy by quoting Scripture: *"You shall worship the Lord your God, and Him only you shall serve"* (v. 8; Deut. 6:13).

The Lord defeated the devil's third solicitation to cast Himself down from the pinnacle of the temple to prove that He was the Son of God (vv. 9-11) by quoting Deuteronomy 6:12: *"You shall not tempt the Lord your God"* (v. 7). Notice that in this solicitation the devil refers to Psalm 91:11-12. First, he does not quote from the Hebrew text, but from the Septuagint, as the translators had added *"at any time"* (see Matt. 4:6; KJV). Second, he left out *"to keep you in all your ways"* to change the context of the passage. The devil is never more dangerous than when he quotes (misquotes) God's Word, for he does so with the purpose to deceive. After observing this fact, F. B. Hole challenges all believers:

> The devil always sows doubts on the Divine Word. No sooner has God said, "This is My beloved Son," than the devil says twice over, *"If* Thou be the Son of God" (Matt. 3:17, 4:3, 6). The little word "if" is a great favorite with the devil! Jesus appropriately met him with the Word of God. That Word is indispensable to Man's spiritual life just as bread is to his natural life. And man needs *every* word that God has spoken, and not just a few special passages only. Are we all finding our spiritual life in "every word that proceeds out of the mouth of God"?[19]

After the final attempt, Matthew tells us that the Lord commanded the devil to depart, which he did (Matt. 4:11). This demonstrated that Jesus Christ is the Son of God and has authority over all angelic beings (e.g., Jude 9). After the testing was completed, angels came to minister to a hungry and victorious Messiah (Matt. 4:11). Luke reminds us that the devil was not finished trying to thwart God's Messiah, but he was waiting for "an opportune time" (v. 13).

What was Satan's overall objective by tempting Christ? If Christ would have turned the stones to bread, He would have knelt before the devil to gather them off the ground. If Christ would have cast Himself down from the temple, He would have lowered Himself before the devil. If Christ would have bowed down to the devil to obtain those earthly kingdoms under his dominion, He would have exalted the devil and disdained His Father. The devil thought to gain the high ground over the Lord Jesus and cause Him to act outside of the Father's will, but because Christ accurately quoted and applied God's Word – Satan was defeated.

If we follow the Lord's example, we too will evade the lion's attack and trample the serpent under our feet (Ps. 91:13). Both metaphors are used in the New Testament in the context of a believer's victory in Christ over Satan (Rom. 16:19-20; 1 Pet. 5:7-9). As shown by Christ during His forty days of testing, it is God who supplies our sustenance, guides our service, and bestows to us honor and authority, not the devil.

There is an obvious difference in the order of satanic attacks on the Lord Jesus as recorded in Matthew 4 and Luke 4. The order maintained by each writer is for the purpose of upholding the prevalent theme of each Gospel. In Matthew, Satan first asks the Lord Jesus to turn the stones into bread, then bids Him to cast Himself down from the pinnacle of the temple, and, third, the devil offers to Christ all the kingdoms of this world, if Christ will only worship him. Luke's order, however, is first the request to turn the stones into bread, then the offer of earthly kingdoms, and finally Satan adjures Christ to cast Himself down from the pinnacle of the temple to prove that the angels will protect Him. Why the different order? Arthur Pink explains:

> In Matthew, the order is arranged climactically, so as to make Rulership over all the kingdoms of the world the final bait which the Devil dangled before the Son of David. But in Luke we have the chronological order, the order in which they actually occurred, and these correspond with the order of temptation of the first man and his wife in Eden, where the appeal was made, as in Luke, to the lust of the flesh, the lust of the eyes, and the pride of life (1 Jn. 2:16; Gen. 3:6).[20]

Sovereign design explains the variation of the temptation accounts, which serves to further declare the wisdom of God and the distinct glories of His Son. Luke's order of temptations is chronological, while Matthew arranged it climactically unto kingship. It is worthy to note that John does not record the temptation of Christ, as that would be contrary to his theme. John presents Christ as God made flesh (John 1:14), and as James insists, *"God cannot be tempted"* (Jas. 1:13). This fact refutes any degrading doctrines that pertain to the Lord's ability to sin or to His members having the capacity to be enticed to sin. He was not only sinless, but His nature was impeccable; there was nothing in Him that could respond to sin (Heb. 4:15).

Christ Commences His Public Ministry in Galilee (vv. 14-15)

After the devil's failed attempts to cause Christ to sin, the Lord was led by the Holy Spirit into Galilee to begin His public ministry (v. 14). He taught in various synagogues throughout the region and the news of Him spread quickly throughout Galilee (v. 15).

Matthew and Mark concentrate more intensely on the Lord's two-year Galilean ministry than Luke. However, Luke provides more information concerning the Lord's Judean and Perean ministries in the closing months of His earthly ministry.

Christ Rejected in the Synagogue at Nazareth (vv. 16-30)

Only Luke provides the age of the Lord when He entered His public ministry after His baptism and anointing (3:23). He was *about* thirty years old, the same age in which a priest could sacrifice in the temple and a Jewish man could publicly read Scripture in the synagogue. The Lord did both, but the former was done outside the camp of Judaism (Heb. 13:12-14) at a place called Golgotha.

Christ maintained every aspect of Jewish Law, including keeping the feasts of Jehovah and keeping the Sabbath day holy. It was His custom to visit the local synagogue on the Sabbath (v. 16). Only Luke records the details of one particular Sabbath day in His hometown synagogue of Nazareth. He was handed a scroll of Isaiah to read from. After announcing that the Spirit of the Lord was upon Him, He read Isaiah 61 verse 1 and half of verse 2:

> *"The Spirit of the Lord is upon Me, because He has anointed Me to preach the gospel to the poor; He has sent Me to heal the brokenhearted, to proclaim liberty to the captives and recovery of sight to the blind, to set at liberty those who are oppressed; to proclaim the acceptable year of the Lord"* (vv. 18-19).

Notice that the Lord Jesus had to open the book and find the portion of Scripture to be read. The Lord had to expend effort to locate the portion of sacred text, just as you and I must turn pages in our Bibles. After reading from Isaiah 61, He closed the book, returned it to the attendant, and sat down (v. 20). With every eye in the synagogue fixed on Him, the Lord then declared, *"Today this Scripture is fulfilled in your hearing"* (v. 21). As foreshadowed in the year of Jubilee (Lev. 25), a new era of reviving joy was dawning in Israel. The Lord Jesus discontinued His reading of Isaiah's prophecy in the middle of a sentence to highlight His two advents to the earth. The remainder of Isaiah 61:2 reads, **"and the day of vengeance of our God**; *to comfort all that mourn."*

The Jews understood that the Lord was claiming to be the One Isaiah was prophesying of, that is, the Messiah. They became so enraged by His claim that they sought to push Him over a cliff. The Lord did not read the remaining portion of verse 2 or verse 3 (which mentions consoling those who mourn in Zion), as that content pertained to His second advent. At that time, He will return to judge the nations and restore Israel to a proper place of honor. For Israel, the Lord's promise to comfort those who mourn will be realized after the Tribulation Period. Obviously, believers in the Church Age can always approach the throne of grace for help when needed (Heb. 4:16), but this prophecy confirms the type of special comfort God provides for a particular group of mourners.

In His incarnation, the Son of God had come to *"seek and to save,"* not to judge the wicked. When Christ was born, He brought God's offer of peace to the earth, as the angels declared on the night of His birth and He Himself declared to His disciples on resurrection day. Praise God that the Lord Jesus abruptly stopped when He did, or all humanity would have received God's retribution for sin. Thankfully, that has been reserved for another day!

Those who heard Christ speak were amazed at the gracious words that proceeded out of His mouth (v. 22). But they could not understand how the son of Joseph, whom they had watched grow up among them, could be any more than an uneducated carpenter's son. The Lord, knowing their thoughts said to them, *"You will surely say this proverb to Me, 'Physician, heal yourself! Whatever we have heard done in Capernaum, do also here in Your country'"* (v. 23). Indeed, the words that Christ spoke were amazing, but the people were not interested in His message; they wanted to see Him perform miracles like the ones they had heard that He had done in Capernaum. The Lord then linked their unbelief with a well-known axiom, *"no prophet is accepted in his own country"* (v. 24). He then provided two historical examples to illustrate Israel's propensity to reject the prophets that God had sent to them.

First, He notes that during the famine that Elijah had pronounced on Israel for their stubborn idolatry, Elijah did not obtain food and shelter from any widows in Israel, but from a Gentile widow in Zarephath (vv. 25-26). As a result, the widow from Zarephath was blessed by God, and she and her son were sustained through the famine.

Second, although there were many lepers in Israel, only the Syrian Naaman came to the prophet Elisha for healing and was cleansed (v. 27). Israel's disobedience to God's Word restricted God's blessing upon them, but Gentiles exercising faith in God's Word had been blessed.

Likewise, because the lost sheep of Israel in Nazareth were rejecting God's Word that He had spoken to them, they would not see God's blessing. In short, He could not perform many miracles in Nazareth because of the people's disbelief (Matt. 13:58). His audience became enraged after hearing these words and put the Lord out of the synagogue and the city (v. 28). They led Him up to a brow of a hill that the city was built on and sought to kill Him by throwing Him down over the cliff, but He passed through the midst of them and went His way (vv. 29-30). God had determined the specific hour of His Son's death, and this was neither the time, nor the place, nor the means in which He would die.

Christ Casts Out Demons in Capernaum (vv. 31-37)

Christ and His disciples journeyed to Capernaum, and shortly after arriving, they entered a synagogue on the Sabbath (v. 31). The Lord began to teach the people, who were astonished at His ability, for He taught as if He owned the Scriptures. Christ's knowledge of Scripture and His passion for God exuded an authority that the scribes, who simply taught the Law's regulations, were missing (v. 32).

There was a man in the synagogue who had an unclean spirit and, in fact, was indwelt by several demons (v. 33). Using the man's vocal cords, the demons cried out, *"Let us alone! What have we to do with You, Jesus of Nazareth? Did You come to destroy us? I know who You are – the Holy One of God"* (v. 34). The demons knew who Christ was, that He had authority over them, and that they would ultimately be destroyed by Him. The Lord commanded the evil spirits in the man to be silent and to come out of him (v. 35). After the man convulsed and cried out with a loud voice, the demonic spirits departed their host.

Those at the synagogue had never seen anything like this before and they inquired among themselves who Jesus was and about His unfamiliar teachings (v. 36). Christ taught with authority and exercised authority over unclean spirits – could Jesus of Nazareth be the Holy One of God as the demons had declared? The news of what He had done in the synagogue that day quickly spread throughout Galilee (v. 37).

Christ Heals Peter's Mother-in-Law (vv. 38-39)

Mark informs us that Simon Peter and Andrew lived in the same house in Capernaum, that Peter was married, and that his mother-in-law also resided in their home. There is no evidence in Scripture that any of the other disciples were married at this juncture, which might explain why so much of the Lord's Galilean ministry was at Capernaum and the surrounding villages.

The Lord and his disciples departed the synagogue and went to Peter and Andrew's home (v. 38). The Lord Jesus was made aware that Peter's mother-in-law lay sick in bed with a high fever. He went to her side and rebuked the fever and immediately she was well (v. 39). Being well, she immediately began serving their many household guests. Her service

The Man and Your God

refreshed the Lord and His disciples, who would be engaging in long hours of ministry throughout the remainder of the day.

This is a good reminder that those who are born again are healed and strengthened to serve the Lord. This often begins with bearing one's daily burdens to bless others. What the Lord does, He does perfectly. Not only was Peter's mother-in-law's fever gone, but her body was enabled to serve without any diminished capacity after being ill.

More Healings as the Gospel Is Preached (vv. 40-44)

The news of Christ's arrival at Peter's home spread quickly through the city. By evening, there was a line at the door of many sick and demon-possessed people to be healed (v. 40). The Lord healed everyone that journeyed to seek His assistance that evening, and He also prohibited the demons from speaking in His presence (v. 41). The demons knew who He was, "the Christ, the Son of God," but because He was God's Message and Messenger to Israel, no infringement on His mission would be tolerated. He would reveal His identity and the reason of His earthly sojourn according to God's sovereign timing.

The next morning, Mark informs us that the Lord rose long before daylight and quietly went to a solitary place to pray (Mark 1:35). To ensure privacy, the Lord often spent the early morning hours communing with His Father. The Lord received His marching orders for the day during these intimate times of prayer. His soul was refreshed by the presence of His Father despite the heavy, ongoing demands of ministry. This is a good routine for all believers to follow. Service without enjoying God's presence will be burdensome to our souls, for *"the joy of the Lord is [our] strength"* (Neh. 8:10).

After dawn came and went, Simon Peter and others began searching for the Lord Jesus (Mark 1:36). After finding Him, Peter said, *"Everyone is looking for You"* (Mark 1:37). The disciples were likely wondering, "Why is Jesus spending so much time in prayer when people are trying to find Him? Doesn't He want to have followers and be famous?" What was the Lord's response when Peter informed Him that *"everyone is looking for You"*? The Lord replied, *"Let us go into the next towns"* (Mark 1:38). Although the people sought to keep Him in Capernaum, the Lord told them, *"I must preach the kingdom of God to the other cities also, because for this purpose I have been sent"* (vv. 42-43). For the next few months, the Lord spoke in synagogues throughout Galilee (v. 44).

Luke Chapter 5

The Lord Begins Calling His Disciples (vv. 1-11)

Luke then recounts how the Lord called His first disciples into ministry. These and other disciples would continue their ministry between the initial offering of the kingdom and its realization later.

While walking along the shore of the Sea of Galilee near Gennesaret, the crowds were following the Lord to hear God's message to them (v. 1). The Lord saw two empty boats on the shoreline and fishermen working nearby washing their nets (v. 2). The Lord stepped into Simon's boat and asked the fisherman to push out a little from the shoreline so that He could teach the people without being pressed upon (v. 3). Simon complied and the Lord sat down in the boat and taught the people.

This was not the Lord and Simon's first meeting, for previously the Lord had called Simon to follow Him while he and his brother Andrew were fishing from their boat (Matt. 4:18). Initially, Peter forsook his fishing nets to follow Christ after His bidding (Matt. 4:20). But Peter had returned to fishing, so the Lord had to again call Peter to follow Him. Hereafter, Peter would be a fisher of men.

After Christ finished speaking, He instructed Peter to launch the boat out further into deeper water and to let down his nets for a catch (v. 4). Apparently, Peter and Andrew and their partners James and John had been fishing all night without catching a single fish (v. 5). So, Peter balked at this idea because of their long, weary night of catching nothing. Furthermore, a line and hook were normally used to catch fish during daytime hours and a net in deeper water at night, so what the Lord was asking Peter, an experienced fisherman, to do was not sensible. But Peter relented, saying that because He had requested him to do it, he would let down "the net" (v. 5). The net quickly filled with a great number of fish and Peter signaled to his partners for assistance. There were so many fish that the net tore and some fish escaped, but the catch was so significant that both boats began to sink from the fish that had been harvested (vv. 6-7).

When Peter saw what had happened, he fell on his knees before the Lord and said, *"Depart from me, for I am a sinful man, O Lord"* (v. 8). There were at least two things on Peter's mind. First, the Lord had said to let down his nets and Peter had let down only one net which tore under the strain of the catch. His partial obedience had limited Christ's blessing to him. May we remember that partial obedience is still disobedience. Second, the Lord had called Peter to follow Him previously and Peter responded by forsaking his fishing nets, but then he returned to fishing (Mark 1:18).

Luke tells us that the crowd was astonished at the catch of fish, but evidently not at the words Christ spoke (v. 9). Even Simon's fishing partners were amazed at the size of the catch (v. 10). The Lord then told Peter not to be afraid, for in the future he would be a fisher of men. At this declaration, Peter forsook all and followed the Lord (v. 11).

A Leper Is Cleansed (vv. 12-16)

The prophet Isaiah predicted that when the Messiah arrived in Israel, He would heal blindness, deafness, lameness, dumbness, and various diseases (Isa. 35:5-6, 53:4). Having concluded His lengthy *Sermon on the Mount* (which Luke does not record), the Lord descended the mount and was followed by a large crowd (Matt. 8:1). A man full of leprosy saw Jesus Christ and came to worship Him, saying, *"Lord, if You are willing, You can make me clean"* (v. 12; Matt. 8:2). The Lord was moved with compassion and stretched out His hand and touched the leper and said to Him, *"I am willing; be cleansed"* and immediately his leprosy was gone (v. 13).

The Lord then told the cleansed leper not to tell others of what had happened, but to immediately go to the temple and be inspected by the priests and offer the gift required by the Law (Lev. 14). This would serve as a testimony of Himself before all the priests (v. 14). It is likely that the cleansed leper eventually arrived at the temple to undergo the cleansing ritual after being healed, but he also largely published the miracle along the way – so much so that Christ and His disciples had to depart the city for a remote region to avoid the swelling numbers of people desiring His assistance (Mark 1:45). Many still came to Him in the wilderness for healing (v. 15). However, being in a deserted place made His ministry more manageable, as only those who really believed that He could help them would make the journey to find Him. This more isolated location provided the Lord ample opportunities to slip away to pray privately also (v. 16).

Whether the Lord did not want the cleansed leper to speak of the miracles to others or just not to be delayed in going to the temple by doing so is unclear. However, the Lord often instructed those He had healed or who had observed a healing to keep quiet about the miracle. This was most likely to avoid being prematurely enthroned by the Jewish populace wanting relief from Roman rule. His countrymen must understand and accept the spiritual aspects of His kingdom offer before He could ever sit on a throne in Israel.

While today there is effective treatment for leprosy, there was none in Old Testament days, meaning that if someone contracted the disease, he or she was isolated from Jewish society to suffer a slowly deteriorating and miserable existence. To prevent the spread of the disease, lepers normally communed together in remote colonies and were dependent on loved ones to supply their necessities. For this reason, leprosy was intensely feared and caused understandable paranoia among the Jews.

Besides healing the leper, the Lord Jesus showed compassion in two additional ways. First, He was not afraid to convey love to the leper by touching him, even though the Law declared him to be untouchable. Not only did the Lord have power to heal the disease, but He also showed that He could not be brought under its corrupting power. He thus remained a fit and clean sacrificial Lamb for God. Second, by sending the healed leper immediately to the priests, He was able to declare the gospel message to hard-to-reach religious leaders sequestered in the temple. Healing a blind or lame person would not accomplish this, as there was no requirement in the Law for them to be inspected and ceremonially cleansed.

One can only imagine the shock on the priests' faces when this exuberant pilgrim began to tell them his story: "A man named Jesus touched me, cured my leprosy, and told me to come to you to proclaim what had happened and to offer the appropriate sacrifices!" In reaching out to touch one leper, the Lord Jesus was showing His love, not just for this individual, but also for the religious elite of Israel. The priests laboring at the temple needed to hear the kingdom gospel message too.

There is no Old Testament record of a healed leper ever going through the ceremonial purification process as supervised by Levitical priests (Lev. 14). This meant that there was something new in Israel. Did this mean that Isaiah's prophecy had been fulfilled? Was Messiah in Israel? The Lord Jesus sent a steady stream of healed lepers to the temple over the next three years. As a result, a multitude of Jewish priests believed on Him and were saved (Acts 6:7).

A Paralytic Is Healed and Forgiven (vv. 17-26)

After Christ's rejection by the Gergesenes, He returned with His disciples across the Sea of Galilee to Capernaum (Matt. 9:1). The Lord was teaching a large group of people in a house (Mark 2:1), with Pharisees and teachers of the Law observing Him (v. 17). While He was teaching, four men brought a paralyzed man on a stretcher to the Lord to be healed but they could not gain entrance to the house because of the crowd (v. 18). Therefore, they carried the paralytic to the rooftop, broke through the roof (perhaps removing tiles) and then lowered the disabled man down to Christ through the hole (v. 19). When the Lord saw the faith of the four men and that of the paralytic who desired to be lowered down to Him, despite the possibility of injury, He said to the paralytic, *"Man, your sins are forgiven you"* (v. 20).

When the scribes and Pharisees heard this statement, they said within themselves, *"Who is this who speaks blasphemies?"* for they reasoned that only God can forgive sins (v. 21). Because the Lord Jesus said that He had the authority to forgive sins, He was claiming to be God, which infuriated Israel's religious leaders. The Lord, overhearing their thoughts, asked them two questions (v. 22). First, He asked them why they thought evil of Him for this declaration; if they truly understood who He was, then they would not think that He was blaspheming God. Second, He asked them, *"Which is easier, to say, 'Your sins are forgiven you,' or to say, 'Rise up and walk'?"* (v. 23). The Lord was implying that it was easier for man to engage in religious jargon than to produce spiritual change in one's life.

As the forgiveness of sins was a spiritual matter, it could not be humanly verified. Hence, one could say, "Your sins are forgiven" without knowing if it were true or not. Therefore, to prove that He did have the authority to forgive sins, the Lord commanded the paralytic, *"arise, take up your bed, and go to your house"* (v. 24). This activity could be visually verified. The paralytic was instantly healed and gained the ability to use his muscles in such a way as to carry his bed while walking to his home (v. 25). The healed man did not have to struggle to do what the Lord commanded him to do (i.e., he did not have to learn to walk). Again, we see the Lord not just healing someone, but also fully equipping them to obey what He said to do. When the multitudes saw the miracle, they marveled and glorified God that a mere human could have such power to heal. They said to themselves, *"We have seen strange things today!"* (v. 26).

This scene conveys a wonderful truth about repentance and faith. The Lord Jesus said that unless people repent of their sins, they cannot be saved (13:3, 5). Confession of sin is necessary for forgiveness to be granted (e.g., 17:3). We also know that unless someone believes on Christ as Savior, he or she cannot be saved (John 3:16-18, 5:24). Repentance and faith swing on the same hinge of gospel truth. Repentance agrees with God on the matter of sin and turns away from what displeased God and could never earn His favor. But one must turn from sin to embrace in faith God's solution for sin, Christ. So, although the paralytic did not confess his sin before receiving forgiveness, the Lord knew the condition of the man's heart by the evidence of his faith in Him. The Lord used the incident to again declare to Israel's leaders that He was God's Son and their Messiah.

Verse 24 contains Luke's first reference in his gospel account to "the Son of Man." "The Son of Man" is an Old Testament term to express human association and, thus, links Christ to earth as a man. Luke applies the title to the Lord Jesus twenty-five times in his Gospel, while, in contrast, John, whose theme is the deity of Christ, only refers to the Lord as the Son of Man twelve times. The Lord Jesus spoke more often of Himself as "the Son of Man" than as "the Son of God," for the title identified His mission and not His essence. It is noted that only the Lord Jesus speaks of Himself as "the Son of Man" in the Gospels, some eighty-four times; yet, there are fourteen references to "others" identifying the Lord Jesus as the "Son of God," a title He applies to Himself only five times (all occurrences are rightly placed in John). The Lord normally spoke of His humble station and ministry, while others were privileged to acknowledge His divine rule and essence.

One of the early references in the Bible to the "Son of Man" is found in Psalm 8. This Psalm is then quoted in the epistle to the Hebrews and applied to speak of the incarnation of Christ. The title "Son of Man" is not found in any New Testament epistle, except for the one reference in Hebrews 2:6-9, which refers to Psalm 8.

The Epistles are books of wisdom given to the church to understand the great mysteries of God, which were before hidden in the recesses of God's mind. The Church, in Christ, has a heavenly, not an earthly, calling. The Lord Jesus will always be a man, but now He is highly exalted and at the right hand of God in heaven. It would now be inappropriate to address Him personally as the "Son of Man." This is why the expression is not found in the Epistles, save once in Hebrews as an explanation of Psalm 8. Christ finished that mission to earth, and consequently, at the pleasure of the Father, now has a name above all names.

The Call of Matthew (vv. 27-32)

The Lord then went to the Sea of Galilee at Capernaum to teach the multitudes (Mark 2:13). His teaching ministry was ongoing in that city, and one day He walked by a tax office and saw a man named Levi (Matthew) sitting within. The Lord said to him, *"Follow Me"* (v. 27). Matthew instantly obeyed the invitation and was a tax collector no more. Because tax collectors were notoriously crooked and collected for personal gain more from the people than Rome required, they were hated by the Jews. Matthew had probably been disavowed by his Jewish parents for engaging in this occupation. But on this day, he left a lucrative and hated occupation to become a poor but beloved disciple of Christ, who wrote the Gospel according to Matthew for us to appreciate.

After being called to be a disciple, Matthew (Levi) hosted a large gathering in his own home in or near Capernaum so that others, including tax collectors, could hear Christ's teachings (v. 29). The sight of Christ eating a meal with tax collectors and sinners infuriated the Pharisees who asked His disciples why He did so (v. 30). When the Lord heard their indictment, He said, *"Those who are well have no need of a physician, but those who are sick. I did not come to call the righteous, but sinners, to repentance"* (vv. 31-32).

The Pharisees believed that they were spiritually well and righteous before God; therefore, they did not need to repent and be saved by Jesus Christ. However, the outcasts of society, like the tax collectors, being less hindered by self-righteousness, were more open to listen to the Lord's message. These sinners were more willing to acknowledge the true condition of their souls and seek God's forgiveness through Christ. The fact is, wherever the Lord went, He associated with sinners, for He came to seek and to save the lost. The self-righteous Pharisees did not want what the Lord was offering them, so He did not waste time speaking to those who had no interest in His message of salvation.

For this reason, Matthew informs us that the Lord told the Pharisees, *"But go and learn what this means: 'I desire mercy and not sacrifice.' For I did not come to call the righteous, but sinners, to repentance"* (Matt. 9:13). This quotation from Hosea 6:6 was to prove that God did not want ritualistic worship and cold religiosity from those who called upon Him, but rather inward humility, righteousness, and holiness. The Pharisees looked good outwardly, but inwardly, they were just as lost as the tax collectors; they were in a much more dangerous situation, as they did not believe that they were lost before God.

The Lord's Disciples Do Not Fast (vv. 33-39)

John the baptizer was likely in prison when John's disciples came to the Lord Jesus with a question about fasting (Mark 2:18). Luke indicates that the Pharisees were also present when this question was asked (vv. 30, 33). Apparently, John's disciples were fasting often, as were the Pharisees, but they had noticed that the Lord's disciples were not fasting (v. 33). The Lord affirmed that His disciples were not given to fasting because the bridegroom (Himself) was still with them, but soon He would not be – then they would regularly fast (vv. 34-35). His answer indicated that a new dispensation was coming.

A dispensation in Scripture is not an era of time per se, but rather an economy of truth that God reveals to man and holds him accountable to obey. Dispensations do have their outworking in time and may overlap to some extent. For example, the dispensation of human government established in Genesis 9 was concurrent with the dispensation of the Law instituted with Israel at Mount Sinai and is still in effect today.

The Lord cited two examples (these were likely His first spoken parables), a new cloth on an old garment and new wine in an old wineskin, to show that the purposes of the dispensations of the Law and of Grace were quite different (vv. 36-39). The Law of Moses was rigid in that, if broken, it did not offer mercy, only condemnation. Accordingly, Paul explains that the purpose of the Law was to show sin (Rom. 3:20) and point guilty sinners to the solution – Christ (Gal. 3:24).

The Law only brought condemnation, as no one could keep all of its precepts. But grace through Christ was offered to those who realized that they had fallen short of God's righteousness and needed to be justified by Him to be acceptable before Him (1 Tim. 2:3-6). Grace is receiving the unmerited favor of God.

In summary, lost souls may approach God through law-keeping (i.e., by self-justification) and be found wanting, or by humbly acknowledging their sinful state and receiving redemption and justification through Christ by grace. Consequently, the purpose of both parables was to show that one can choose to live by the Law or by Grace, but not both; the two systems cannot be mixed (Rom. 4:4-5). The purpose of the first was to show the necessity of the second for salvation.

Both parables illustrate this point. A piece of new cloth (unshrunk material) is a poor patch for an old garment, for after it becomes wet and dries, it will shrink and pull away from the old cloth. The latter situation creates a worse outcome than the original problem. Likewise, those trying to mix efforts of self-reformation with God's work of grace will become more resistant to the truth of the gospel message, which has its basis in grace alone. For the same reason, putting new wine in an old wineskin (which has no elasticity) will result in a bad outcome. As the new wine ferments, it will expand and burst the old wineskin, making it unusable. It would have been better to hold to the Law alone than to try to mix Law-keeping with God's grace for salvation. Grace plus a nickel is not grace! The Lord also highlighted our human tendency to embrace religious legalism rather than to humbly receive God's grace by noting that those who drink older wine will not prefer the newer vintage.

The Law was stringent and rigid; its purpose was to condemn, not to save. The Law was designed to highlight man's lost state before God and show his need for God's Savior. Because Christ was born under the Law and completely kept the Law, He was proven to be an acceptable substitute for sacrifice on the account of the guilty (i.e., everyone). Through the process of substitution, then, God was able to righteously judge human sin and offer forgiveness and acceptance through Christ. This means that those who resort to Law-keeping to earn God's favor instead of believing in Christ's redemptive work alone are telling God, "Your Son did not do enough to save me; You need my help too." This is an offensive notion to God. Let us be careful of mixing any elements of the Law with all that God wants us to appreciate in grace!

Luke Chapter 6

Laboring on the Sabbath Controversy (vv. 1-5)

While venturing through ripened grainfields near Capernaum on the Sabbath Day (Mark 2:1), the Lord's hungry disciples plucked a few heads of grain, rubbed the chaff away in their hands, and then ate the kernels (v. 1). This apparently happened a week after the Lord healed the paralytic on the Sabbath Day. The disciples' actions were abruptly challenged by the Pharisees who said, *"Why are you doing what is not lawful to do on the Sabbath?"* (v. 2). The Pharisees' accusation afforded the Lord Jesus with an opportunity to rebuke their religious pride, which had blinded them from comprehending who He really was. He was not the son of a fornicator, nor a Samaritan, nor a man possessed by demons, as they claimed. Rather, He was their Messiah – the Son of God. The Lord's rebuttal contained one historical illustration and a reference to priestly temple service.

First, the Lord Jesus reminded them of what David and his men had done to alleviate their hunger; they entered the house of God and ate the showbread (vv. 3-4). Only the priests were allowed into the tabernacle or temple and only the priests could eat the twelve unleavened cakes, and then only on the Sabbath Day. Yet, David and his men were not punished by God for their actions. Why? It was because David was a righteous man, God's chosen man, who had been rejected by the nation under King Saul's reign. Given their dire and unjust situation, their necessary action was permitted – it would never have occurred if David had been treated properly by Saul.

This historical example was chosen for its direct correlation between David and his men and the Lord and His disciples. Just as David's leadership had been rejected by the nation under Saul's reign, the Pharisees had prompted the people to reject Jesus Christ as their Messiah. If the Pharisees had received Jesus as their Messiah, His disciples would not have been scavenging for food. Thus, the Lord's rebuke in verse 5: *"The Son of Man is also Lord of the Sabbath."*

The Man and Your God

Healing on the Sabbath Controversy (vv. 6-11)

The Lord ceased His dialogue with the Pharisees, but then ventured into "their" synagogue on another Sabbath day (Matt. 12:9). Previously, He had proclaimed that *"the Son of Man is the Lord of the Sabbath"* (v. 5). He, as God, had created the Sabbath for man, and therefore, He was the One who could best explain its meaning and purpose. The Lord Jesus would validate His claim by performing a miracle on the Sabbath, which would also illustrate the purpose the Lord of the Sabbath had for His Sabbath.

There was a man with a withered hand present in the synagogue (Luke informs us that it was his right hand; v. 6). Looking for an opportunity to accuse the Lord of wrongdoing, the Pharisees were watching Him closely to see if He would heal the man (v. 7). Based on Matthew's account, the man may have been "planted" in the synagogue by the Pharisees, for they asked the Lord, *"Is it lawful to heal on the Sabbath"* before the Lord said anything (Matt. 12:10). The Lord Jesus responded to their contrary disposition by telling the man with the withered hand to stand before Him, which he did (v. 8).

The Lord then asked His audience, *"Is it lawful on the Sabbath to do good or to do evil, to save life or to destroy?"* (v. 9). The Pharisees did not answer the Lord's question. It is noted that during the Maccabean revolt against invaders in the second century B.C., the Jews did engage in warfare on the Sabbath day. The Lord never meant for His people to be slaughtered by aggressors if attacked on the Sabbath.

Matthew tells us that the Lord further expounded on His question by pointing out the fact that any one of the Pharisees would rescue one of his sheep if it had fallen into a pit on the Sabbath day (Matt. 12:11). Yet, to God, a man is much more valuable than a sheep; so, it would be *"lawful to do good on the Sabbath"* (Matt. 12:12). Showing compassion and selfless love to others always honors God, regardless of what day it is.

The self-righteous, coldhearted attitudes of the Pharisees angered the Lord. According to their oral law, one could not make a sick person better on the Sabbath, as that would be considered work. As Israel's leaders, they were to exemplify God's holy and loving character to the people but were failing miserably to do so. The Lord demonstrated what He had been teaching about the Sabbath and the true nature of God by commanding the man with the withered hand to stretch his hand out. The man obeyed the Lord, and the Lord immediately and fully restored the disabled man's hand (v. 10). There was now no functional difference between either of his hands. The Pharisees were enraged that the Lord had healed on the Sabbath, and therefore discussed among themselves what should be done concerning Jesus (v. 11).

The Twelve Are Chosen (vv. 12-21)

The Lord went up on a mountain to pray. Luke tells us that the Lord prayed throughout the night before commissioning His disciples the next day (vv. 12-13). The Lord's example emphasizes the importance of God's people engaging in adequate prayer to know the mind of the Lord before making important ministry decisions.

Luke lists the names of the chosen twelve apostles: *"Simon, whom He also named Peter, and Andrew his brother; James and John; Philip and Bartholomew; Matthew and Thomas; James the son of Alphaeus, Thaddaeus, and Simon the Canaanite; Judas the son of James, and Judas Iscariot, who also became a traitor"* (vv. 14-16).

Although it was Andrew who first introduced his brother Peter to the Lord, the inner circle of disciples closest to the Lord later became Peter, James, and John. The Lord referred to the latter two brothers as the "Sons of Thunder." James was the first of the twelve to be martyred in the Church Age (killed by Herod; Acts 12:2). John was the "beloved" disciple and the one to whom the Lord entrusted the care of His mother (John 19:26). All four men were fishermen by trade before following Christ.

Philip was from Bethsaida and introduced Nathanael (or Bartholomew), the man without guile, to the Lord (John 1:47). Thomas had doubts about Christ's resurrection later, but also declared Christ as Lord and God (John 20:28). Matthew was a former tax collector and likely the wealthiest of the disciples called into ministry; he wrote the Gospel of Matthew. Not much is known about James, the less, the son of Alphaeus; Thaddaeus (also called Judas and Lebbaeus), the son of James (v. 16); and Simon, the Canaanite, previously a Jewish Zealot that opposed Roman rule (v. 15). Judas Iscariot betrayed the Lord.

Matthew, a publican and an employee of Rome and Simon, a radical defender of Jewish life, represent the extreme viewpoints in Israel at that time, yet, as Christ's disciples, both men found common ground and there is no record of any hostility between them.

The Sermon on the Level Place (vv. 17-39)

Christ and His disciples came down from the mountain to find an enormous gathering below. Besides Christ's disciples in Galilee, there were many from Jerusalem and Judea in the south and from the coastal cities of Tyre and Sidon in the north that had come to hear Jesus and be healed by Him (v. 17). Indeed, there were many with various infirmities and unclean spirits that were healed (v. 18). Many sought to merely touch the Lord to be healed, and power came out of Him to heal all who did seek His help (v. 19). Although many of Christ's miracles and signs were accomplished by the Holy Spirit, Luke mentions that, in this instance, power came out of the Lord to achieve the healings.

Matthew describes a famous scene and message in Christ's ministry – *The Sermon on the Mount*. Matthew devotes three chapters to Christ's dissertation (chs. 5-7), which occurred on a mountain and contained blessings, but no woes. The message in this chapter contains four blessings and four woes. Luke's record here is of a similar message that Christ gave, but at a different location and a different time. The Sermon on the Mount occurred just prior to the leper being cleansed (Matt. 8). The leper in the last chapter was healed after the Sermon on the Mount, but before this message was given. The Lord's audience is also gathered on a level place (not a mountain, as in Matthew).

The Sermon on the Mount in Matthew is the manifesto of the King, literally the kingdom's constitution declaring how those who are in a right relationship with God should behave. In that message, the Lord addressed the ideal character and conduct of the subjects of His kingdom and what their circle of influence and testimony ought to be. *The Sermon on the Level Place* in Luke pertains more to the lifestyle of the disciples in personal witnessing. For example: in Matthew, the Lord pronounced a blessing upon *"the poor in spirit"* (Matt. 5:3), but in Luke the blessing is to *"the poor"* (v. 20). The former speaks of humility, the latter, of suffering poverty for being faithful to Christ in the world. In summary, Christ is not promising to bless the poor, the hungry, and the afflicted per se, but rather those choosing to be poor, to be hungry, and to suffer affliction for His sake.

It is in this vein that the Lord commenced disclosure of four beatitudes. The first beatitude was a pronouncement of blessing on those who are "poor" (v. 20). The second blessing was for those who were "hungry" (v. 21). The third, for those who "weep" and the fourth, for

Luke

those "hated" and "reviled" by men *"for the Son of Man's sake"* (v. 22). The Lord had just chosen His twelve disciples for service. How did He plan to send them into the world to evangelize the lost? They would carry His name to the nations while suffering poverty, hunger, sorrow, and the hatred of the world; they would suffer oppression for His name (John 15:18-20). This was not a new concept of heralding God's Word, for God had previously sent out His prophets to confront His wayward people and they had been rejected, reviled, and oppressed for doing so (v. 23).

But those servants who choose to sacrificially serve the Savior and to endure suffering in His name now can expect to inherit the kingdom of God. At that time, the Savior will satisfy all their needs, cause them to have great joy, and they will be rewarded for their faithfulness (v. 23).

In contrast with the four beatitudes for faithful service in His name, the Lord levies four woes to those who will be considered least in His kingdom. These servants valued things of the world more important than being His witnesses in the world. Those believers who live for the moment instead of eternity will value things of this world more important than winning souls to Christ.

First, the Lord condemns the hoarding of wealth, instead of using what has been received from the Lord to meet the needs of others (v. 24). To ignore those who are hungry while one has plenty of food and provisions constituted the second woe. Those servants choosing the amusements and entertainment of the world to be happy rather than suffering for the cause of Christ will have much regret later when they suffer loss at Christ's judgment seat. The fourth woe pertained to seeking the acceptance or praise of worldlings instead of pleasing the Lord with faithful service. While those of the world may respect believers living for Christ daily, children of the devil will not speak well of them, for that would endorse Christ and His message, which condemns them.

The Lord then conveys a fourfold exhortation to His servants to describe the type of disposition they should have towards those who persecute them: They should love their enemies, do good to those who hate them, bless those who curse them, and pray for those who mistreat them (vv. 27-28).

The Lord follows the exhortations with a fourfold illustration as to what such conduct might look like. First, if someone strikes you on one cheek, do not strike back, for that is how the world behaves, but rather turn your other cheek towards the striker that your meekness might speak to his conscience (v. 29). Second, if someone steals or takes advantage of you, do not withhold what else is desired, to again invoke his conscience concerning his wrongdoing. Third, give to those who ask for your assistance, to show the generosity of the Lord (v. 30). Fourth, if someone borrows something from you and does not return it, do not ask for it back. Every time that the borrower looks on what is yours, he will be reminded of your longsuffering nature. In short, servants of the Lord should treat others as they would desire to be treated (v. 31).

Demonstrating the character of Christ in all that we do and say to the unregenerate is more important than what we have or what we lack (Phil. 1:20, 4:12-13). Worldlings will love those who love them and do good to those who do good to them, but to convey a message from beyond this world means that those representing it must have a temperament and behavior out of this world. Therefore, believers are to love those who hate them, and to do good to those who oppress them (vv. 32-33).

Sinners loan to others with the expectation of receiving back what was lent plus interest. However, a child of God sees what was loaned and not returned as a means of expressing Christ's love to the individual that wronged them by keeping what was loaned (v. 34). In verse 35, the Lord summarized His message, love your enemies, and do good to them, and do not give to others with an expectation of benefit, and do not loan with an expectation of receiving again what was lent.

What God has entrusted to us should never keep us from fulfilling our divine calling but is to be used to supply legitimate needs and to support His work. We are to care for loved ones, our neighbors, and to show love to the unregenerate. Saints will have differing views on what it means to forsake all to follow Christ and still maintain the means to care for loved ones. As no one lives completely by faith, the Lord begins with a warning about judging others in areas of life that we should not.

The Lord promised to amply reward all those who behaved accordingly, for by their good works they demonstrated what is important to them. This is how children of "the Most High" are to behave, for their heavenly Father is kind to the unthankful and merciful to the wicked (v. 36).

Turning from having proper behavior among worldlings, Christ next addresses proper motives for serving Him with a fourfold exhortation: Do not judge or condemn others and be forgiving and charitable to them (vv. 37-38). Anything that a believer loses in this world for the cause of Christ, will be amply measured back to them by the Lord at His judgment seat. The Greek verb *hyperekchyno* rendered "running over" means "to

Luke

pour out beyond measure." This "super running over" describes the abundant heavenly reward that believers will receive for esteeming Christ more important than anything the world could offer them during their earthly sojourn.

The Lord said, *"Judge not, and you shall not be judged"* (v. 37). It is often the wayward that quote this verse to avoid personal accountability for their sin. There are at least two important applications of this verse. First, as the verses that follow explain (e.g., vv. 43-45), the context of what the Lord is saying is not that God's people should not judge each other in matters of sin, but rather we should not do so with un-Christ-like attitudes, and we should not judge in areas that we have no authority to. Second, the Greek verb tense for the English word rendered "judged" in this verse is aorist. This indicates that all believers will stand before the Lord in a coming day for a once-for-all-time judgment; knowing of this accountability, we should be actively judging ourselves now (1 Cor. 3:11-15; 2 Cor. 5:8).

Scripture commands Christians to judge each other in the areas of life and doctrine. Paul instructed the assembly at Corinth to put out a man from the assembly fellowship who was committing blatant acts of immorality and then bragging about it (1 Cor. 5). When someone is in unrepentant sin, he or she cannot be in fellowship with God, nor His people. Believers can only enjoy Christ's fellowship with each other while being in unbroken communion with Him. Paul instructed the believers at Thessalonica not to have close association with those claiming to be Christians, but that were not holding to the apostles' teaching (2 Thess. 3:6, 14). Believers are required to judge others identifying with Christ in doctrine and life to determine whether association is permitted.

While believers are to judge each other to confirm soundness of doctrine and life, the Lord issued a warning in how this was to be accomplished (vv. 39-42). For example, we cannot properly see to pull a speck from our brother's eye if we have a plank in our own eye. The plank may be unconfessed sin, but more often it is simply un-Christ-like attitudes that keep us from responding as Christ would in the situation. If we are blinded by pride and selfish bents, we cannot lead others in the way they should go. If the blind lead the blind there will be terrible consequences, like falling into a ditch.

It is often those initial thoughts that come to mind, when someone abruptly intrudes into our day with their problems, that give evidence of the plank: "Why is she calling me again with the same old issue?" "I wish he would get his act together and quit bothering me." "I hope that he will tell others how I helped him." If we are not motivated by selfless love for others, we will not be able to skillfully remove the speck from another's eye as Christ would. We need to first confess our own failures, wrong motives, and bad attitudes before we can help others.

It is also good for us to remember that, though we are to judge the behavior and doctrine of others, we are not to judge fellow believers in the following areas: their personal liberty (Rom. 14:1-3), their motivation for service (7:1-5), their ministry's profitability (1 Cor. 4:1-4) or their salvation in Christ (John 5:21-24). Concerning the matters of Christian liberty, someone's motives, the value of someone's ministry, and the validity of their salvation – only the Lord knows what is in our hearts and why we do what we do, so let us be careful judging such things.

For this reason, Paul warns fellow servants of Christ not to judge each other, for only the master will judge his own servants: *"Who are you to judge another's servant? To his own master he stands or falls"* (Rom. 14:4). If we can help others, let us behave as Christ would and let us not intrude in matters that only He can judge properly.

The main objective of discipleship is to learn Christ, completely identify with Him, and to become like Him (v. 40). This is accomplished by yielding to His yoke (His Lordship). True disciples of Christ never gain disciples to themselves – they point others to Christ. The Greek word for "disciple" is *mathetes*, which literally means "a learner." The pursuit of the disciple is to learn Christ and His mind, so that we will behave as He would in every situation. If we have the mind of Christ, we will be able to lead others Christward without any mishaps.

The virtue of one's character validates the source of the message. Like a bad tree, an unregenerate person cannot produce spiritual fruit pleasing to God; only someone that has been born again (a good tree) can bear such good fruit (v. 43). Nature teaches us that a tree bears fruit in accordance with its nature: men do not gather figs from a thorn bush or grapes from a bramble bush (v. 44). Because evil resides in the heart of the unregenerate, nothing out of their mouths can be found acceptable to God (v. 45). The spiritual reality of the root and of the tree is observed in the fruit that appears on the branches. A good tree consistently bears good fruit, while a bad tree cannot produce what is good. Morally pure and spiritually healthy saints will speak well of the Lord Jesus.

Much of the Lord's sermon was a flat rejection of the traditions and practices of the Pharisees (i.e., their religiosity) and the overall disposition of Gentile authority (i.e., their worldliness). To represent Him properly to the unregenerate, His disciples must not be given over to legalism or worldliness.

As many in His audience identified with Him, He warned them not to enthrone themselves and reject Him as their Lord: *"But why do you call Me 'Lord, Lord,' and not do the things which I say?"* The crux of the Lord's message was, "Don't call Me Lord if you are not going to do what I say." It is mockery to refer to Jesus Christ as Lord, but then do what we want regardless of what He commands.

Normally, when Scripture speaks of the will of God, it explicitly states what it is. There is no mystery about it; God has declared to us His general will for our lives. Consequently, the more pertinent question becomes, not what the will of God is for my life, but will I obey the revealed will of God for my life? The Lord Jesus told His disciples, *"If you love Me, keep My commandments"* (John 14:15). Obedience to the Lord practically proves our love for Him. A lack of love for the Lord will be shown through an unyielded spirit and through disobedience. There is such an intimate tie between genuine love for the Lord and obedience to the Lord that Paul bluntly states, *"If any man love not the Lord Jesus Christ, let him be Anathema* [eternally condemned]" (1 Cor. 16:22).

The Lord commands those identifying with Him in a profession of faith to be publicly baptized in His name (Matt. 28:19-20). Yet, many who say that they have trusted Christ as Savior flaunt various reasons for not being baptized. The Lord commanded His disciples to remember Him often by keeping the Lord's Supper (Luke 22:19-20). Regrettably, many believers disobey the Lord's command for the most superfluous reasons. Believers are also commanded not to forsake the assembling of themselves together for meetings of the Church (Heb. 10:25). Any time a believer willingly chooses to miss meetings of the church for illegitimate reasons, he or she casts a vote to close down the church. If Christ is Lord, let us honor Him with our obedience.

In the closing of His message (vv. 46-49), He told the people that they were now accountable for what they had heard: Would they follow Him and build their lives upon His teachings, or would they continue to follow empty religious traditions and human reasoning (i.e., building their house on a foundation of sand)? When the storms of life would come, the latter would prove to be a total "washout," while those who built upon His Word (the rock) would stand fast and enjoy an abiding peace in life, despite difficulties.

Luke Chapter 7

Christ Heals the Centurion's Servant (vv. 1-10)

After finishing *The Sermon on the Level Place*, the Lord returned to Capernaum, presumably with His disciples. Luke's account of this story affords a few more details than what Matthew provided. Apparently, after hearing of the Lord's arrival at Capernaum, a Roman centurion sent Jewish elders to ask Him for assistance. The centurion had a faithful servant that was suffering from severe paralysis and was near death (v. 2; Matt. 8:5-6). This scene is ironic, as we have Jewish leaders that did not believe that Jesus was the Christ being compelled to beseech Him for Messianic power on behalf of a Gentile that they esteemed more important than Himself (v. 3). The elders told the Lord that the centurion loved the Jewish people and was kind to them; he had even built them a synagogue (vv. 4-5). This was to convince the Lord that the centurion was worthy of His help.

The Lord agreed to go, but before arriving at the centurion's home, the officer sent messengers to tell the Lord not to trouble Himself any further, but just say the word and his servant would be healed (v. 6). The messengers then explained that as an officer in authority, the centurion commanded the affairs of his soldiers; he understood that one must be under authority to exercise authority (v. 8). Since the Lord Jesus had authority over diseases, the centurion knew that He was under divine authority and could therefore heal his servant. Furthermore, the honorable centurion did not feel that he was worthy enough for the Lord to come under his roof (v. 7).

The Lord was astonished by the officer's response and said to the crowd, *"I say to you, I have not found such great faith, not even in Israel!"* (v. 9). The centurion possessed little truth, but enough to exercise tremendous faith, which the Lord praised. There are only two authority structures today: God-ordained and Satanic-controlled. Remaining under God's authority enables us to exercise His authority and bless others. But those who reject His authority do not escape authority, but rather find themselves under Satan's authority, and there is only misery to be found there.

Matthew testifies that the centurion's confession caused the Lord to point out that in His kingdom, believing Gentiles would enjoy fellowship with the Jewish patriarchs. However, "the sons of the kingdom" (i.e., those who were privileged to have a Jewish heritage, but did not believe the truth revealed to them about Jesus Christ) will be cast into outer darkness (i.e., eternal judgment in Hell; Matt. 8:11-12). The benefit of more revelation also results in more accountability if rejected (10:13-16). The Lord honored the centurion's faith by healing his servant (v. 10).

At this point in His ministry, the Lord Jesus was seeking the lost sheep of Israel to receive Him as their Messiah; His efforts were not directed to the Gentiles. This explains why He performed only two miracles in association with Gentiles. Both healings were performed at a distance on behalf of a Gentile who had great compassion for someone else who was suffering and great faith in the Lord to resolve the issue. The Canaanite woman seeking help for her demon-possessed daughter is the other occurrence (Matt. 15:21-28). The Lord was thrilled by their sincere faith and granted their requests. A. C. Gaebelein summarizes how these Gentile healings point to dispensational truth:

> Whenever the Lord heals by touch it has reference, dispensationally, to His personal presence on the earth and His merciful dealing with Israel. When He heals by His Word, absent in person, ... or if He is touched in faith, it refers to the time when He is absent from the earth, and Gentiles approaching Him in faith are healed by Him.[21]

This explains why the prophet Elisha, who prefigured Christ's ministry, also healed Naaman, the Gentile captain, of his leprosy from a distance, but healed his Jewish countrymen in person. Elijah, who called the nation of Israel to repentance, typified the ministry of John the baptizer, but Elisha was a champion of the people and engaged in personalized ministry to heal and assist his countrymen.

Christ Raises the Widow's Son From the Dead (vv. 11-18)

Directly after healing the centurion's servant, the Lord with His disciples and many others departed Capernaum and journeyed to the southwest around the Sea of Galilee. The next day, just as the Lord was about to enter the small city of Nain, a funeral procession came out of the city gate (vv. 11-12). Nain is located about twenty-five miles southwest of Capernaum and six miles southeast of Nazareth. The only son of a widow from Nain had died and there was a large crowd accompanying her to the burial site.

As the Jews typically buried their dead on the same day (Deut. 21:23; Acts 5:5-10) it is likely that the Lord and His disciples arrived at Nain late afternoon of the day that the boy had died. He had not been summoned to Nain to work a miracle, as the lad was still alive when they had departed Capernaum the day before. But knowing what would happen, He took a lengthy journey to bless one distraught widow.

Seeing the plight of the widow, the Lord had compassion for her and told her, *"Do not weep"* (v. 13). He stepped near the open coffin that was being carried and those who bore the lad's corpse stood still (v. 14). The Lord said to the deceased, *"Young man, I say to you, arise."* Immediately, the young man sat up, began to speak, and then He went to console his mother (v. 15). It is at this juncture that Luke refers to Jesus as "the Lord" for the first time in his gospel record (v. 13). Norman Crawford explains why this declaration is significant:

> It is significant that he ascribes this great miracle to the Lord. Death could not exist in His presence. It is recorded that the Lord attended a wedding (John 2:1–11), but it is not recorded that he attended a funeral, or at least when He did, He raised the dead to life. If He had been in Bethany when Lazarus was dying, there would have been no death.[22]

While Mark portrays the busy ministry of the Lord in his gospel account, Luke adds more personal information about the miracles Christ performed to highlight Christ's compassion for others. For example, only Luke records: the resurrection of the widow of Nain's **only** son from the dead (7:12), that Jairus' daughter, also raised from the dead, was his **only** daughter (8:42) and that the demon-possessed boy, whom the Lord healed, was his father's **only** child (9:38).

Two large crowds had merged to witness this miracle. Fear came upon everyone as they gave praise to God and said, *"A great prophet has risen up among us"* and *"God has visited His people"* (v. 16). The news of the widow's son being raised from the dead quickly spread throughout Judea and Galilee (v. 17). Although John had been imprisoned by Herod (perhaps at Machaerus on the eastern shore of the Dead Sea), his disciples informed him of the spectacular event (v. 18).

Luke

Christ Reassures His Forerunner (vv. 19-28)

After commissioning and sending out the twelve disciples to preach the Kingdom Gospel message throughout Galilee, the Lord Jesus returned to teach and preach in the cities of that region where the disciples had previously lived (Matt. 11:1).

John the baptizer had been in prison for several months by this time (3:19-20). He had been accustomed to residing in the vast freedom of the wilderness, so the harsh and lonely confinement of prison would have been an emotional and physical strain on him. No doubt He wondered why Jesus had not ushered in His kingdom and liberated him from prison. Being discouraged with his situation, John sent two of his disciples to ask Jesus if he was the One (i.e., the Jewish Messiah) of whom the prophets had foretold of or if they should be looking for another (vv. 19-20).

After hearing John's inquiry through his disciples, the Lord affirmed to them that He was the prophesied Messiah and noted that the types of miracles that He was performing were a direct fulfillment of Isaiah's prophecies: the blind see, the deaf hear, and the lame walk (vv. 22-22; Isa. 35:5-6), and lepers had been cleansed (Isa. 53:4). Having performed these predicted miracles, the Lord Jesus had proved that He was the Messiah. He had even gone beyond these prophesied feats to raise the dead. The Lord told John's disciples to inform John that the gospel message was being preached throughout the land; even the poor (Isa. 61:1), who were often neglected, were hearing and receiving His message.

Lastly, the Lord told John's disciples, *"And blessed is he who is not offended because of Me"* (v. 23). The Lord's lowly, servant style of leadership was out of step with the self-exalting character of civil rulers and the self-promoting disposition of the religious leaders. The Lord's methods and demeanor would stand in sharp contrast to any kind of leadership that the people were accustomed to at that time. He was not operating in the flesh, but in the power and the character of God. Christ served others; He did not come to be served. No doubt John and other Jews were looking forward to being liberated from all Gentile oppression by the promised Messiah as prophesied, but that would not be accomplished until Christ's second advent to the earth.

After John's disciples departed to deliver Christ's message to John, the Lord turned to the multitude and expressed glowing praise for John.

He reminded the crowd that when they had previously ventured out to the wilderness to hear John's message, they observed a man fully controlled by the power of God. He was not some bent papyrus reed that had no strength to stand firm against the winds of adversity, speaking of religious opposition and vacillating human opinions (v. 24). Even John's simple diet and modest attire were a rebuke against the luxurious and materialistic disposition of the Jewish leaders. John lived the message that He preached while those who were to lead and to serve God's covenant people served themselves (v. 25).

Had the Jews gone to the wilderness to see a prophet (v. 26)? Indeed, John was a prophet, and in fact the greatest of the prophets because he was chosen by God from the womb to be Christ's forerunner and to prepare the Jewish nation for Messiah's coming. This high status did not relate to John's personal character or even to the quality of his service, but rather to the important role that was assigned him. There were many Old Testament prophets that were bold and zealous messengers for God, even losing their lives to complete their assigned callings, but only John was given the honor of pointing Israel to *"the Lamb of God who takes away the sin of the world!"* (John 1:29). It was not that John was greater in character or eloquence than those preaching before him, but his task of being the Messiah-King's herald was greater in grandeur than the assigned duties of previous prophets (v. 27). This was why the Lord gave John such a high accolade.

The Lord's next statement proves that He was speaking of John's honor to a specific service rather than his personal character: *"He who is least in the kingdom of God is greater than he* [John]*"* (v. 28). To be a citizen of Christ's kingdom, positionally speaking, is a greater privilege than just being the one who announced that the kingdom was coming. John had a spectacular ministry and did great things for the Lord, but those things are not even comparable with what believers in the Church Age have in Christ and the eternal inheritance secured in Him.

The Rejection of This Generation (vv. 29-35)

Many were moved by Christ's testimony of John and of the necessity of believing the message that John had preached – one must repent and receive the Messiah to be accepted by God. As a result, many (even some tax collectors) who had repented of their sins and had been baptized with the baptism of John praised God (v. 29).

In contrast, the Pharisees and lawyers that were present rejected God's revealed will as expressed through John's message and baptism of repentance. While the Pharisees held the respect of the people, they did not have God's favor. They were self-exalting and self-focused; they measured the spirituality of others by their own standards of religiosity. The Lord told this parable to rebuke those of "this generation" who were of this spiritual disposition. Hence, He is mainly speaking to the Pharisees and scribes, who were supposed to be the spiritual leaders of the people (v. 30). The Lord likened the Pharisees to children in the street dancing to their own piped songs (vv. 31-32). MacDonald writes:

> They didn't want to play either wedding or funeral. They were perverse, wayward, unpredictable, and refractory. No matter what ministry God used among them, they took exception to it.[23]

Anyone who did not join their religious escapades was rejected by them. For example, John the baptizer lived a simple existence in the wilderness while he fulfilled his ministry, yet the religious leaders rejected him, saying, *"He has a demon"* (v. 33). Additionally, the Pharisees accused the Son of Man, the Lord Jesus, of extravagant living because He ate and drank with those He came to save (v. 34). Neither John's near-impoverished lifestyle in the wilderness while calling sinners to repentance nor the Lord's compassionate efforts to awaken the wealthy of their spiritual need had their approval.

Only Luke refers to the Lord as *"a friend of tax collectors and sinners"* (v. 34). The Lord often visited them in their homes to speak of spiritual matters. The Lord was available to anyone who was concerned about his or her soul. He spoke to the vile, the demon possessed, the immoral, the distressed, and the brokenhearted – and met each one of their needs. The Lord loves sinners, but still hates their sin. We should follow the Lord's example and not be afraid to interact with the lost.

Religious moralizers will attack those faithfully declaring God's Word in whatever way they can to avoid considering what God wants them to hear. The Old Testament prophets repeatedly suffered this type of abuse and at times were imprisoned or put to death to suppress their preaching. Clearly, those who live for the Lord will never be able to please the Pharisaical mentality. Whether today or in Christ's day, Pharisees only dance to their own music! Israel's leaders had lulled themselves into a self-absorbed sway and willful complacency of the things important to God, especially the care of His people.

Thankfully, the Lord Jesus was not distracted by their criticism or by their rejection of His message. Rather, He ignored their opposition and kept to the work that God gave Him to do. When faced with pharisaical pride, this is a good example for us to follow also. If you are faithfully serving the Lord in your divine calling, you will be criticized; so, expect it. Benefit from what is profitable, and forget what is not, but keep serving the Lord regardless. If the devil can get us defending ourselves against unjust criticism instead of serving God – he wins! Satan gains a victory when he pulls us out of God's work into his own wicked agenda!

The Lord concludes His rebuke of the Pharisees with this statement, *"But wisdom is justified by all her children"* (v. 35). In this statement, "wisdom" represents the Lord Himself; He is the holder of divine truth and wisdom. Those who honor Him are "wisdom's children." Although many in Israel would reject Jesus Christ, those who truly repented of their sins and received Him as their Savior would vindicate the Lord's message as true, by living holy lives devoted to God.

The Two Debtors (vv. 36-50)

A Pharisee named Simon invited the Lord to his home in Capernaum for a meal and the Lord accepted the invitation (v. 36). While they were eating, a woman of ill repute came into his house with an alabaster flask of fragrant oil (v. 37). Jewish Rabbis did not talk to or eat with women in public, nor were women invited to banquets such as the one Simon was hosting. Yet, she knew that Jesus was there, so she came anyway, knowing that she would be disdained by those at the feast.

The weeping woman washed the Lord's feet with her tears and wiped them clean with her hair. She then kissed the Lord's feet and anointed them with fragrant oil (v. 38). The woman was publicly showing her appreciation for Christ; she believed His message of reconciliation.

Most roads were unpaved at this time and the normal footwear of the day was sandals. This meant that the feet of those traveling on foot often became caked with dust or mud. For this reason, it was customary for the host to provide a servant to wash the feet of those who had arrived at his home or at least some provision for washing up, but Simon had not done so. But the woman saw the opportunity to refresh the Lord and did what Simon had failed to do. However, because of her sinful background (i.e., prostitution), Simon thought less of the Lord for willfully receiving her expression of gratitude: *"This Man, if He were a prophet, would know who and what manner of woman this is who is touching Him, for she is a sinner"* (v. 39). In other words, "If this man was really a prophet of God, he would know the depravity of this woman and would shun her, instead of welcoming her actions."

As shown by the woman, a kiss was a symbol of true repentance – she was honoring God's Son in an appropriate way. In contrast, Judas rejected Christ's Lordship and betrayed the Lord with the sign of a kiss (Matt. 26:49). To refuse God's offer of salvation in His Son results in God's judgment (Ps. 2:11), but Judas committed a greater offense: He mocked God's Son by a sign of affection and repentance to have Him arrested and abused. Ultimately, all of us must decide whether we will respect the One God loves and honors, His Son, or be wise in our own conceit.

Returning to the narrative, the Lord, who overheard Simon's thoughts about Him, told the Pharisee that He had something to say to him. Simon told the Lord to do so (v. 40). The Lord then told him a story about two forgiven debtors to rebuke his cold-hearted attitude (vv. 41-42). One debtor was forgiven much and another not so much. Simon understood the point of the parable: Those who have been forgiven much love much (v. 43).

The woman, an outcast of society with few resources, had done much more to refresh Him than influential Simon had done even though he was hosting the Lord in his home. The Lord called Simon's attention to her good works: *"Do you see this woman?"* (v. 44). He then told the woman that though her sins were many, they had been forgiven. *"Your faith has saved you. Go in peace"* (v. 50).

The woman's testimony was used to rebuke Simon in two ways. First, James tells us that *"Faith by itself, if it does not have works, is dead"* (Jas. 2:17). Simon may have been curious about what Jesus was teaching, but his actions showed that he had not trusted in His message, or he would have demonstrated his appreciation for being forgiven also. Second, the Lord affirmed *"to whom little is forgiven, the same loves little"* (v. 47)! The portion that we return of what we have received from the Lord directly reflects how much we believe we have been forgiven and how much we love Christ. Indeed, those forgiven much – love and give much (v. 43)!

Luke Chapter 8

Women Serving the Lord During Galilean Ministry (vv. 1-3)

Furthering the kingdom of God requires all the Lord's people to be involved in the work. All believers have been given spiritual gifts, natural abilities, and earthly resources to invest into eternity. While Christ and His disciples were busy attending to the sick and demon-possessed, and teaching the people, there were a variety of others behind the scenes in support roles (v. 1).

Luke mentions that several women, some of which had been healed of infirmities or demonic oppression, were faithfully serving the Lord and supplying financial support for His ministry (vv. 2-3). Mary, called Magdalene, Joanna, the wife of Chuza (Herod's steward), and Susanna are specifically mentioned. The Lord cast seven demons out of Mary. The fact that many of these women traveled with the Lord and His disciples likely meant that they were assisting them by obtaining provisions and necessities, preparing meals, washing clothes, etc.

Obviously, the Lord knew how to prepare a meal (John 21:9), but to be alleviated of that responsibility meant that He could more freely teach God's Word and heal the sick and the oppressed. The women could not do that, but the Lord could, and they wanted Him to do as much as He could without being hindered by activities that they could assist with. While many men confronted and mistreated the Lord during His earthly sojourn, there is no record of any woman opposing or rejecting Him.

The Parable of the Sower and the Soils (vv. 1-15)

In Matthew's account, the Lord strung together seven parables to chronologically reveal events associated with the *Mystery of the Kingdom* to His audience (Matt. 13). These parables spanned from the time of His first advent (which was a seed-sowing mission) until His return to rule the world in peace (which would require the judgment of the wicked and their removal from the earth). Matthew indicates that the Lord did not speak of any "mysteries" pertaining to the kingdom of heaven until after His withdrawal from public ministry because of Jewish rejection. That distinction is not as noticeable in Luke's account.

The disciples noticed that the Lord was speaking more parables in His public addresses and asked Him, *"Why do You speak to them in parables?"* (Matt. 13:10). The Lord Jesus then explained that He intentionally spoke in parables to reveal truth, but in a partially-veiled manner that would test His audience (Matt. 13:11-12). The parables were not just enjoyable stories but served as a test to the hearers. The casual onlooker, the "window shopper," would hear and not understand, nor would he or she desire any more insight concerning the parable – "thanks for the good story." This fulfilled Isaiah's prophecy that at Messiah's first advent, Israel would hear but not understand, and see but not perceive the truth being proclaimed (Matt. 13:13-15; Isa. 6:9-10). The Jewish nation, being spiritually despondent, would not regard the Messiah's message of life.

But those individuals longing to understand the spiritual significance of the parable would seek the Lord for further instruction (Mark 4:10-12); those who merely enjoyed the story would go their own way. Often it was only the Lord's disciples who sought to learn the deeper meaning of His stories. By design, then, a parable is concealed truth that tests the heart of each one who hears the story.

A great multitude from cities throughout the region had come to hear the Lord's teaching (v. 3). The Jews were a nation composed of shepherds and farmers, so He spoke to them the parable that they could understand, *The Sower and the Soils* (vv. 5-10). He then explained the parable in verses 11-15.

The ground in which the seed (God's Word) is sown is likened to the various dispositions of the human heart. Four types of "soils" or hearts are identified: the wayside, stony, thorny, and fruitful ground. Matthew provides a few more details in the story than Luke does. The key components of this parable must be properly identified if we are to understand its meaning:

The seed = the Word of God (specifically the Kingdom message).

The sower = Christ primarily.

The soils = various human hearts (i.e., as God knows them).

The birds = Satan's opposition to God's Word being shared.

The sun/lack of moisture = persecution and suffering (Matt. 13:6).

The thorns = the influence of humanism and worldly affairs.

The plant = the visible evidence of God's Word at work.

The fruit = the visible evidence of true salvation.

The wayside = someone with no time for or interest in God's Word.

The stony ground = someone emotionally affected by God's Word.

The thorny ground = those who allow worldliness to negate the Word.

This parable represents the proclamation and offering of the kingdom to Israel by a sower, who primarily represents Christ, but may include John the baptizer also (Matt. 3:2, 4:17). The seed in the parable is God's Word, which is "living and powerful" (Heb. 4:12). A seed contains life and God's Word offers life to those who will receive it in faith. Specifically, the seed in this parable represents the kingdom message offered by Christ to the Jewish nation; this invitation could not be received without genuine repentance. The various soils represent the spiritual disposition of human hearts that God's message would confront. Only those having a softened and prepared heart received God's message and became fruitful to Him.

The birds depict Satan's adverse efforts to oppose the receipt of God's Word once sown among the populace. Birds are often used in Scripture to metaphorically convey satanic opposition. For example, even after Abram had obeyed God's word and prepared animals and birds for an offering, he still had to drive the unclean birds from devouring his sacrifice until later in the day when God confirmed His covenant with Abram (Gen. 15). Satan was opposing God's covenant with Abram and thus the forthcoming Messiah that would come through it – the One who would bless all families of the earth (Gen. 12:3). Likewise, in this parable, the birds symbolize Satan's evil influence and operations to oppose God's kingdom and the efforts of Messiah to establish His kingdom.

Many have interpreted the visible plant in the parable as a sign of conversion and regeneration, but the Lord clarifies in the explanation that that is not the case. What is seen above the ground is a counterfeit life because the plant does not have a root of faith below the ground (i.e., in the heart; Matt. 13:6). Only God sees what is in each of our hearts, that is, what is below the ground in the parable. We can only see the outward manifestation of the heart in visible behavior. The plants in this parable represent the visible evidence that the Word of God has had an impact on a person's heart, but it is not necessarily conversion.

Some people feel conviction and guilt after being confronted with the gospel message and respond by self-reformation, rather than by true repentance and acceptance of Christ. In time, trials (intense sunlight) and the cares of the world (the thorns) reveal the true reality of things – no true conversion (no root below ground). In this parable, the plants associated with the stony and thorny ground do not represent true life, but merely an emotional response to God's Word. Only the ground that produced fruit represents a true conversion – there can be no fruitfulness to God unless His seed has produced a root of faith in the human heart.

The Lord Jesus said that you will know a tree (a true believer) by whether he or she bears good fruit (behavior and deeds which honor God) or not (Matt. 7:17-18): *"Therefore by their fruits you will know them"* (Matt. 7:20). This means that at times we may be conned by well-meaning, moral, and Christ-identifying people, but the Lord is not fooled by the facade of an unregenerate person. In fact, the Lord said there are many who know things about Him, but have not trusted Him for salvation; hence, they have not shown Christ to be their Lord (Matt. 7:21-23). Clearly, it is possible to know a lot about the Lord and do things in His name without ever being born again. The Lord knows who are truly His and who the counterfeits are. Many identifying with Christ, even calling Him Lord, are not actually saved. The true test of knowing and serving the Lord is found in our desire to do God's will – this is true fruit-bearing. Only those who do the will of God are really His people (Mark 3:35).

The following summarizes the four kinds of soils identified in this parable.

The wayside: The heart that has no interest in the things of God and blatantly rejects the gospel message. The Word had no visible influence on the hearer.

The stony ground: The heart in which the Word of God did not penetrate deep enough to cause the reality of new birth. These people are mere professors in religious camouflage; they had an emotional response to the gospel message instead of brokenness and repentance before God. A little suffering shows them for who they really are.

The thorny ground: The heart in which the Word of God causes the individual to feel guilt and to change his or her conduct through self-effort, but because there is no true conversion, the cares of the world quickly choke out the effect of God's Word in this life.

The good ground: The heart that is well-prepared and receives the Word of God by faith alone unto salvation. True salvation is evidenced by fruit-bearing.

The Parable of the Lighted Lamp (vv. 16-18)

While still speaking to a large audience which included many followers, the Lord likened the testimony of true believers to that of light. In Matthew's account of this parable, the Lord, speaking directly to His disciples, said, *"You are the light of the world"* (Matt. 5:14). A lighted lamp that is hidden under a vessel or put under a bed has little benefit to illuminate its surroundings (v. 16). Rather, for a lit lamp to be seen, it must be placed in an unobscured location, such as a lampstand. Light exposes the true nature of things as it causes what was hidden to be seen (v. 17).

In application, a believer who no longer lives to declare the goodness of Christ in word and by deed has become useless in furthering the cause of Christ. There is no testimony of the Savior for the children of the devil to notice or consider. The disciples were thus encouraged to let their lights shine in a world that desperately needs to see Christ in their good works – such behavior would glorify their Father in heaven (Matt. 5:16).

The more revelation of the truth that they understood meant that they had more accountability with God if they did not to share it with others (v. 18). Their light must be available for others to see divine truth. The disciples were not accountable to God if those having their sin exposed by their light chose to walk in darkness afterwards.

A New Relationship (vv. 19-21)

While the Lord Jesus was still speaking, He was informed by someone in the audience that His mother and brothers had arrived and desired to speak to Him (vv. 46-47). The Lord used this interruption and information to speak of a spiritual union that was more intimate than natural relationships. He said to those listening to Him, *"My mother and My brothers are these who hear the word of God and do it"* (v. 21).

Mary and His half-siblings represented the nation of Israel, which had largely rejected Him and His message (even Christ's half-siblings did not believe that He was the Messiah; John 7:5). Consequently, the

Luke

Lord was giving an open invitation to anyone who wanted to receive Him to do the will of His Father (e.g., Matt. 11:28-30).

The Lord was not belittling His earthly family or denying His love for them, but rather He was highlighting that having a spiritual relationship with Him was much more important. Our natural relationships all end with death, but our spiritual union with Christ lasts forever. In Him is life and in His presence is unspeakable joy and complete satisfaction.

Jesus Christ Calms a Windstorm (vv. 22-25)

Not long after this speech, the Lord entered a boat with His disciples. They departed Capernaum and journey southeastward across the sea to the country of the Gadarenes (Gergesenes; v. 22). Mark informs us that it was evening when they left Capernaum (Mark 4:35). The Lord went to the stern of the boat and laid down on a pillow and went to sleep (v. 23; Mark 4:38). But before doing so, He told His disciples, *"Let us cross over to the other side of the lake"* (v. 22). Thus, the will of the Lord had been clearly expressed and could be taken as a promise of safety. As the disciples were rowing, a violent tempest suddenly arose, which caused huge waves to beat against the boat and fill it with water.

This is the only time in Scripture that we read of the Lord sleeping. Can you imagine the life of the Lord Jesus? Day in and day out, at any time of day or night, people were coming to Him with their problems and ailments, while others were rejecting His message and even plotting His death. No wonder He fell asleep in the stern of a boat and did not wake up when the boat was being tossed to and fro in a violent storm. The weariness of His perfect manhood required the rejuvenation of restful sleep.

The desperate disciples woke the Lord and pleaded with Him to save them before they perished (v. 24). He then stood up and rebuked the wind and the sea and there was a sudden great calm. The Lord then rebuked His disciples by asking them the question, *"Where is your faith?"* (v. 25). He had already told them that they needed to cross the sea. Why did they doubt His word? Did they really think that His heavenly Father would allow Him to perish in the sea before completing His mission?

Having witnessed this powerful feat, the disciples said to themselves, *"Who can this be? For He commands even the winds and water, and they obey Him"* (v. 27). Obviously, they were still growing in their understanding of who Jesus Christ is, the Master of all creation. He is the Son of God who created all things and by Him all things consist (John 1:3; Col. 1:17). Thus, there was no need to awaken Him; they were safer with Him in the stormy sea than any other place on earth without Him.

Power Over the Demons at Gadara (vv. 26-39)

The Lord Jesus often cast out demons to heal the populace of their physical and mental infirmities and spiritual oppression. In this story, our Lord was willing to sail to the southeast shore of the Sea of Galilee with His disciples to meet one demon-possessed man in much turmoil. This was the region of the Gadarenes (or Gerasenes, or Gergesenes) and was settled by the tribe of Gad in Joshua's day. The town of Gadara was about seven miles southeast of the seashore. The Lord teaches us to go the extra mile to assist those suffering affliction.

Matthew records that there were two "exceedingly fierce" demon-possessed men residing in the tombs near the shoreline (Matt. 8:28). These men were so violent that no one could safely travel through the area. Though there were two possessed men, the story centers around the one called Legion. We are not told if the other man was healed or not.

One of the possessed men immediately came out of the tombs to meet the Lord (Matt. 8:29). Luke tells us that he was naked and had been demon-possessed for a long time (v. 27). He had often been shackled and chained but broke his bonds (v. 29). Day and night the demoniac was screaming and cutting himself with stones (Mark 5:5). His condition was one of utter misery. After seeing the Lord, he fell down before Him and acknowledged His authority as the Son of God (v. 28). The demons speaking through the man were afraid that Christ had come early to render final judgment on them, but that was not the case.

The Lord asked the possessed man his name and the man responded, "Legion," for there were many demons that had entered him (v. 30). The demons sensed that the Lord was about to cast them out of the man, so they begged Him for permission to enter a herd of swine (about 2,000 pigs), rather than being cast into the abyss (vv. 31-32). The Lord permitted this course of action and the demons yielded to His authority by coming out of the man. They then entered the large herd of swine, which ran violently off a cliff and perished in the sea (v. 33). Those who were attending to the swine immediately departed and fled to the city to inform others of what had happened (v. 34).

But why would the Lord grant the demon's request to enter the swine? Scripture is silent on this matter, but William MacDonald offers two possible reasons:

> Why should the Sovereign Lord accede to the request of demons? To understand His action, we must remember two facts. First, demons shun the disembodied state; they want to indwell human beings, or, if that is not possible, animals or other creatures. Second, the purpose of demons is without exception to destroy. If Jesus had simply cast them out of the maniacs, the demons would have been a menace to the other people of the area. By allowing them to go into the swine, He prevented their entering men and women and confined their destructive power to animals. It was not yet time for their final destruction by the Lord.[24]

Additionally, it is observed that the Law deemed swine as unclean animals. The Jews were not to touch or eat nor offer to the Lord what was unclean (Deut. 14:8). By permitting the demons to go into the swine, which brought about their destruction, the Lord was reproving His countrymen for their disobedience of the Law. The Lord demonstrates His authority over rebel spirits and disobedient men to the glory of God.

When the townsfolk heard of what happened, they traveled to the location of the miracle and found the previously possessed man sitting, clothed, and in his right mind (vv. 35-36). This meant that the one who had accomplished this miracle was more powerful than a multitude of demons and they were afraid; they even asked the Lord to leave the region (v. 37). The presence and power of God will always frighten worldlings yearning for comfort and prosperity in a realm presently under Satan's control. Regrettably, they did not want to receive the One who had shown Himself more powerful than an entire legion of demons!

Notice that the healed man was clothed. Perhaps a disciple donated clothing, but it seems more likely that Christ crossed the sea with every provision to resolve this man's pain and shame. If we decide to help someone, let us do our best to do so and in a way that restores dignity.

In response to the Gadarenes' request, the Lord Jesus entered into a boat to depart from them (v. 37). The healed man begged the Lord to let him come with them, but the Lord denied his request, saying, *"Return to your own house, and tell what great things God has done for you"* (vv. 38-39). The man obeyed the Lord and spread the news of how he had been healed *"throughout the whole city."* He was a lit lampstand and desired that everyone would hear and know the truth about Christ (v. 16).

Christ Has Power Over Hemorrhaging and Death (vv. 40-56)

The Lord and His disciples return to Capernaum, where a multitude of people were waiting to welcome Him (v. 40). A ruler of the synagogue named Jairus quickly fell down before the Lord and begged Him to come to his home, for his only daughter (of about twelve years of age) was dying (v. 41). Apparently, his daughter was in a coma and near death when Jairus departed to petition Jesus Christ for help (v. 42; Matt. 9:18). In his initial conversation with the Lord, Jairus may have presumed that his daughter was likely deceased by that time. Regardless, the Lord agreed to help, but navigating through the crowd caused a delay.

While en route, a woman who had an ongoing flow of blood for twelve years touched the hem of the Lord's garment to be made well and she was cured (vv. 43-44). Luke, the physician, mentions that this woman had spent all her livelihood on physicians, but no one could cure her hemorrhaging, which Mark states was worsening (Mark 5:26) – that is, until she came to the Great Physician.

The Lord, knowing that power had come out of Him to accomplish the miracle, did not want the matter of the woman's faith and healing to be a secret, so He asked, *"Who touched Me?"* (v. 45). Of course, the disciples did not understand the Lord's question as they were trying to pass through a large crowd of people as they followed Jairus – a lot of people were touching the Lord (v. 46). However, the Lord clarified the situation: power had gone out of Him to heal someone. Rather than permitting the healed woman to secretly retreat from the crowd, Christ's statement posed an opportunity for her to meet her Savior and to glorify God for the miracle. Although the disciples did not know what was going on, the healed woman did, and she came trembling and fell at the Lord's feet and publicly confessed to what she had done and why (v. 47).

The Lord commended her testimony, *"Daughter, be of good cheer; your faith has made you well. Go in peace"* (v. 48). Whenever someone professes Christ in a spirit of humility, His peace and commendation will follow. Interestingly, "has made" and "well" in this statement are derived from the same Greek verb *sozo* in the perfect tense. *Sozo* is usually rendered "save" in the New Testament. Literally, then, the woman's faith "saved her safe" forever. When Christ heals or saves, a permanent state of physical or spiritual wellness is always received.

True faith is always appreciated by the Lord. Because He chose to handle the situation in this manner, the woman who had been perpetually deemed *unclean* by the Law for years would now be able to resume normal life in Jewish society, for she had been healed and declared "well" by Christ. This is what Christ came to do – make those declared unclean by the Law to be clean before God by grace through faith.

After the woman was healed, a servant of Jairus arrived to inform him that his daughter had died and that there was no need to trouble "the Teacher" (v. 49). Apparently, all attempts to revive her had failed and she was now past any hope of resuscitation. The Lord consoled the grieving father, *"Do not be afraid; only believe, and she will be made well"* (v. 50). Matthew records Jairus' declaration of faith; he believed that if the Lord simply put His hand on his daughter, she would live (Matt. 9:18). This was an incredible statement, as the last resurrection of the dead recorded in Scripture (the Old Testament) had occurred in the days of the prophet Elisha, more than eight centuries previous.

Sometime later, the Lord arrived at Jairus' home, which was crowded with wailing people and hired flute players (Matt. 9:23). The Lord said to them, *"Do not weep; she is not dead, but sleeping"* (v. 52). The Lord knew the outcome of what He was about to do and did not want the fame of it to be publicized, so He poetically describes her as merely "sleeping" rather than being permanently or irrevocably dead. Paul also speaks of those who have died in Christ and are awaiting resurrection as being poetically "asleep" (e.g., 1 Thess. 4:13). Luke, the beloved physician, states the clinical facts of the situation, *"They ridiculed Him, knowing that she was dead"* (v. 53).

The Lord responded to their mockery by putting them all out of the house, especially the noisy professional mourners (v. 54). The Lord only permitted the girl's parents and Peter, James, and John to accompany Him to where the dead girl was lying (v. 51). The Lord took the child's hand and said, *"Little girl, arise"* (v. 54; Mark 5:41).

Her spirit returned to her and to everyone's amazement, the girl immediately arose and walked (v. 55; Mark 5:42). The Lord not only resolved the problem (death), but He did so in such a way that the girl was not living in a reduced condition, for she could walk about and digest food normally. This is the second resurrection recorded in the New Testament and the fifth in the whole of Scripture. The Lord charged those who had observed the miracle to keep it secret and that her parents should give their daughter something to eat (v. 56).

Luke Chapter 9

The Twelve Are Sent Into the Fields of Galilee (vv. 1-6)
Before the Lord commissions the twelve disciples to preach the gospel of the kingdom throughout Galilee, Matthew tells us what motivated His actions. The Lord was moved with anguish and compassion over the spiritual plight of His countrymen, *"because they were weary and scattered, like sheep having no shepherd"* (Matt. 9:36).

The Lord not only commissioned His disciples to preach the kingdom message to the lost sheep of Israel in Galilee (Matt. 10:5-6), but He also gave them authority over unclean spirits and all kinds of ailments (vv. 1-2). God wanted His covenant people to know that their promised King and Messiah was willing to dwell with and to reign over them if they would repent and humbly receive Him.

Mark informs us that the disciples went out in groups of two (Mark 6:7). Whenever the Lord places responsibility, He also fully equips His servants to accomplish all that He desires them to do. Warren Wiersbe describes what was to be accomplished by the authority the disciples had received from the Lord:

> These Apostles were given special power and authority from Christ to perform miracles. These miracles were a part of their "official credentials" (Acts 2:43; 5:12; Heb. 2:1–4). They healed the sick (and note that this included *all* kinds of diseases), cleansed the lepers, cast out demons, and even raised the dead. These four ministries paralleled the miracles that Jesus performed in Matthew 8 and 9. In a definite way, the Apostles represented the King and extended His work.[25]

Although the Lord has not given His servants today the same specialized ministry and authority of the twelve, He has given each believer a calling and spiritual gift(s) to accomplish it (Eph. 4:11-12). All believers are to be Christ's witnesses in the world (Acts 1:8).

The Lord told His disciples that their ministry was to be free of charge and that they were to depend on the Lord for their support (v. 3).

Luke

This would demonstrate that the nature of the kingdom message itself was founded in grace and not the Law. Isaiah foretold the nature of Messiah's message centuries earlier: *"Everyone who thirsts, come to the waters; and you who have no money, come, buy and eat. Yes, come, buy wine and milk without money and without price"* (Isa. 55:1). While it is true that God does supply the physical needs of those who trust in Him, the primary focus of this invitation is the spiritual satisfaction of individuals in the Jewish nation. Why spend money on bread which cannot satisfy one's true need? It would be wise to receive from God that which abundantly delights the soul forever.

God promises to satisfy our spirit's deepest need without any human compensation (i.e., no one can buy or earn His forgiveness through payment or doing "good works"). For this reason, the disciples were to freely receive from those responding to their no-cost message (v. 4). They were not to worry about where their next meal would come from. Neither were they to hoard funds and store up provisions for their journey; these would only encumber them in performing the task that they had been assigned. Storing up what might be needed would also hinder them from seeing God's hand in providing for their daily needs.

As the disciples went from town to town with the kingdom message, some would graciously receive them because they recognized that the disciples were representing the Messiah. Because they were relying on the Lord to supply their needs, the disciples would have limited ability to return such kindness, but they were not to fret; the Lord would reward those who showed them hospitality (Matt. 10:41).

The disciples were to go forth into the harvest being completely dependent on the Lord to direct their way, to empower their ministry, and to provide whatever they needed in shelter, clothing, and food. If a town or city rejected their message, they were to depart that place, shake off the dust from their sandals, and go to the next town (v. 5). The act of shaking off the dust from one's sandal was to visibly indicate that the recipients of the gospel had rejected Christ and therefore would not receive His peace, but rather His wrath in the day of judgment (Matt. 10:14-15). Thus, the apostles were leaving the house remaining under judgment (including its dust), as it had been when they entered it (e.g., Acts 13:51).

The disciples then departed Capernaum in pairs, two by two. They were under Christ's authority to preach the gospel and to perform healings and to cast out demons. The signs that they worked were a confirmation of the message they heralded (Heb. 2:3-4). They toured throughout Galilee for many days before returning to the Lord and giving him a ministry report (v. 6).

Herod Is Baffled by Jesus Christ (vv. 7-9)

Through feminine scheming, Herodias, Herod's illegitimate wife, bamboozled him into beheading John the baptizer. John's death apparently occurred while the disciples were evangelizing Galilee. Some thought that John was the prophesied return of Elijah or of the Prophet that Moses had foretold would come to Israel in a future day (v. 8).

Herod had such high esteem for John that he thought that Jesus of Nazareth had somehow inherited John's power and authority after John had been executed, and in this sense, John had come back from the dead to haunt him (v. 7). Consequently, Herod was baffled over the things that he had heard about Jesus of Nazareth and wanted to find out more about Him through a personal interview (v. 9). This desired meeting did not occur until a few hours before the Lord was crucified, and while being interrogated by Herod, the Lord Jesus answered him nothing.

The Disciples Return (vv. 10-11)

The excited disciples returned with joyous news concerning their Galilean ministry (v. 10). It was a bittersweet moment, for the Lord had just been told of John's death. Given all that had just happened, the Lord told His disciples that it was time to come aside to rest for a while (i.e., time to separate themselves from the crowds and daily ministry). He took them to a deserted place near the city of Bethsaida.

The Lord teaches us that there should be a legitimate time to grieve the loss of a loved one and that we need times of physical and mental rest from ministry also. Proper grieving requires time away from life's normal responsibilities to reflect and settle one's soul in prayer and reading His Word. The disciples departed *together* to journey to a deserted place to achieve solitude. Notice that they did not isolate from each other during this time. To be free from responsibilities and distractions during the grieving process is important but isolating from friends and family is dangerous. It is at such times as this that we need our closest friends and family members nearby to anchor our minds in the truth and to weep with us. To give a grieving person a hug from the

Lord when the bottom has dropped out of his or her world is a tremendous blessing.

After an unknown time of solitude, the crowds became aware of their location and sought them. When the Lord saw the multitude, He was moved with compassion and began to serve them (v. 11; Mark 6:34). Indeed, we should take time to mourn the death of a loved one, but the Lord shows us that there is also a time to get back to serving others.

Five Thousand Fed (vv. 12-17)

On two different occasions, the Lord Jesus performed miracles to feed the multitudes that had gathered in remote locations to hear His message. Matthew and Mark record both events. The feeding of the five thousand is the only miracle recorded in all four Gospels and signals the close of Christ's two-year Galilean ministry. After this, Christ will travel to Phoenicia, Decapolis, Caesarea-Philippi, Judea, Perea, and then back to Jerusalem for His final days of ministry, culminating with His death, burial, and resurrection.

The first miracle occurred in "a deserted place" that was remotely near Bethsaida, according to Luke (v. 10). However, John refers to the location being near Tiberias, a city on the western shore of the Sea of Galilee (John 6:23). Bethsaida is the hometown of Peter, Andrew, and Philip (John 1:44). But there were two towns that went by this name: Bethsaida Galilee (Tabgha) on the northwest side of the Sea of Galilee and Bethsaida Julias on the north-northeast side of the sea. Luke is apparently referring to Bethsaida Galilee as the location of the miracle, which is just north of the area that John identifies for the event. Two towns named Bethsaida are mentioned: Luke says that the miracle occurred near Bethsaida and Mark states that the Lord told His disciples afterwards to cross the sea to Bethsaida. Yet, the information in the Gospels is not sufficient to emphatically identify the exact location of this miracle; we can, however, speculate about its most likely location.

John, an eyewitness of these events, states that the feeding of the 5,000 occurred near Tiberias (John 6:23). The disciples departed from this location in a boat without the Lord and were told by Him to go to Bethsaida (Mark 6:45). If Bethsaida Julias was meant, that would be an eight-mile journey to the northeast of Magdala directly across the sea, which would be a risky venture at night. John records that the disciples rowed towards Capernaum, which would be in the direction of Bethsaida

The Man and Your God

Galilee (John 6:17). This would be a safer trek north-northwestward as the shoreline would remain in sight (John 6:17).

However, a windstorm throughout the night hindered their progress northward until the Lord came to them walking on the sea in the fourth watch. After He entered the boat, He calmed the sea, and instantly moved the boat to a location just southwest of Capernaum (John 6:24), which allowed them to do ministry in Gennesaret the next day (Mark 6:53). This agrees with John's statement that people came in boats from Tiberias to Capernaum looking for Jesus the next day and found Him (John 6:23-24). If the miracle occurred at Magdala (about four miles south of Bethsaida Galilee and three miles northwest of Tiberias), it might be possible for the news to have spread down to the people from Tiberias overnight, but it seems more likely that these seekers from Tiberias had witnessed the miracle themselves and sought Jesus in the most likely place they might find him, Capernaum. Capernaum was the Lord's home base, so to speak, during His Galilean ministry.

Returning to the text at hand, after a long day of ministry, the disciples came to the Lord and asked Him to send the people away, so that they could journey to surrounding villages and purchase food for themselves before nightfall overtook them (v. 12). The Lord informed His disciples that there was no need to send the people away, but rather they should feed them (v. 13). John's account affirms that there were neither sufficient funds available nor nearby resources to feed a crowd of this size. Moreover, the only food that the disciples had found was a boy's sack lunch of two fish and five loaves which Andrew had spied out (v. 13; John 6:9).

The Lord told His disciples to cause the people to sit down in the grass in groups of fifty and to bring Him the fish and the loaves (v. 14). This was accomplished by the disciples (v. 15). After receiving what was available, the Lord gave thanks for the fish and the bread, broke the bread, and gave the fragments to the disciples to be passed out to the people (v. 16). After everyone had eaten their fill, there were twelve baskets full of fragments that remained.

Three helpful applications are suggested from this story. First, serving will always precede the reward for service, and the reward will be far more than we deserve! There was a basket for each serving disciple, and each received an abundant portion after their service was completed. Second, everyone was completely satisfied with the Lord's provision. He fed an estimated 20,000 people (5,000 men, plus women

Luke

and children; v. 17). The Lord Jesus satisfies all genuine need when we rest in Him. Help may not always come the way we expect it to or when we think it should, but the Lord's provision will never leave us disappointed! Third, the pattern of service in this story is a good one for us to follow: Understand what the Lord has given each of us, be willing to give it back to the Lord, obey how He says to use it, and then preserve the blessing that God supplies afterwards as a testimony of His goodness.

Peter's Confession of Christ (vv. 18-21)

The Lord with His disciples then journeyed to Caesarea Philippi about 25 miles north of the Sea of Galilee (Matt. 16:13). This was the capital city of the region ruled by the tetrarch Philip (not to be confused with Herod Philip). Caesarea Philippi is at 1,147 feet above sea level, a lush location hidden at the base of Mount Hermon and amid three valleys. Several springs around the city are the upper sources for the Jordan River.

While the Lord was alone praying, His disciples joined Him (v. 18). The Lord Jesus asked His disciples a question: *"Who do the crowds say that I am?"* The disciples responded by saying that some believed that He was John the baptizer, others thought Him to be Elijah, or another of the Old Testament prophets (v. 19). While anyone else would have been honored to be considered alongside these great men of faith from the past, these views of Jesus were lacking. He was not Messiah's forerunner prophesied by Isaiah (Isa. 40:3) or merely one of God's prophets; rather, He was "the Prophet" that Moses foretold would come to show Israel the way back to God (Deut. 18:15-19). He was God incarnate, Israel's Messiah, and any other view of Him was deficient and insulting.

Then the Lord asked a more important question, *"Who do you say that I am?"* (v. 20). Peter did not hesitate to answer, *"The Christ of God."* Although Peter was still learning the greatness of His Savior, he did understand that Jesus Christ was the Son of God and had come from heaven to the earth to do His Father's will (Matt. 16:16).

The Lord Jesus had been preaching with His disciples in northern Israel for about two years but had been widely rejected. Consequently, He instructed His disciples not to publicize that He was the Christ (v. 21). The people enjoyed His stories and benefited from His miracles, but generally they were not interested in the spiritual ramifications of His message. The Jews longed to be delivered from the Romans, but not from themselves through inward reflection, humble repentance, and subjection to Christ. This was the deliverance God wanted for His covenant people, but they were blind to it. Christ's early popularity had waned, and going forward, His course was steadfast to Calvary.

Although Jesus was God's Christ, it was not the appropriate time for that information to be affirmed publicly. Besides that, the disciples needed more time to grow in their understanding of who He was and why He had been sent to the earth.

There are seven important events pertaining to Christ's ministry that are recorded in all four Gospels: The ministry of John the baptizer as the forerunner of Christ, the feeding of the 5000, Peter's confession of Jesus being the Christ, the Triumphal Entry presentation of Messiah, and the crucifixion, burial, and resurrection of the Lord.

Jesus Christ Foretells His Death (v. 22)

It is at this time that the Lord plainly informs His disciples that He must go to Jerusalem and suffer many things by Israel's religious leaders, including being put to death. But this was not the end of the story; He would be raised from the dead on the third day (v. 22). Luke does not record Peter's rejection of the Lord's statement (Matt. 16:22). There is no doubt that Peter loved the Lord Jesus and did not want Him to suffer any harm, yet he was not speaking for God on this matter.

The Cost of Discipleship (vv. 23-27)

After speaking of what doing God's will would cost Him, the Lord spoke of what following Him would cost the disciples: *"If anyone desires to come after Me, let him deny himself, and take up his cross daily, and follow Me"* (v. 23). The Lord speaks of three critical mindsets that those identifying with Him must have: self-denial, taking up one's own cross, and following Him.

First, a true disciple of Christ must deny himself. Complete identification with Christ means that we practically reckon who we were in Adam (i.e., in our unregenerate state) is dead and gone, and we are alive in Christ. Paul put the matter this way: *"I have been crucified with Christ; it is no longer I who live, but Christ lives in me; and the life which I now live in the flesh I live by faith in the Son of God, who loved me and gave Himself for me"* (Gal. 2:20; also see Gal. 6:14). The Greek verb rendered "crucified" in this verse has a passive voice and a perfect tense, meaning that God has once and for all carved us out of the world by the cross of His dear Son, and we are now to live for Him. We are one with Christ forever and must seek to live out His life in the way that He desires us to. To deny self, one must be willing to recognize Christ's lordship in all areas of life and to renounce our claims to plan and choose without His approval. This new calling precludes self-ambition, self-sufficiency, self-exaltation, and self-gratification (i.e., beyond what has God's approval).

Second, a true disciple must take up his or her cross daily. The Jewish historian Josephus wrote that hundreds of Jewish insurrectionists had been crucified in Galilee by Rome and also earlier by the Greeks.[26] A few years later, during the Roman conquest of Jerusalem in 70 A.D., about 500 Jews were crucified daily according to Josephus.[27] All this to say that the disciples understood that the cross symbolized more than just a burden; it was an instrument of death also.

Anyone being nailed to the cross in ancient days meant that he or she was going to die a slow, agonizing death. Those crucified had nothing on their daily planners for the following week. Dying daily means, "Not my will, but Your will be done, Lord." Additionally, when one's hands were nailed to the cross, it made it impossible to grab anything. Bearing one's cross daily means that believers cannot engage in carnal appetites or get sidetracked by worldly pursuits.

Paul identifies what is necessary for Christians to adequately display the name of Christ: *"Let everyone who names the name of Christ depart from iniquity"* (2 Tim. 2:19). Believers cannot pretend to be holy; their conduct will either honor a sin-hating Savior or endorse a Savior-hating system. To declare the name of Christ is a great privilege, but to fully associate with His name is the highest honor. To be identified as a "Christian" is one and the same as acknowledging Christ's call to live as He did – a holy, selfless, consecrated life to God. William MacDonald summarizes what it means to bear one's cross:

> To **take up the cross** means to deliberately choose the kind of life He lived. This involves:
> - The opposition of loved ones.
> - The reproach of the world.
> - Forsaking family and house and lands and the comforts of this life.
> - Complete dependence on God.
> - Obedience to the leading of the Holy Spirit.

- Proclamation of an unpopular message.
- A pathway of loneliness.
- Organized attacks from established religious leaders.
- Suffering for righteousness' sake.
- Slander and shame.
- Pouring out one's life for others.
- Death to self and to the world.[28]

Accordingly, we come to Christ's cross and leave with our own cross. The cross is a symbol of shame and death, and Christ asks those who believe in Him to follow His selfless example of faithfulness, even unto death. On the night before His crucifixion, the Lord told His disciples that by identifying with Him, they would also experience the world's hatred and persecution (John 15:18-20). The gospel message pleads for the hell-bound sinner to embrace the cross of Christ, and no less so for the heaven-bound saint to take up his or her cross that he or she might enjoy His life now.

Third, a true disciple of Christ must forsake to follow the Lord. Forsaking must occur before following. Otherwise, there are too many anchors to the old life, which will hinder close exposure to the Savior. Our desire to follow Christ is a measure of how much we truly love Him and believe His message. The reason we hold back from being fools for Christ, and thus from seeing the mighty hand of God in our lives, is disbelief – we don't trust God. Through disbelief, the One who was offended for us becomes an offense to us. Those associating with Christ superficially will ultimately find Him loathsome. A true disciple of Christ esteems Him more important than anything this world has to offer: career, wealth, education, prestige, fame, following peers, going with the flow, and even natural relationships.

Many come to Christ's cross for salvation but then neglect to go on with Him and bear their own cross; this is an affront to the discipleship message He taught. The believer was never to flee the cross, but rather is to die daily upon it – only then does his or her life count for eternity (v. 24). Taking up one's cross means that we will follow Christ no matter the personal cost. The Lord Jesus is a perfect gentleman; He will not force us to bear our cross or obey His calling for our lives. However, to ignore His calling is to pursue an existence which has no meaning or eternal value. Christ likens this ideology to a man who gains all the world has to offer, but still loses His own soul in the end (v. 25). What is the profit in that – trading brief luxury and sensual pleasure for an eternal abode without God?

May each of us learn the necessity of denying ourselves, taking up our cross, and following the Lord with all our heart. There is a coming day in which all true disciples of Christ will be rewarded for following the Savior (v. 26). For those in the Church Age, this will occur at the Judgment Seat of Christ directly after the Church is raptured from the earth (Rom. 14:10-12; 2 Cor. 5:10). The Lord then said something that certainly perked up the ears of the disciples, *"There are some standing here who shall not taste death till they see the kingdom of God"* (v. 27). We learn later that the Lord was speaking of what Peter, James, and John witnessed on the Mount of Transfiguration (vv. 29-32) – a preview of Christ's glory in His kingdom (2 Pet. 1:16). This event did occur before the disciples "tasted death," that is, before they fully experienced death (Heb. 2:9). The disciples would later be tortured, and most would be put to death for the cause of Christ.

As the last living disciple, an elderly John was banished to the isle of Patmos as a Roman prisoner. While there, John witnessed the apocalypse, the revelation of Jesus Christ in various visions. For our benefit, he recorded what he witnessed in heavenly realms. His chronicle of future events has been preserved for us in the book of Revelation. All this to say that John was blessed with two revelations of Christ's glory.

The Transfiguration of Christ (vv. 28-36)

About eight days after the incident in Caesarea Philippi, the Lord took Peter, James, and John up to a high mountain in Galilee to pray (v. 28). Matthew states that it was after about six days (Matt. 17:1). As neither apostle uses exactness in the record, and Luke may be including the terminal days as well as the intervening days, we may conclude that the transfiguration occurred approximately a week after Peter's confession of faith at Caesarea Philippi. But why did the Lord choose to display His glory to His disciples at this juncture in His ministry? F. B. Hole suggests a reason why the transfiguration occurred at this moment:

> The Lord knew that these words of His would fall as a blow upon the minds of the disciples, and therefore He at once ministered to them great encouragement, not by words so much as by giving them a sight of His glory. This was granted not to all but to the chosen three, and they could communicate it to the rest. In the transfiguration they saw

the kingdom of God, since for that brief moment they were "eyewitnesses of His majesty" (2 Pet. 1:16).[29]

Mount Tabor, about fifteen miles southwest of Tiberias, is the traditional site for Christ's transfiguration, but this seems unlikely as there was an ancient, fortified city on top of Tabor (1 Chron. 6:77) that was garrisoned by Roman soldiers during the time of Christ. Furthermore, the Lord and His disciples had been in the region of Decapolis for some time and recently as far north as Caesarea Philippi. This region, loosely considered to be Galilee, boasted many high mountains in which this event may have occurred. Given that the Lord had been in Caesarea Philippi (Matt. 16:28) and was back in Capernaum directly afterwards (Matt. 17:24), a trip to Mount Tabor (about twenty miles southwest of Capernaum and fifty miles south of Caesarea Philippi) seems unlikely. Scripture is silent on where this event occurred.

Luke infers that the Lord and His three disciples spent the night on the mountain and came down the next day (vv. 32, 37). This means that the following events may have occurred during nighttime hours.

When applied metaphorically, mountains in Scripture symbolize governmental authorities or kingdoms. Both Isaiah and Micah foretold of God's glorious mountain on earth, speaking of Messiah's future earthly kingdom (Isa. 2:2; Micah 4:1-3). This future reality is momentarily displayed when the brilliance of Christ's intrinsic glory is revealed on a mountaintop in Galilee. Luke describes what happened: *"As He prayed, the appearance of His face was altered, and His robe became white and glistening"* (v. 29). Matthew also describes the scene: *"He was transfigured before them. His face shone like the sun, and His clothes became as white as the light"* (Matt. 17:2). One can only imagine the dazzling glory of the Lord on this high, remote mountain and apparently at night.

The Lord Jesus had said that some of the disciples would not die until they had seen the kingdom of God (v. 27; speaking of Christ coming into His glorious kingdom; Matt. 16:28). Years later, Peter affirmed what was declared by this incident: *"the power and coming of our Lord Jesus Christ"* – the revealing of *"His majesty"* (2 Pet. 1:16). For a moment the disciples were given a foretaste of the coming kingdom.

Luke then explains that both Moses and Elijah appeared and spoke with the Lord about His decease, which was to be accomplished at Jerusalem (vv. 30-31). The presence of both Moses and Elijah is significant, as Moses represents the Law and Elijah the prophets. All that the Law and the prophets reveal about Israel's coming Messiah will be fulfilled by Jesus Christ. Just as the disciples saw Christ on earth in His glory, in a coming day the entire world will see His glorious kingdom!

The disciples were sleeping but were awoken by this dazzling display of glory (v. 32). Peter somehow realized, perhaps by overhearing their conversation, that the two men speaking with the Lord were Moses and Elijah, for he interrupted their conversation to offer to build each one of them a booth (v. 33). But it was not time for Christ's kingdom to come.

Peter's suggestion of erecting three tents showed a lack of discernment for the Lord's proper place in the kingdom. Yet, his unintentional blunder was immediately checked when a sudden bright cloud overshadowed them and God the Father declared, *"This is My beloved Son, hear Him"* (vv. 34-35). Matthew tells us that the disciples fell to the ground in fear, but the Lord touched them and when they looked up, they only saw the Lord and in His normal appearance (Matt. 17:6-8). There is a glorious earthly kingdom coming in which Jesus Christ will be wonderfully recognized as God's only begotten Son. He will rule the earth with full glory, honor, and authority as God's faithful Son.

The Lord asked Peter, James, and John not to reveal what had happened on the mountain until after His resurrection (v. 36; Matt. 17:9). The establishment of His kingdom would occur after His second advent to the earth, but His redemptive work of Calvary was yet unfinished business that must be attended to. Suffering must precede glory!

Lack of Prayer – Lack of Power (vv. 37-43)

The fact the disciples were sleeping when the transfiguration of Christ occurred and that the Lord, Peter, James, and John came down the mount the next day indicates that the event occurred at night (v. 37).

The twelve disciples had just returned from preaching the kingdom message throughout Galilee. The Lord had given them authority over demons and the power to cure infirmities as they went (v. 1). Immediately after the Lord and His disciples descended the mountain, they were met by a large crowd. A man came to the Lord and kneeled before Him with an urgent request: *"Teacher, I implore You, look on my son, for he is my only child"* (v. 38). The father went on to describe the foaming at the mouth convulsions (epileptic fits) that he suffered, which often caused his son to fall into the fire or open water (v. 39; Matt. 17:15-16). The father had brought his son to the Lord's disciples, but they could not help him (v. 40).

To have Christ's authority and not reflect His ability in ministry is an offense to the Lord. Accordingly, the Lord publicly chided His disciples for lacking faith to heal the man's son. They were acting like the general Jewish populace, from which they had been called, *"a faithless and perverse generation"* (v. 41). The Lord then asked the father to bring his son to Him, which he did. The epileptic symptoms were resulting from demon possession, so the Lord rebuked the demon residing within the boy and he was instantly cured (v. 42). Everyone marveled at the miracle which had keenly displayed the majesty of God (v. 43).

Matthew tells us that afterwards, the disciples came to the Lord Jesus privately and asked, *"Why could we not cast it out?"* (Matt. 17:19). The Lord answered their query by stating that they lacked faith to cast out the demon. Even a little faith in God, as likened to the small size of a mustard seed, can move mountains. Mountains here speak of seemingly insurmountable difficulties. True faith that discerns the will of God will lay hold of the power of God through prayer and fasting (Matt. 17:21). Prayerless believers will be powerless failures in serving the Lord! The Christian life should be marked by prayer and fasting. A believer who fails to pray will fail at everything.

Christ Foretells of His Death and Resurrection (vv. 44-45)

While still in Galilee, the Lord again reminded His disciples of the sorrow that awaited Him in Jerusalem. This is the second time in this chapter that the Lord Jesus has spoken of His forthcoming betrayal, death, and resurrection. Because the meaning of this statement was hidden from the disciples, they did not fully understand what the Lord meant, but after hearing His words, they were "exceedingly sorrowful" regardless and were afraid to ask Him about His declaration (v. 45; Matt. 17:23).

Lack of Humility – Lack of Greatness (vv. 46-48)

The disciples were having a dispute among themselves as to who would be the greatest in the kingdom (v. 46). Knowing what was lurking in their hearts, He took a small child and set him down by Him (v. 47). Having His object lesson before His disciples, the Lord then spoke to them, *"Whoever receives this little child in My name receives Me; and whoever receives Me receives Him who sent Me. For he who is least among you will be great"* (v. 48).

The Lord said that greatness in His kingdom would be achieved by humbling oneself in Matthew's account (Matt. 18:4), but in verse 48, He adds the necessity of demonstrating His love and humility to the lowliest believer. Our esteem for the lowliest believer in the Church shows how much we love the Lord Jesus (Matt. 25:40). The disciples had been thinking of their own greatness and as a result, they lacked power in the Lord's work, and they lacked wisdom and commitment to properly do what the Lord tasked them to do (vv. 40, 54-56).

The physical kingdom would not be established for some time, but the inward or spiritual realities of the kingdom would be revealed in Spirit-filled believers during the Church Age. Greatness is obtained in the kingdom by assuming a humble attitude before others to best serve them: Do we willingly serve others before ourselves? Do we quickly sacrifice our rights for the good of others (1 Cor. 9:19)? Do we serve to insert our personal opinions? Do we desire visibility or recognition for serving? How do we respond when treated like a servant (John 3:29-30)? Do we complain while serving? Do we gloat over our doings? Do we listen or seek to promote ourselves?

> The greatest test of whether the holiness we profess to seek or to attain is truth and life will be whether it produces an increasing humility in us. In man, humility is the one thing needed to allow God's holiness to dwell in him and shine through him. The chief mark of counterfeit holiness is the lack of humility. The holiest will be the humblest.
>
> – Andrew Murray

Sectarianism Is Rebuked (vv. 49-50)

John then asked the Lord a question. This is the only time that John is directly quoted by his given name: *"Master, we saw someone casting out demons in Your name, and we forbade him because he does not follow with us"* (v. 49). But the Lord corrected their behavior, *"Do not forbid him, for he who is not against us is on our side"* (v. 50).

The Lord admonishes His disciples for their sectarian spirit. They had witnessed someone casting out demons in the Lord's name and told the man to cease liberating the possessed because he was not specifically associating with Christ, or with them. The man was not teaching false doctrine or doing anything immoral; he just sought to help others and further the cause of Christ.

The Lord told His disciples not to hinder the man, for if he had enough truth and faith in Christ to cast out demons, he was on His side. This meant that the man was confronting Satan and therefore would not be speaking ill of Christ. Anyone believing that Christ was the Son of God was on the right side; they were not working against the Lord.

It is easy for us to think of other believers as "us" and "them" because they do not associate with us, or they think differently than we do. Yet, the Lord affirmed the oneness and the equal standing of all believers when He told His disciples, *"For one is your Teacher, the Christ, and you are all brethren"* (Matt. 23:8). Christians are identified by biblical names such as Christians, believers, saints, and brethren. No denominations, cliques, or separate followings should be found in the Body of Christ. Paul asked the Corinthians, who were bestowing special honors to particular preachers instead of following Christ, *"Is Christ divided?"* (1 Cor. 1:13). The act of identifying with anyone or any organization instead of Christ is completely unbiblical. Rather, we should identify with David's thinking, *"I am a companion of all who fear You, and of those who keep Your precepts"* (Ps. 119:63).

> However sweet the word may sound; any sectarian boasting is but the babbling of a babe. The divisions in the Church are due to no other cause than to lack of love and walking after the flesh.
>
> – Watchman Nee

Jesus Christ Passes Through Samaria (vv. 51-56)

Luke does not report much of the Lord's ministry in Decapolis. Having wrapped up His ministry in Galilee and Decapolis, the Lord ventures south through Samaria to begin His Judean ministry and the final year of His earthly sojourn. He was ever moving closer to His ultimate fate (the sacrifice of Himself) in Jerusalem (v. 51).

As the Lord and His disciples traveled through Samaria, messengers went before them into a village in Samaria to prepare for His arrival (v. 52). But seeing that the Lord Jesus was determined to journey to Jerusalem and not remain with them, the Samaritans did not warmly welcome Him (v. 53). Clearly, racial pride was hindering the Samaritans from hearing and considering Christ's message.

When James and John saw how the Samaritans snubbed the Lord, they asked Him if they, like Elijah had done centuries earlier, should call down fire out of heaven and consume them (v. 54). Racial pride was affecting their motive for sharing Christ with others also. Over the course of the previous months, they had watched many others reject the Lord's message, but had not suggested such a severe judgment. But clearly, the sons of thunder did not feel that the Samaritans where worthy of a second chance of receiving the grace of God through Christ.

The Lord immediately saw through their wrong attitudes and rebuked them, *"You do not know what manner of spirit you are of. For the Son of Man did not come to destroy men's lives but to save them"* (vv. 55-56). The actions of James and John were not motivated out of concern for the Lord's honor or for the furtherance of the gospel. They were put out because of the Samaritans' attitude toward them, and thus, they deserved to be punished by God. This was the spirit of the flesh at work, not the Spirit of God accomplishing Christ's mission of compassion.

During the Lord's first advent, His mission was to seek and to save the lost through the offer of Himself for humanity at Calvary. At His second advent, He will judge the wicked and all those who had rejected Him, but now was not the time of condemnation, except for His own, and He fully embraced it. The Samaritan's rejection of Him was nothing in comparison to what waited for Him in Jerusalem in about a year's time.

Resistance to Christ's Authority (vv. 57-62)

Because there was a crowd following Him, the Lord instructed His disciples that they should leave Capernaum and cross over to the opposite shore of the Sea of Galilee (Matt. 8:18). Apparently, many wanted to follow the Lord at this time, which provided Him an opportunity to speak about what it meant to be a true disciple of His. Matthew records the Lord's dialog with two men (a scribe and another man who wanted to follow Him), while Luke identifies three men in the story.

The first man is enthusiastic and volunteered to follow the Lord anywhere, no matter what the cost might be (v. 57). But the Lord reminded him that He was a homeless wanderer; He did not even have a pillow to lay His head on at night (v. 58). The implication was, "Are you really ready to give up all the material comforts of life to follow me?" Apparently not, as we hear no more from him.

The second man did not volunteer, as the first man did, but rather the Lord called him to be His follower (v. 59). This man was interested, but he had something he wanted to do first. Burying one's father is an important task, but certainly the Lord would have known all about it, yet He still called the man. Under the Law, anyone touching a dead person was unclean for seven days (Num. 19:11), which meant that the man was putting the Lord off for a week to bury His father. Anytime we say, "Lord, let me first," we have sinned against Him. He is never to have second place in anything.

The Lord told this man to *"Let the dead* [the spiritually lost] *bury their own dead* [their deceased], *but you go and preach the kingdom of God"* (v. 60). It was far more important to preach the gospel to the living that they might inherit eternal life, than to bury the corpse of someone whose eternal state had already been determined (Heb. 9:27).

The third man resembled the first in that he volunteered to follow the Lord (v. 61). Yet, he is like the second in that he used those same contradictory words, "Lord, let me first...." There is certainly nothing wrong with showing love to one's family by bidding them farewell, but the man permitted his family ties to supersede Christ's proper place. The Lord responded to him, *"No one, having put his hand to the plow, and looking back, is fit for the kingdom of God"* (v. 62).

The Lord's illustrative response concerning the hard and focused work of plowing indicated that His disciples could not be self-centered in following Him; rather, they must remain fully focused on the tasks He gives them. Earthly comforts, jobs and important doings, and tender relationships still hinder people from following the Lord today. This is a remarkable illustration of three would-be disciples who allowed something to hinder their dedication to Christ.

In reviewing the Lord's teaching in Luke 9, we learn that when believers lack proper attitudes, their service for the Lord will also be lacking. First, the disciples lacked power because they lacked time in prayer and fasting (vv. 37-43). Second, the lack of humility created a lack of unity among the Lord's servants (vv. 46-48). Third, the lack of compassion resulted in a lack of grace and a judgmental spirit (vv. 51-56). Fourth, a lack of commitment to the Lord resulted in a lack of acceptable service for the Lord (vv. 57-62).

Luke Chapter 10

The Seventy Are Sent Throughout Judea (vv. 1-24)

While in Galilee, the Lord had sent His twelve main disciples out in pairs to preach the gospel and to heal the sick and oppressed (9:1). Having arrived in Judea, the Lord likewise sent seventy disciples out in pairs to preach the kingdom message throughout Judea and Perea. The Lord then planned to follow behind them going from city to city with the kingdom offer.

The Lord saw Judea as a field of souls to be harvested for the kingdom of God, but there were few laborers to accomplish the work (v. 2). Therefore, He asked the disciples to pray that the Lord of the harvest would send out laborers into His harvest. And then He sent them out as lambs among wolves, meaning that their evangelical activities would often occur in hostile and even dangerous environments (v. 3).

The Lord's instructions to the seventy evangelists were similar to those He had given after commissioning the twelve to preach the kingdom message in Galilee previously. The Lord told His disciples that their ministry was to be free of charge and that they were to depend on the Lord for their support. Hence, they were to take only the bare necessities with them. Carrying extra resources with them, such as sandals, clothing, or a money bag, would just slow them down (v. 4). Additionally, storing up what might be needed would also hinder them from seeing God's hand in providing for their daily needs. They also were to stay focused on the mission and not to be distracted by superficial conversations while journeying from town to town.

For this reason, the disciples were to freely receive from and bless those responding to their no-cost message (vv. 5-7). They were to accept hospitality when offered without any idea of possibly bettering their accommodations if another hosting offer was received. The Lord's emissaries were also to eat the food supplied by their host and be thankful for it without coveting a better meal. They were not to worry about where their next meal would come from. The disciples were to go forth into the harvest being completely dependent on the Lord to direct their way, to empower their ministry, and to provide whatever they needed in shelter, clothing, and food.

If a town or city rejected their message, they were to depart that place, shake off the dust from their sandals, and go to the next town (vv. 8-11). The act of shaking off the dust from one's sandal was to visibly indicate that the recipients of the gospel had rejected Christ and therefore would not receive His peace, but rather His wrath in the day of judgment (vv. 14-15). Thus, the apostles were leaving the house remaining under judgment (including its dust), as it had been when they entered it (e.g., Acts 13:51). The kingdom of God had come near to them, but had been rejected; therefore in a coming day, Christ would judge these cities more sternly than Sodom (v. 12).

How is it possible for the Lord to be more tolerant of wicked cities such as Tyre, Sidon, and Sodom in the day of judgment than the Jewish cities such as Chorazin, Bethsaida, and Capernaum (vv. 13-14)? Because where God extends greater responsibility there will always be greater accountability. The former cities had little revelation of truth to reject (Sodom only had the half-hearted testimony of one carnal believer named Lot), but the latter cities had the Son of God standing in their midst and they, being lifted up in pride, rejected His message (v. 15). The disciples were Christ's ambassadors, His representatives of His kingdom. Anyone rejecting them was rejecting Him, and being the Son of God, that also meant that they were rejecting God the Father, who had sent His Son to the nation of Israel (v. 16).

Just as there are different rewards in heaven for faithfulness, there are differing degrees of eternal judgment depending on how much truth was rejected (e.g., 12:41-48, 20:47). Everyone is given some divine truth to consider. For example, Paul explains that sophistication of creation demands a Creator, and that the human conscience contains moral reckoning of God's Law (Rom. 1:19-20; 2:11-15). Some individuals do receive more truth to consider, but these also have more accountability with God, if they reject what is revealed.

The prophet Ezekiel foretold that many of the Jewish cities destroyed by Gentile rulers would be rebuilt and resettled in the original locations after God gathers His covenant people back to their homeland in the Kingdom Age (Ezek. 36:11, 24). Today, there are many cities in Israel that bear the ancient names of previous biblical cities: Cana, Jericho, Nain, Bethany, Bethlehem, Hebron, Gaza, etc. However, only a few ruins remain of those cities which the Lord Jesus cursed, Chorazin,

Luke

Bethsaida, and Capernaum, for their rejection of His message. No one can escape His righteous judgments.

The disciples returned to the Lord rejoicing because many had believed Christ's word and many miracles had been done in His name and even the demons were subject to them in Christ's name (v. 17). The demons were not subject to the disciples, but to Christ's authority that had been given to them. After hearing their exuberant report, the Lord said to them, *"I saw Satan fall like lightning from heaven"* (v. 18). Was the Lord speaking of a past event, Satan's fall from heaven, that He witnessed long ago, or of the powerful ministry accomplished by the disciples as an extension of His authority, or of Satan's future and final judgment in the Lake of Fire?

The Greek verb *theoreo*, rendered "I beheld," is in the imperfect tense (observed in the past for a time), and the verb *pipto*, translated "fall," is a participle (a verbal noun) in the aorist tense (a completed action); thus, the idea is that the Lord "beheld Satan fallen" in a plunge as fast as lightning. As the disciples would have already been aware of Satan's fall because of pride (Isa. 14:12-15), that does not seem to be the point of the Lord's statement. Rather, the idea seems to be that Christ's authority that the disciples had exhibited over demonic forces was picturesque of Christ's ultimate victory over Satan (Rev. 20:10). As F. B. Hole explains, at times prophetic statements are posed as a completed event to indicate their certainty in God's sovereign plans:

> The allusion in verse 18 is not, we believe, to the original fall of Satan but to his final dispossession, as predicted in Revelation 12:7-9. The past tense is often used in prophetic utterances to describe future events. It is used in those verses in Revelation, as also in Isaiah 53:3-9. So the Lord confirmed the authority which at that moment He had given them, exerted over all the power of the enemy, but at the same time He indicated something that went beyond all power exerted upon earth.[30]

If the disciples remained holy in conduct and faithful in their mission, they would be invincible under Christ's authority. They could trample serpents and scorpions, and have power over the enemy, such that no harm would come to them as they executed their evangelical mission (v. 19). But any victory over the enemy that was realized was really Christ's victory, thus, they were not to be high-minded about their success, but rather that their names were written in heaven (v. 20). This is likely a reference to *The Lamb's Book of Life*, which is a ledger written before the world was created containing the names of all those who would be eternally saved through the Lamb's redemptive work accomplished at Calvary (Rev. 13:5, 17:8). As all human names are written in the Book of the Living, which both Moses and David refer to, that would not be a notable matter. Names in this book are blotted out, if the individual dies outside of exercising faith in God's revealed truth (Heb. 9:27; Rev. 3:5).

After hearing about the triumphant ministry of His disciples in Judea, the Lord "rejoiced in the Spirit" and was moved to thank His Father for how the gospel message had been received by those exhibiting childlike faith (v. 21). The Lord already knew that such a victory was assured, but after the news was publicly proclaimed by the disciples, it was most appropriate to publicly praise God and give Him thanks for what had been accomplished.

Those governed by human reasoning and religious piety would never receive the good news message. The Father alone understood who the Lord Jesus was, the mission that He had been sent to accomplish, and the blessing to humanity that would result. He was under His Father's authority, and His Father placed everything in His Son's hands to ensure His success (v. 22).

The Lord then reminded His disciples that they had been greatly blessed to see the work of God unfold before their eyes. Prophets of old had foretold the kinds of amazing feats that would occur in Israel when Messiah arrived, but they only saw by faith; the disciples witnessed these things with their own eyes (vv. 23-24).

A Lawyer Tests the Lord (vv. 25-29)

A lawyer engaged the Lord in a conversation about what he could *"do to inherit eternal life"* (v. 25). Although Jewish lawyers were experts in the Mosaic Law, this man lacked much spiritual understanding. First, he did not know to whom he spoke, and second, he did not understand that eternal life could not be inherited or earned. The lawyer was not serious about the subject matter, but rather was hoping to somehow trip the Lord up in His words through probing questions. He had come to test the Lord rather than to consider His message with an open heart. Regardless of his motivation, the lawyer desired to be justified before others rather than being justified by God. The Lord answered the lawyer's question about how to obtain eternal life with two of His own: *"What is written in the law?"* and *"What is your reading of it?"* (v. 26).

First, the Lord caused the man to consider what the Word of God stated about the matter of salvation. An individual cannot repent and receive Christ as Savior without first understanding the Word of God, for *"faith comes by hearing, and hearing by the word of God"* (Rom. 10:17). Believers today would do well to remember that we are merely facilitators of Scripture; we say no more than what God has commissioned us to speak.

Second, the Holy Spirit is the One responsible for working in the hearts of those who hear God's Word. Conversion is impossible without the work of the Holy Spirit to convince the sinner of his or her sin, the need for a righteous standing before God, and of forthcoming judgment for those who rebel (John 16:7-11; 1 Cor. 2:8-15). If Christians would follow the Lord's example of asking questions and referring their listeners to God's Word for the answers, they would avoid most arguments. It is the injection of our words, feelings, traditions, and methods into conversations which hinder the work of God on the unregenerate. The gospel message by nature is offensive to the unregenerate, but our approach in sharing the gospel should not be offensive or ambiguous; all that matters in evangelism is the accurate conveyance of God's Word and the ministry of God's Spirit.

The lawyer answered the Lord's questions correctly by first quoting Deuteronomy 6:5 and then Leviticus 19:18 – to sacrificially love God with your whole being and then to demonstrate that same kind of genuine love to others pleases God. The Lord not only stated that the lawyer's answer was correct, but also applied its meaning – if anyone fully lived in this way, they would be accepted by God. The Lord Jesus would later state that all the tenets of the Law hung on these two commandments – properly loving God and our fellow man (Matt. 22:40). The first four of the Ten Commandments relate to the former idea and the last six to the latter one.

Because the lawyer had affirmed God's commands contained in the Law, the Lord replied, *"Do this and you will live"* (v. 28). In saying this, the Lord was affirming the need to declare one's sin as the first step in receiving salvation. If the lawyer wanted to approach God through Law-keeping, he would never be justified before God, for no one can keep the Law (Rom. 3:20). But instead of allowing the Law to condemn his behavior, the Lawyer sought to justify himself, by asking the Lord another testing question, *"Who is my neighbor?"* (v. 29). Why did the Lawyer seek to justify himself when no one had accused him of wrongdoing? The reason is that his conscience accused him and caused him to feel guilt, which his religious pride then immediately resisted. Regardless, the Lord answered this question by telling him a parable, as the Lord desires that all testy lawyer-types become good neighbors.

The Good Samaritan (vv. 30-37)

The parable of *The Good Samaritan* is only found in the Gospel of Luke. The story was spoken to a lawyer during the Lord's Judean Ministry (about six months before Calvary). The text informs us that the lawyer was not truly interested in gaining eternal life, but rather sought an opportunity to test the Lord and justify himself. The Lord spoke the parable of *The Good Samaritan* in response to the lawyer's question, "Who is my neighbor?" Rather than asking the Lord this question, the lawyer should have asked himself, "Am I a good neighbor?"

The priest and the Levite in the story had a legitimate opportunity to demonstrate love for the wounded man, their neighbor, but they declined to do so. However, a Samaritan passing by and seeing the injured party was moved with compassion and did his best to ensure his recovery. The robbed man was apparently a Jew, so the act of the Samaritan was especially kind, as ethnic hatred and religious etiquette kept the two people groups apart. The Jews considered the Samaritans as unclean dogs. The Samaritans were a mixed Jewish-Gentile people group which developed in central Israel after the Assyrian invasion of the Northern Kingdom in the eighth century B.C.

> The first question which the priest and the Levite asked was: "If I stop to help this man, what will happen to me?" But the good Samaritan reversed the question: "If I do not stop to help this man, what will happen to him?"
>
> – Martin Luther King Jr.

The racial hatred of the Jewish lawyer was exhibited after the Lord asked him who had been a good neighbor to the injured man in the story. The lawyer could not force himself to utter the word "Samaritan" in his response, but rather said "he who had mercy." Regardless of their social abhorrence of the Samaritans, the Jews listening to the Lord's story were all wishing that they could be like the good Samaritan in the parable!

The Lord's response to the lawyer's first question was intended to speak to his conscience: only perfect Law-keepers would have God's approval and receive eternal life. The purpose of the parable was to cause the hearers to look beyond the impossibility of self-justification to being justified through Himself, their Savior. The crux of the story is this: If the needy man in the story could receive help from a Samaritan, why will you not receive help from Me concerning your dire situation of sin?

Mary and Martha in Contrast (vv. 38-42)

The home of two sisters, Mary and Martha (and perhaps of their brother Lazarus), became a frequent resting place for the Lord (v. 38). They lived in Bethany, which was located only two miles east of Jerusalem (John 11:1). During one such visit, the Lord took the opportunity to teach those who had gathered in their home to hear Him. Mary chose to sit at the Lord's feet and listen to Him, which frustrated her sister Martha, who was encumbered with much serving (vv. 39-40). She even asked the Lord to rebuke her sister so that she would rise and help her.

The Lord gently corrected Martha by saying that Mary had chosen what was best and would be blessed for doing so (vv. 41-42). Obviously, serving the Lord as He has called us to do is expected, but what we see others doing, or not doing, should not make us anxious (they are accountable to the Lord for their own actions), and our ministry should never replace having spiritual intimacy with the Lord. Certainly, what Martha was doing would benefit others, but fretting about what does not matter robs our joy in serving and keeps others from appreciating it too.

There are at least two things that we can glean from Mary's behavior: First, she had to say "no" to some legitimate activities to have time to sit at the Lord's feet and learn from Him. Second, after doing so, she was misunderstood by someone that did not have the same conviction. Regardless, Mary was complimented by the Lord in front of everyone for making the best choice. If we feel ourselves getting anxious or judgmental of others while engaged in ministry, it is time to come aside and sit at the Lord's feet and be refreshed by Him. This is the "good part" for our souls, although others may not agree. If we become so busy working for Christ that we have no time to love Him, we too should expect His rebuke. Christ is more concerned that hearts beat for Him, than that hands merely labor for Him.

Luke Chapter 11

Christ Teaches His Disciples About Prayer (vv. 1-4)

The disciples, after observing the Lord's intimate prayer-life, wanted to have the same kind of experience with God; hence, one of them asked, *"Lord, teach us to pray, as John also taught his disciples"* (v. 1). The Lord Jesus then taught His disciples to pray by providing them with a model prayer, but not one to be repetitiously prayed. Interestingly, the Lord had already taught them this pattern for praying about a year and a half earlier on the Mount of Olives (Matt. 6:9-13). Apparently, after observing the Lord's passionate prayer-life, they still felt deficient in how they were conversing with God.

The Lord began, *"Our Father in heaven, Hallowed be Your name"* (v. 2). God, His name, and His dwelling place transcend all that is common and earthly. God is Holy; He is separate from all else! All that is associated with Him, including His name, should be revered. The Lord Jesus compels us to first ponder the character and attributes of God when approaching Him in prayer. Why? The more we understand of our God's awesome nature, the faster the enormity of our problems diminish by comparison. C. H. Spurgeon, commenting on verse 9, wrote:

> The proper study of a Christian is the Godhead. The highest science, the loftiest speculation, the mightiest philosophy which can ever engage the attention of a child of God is the name, the person, the work, the doings, and the existence of the great God whom he calls his Father.[31]

Next, we are to pray for the advancement of all that God desires, which means that we must know His will, as expressed in His Word, to pray in this way: *"Your kingdom come. Your will be done"* (v. 2). To pray "on earth as it is in heaven" is to ask God to powerfully declare His holiness, His kingdom, and His sovereign rulership in such a way to make it permanent on the Earth.

After putting what is important to God first, we are to acknowledge our own needs, including spiritual and physical food to nurture our souls and bodies (v. 3). Next, we must have hearts free of bitterness and hatred if we want to enjoy fellowship with God (v. 4). We understand that by praying, *"Forgive us our sins, for we also forgive everyone who is indebted to us,"* we have a debt of sin that needs God's forgiveness. To pray, *"forgive us our debts, as we forgive our debtors"* (Matt. 6:12), means that we understand that because of our sin, we owe God a debt that cannot be repaid.

Because the Lord instructs us to plead with God to show mercy by granting the forgiveness of what we could not repay, we also should be willing to show the mercy to others who have sinned against us. We would only reject this behavior if we had an erroneous appreciation of God's forgiveness to us through Christ. Thus, an unforgiving heart in the non-believer would show that he or she was still in their sins (i.e., had not received God's judicial forgiveness), while the unforgiving believer would forfeit God's parental forgiveness and invite His chastening hand.

God is a merciful God, who wants us to experience His forgiveness and liberation from sin. This means that those who are truly His children must release, to God's judicial care, those offenses committed against us, so that we may enjoy unhindered communion with Him. Christ is not saying that God's judicial forgiveness for sin can be received by forgiving others, or for any other reason, for that matter. But a forgiving heart is a testimony that someone has received His forgiveness and experienced His mercy.

To petition God not to "lead us into temptation" does not mean that He may choose to entice us to sin; it is our flesh, the world, and the devil who do that, not God (v. 4; Jas. 1:13). Rather, we are admitting to God that our flesh is weak and that our full confidence is in Him to preserve us when we are solicited to sin. To be divinely delivered from evil's grasp means that we were not led into temptation. However, the Greek word rendered "temptation" carries the connotation of "proving the validity" of something, that is, a testing that proves the reality of something. James tells his audience, "The testing of your faith produces patience" (Jas. 1:3). Hence, we should not expect God to remove us from those difficulties which He has predetermined to use to refine us and cause us to act more like His Son (Rom. 8:29).

The Friend at Midnight and Fatherhood (vv. 5-13)

The parables of *The Friend at Midnight* (vv. 5-10) and *Fatherhood* (vv. 11-13) were spoken directly after the Lord shared with His disciples a pattern of prayer to follow (not a prayer to be repeated by rote). Both stories further exemplified important aspects of fruitful prayer-life.

Both parables convey the idea of persistent praying...asking, seeking, knocking, until the God of heaven provides answers to that which is burdening our hearts (vv. 9-10). Besides *yes*, *no*, or *different* answers to our prayers, we must realize that our tunnel vision perception of things often inhibits us from waiting for a sovereign God to work out His will in time. It will always be His best for us to wait for what God has for us. As the prophet Habakkuk learned, what often seems to be a *delayed* answer to our prayers is rather a legitimate response of a loving and holy God at work.

We should not think that these parables infer that God is somehow annoyed at our persistent praying or that He will be forced to answer a prayer in a particular way because He has heard it many times. Rather, the idea is that if a reluctant friend will respond to the inconvenient request of his neighbor for three loaves of bread, how much more likely is God to grant our requests (vv. 5-8). We are not unwelcomed neighbors, for God has invited every believer to come boldly into His presence to receive His help in time of need (Heb. 4:16). We have confidence that if we are praying in the will of God, such prayers will be answered appropriately to honor His name.

Similarly, in the second parable, it is expected and appropriate for a father to feed his children, rather than allowing them to hunger because of neglect (vv. 11-12). How much more then should we expect our heavenly Father to bestow goodness to His children so that they do not needlessly lack (v. 13)! *"Every good gift and every perfect gift is from above, and comes down from the Father of lights, with whom there is no variation or shadow of turning"* (Jas. 1:17).

We read of the Lord Jesus instructing His disciples seven times in the Gospel of John to pray only in His name. Such prayers are to be founded in God's Word and directed to the Father: *"And whatever you ask in My name, that I will do, that the Father may be glorified in the Son. If you ask anything in My name, I will do it. If you love Me, keep My commandments"* (John 14:13-15). *"Whatever you ask the Father in My name He may give you"* (John 15:16). If *friendship* caused the hesitant neighbor to supply the requested bread in the parable, how much more will *sonship* prompt the ever-willing Father to supply all our needs in real life?

Christ Heals a Demoniac Boy (v. 14)

Although the Lord had healed people suffering muteness previously (e.g., Matt. 9:32-34), this miracle is only recorded by Luke. A boy was suffering muteness because of demon possession. The Lord cast out the demon and the boy's muteness was healed and the multitude observing the miracle marveled.

Blasphemy of the Holy Spirit (vv. 15-23)

Although the crowd was amazed by the miracle that Jesus Christ had just performed in healing the mute boy, the Pharisees were not impressed (Matt. 12:24). Not only did they reject Christ's message, but they also accused Him of performing a counterfeit miracle because He was in league with Beelzebub, the ruler of the demons (v. 15). Luke states that "some of them" accused the Lord of doing this, which may mean that others were complicit with the Pharisees in the accusation. In short, they were saying that Jesus had received power and authority from Satan to accomplish the miracle. Additionally, having rejected the validity of the miracle just performed, they requested that the Lord show them an irrefutable *"sign from heaven"* to validate the authority of His ministry (v. 16). Both ideas were extremely offensive to the Lord Jesus.

All the miracles that Christ did were signs (undeniable evidence) to Israel that Christ was who He claimed to be – the Messiah. The Lord's preaching and signs composed the kingdom message to the Jews. Though the signs provided proof that Jesus was the Christ, they would prove insufficient to cause the people to trust the Messiah for salvation. For *"without faith it is impossible to please Him* [God]*"* (Heb. 11:6), and faith requires the soul to venture beyond what the senses can verify. Because the Pharisees were unwilling to believe what they heard from Christ, they would never see His performed miracles as legitimate, even if they saw a spectacular sign in heaven.

To confront the Pharisees' behavior, the Lord laid out several condemning points. First, the Lord pointed out that such a conclusion was not logical because a kingdom divided against itself cannot stand (v. 17). If Satan casts out Satan, how can his kingdom stand (v. 18)?

Second, the Lord pointed out that Jewish exorcists (the Pharisees' sons, so to speak) claimed to cast out demons (v. 19). Although the Lord did not affirm or deny their assertion, His point was that they too must be in league with Satan, for if the power to cast out demons came from Satan, then whoever exercised that power was under Satan's authority. But the Jewish exorcists would strongly reject such a notion; they believed that God was enabling them to perform exorcisms. This meant that the Jewish exorcists would judge the Pharisees as being inconsistent in their reasoning by concluding that Jesus Christ had cast out demons by Satan's authority.

The Lord then states a more logical conclusion: If He was casting out demons by the Spirit of God, then certainly the kingdom of God had come (v. 20). For the kingdom of God to be powerfully proclaimed by Christ meant that the "strong man" of the house (Satan's authority on earth) must first be constrained (v. 21). There could be no middle ground in this matter; one must believe who the Lord Jesus proclaimed Himself to be – God's sent Messiah – or reject His claim and remain under Satan's control (v. 22). There are only two authorities in the world today – God's authority and Satan's rebellious authority, which our Sovereign Creator limits to accomplish His own purposes. Thus, the Lord concluded, *"He who is not with Me is against Me, and he who does not gather with Me scatters abroad"* (v. 23).

Matthew further explains that the Pharisees, by attributing a miracle Christ had performed in their midst to Satan, had committed the unpardonable sin – they had blasphemed the Holy Spirit. Anyone committing this offense cannot be saved. This type of sin cannot be committed today, as Christ is not on the earth working miracles; however, there does remain an unforgivable sin today – those who reject Christ's Good News message cannot be saved.

Self-Reformation Is Worthless (vv. 24-26)

The Lord offers an allegory to summarize unbelieving Israel's past, present, and future. The man in the story represents the Jewish nation, while the unclean spirit typifies Israel's stubborn, idolatrous tendency throughout their history. From the Egyptian exodus in the fifteenth century B.C. to the Babylonian dispersion in the sixth century B.C., God repeatedly judged His covenant people for their blatant idolatry.

The destruction of Jerusalem and the Babylonian exile did largely purge idolatry from the surviving Jewish population. This is what is referred to in the story when the unclean spirit departs from the man (i.e., the house was swept clean of the idolatrous spirit by divine judgment; vv. 24-25). However, as William MacDonald suggests, "the empty house speaks of a spiritual vacuum – a dangerous condition, as the sequel shows. Reformation is not enough. There must be the positive acceptance of the Savior."[32] After the Jews returned to Israel from their Babylonian captivity, a system of religious doings developed in Israel that circumvented the necessity of substitutional sacrifices for sin.

Modern-day Judaism continues to blind the Jewish people from recognizing their need for God's solution for sin, His provided Savior. The purpose of the Law is to show sin (Rom. 3:20) and point the Jews to the only One who could redeem and cleanse them – Jesus Christ (Gal. 3:24). So, though Israel was swept clean of idolatry by God's Babylonian chastisement, Israel's humanized religion of doings to earn God's favor was a worse travesty than their previous idolatry. This is pictured in the disposed unclean spirit returning with seven evil spirits more wicked than himself to indwell the previously possessed and cleansed man (v. 26). The latter situation is much worse than Israel's previous idolatry, for, having rejected Christ, the Jewish people must work to save themselves. As F. B. Hole explains, the full outcome of the seven spirits will be realized during the Tribulation Period when the apostate Jewish nation will worship the Antichrist:

> Verses 24-26 are evidently prophetic. At that moment the unclean spirit of their ancient idolatry had gone out of Israel, but though they were "swept and garnished" in an outward way, they were engaged in refusing the One sent of God to occupy the house. As a result, the old unclean spirit would return with others worse than himself, and so their state be worse than at the beginning. This word of Jesus will be fulfilled when unbelieving Israel receives Antichrist in the last days.[33]

Modern Judaism is not idolatry in the sense that the Jews are worshiping false gods instead of Jehovah, but rather, the Jews do not need God's provided Savior. They can atone for their own sins and earn God's favor by doing good works. Jewish Rabbis no longer teach that blood sacrifices are necessary to atone for sin, but that repentance, good deeds, or prayer have atoning value and thus replace the animal sacrifices demanded by Scripture. Yet, these all pictured the future, once-for-all blood sacrifice of Christ providing propitiation for human sin. Judaism teaches that individuals can make atonement for their personal sins against God without shedding blood (quotes from *Everyman's Talmud* by Abraham Cohen):

> What can be a substitute for the bulls which we used to offer before thee? Our lips, with the prayer which we pray unto thee (Pesikta 165*b*; p. 158).
>
> If one has been utterly wicked throughout his life and repents in the end, his wickedness is never again remembered (by God) against him (Kid. 40*b*; p. 109).
>
> Whence is it derived that if one repents, it is imputed to him as if he had gone up to Jerusalem, built the Temple, erected an altar and offered upon it all the sacrifices enumerated in the Torah? (Lev. R. VII. 2; p. 105).

This idea of alternative atonement (doing good works to atone for one's sins) is utterly contrary to Scripture: *"For the life of the flesh is in the blood, and I have given it to you upon the altar to make atonement for your souls; for it is the blood that makes atonement for the soul"* (Lev. 17:11). God's justice concerning a guilty sinner is satisfied through the judging of an innocent substitute – God's own Son paid the price for our sin by giving up His own life. So, the idea that the Jews could save themselves through self-reform and self-effort is deeply offensive to God, for it devalues the sacrifice of His Son.

A New Relationship (vv. 27-28)

A certain woman raised her voice and interrupted the Lord's rebuke of the Pharisees by saying, *"Blessed is the womb that bore You, and the breasts which nursed You!"* (v. 27). Evidently, this interruption occurred because Mary had just arrived on the scene. For Matthew tells us that someone in the audience had informed the Lord that His mother and brothers had arrived and desired to speak to Him (Matt. 12:46-47). The Lord used this interruption and information to speak of a spiritual union that was more intimate than natural relationships. He asked, *"Who is My mother and who are My brothers?"* (Matt. 12:48). Then, while pointing to His disciples, He answered His own question: *"Here are My mother and My brothers"* (Matt. 12:49)!

Luke

Indeed, the Lord was thankful for Mary, his mother, and for His half-siblings, but the crucial matter of obtaining God's blessing was tied to obeying His word (v. 28). Those who do the will of His Father in heaven are His family. Mary and His half-siblings represented the nation of Israel, which had largely rejected Him and His message (even Christ's half-siblings did not believe that He was the Messiah; John 7:5). The Lord was now giving an open invitation to anyone who wanted to receive Him to do the will of His Father.

The Lord was not belittling His earthly family or denying His love for them, but rather He was highlighting that having a spiritual relationship with Him was much more important. Our natural relationships all end with death, but our spiritual union with Christ lasts forever. In Him is life and in His presence is unspeakable joy and complete satisfaction. Indeed, Mary, as a young virgin, was blessed to give birth to her Savior, but she was more blessed to hear and obey God's Word concerning her firstborn son, Israel's Messiah.

The Sign of Jonah and the Queen of the South (vv. 29-32)

The word "miracle" is not found in Matthew's Gospel and is only rendered once in Luke's account (23:8). Generally speaking, the miracles that the Lord performed are referred to as "signs." These signs witnessed by Israel were irrefutable evidence proving that Christ was who He claimed to be – the Messiah. The Lord's preaching and signs composed the kingdom message to the Jews. Though the signs provided proof that Jesus was the Christ, they would prove insufficient to cause the people to trust the Messiah for salvation.

The Lord Jesus stated that it was the unrighteous who wanted to see a "sign or a wonder" to believe in Him. He called these "sign seekers" an evil generation (v. 29). Even those people who had witnessed the miracle of the feeding of the 5,000 were pestering the Lord the very next day: *"What sign will You perform then, that we **may see it and believe You?"*** (John 6:30). Did they not recall the miracle the day before? Did they not fill their bellies with a boy's multiplied sack lunch? The Israelites saw miracles every day in the wilderness for forty years, yet it did not increase their spirituality – for they constantly murmured against God and His leadership. This shallow spiritual mentality was evident while the Lord Jesus was hanging on the cross: *"Let the Christ, the King* *of Israel, descend now from the cross, that we **may see and believe***" (Mark 15:32).

Although the crowds wanted to see the Lord work another miracle, He declined to as it would not cause them to believe His message. Rather, the only sign that He would offer them in the future as Messianic evidence was the sign of the prophet Jonah. Jonah is a type of Christ in many respects. First, like Christ, Jonah was from Galilee (Gath-Hepher, Jonah's hometown, was only three to four miles from Nazareth). Second, the Jewish leaders were in error when they said to Nicodemus: *"Search and look, for no prophet has arisen out of Galilee"* (John 7:52). In their proud religiosity, the Pharisees probably ignored Jonah because he preached to Gentiles; they simply could not bear the thought that God's grace should benefit publicans and sinners. Likewise, the Sanhedrin despised Jesus from Galilee and His mission. Third, the Lord referred to the "three days" Jonah was in the belly of the great fish to foretell His death, burial, and resurrection. However, our Lord tasted death in all its appalling reality as the righteous judgment of God against sin, your sin and mine (Heb. 2:9), whereas Jonah suffered for his own disobedience.

Hence, the Lord Jesus offered a prophetic sign to the Pharisees: *"For as Jonah was three days and three nights in the belly of the great fish, so will the Son of Man be three days and three nights in the heart of the earth"* (Matt. 12:40). Later, the Lord clarified the exact meaning of His earlier statement about His own resurrection: He would be *"killed, and be raised up **on the third day**"* (Matt. 17:23; NASB), but also be *"killed, and **after three days** rise again"* (Mark 8:31). The Lord Jesus implies that these are interchangeable expressions though appearing contradictory to us. In fact, most references speaking of the resurrection declare that it would occur **on** the third day (9:22, 18:33; Matt. 17:23, 20:19) or **in** the third day (John 2:19-22). The Lord Jesus used Jonah as a type to signify to the Pharisees what was going to happen to Him: three days and three nights Jonah was in the belly of a great fish; likewise, for three days the Son of Man shall be in the earth (the grave).

Jonah told the Ninevites that their sins had reached up to heaven and that God was going to destroy their city in forty days. The Ninevites humbled themselves and repented after hearing Jonah's message. Now, One greater than the prophet Jonah was in Israel, but His divine message and personage were being blatantly rejected by God's covenant people. Therefore, on judgment day those rejecting a greater message and Messenger will stand guilty before the pagan Ninevites who repented after heeding Jonah's warning (v. 32). As Gentiles, the Ninevites had less privilege and less light, but were spared judgment because they believed Jonah's message and humbled themselves before God.

In verse 31, the Lord mentions another instance of a Gentile being blessed by God for eagerly validating what she had heard about Him to be true. The queen of the South is the queen of Sheba mentioned in 1 Kings 10:1-13 and 2 Chronicles 9:1-12. After hearing of Solomon's fame, the queen of Sheba (Yemen in Arabia) traveled nearly 1,200 miles to test his wisdom with hard questions. Solomon's mercantile navy operated along the Arabian coast and would have had contact with this influential Arabian kingdom.

The queen's large caravan brought exceptional spices, gold in abundance, and precious stones as gifts for Solomon. Such spectacular presents corroborated her prestige and wealth. The queen spoke with Solomon about all that was in her heart, and he explicitly answered all of her questions expertly. Her interaction with Solomon was beyond anything she could have imagined. The king's incredible wisdom, immense wealth, enormous table provisions, and the incredible accomplishments were all true. In fact, she concluded that the half had not been told to her.

The queen gave Solomon all the gifts that she had transported from her homeland: 120 talents of gold (about 4.5 tons), and an abundance of rare spices and precious stones (2 Chron. 9:9). In return, King Solomon gave to her *"all she desired, whatever she asked, much more than she had brought to the king,"* and then she returned to her own country.

By referring to the queen of Sheba's thorough investigation of Solomon, the Lord was reprimanding the careless attitude of the Jewish nation towards Him. Despite the incredible expense and great distance, she wanted to know for herself if the stories concerning Solomon were true. She neither requested nor witnessed any miracles, but examined the evidence with an open mind; however, the Jews in Christ's Day were not willing to follow her diligent example.

In contrast, God had sent His own Son directly to Israel; the Jews did not have to travel to a faraway land to hear God's message to them. Yet, they had no room in their hearts for their Messiah, even though He was far greater than Solomon. The queen of Sheba's testimony was a rebuke of the callous attitude that the Jewish nation had towards Christ.

The Lit Lamp (vv. 33-36)

The Lord then spoke a similitude that He had previously used, namely that of the *Lit Lamp* (8:16). The Lord affirmed that a lit lamp must be set on a stand to illuminate its surroundings (v. 33). Hence, it would be absurd to put a burning lamp in a hidden place, such as under a basket; its light must be seen to be beneficial. Light portrays the meaning of undefiled truth in Scripture: *"God is light and in Him is no darkness at all"* (1 Jn. 1:5).

Previously, the Lord had used the similitude to exhort true believers to live out what they knew to be truth, but in this scenario, the Lord is rebuking His unbelieving audience to trust what God is revealing to them through the light of His Word. The Ninevites and the Queen of Sheba had heeded God's lamp of truth and were blessed.

The eye responds to light to guide the body appropriately (v. 34). The Jewish problem of unbelief was not that there was not light, but that they were not responding to it with open hearts (v. 35). God had lit a lamp and illuminated the world with the revelation of His Son. The Lord charged His audience to respond to the truth that God's Word had revealed to them concerning Himself – their Messiah was standing before them. It is not God's fault if anyone chooses to ignore the light from God's lamp.

Pronouncing Woes on the Pharisees (vv. 37-54)

After listening to His message, a certain Pharisee invited the Lord Jesus to His home to share in a meal (v. 37). The Lord accepted this invitation, but he sat down to eat after arriving at the Pharisee's home without first washing His hands (i.e., he did not perform the ceremonial washing of hands required by Rabbinical law).

The Pharisee was stunned that the Lord ignored the traditional practice, which the Pharisees highly esteemed (v. 38). Obviously, the Lord knew that the Pharisee would notice His negligence in holding to this human tradition, which was by design. The Lord used the awkward situation to deliver a message of woes on Israel's religious leaders.

This message is different than the one occurring several months later as recorded in Matthew 23. In Matthew's account, the Lord is speaking publicly in the temple and on the Tuesday before His crucifixion. At that time, He pronounced eight woes on the Pharisees. In the message before us, there are six woes pronounced and one implied for a total of seven.

Although many of these judgments are similar, the woes listed in Luke and in Matthew have a different order and some are unique.

The first woe, which is implied because of the Pharisees' foolishness and wickedness, pertained to externalism (vv. 39-41). The Pharisees were more concerned in maintaining an outward moral and religious facade than exercising introspection that would lead to repentance and humility before God. They were more concerned about what others thought of them than God's evaluation of their spirituality. The Lord likened this disposition to that of a cup or a dish that had been thoroughly washed on the outside but was full of impurities on the inside, such as extortion and self-indulgence. Who wants to drink out of a cup that is filthy on the inside? Spiritually speaking, the Pharisees did not care about the inside condition of the cup if it appeared outwardly clean. The Lord rebukes their externalism. The Pharisees needed to get their hearts right with the Lord, rather than worrying about what the people thought of them.

The second woe pronounced was for concentrating on minor rituals and neglecting the weightier matters of Scripture (v. 42). They were meticulous to render to God one tenth of the most insignificant herbs that they grew, but then exonerated themselves from displaying the greater matters of the Law, such as justice and mercy. The Lord was not saying that they should not pay their tithe to the Lord as required by the Law, but rather heretical teaching is typified by out-of-balanced thinking. Majoring on a minor or majoring on one truth at the exclusion of other truth will eventually cause division among God's people. The truth is in the whole of God's Word, and nothing should be neglected. The Pharisees were focused on the minutiae of the Law, but blind to the justice, honesty, generosity, and holiness that were foundational aspects of the Law.

The third woe pronounced against Israel's religious leaders was for desiring the esteem and praise of men more than having the approval and honor of God (v. 43). The Pharisees delighted in religious showmanship. Hence, they desired to have the chief seats in the synagogues and delighted in public greetings from the people that acknowledged their influential status among them.

The fourth woe pronounced on the scribes and Pharisees was for their fake spirituality (v. 44). The Lord likened the Pharisees to *"graves which are not seen."* The Pharisees were dead in trespasses and sins, but they and those who followed them failed to recognize their spiritual condition.

The Man and Your God

They gave a show of spirituality, but by acting righteous, when they were spiritually dead, they were being like an unmarked grave. In a similar woe recorded by Matthew, the Lord reversed this metaphor; the Pharisees were like whitewashed sepulchers with a rotting corpse inside (Matt. 23:27). The Pharisees looked good on the outside, but inwardly they were full of corruption. They strived to appear upright before men, but God saw directly into their depraved hearts and what He found there was as putrid as a rotting body.

One of the lawyers then interrupted the Lord's monologue to declare that what He was saying was offensive to them: *"by saying these things You reproach us"* (v. 45). There were many things that the Lord taught that Israel's leaders could not understand because they were blinded by human traditions, but on this point, the lawyer had perceived things correctly. Since a lawyer had interrupted His message, the next woe was directed to the lawyers.

The fifth woe was pronounced on the lawyers for loading their countrymen down with man-made rules (burdens) which the religious leaders did not follow themselves (v. 46). Furthermore, they taught the people traditions and practices which undermined scriptural truth, such as honoring vows made to the Lord. When spiritual leaders take away from the truth or add to it, the result will always burden God's people.

The sixth woe against Israel's religious leaders pertained to their homage to God's murdered prophets to justify themselves before the people (vv. 47-48). To honor the Old Testament prophets, the Pharisees maintained their tombs and monuments and decorated them with wreaths. What did this activity indicate to the people? The idea being that if those prophets had been speaking to them, they would have received their message and not put them to death.

The Lord reminded them that, by their own admission, their forefathers had murdered God's prophets, therefore the judgment of God was not only on their forefathers but would have repercussions for their sons (descendants) also (vv. 50-51). By mentioning Abel, the first martyr (Gen. 4:8) and then the martyred priest Zechariah at the end of the Old Testament (2 Chron. 24:21), the Lord was including all God's witnesses in between who had faithfully declared the truth and died for doing so.

The "wisdom of God" in verse 49, who will send the prophets even though many would be put to death, is a reference to Christ. He would be sending prophets and apostles to men in His generation, but just as the previous messengers of God had been persecuted and killed by their

Luke

forefathers, He and His messengers would also suffer the same fate. The point being that just as their forefathers had rejected God's messengers and put them to death, they were rejecting Him, God's chief Messenger, and were plotting His death at that moment. Nothing had changed; they were just as rebellious as their forefathers.

The seventh and final woe pronounced against the lawyers was for their spiritual obstructionism (v. 52). Not only did they reject Christ's kingdom message, but they also aggressively hindered others from believing it. The idea that one needs to repent to receive God's grace is putrid to the natural man, so those rejecting Christ's message could not enter the kingdom of God.

The Lord's message to Israel's religious leaders greatly riled them (vv. 53-54). They vehemently assailed Him and cross-examined Him over many things, hoping to find some fault that they could then publicly accuse Him of. But it was not to be; humanized religion will never be able to refute divine truth – and Christ is God's truth incarnate.

It is easy to see the ills of humanized religion in the behavior of the Pharisees, but not in ourselves. Our natural tendency is to develop routine patterns and traditions that often result in unscriptural or out of balanced behavior over time. We, too, can neglect *"the weightier matters of the law: justice and mercy and faith"* (Matt. 23:23). Although no teaching in Scripture should be neglected or ignored, the Lord did affirm that there were weightier matters of doctrine to consider first. It would be good for us to weigh out what we believe Scripture is teaching in doctrine and in pattern and categorize each aspect under what is essential, what is important, and what is a preference. It is important to discern between what is commanded in Scripture and what was merely a pattern of the early Church.

For example, the Lord said to remember Him often by keeping the Lord's Supper (22:19-20). The early Church settled on a practice of remembering the Lord each Sunday by breaking the bread. Because this was the practice of the apostles, we may consider this a safe form to follow, but there is nothing wrong with meeting on other days of the week or more or less often to break bread. A practice of the Church in Scripture does not trump scriptural commands for the Church to obey.

Obviously, essential teachings concerning the doctrines of salvation, the study of God, and the inspiration of Scripture cannot be compromised, but let us be careful not to erect non-essential matters on the scriptural foundation in which our faith alone must rest.

Luke Chapter 12

Beware of the Leaven of the Pharisees (vv. 1-15)

A great multitude had gathered to the Lord Jesus. No doubt many were stunned and elated by His fearless denunciation of Israel's hypocritical shepherds. After condemning Israel's religious leaders, the Lord warned His disciples: *"Beware of the leaven of the Pharisees, which is hypocrisy"* (v. 1). Leaven, in Scripture, speaks of sin, corruption, or evil doctrine (Matt. 13:33; 1 Cor. 5:8). Because leaven (yeast) is used in the fermentation process, it is a perfect symbol of decay and corruption, which is why, spiritually speaking, we should not be contaminated by it. The leaven of hypocrisy that He was speaking of was the oral traditions that the Pharisees levied on the people in religious piety but did not always keep themselves.

This same pharisaical leaven infests the Church today. For example, Church traditions have caused many professing Christians to ignore Christ's command to remember Him often through the Lord's Supper or to transform the memorial feast into some unscriptural practice. Some have even associated the eating of the bread and the drinking of the wine in the Lord's Supper with receiving or maintaining their salvation. This kind of leaven (i.e., false teaching) undermines the gospel message of grace declared repeatedly in the New Testament (e.g., Gal. 1:6-9).

All such corruption will be exposed for what it is in a coming day, and everything done in the darkness (wicked deception) will be exposed to the light of truth and be judged by Christ (v. 2). Darkness cannot suppress light. Therefore, the Lord also knew that after His passion, His disciples in training, who still had unheard voices, would be powerfully shouting the truth from housetops (v. 3).

The Lord warmly affirmed that they were "His friends" and that they should never be ashamed of His intimate friendship with them under any circumstances (v. 4). The believer's eternal union with Christ ensures that everything that comes into our lives also comes into His, and He is able to rise above every perceived obstacle and hardship. We have lived our yesterdays, but God has already lived our tomorrows. Indeed, the

Luke

Lord proves His ongoing friendship and faithfulness and asks us to do the same: *"You are My friends if you do whatever I command you"* (John 15:14). Accordingly, believers are only to fear the Lord and not those opposing His message, nor are they to fret about the necessities of life while doing God's will – He will not neglect His servants.

Thus, the Lord challenged His disciples, *"Do not be afraid of those who kill the body, and after that have no more that they can do"* (v. 4). The most the devil can do is to take the life of a believer, which releases their soul to be with the Lord in heaven (2 Cor. 5:8). The devil cannot harm the soul of the deceased. Therefore, the disciples should only revere with fear the One who has the power to cast the souls of the deceased into hell (v. 5).

God is completely sovereign over His creation; He sees all, knows all, and controls all things. Although a sparrow is nearly a worthless bird (for five sparrows were sold for two copper coins), not one falls to the ground unnoticed by the Creator (v. 6). Certainly, one of His children is much more valuable than many sparrows. At any given time, the Lord knows the number of hairs on each of our heads, a situation which is constantly changing (v. 7). Therefore, given God's acute sovereignty over all His creation, believers do not need to fret over anything; nothing occurs in our lives that He is unaware of and does not have His approval, though we may not always understand His ways at times.

If the disciples confessed Him before men, then they could have great confidence in the Lord to confess them before the angels of God in heaven (v. 8). For those who deny Him before men, He will also deny them before the angels in heaven (v. 9). The Greek verb rendered "denies" in verse 9 means to "utterly deny or reject." The verb is in the middle voice meaning that the subject (any individual) had willfully chosen on their own behalf to reject Christ. In a moment of weakness, Peter would later briefly deny the Lord, but He never rejected the Savior. As previously discussed in Luke 11:15-23, one can be forgiven of speaking ill of the Lord Jesus, but blasphemies spoken against the Holy Spirit will not be forgiven (v. 10).

John's Gospel elaborates on the various enabling ministries that the Holy Spirit will have once He indwells believers in the Church Age. He will enable them to progress to spiritual maturity, guide them into all truth, and teach them what pertains to Christ (John 16:12-14). At this juncture, the Lord told His disciples that when they are brought before governing authorities who oppose their message, they do not need to worry about what to say, for the Holy Spirit will provide the appropriate words at the appropriate time (vv. 11-12). However, as William MacDonald suggests, this promise should not be used to promote laziness in the study of God's Word or in prayer:

> The Holy Spirit would put the proper words in their mouths whenever it was necessary. This does *not* mean that servants of the Lord should not spend time in prayer and study before preaching the gospel or teaching the Word of God. It should not be used as an excuse for laziness! However, it is a definite promise from the Lord that those who are placed on trial for their witness for Christ will be given special help from the Holy Spirit.[34]

Every aspect of their ministry must be marked by obedience to Him as enabled by the Holy Spirit. If believers are walking in the Spirit, they will receive suitable words to speak in times of crisis.

A man in the crowd then interrupted the Lord by requesting Him to tell his brother to divide their father's inheritance with him (v. 13). We are not told if the man was being taken advantage of or if he was wanting more than was prudent in the situation; it did not matter, for Christ would not be judging such trivial things. Rather, the Father had sent His Son to seek and to save the lost by giving Himself as a ransom for humanity. During His first advent, He was not tasked with judging the world's injustices (v. 14); however, when He returned to establish His kingdom on earth, all things would be set right.

Although He would not judge the matter that had been brought to His attention, He did warn His audience, *"beware of covetousness"* (v. 15). If people love things, they will ignore God's calling for them and abuse others, but if people love the Lord, they will use things to serve others. Believers must remember that our lives are much more than the things we collect during our brief earthly sojourn and completely lose at death; our life is in Christ. The Lord then told the parable of *The Rich Fool* to illustrate this truth.

The Rich Fool (vv. 16-21)

This parable was spoken towards the end of the Lord's Judean Ministry, just before the *Feast of Dedication* in December. Instead of sharing the blessings of a bountiful harvest with others, the rich man built more barns to hoard for himself what God had entrusted to Him (vv. 16-

18). His needs were amply met, so he could have avoided the needless construction expenses by distributing the excess to those in need. But this was not his choice. Rather, given the surplus, he hoped to retire early and "eat, drink, and be merry" (v. 19).

God severely judged the rich man for his poor stewardship – he had used what God had given him to exalt himself and to gain prosperity instead of assisting others (v. 20). When God supplies beyond our needs, our first recourse should be to discern why, and who He would desire us to bless. The rich man valued temporary wealth over eternal riches; let us not follow his example.

Not only did the rich man lose everything that he valued on earth, but his life was forfeited also. He had expended his time and resources to achieve temporal advancement, but he had gained nothing that counted for eternity (v. 21). Those who desire to live independently from God ultimately have an existence apart from Him – this is called "death" in Scripture.

What is the application for us today? We are all stewards of what God has given us and we all must give an account to Him; may we all be found faithful on that day (1 Cor. 4:2). Believers should not hoard God's blessings, but rather keep His provisions in circulation so that others can experience the goodness of God also. This describes the spirit of equality that Paul says should exist among God's people (2 Cor. 8:13-14). Our lives must not be defined by what we think we have, but rather by what Christ has that we are to share with others.

Consequently, the Lord followed the parable with an exhortation and a promise to His disciples (Luke 12:22-24). The disciples were not to worry about life's necessities – God would take care of them. Hence, they were not to focus their attention on temporal things, but instead on what benefited God's kingdom.

Why Worry? (vv. 22-34)

After telling *The Rich Fool* parable, the Lord expounded its application to His disciples. The primary focus of their lives was to be the furtherance of His kingdom, not on their own needs. They did not need to worry about adequate clothing or where their next meal was coming from (v. 22). He would be faithful to supply what was needed to sustain them physically, but they must be faithful to engage in the spiritual ministry of saving souls that He had tasked them with (v. 23).

The Man and Your God

The Lord then gives an illustration of God's faithfulness by referring to the ravens, who neither sow nor reap, nor have barns to store provisions for the future (v. 24). The disciples were worth far more than ravens to God, so certainly they could expect Him to supply all their essential needs also. This meant that there was no reason to fret about their future needs. Besides that, worrying about the future cannot change it, any more than thinking about your height, or perhaps your life span, can add inches or years to either (vv. 25-26).

The meaning of "anxiety" is to be pulled in different directions at the same time, and the idea of "worry" is to be strangled. Anxiety and worry are the principal thieves of the believer's joy. Yet, we cannot be robbed of God's peace if we choose to rejoice in Him instead of seeking satisfaction and happiness in favorable circumstances. The prophet Isaiah tells us that this is how we can enjoy God's *"perfect peace"* of mind: *"You will keep him in perfect peace, whose mind is stayed on You, because he trusts in You. Trust in the Lord forever, for in YAH, the Lord, is everlasting strength"* (Isa. 26:3-4). Nearness to God is the best defense against depression and the best means of promoting a stable mind.

> Worry does not empty tomorrow of its sorrow. It empties today of its strength.
> – Corrie Ten Boom

Paul reminded the Corinthians that all we have is from the Lord and is given to us to enjoy life by living for Him (1 Cor. 4:7): *"We brought nothing into the world, and it is certain that we can carry nothing out"* (v. 7). Clearly then, if God wanted us to have more than we have, He would gladly give it to us. God wants us to have that which is best for us: *"Every good gift and every perfect gift is from above, and comes down from the Father of lights"* (Jas. 1:17). Being thankful for God's provision defeats the temptation to be dissatisfied, to be anxious, and to complain against God (Phil. 4:11-12).

In a second example of God's faithfulness, the Lord Jesus asks His disciples to consider the lilies, which grow without toiling to do so and yet have a beautiful splendor for all to appreciate (v. 27). Likewise, God clothes the fields annually with grass for a particular season before it is removed and burned afterwards (v. 28). Obviously, the disciples were much more valuable to God than a field, therefore He would certainly supply their needs in a faithful manner also. The disciples were not to be

Luke

lacking in faith nor were they to be anxious about food and drink (v. 29). Worldlings often fret about such temporal things, but the disciples were God's children and His servants, and He both knew what they needed and was able to provide what was needed at the appropriate time (v. 30). If they lived for the kingdom of God, they would not lack anything necessary to serve Him (v. 31).

The disciples were God's "little flock" that was destined to inherit the coming kingdom when Christ established it (v. 32). Their destiny, their reward, their inheritance, and their honor were all secured in Christ; thus, there was nothing for them to worry about. In fact, the less self-focus they had on preserving temporal things the better, for what they used to further the kingdom provided eternal heavenly reward (v. 33). While men may steal your earthly possessions, what was reserved in heaven for them could not be taken or corrupted; it was eternal and protected by God.

Finally, the Lord told His disciples, *"For where your treasure is, there your heart will be also"* (v. 34). What we think about, what we desire, and what we glory in reveals to us what is important to us, that is, what is our treasure. We live for what we treasure. If we treasure Christ above all else, then we will live for Him without reservation. This type of attitude will ensure that our service will not be hindered by fretting about temporal things.

Watchfulness Is Required (vv. 35-40)

In verse 34, the Lord reminded His disciples that they would live for what they treasured in life. If they deeply valued Him and His heavenly mission for them, they must be walking in the light and be unhindered by worldly affairs to progress forward. Disciples of Christ must forsake to follow Him. This means that believers must be willing to remove those things which hinder their spiritual growth and testimony for Him.

Olive oil, the fuel of a lamp, is a type of the Holy Spirit in Scripture and the lamp's light refers to the testimony of His divine power at work (Zech. 4:2-6; Rev. 4:5). Girding one's robe about one's waist enabled unencumbered movement and a burning lamp ensured adequate light to illuminate the way in which one was moving. The point being that believers must remove anything from their lives that is hindering their spiritual growth and service to Christ, such as worldly entanglements. Likewise, they must be in God's Word and in fellowship with Him to be guided by the Holy Spirit as to where and how they should serve Him.

The Man and Your God

The Lord likens this state of readiness to servants waiting for their master to return home from a wedding (vv. 36-40). The wedding here is used as an illustration and should not be taken as an allegory of some prophetic event, such as the *Marriage Supper of the Lamb*. The Lord could have used any circumstance which caused the master to journey from his home and returned afterwards unannounced. His servants were to be undistracted and unhindered so that they could immediately attend to their master whenever he did return.

The master will be excited to observe his servants eagerly watching for him, so much so that he takes up the apron and causes his servants to sit down while he serves them (v. 37). This is a touching analogy that portrays the Lord's humble attitude in serving those He loves. Although He deserves all the honor and glory in His own home, He lowers Himself to honor and to refresh others. Thus, the watchful and waiting servants will be blessed by such a master, no matter when he arrives home, even in the middle of the night (i.e., during the second or third watch; v. 38).

The Lord then warns that it would be prudent for humanity to realize that judgment is coming. If a man knows that his home is going to be broken into by thieves, he will be watching and waiting for them, even though he does not know when they are coming (vv. 39-40). The world will not be expecting Christ's sudden appearance to set up His kingdom, but His servants (the Jewish remnant and perhaps Tribulation saints) should be watching and waiting with great expectation for that event (v. 44). A true servant is known by how they behave concerning Christ's coming. Whether it is to snatch the Church from off the earth to heaven or to later rescue the remnant of Israel out of the Antichrist's clutches, faithful servants will be watching and waiting for Christ.

The Lord Jesus never told His disciples to be looking for the Antichrist, but rather to be intently watching and waiting for His unannounced return to the air to take the Church home (1 Cor. 1:7-8; Phil. 1:6, 10; 1 Thess. 5:9; 2 Thess. 1:10). It is noted that a few Christians hold to a Partial Rapture view, a position that states that only those believers "watching and waiting" for the Lord's coming will be raptured at various times prior to and during the seven-year Tribulation Period. But both the Lord and Paul confirm that Christ is coming for the Church in its entirety (John 14:1; 1 Cor. 12:13, 15:51-52).

Around the dial of a clock in a church in Strasburg, Germany, are these words: "One of these hours the Lord is coming." We do not know when; it may be today; it may be tomorrow! Therefore, let us be watchful servants while we wait for our Beloved to come. Christ's servants are to live with the ongoing expectation of His coming for them. For this reason, they should have their waist girded and lamps burning!

The Testing of Servants (vv. 41-48)

Peter was confused as to whom the parable concerning watchfulness applied (v. 41). Was He addressing the application to His disciples only or to all people? The latter group would include worldlings who did not follow Him, professors who had identified with Him, and true disciples that were devoted to Him. The Lord responded to Peter's question by telling another parable, which implied that anyone claiming to be a steward of God should heed its meaning.

A master only promotes a faithful and wise steward to oversee the affairs of his household (v. 42). If the steward faithfully cares for all those entrusted to him by his master, the master will bless and promote him after he returns from his journey (v. 43). Indeed, he will put such a proven servant over all that he has (v. 44).

However, if the steward thinks that, because his master will be gone a long time, he can take advantage of the situation for personal gain, then the heart of that servant is revealed (v. 45). A steward that harshly treats other servants and lavishes himself with the master's provisions will be cut off from his stewardship by the master when he returns (v. 46). Because he knew what the master expected of him but chose not to do it, he will be severely punished and not be considered a servant any longer (v. 47). By his actions, he proved that he did not have a heart devoted to the master. He was a servant in title only, but he is and always has been an unbeliever.

The Lord concluded His story by affirming that just as there are different rewards in heaven for faithfulness, there are differing degrees of eternal judgment depending on how much truth was rejected (v. 48, 10:11-16, 12:41-48, 20:47). Everyone is given some divine truth to consider. For example, Paul explains that sophistication of creation demands a Creator, and that the human conscience contains moral reckoning of God's Law (Rom. 1:19-20; 2:11-15). Some individuals do receive more truth to consider, but these also have more accountability with God, if they reject what is revealed. The steward in this story had much revelation and therefore much responsibility; therefore, he received a severe punishment for his treachery.

Division Over Christ (vv. 49-59)

Directly after contemplating how true servants will be rewarded and how unfaithful servants (unbelievers) will be judged by their master, the Lord began to ponder His own mission on the earth. He had come from heaven to seek and to save the lost by delivering Himself to be God's sin offering for humanity at Calvary. He realized that His heavenly mission and message would send a fire on the earth (v. 49). He wished that this fire (the preaching of the gospel in the Church Age) was already spreading in the world, for that would mean His suffering and death would have already occurred.

Regardless, He was aware that He had a baptism that must be accomplished, speaking of His passion. The Greek verb rendered "to be baptized with" is *baptizo* and literally means "to dip or to place into or underneath" something. He was fully aware of the wrath of God that He would be placed into at Calvary and His soul would be distressed until that propitiatory work was accomplished.

Christ's suffering at Calvary is one of six types of baptisms mentioned in Scripture:

1. Jewish Ceremonial Purification (11:38-39) – the Jewish tradition of handwashing, which pictured self-cleansing to earn God's favor.
2. John's Baptism of Repentance (Mark 1:2-4) – the first step of salvation is to acknowledge, "I am a sinner; I need a Savior."
3. Christ's Baptism of Suffering (v. 50) – that Christ would be placed under the wrath of God for our sin.
4. Spiritual Baptism by the Holy Spirit (1 Cor. 12:13) – this act created the Church and places new believers in Christ.
5. Believer's Baptism (Matt. 28:19-20) – the act of personal obedience after becoming a Christian.
6. Baptism of Fire (Matt. 3:11-12) – this speaks of God's judgment of the wicked.

The Lord Jesus frankly told His disciples that the gospel that they were to preach would have a divisive outcome among those hearing it (v. 51). Although believing in His message of life would result in receiving God's peace, it would also cause hostility among family members who chose to reject Him (vv. 52-53). Those who freely chose Christ as Lord and Savior would be isolated and persecuted by those who had not believed on Him.

Matthew likens this dynamic to a sword dividing family members apart (Matt. 10:34). It is evident from Paul's instructions to the saints at Corinth that even marriages were being split apart by the gospel message (1 Cor. 7:12-16). But there can be no middle ground on this matter; true believers understand that all earthly relationships are secondary in comparison to the love and devotion Christ expects of those following Him.

Although the Lord Jesus had been speaking to a large crowd, much of His teaching on being watchful and faithful servants no matter the cost had been directed at His disciples. However, in verse 54, He rebukes the hypocrites listening to Him, that is, those who had witnessed Him heal people and yet still wanted Him to work some spectacular sign in heaven that they might see and then believe in Him.

The Lord uses a meteorological illustration to point out the fallacy of building one's faith on what is visible in the heavens. When they observed a cloud rising in the west, they would rightly forecast rain for that day (v. 54). Likewise, observing a south wind meant that hot weather was coming (v. 55). The Lord then called the Pharisees and Sadducees in His audience, hypocrites, because they could discern the face of the sky, but not the signs of the times – what Scripture declared to be true about Himself, their Messiah (vv. 56-57; Matt. 16:3). These religious leaders had memorized significant portions of the Old Testament, and yet they could not discern by Scripture that their prophesied Messiah was standing before them.

The Lord wanted His audience to discern the truth properly before it was too late and they came under divine judgment. To that end, He said that it would be wise for someone to settle with an adversary who was in the right before the matter was brought before a judge for a ruling (v. 58). It would be better to evaluate the situation reasonably and settle the dispute out of court than to take an ill-perceived position before a righteous judge.

Such a high-minded attitude would land the defendant in prison until he was able to pay the plaintiff. In prison, the guilty would be aware of their folly, but it would be too late to peacefully resolve the matter. The point being that God is the righteous Judge and Executor of true justice. All that He finds guilty will be cast into an eternal prison called "Hell" and no one will ever be able to pay enough to obtain their freedom from that horrible place. Now was the time to repent and to surrender to Him!

Luke Chapter 13

A Gospel Panorama

One of the most beautiful panoramic views of the differing vantage points of Christ is seen in the gospel message itself. There is but one gospel message, yet each writer highlights varying aspects of the gospel as it directly relates to his associated theme.

Matthew's authority theme stresses "repentance" eleven times, but only three times does he speak of the necessity to believe in the Lord Jesus (e.g., Matt. 4:17). In fact, in Matthew, the Lord spends more time criticizing the Jews for not believing John's message of repentance than for not believing on Him.

Mark stresses the need to both repent and to believe in Christ to be saved, but there is clearly a heavier focus on believing (e.g., Mark 1:14-15). He speaks of believing in Christ nearly a dozen times and of the necessity to repent only four times. As Christ is not lauding His kingly authority in Mark, repentance is of a secondary emphasis. Accordingly, it would require real faith to believe on a lowly Servant for salvation.

Luke speaks of believing in the Lord five times but addresses the matter of repentance fourteen times. The beloved physician instead employs terms in his Gospel which appeal to human need and sorrow, such as "perishing" (vv. 3, 5). "Perishing" speaks of dying, and Luke speaks of it more often than the other Gospel writers. On behalf of Christ, Luke petitions the sick, the suffering, and the brokenhearted who are suffering under the effects of sin. The Lord feels our painful infirmities caused by sin. He desires to save the sinner from eternal judgment and to relieve the agonizing aftermath of sin.

John's Gospel expresses the heavenly perspective of the gospel message. While Matthew and Luke stress repentance, for one must acknowledge their sins before salvation can be obtained, John simply declares the overall spiritual situation: In God is life, and apart from God is death (John 1:3-4). Speaking of Christ, John writes: *"All things were made by Him"*; John stresses the fact that man is spiritually dead and must be born again (John 3:3) and made alive (John 5:21). How is this achieved? By believing (John 3:16, 3:36, 5:24). Consequently, the words "repent" and "forgive" are not found in John's account, but the matter of believing is emphasized ninety-nine times! Man is dead in the world. Eternal life is only in Christ and that is received by believing in Him.

Repent or Perish (vv. 1-5)

Whether the Lord was still speaking to the crowd that He just warned to respond properly to revealed truth is unclear. Someone informed Him that Pilate had mingled the blood of certain Galileans with his pagan sacrifices (v. 1). The idea being suggested was that God must have disapproved of these Galileans to permit them to die in such an outrageous way.

After hearing this news, the Lord Jesus asked those with Him if they thought these Galileans were more sinful than other Galileans (v. 2). By this question His audience understood that all men were guilty sinners and deserved God's judicial wrath. Furthermore, His mercy could only be received through personal repentance (v. 3). To illustrate His point, He then mentioned another tragedy and asked if the eighteen men killed when the tower in Siloam collapsed were worse sinners than those living in Jerusalem (v. 4). The implied answer is again "no."

In a world ruined by sin and where all are born with Adam's fallen nature, terrible things will happen to so-called "innocent" people, but no one is truly guiltless before the Lord (Rom. 3:23). Although we cannot avoid certain calamities, we can avoid perishing as sinners through genuine repentance. To stress this point, the Lord repeated His statement in verse 3 – one must repent to be saved from God's wrath (v. 5).

Later, the Lord taught that the confession of sin must occur before forgiveness can be received (e.g., Luke 17:3). We also know that unless someone believes on Christ as Savior, he or she cannot be saved (John 3:16-18, 5:24, 8:24). Repentance and faith swing on the same hinge of gospel truth. Repentance literally means "a change of mind." True repentance agrees with God on the matter of sin and turns away from what displeases God and could never earn His favor. But one must turn from sin to embrace in faith God's solution for sin, Christ.

One who is truly repentant is deeply grieved over personal sin and yearns to turn from iniquity (Jer. 8:6). Those who repent and turn must turn to that which is an effective solution for their sin. They must believe the gospel of the Lord Jesus Christ. This is what the Thessalonians did.

They *"turned to God from idols"* (1 Thess. 1:9). Their salvation was evident in that, despite being persecuted for their faith, they continued to serve the true God. They were the real thing!

God is *"not willing that any should perish but that all should come to repentance"* (2 Pet. 3:9), but a seeking sinner must repent and trust Christ alone for salvation (v. 3; Rom. 10:9).

The Barren Fig Tree (vv. 6-9)

Christ spoke this parable just before the Feast of Dedication and at the conclusion of His Judean ministry, some four months before Calvary.

The Jewish nation is allegorically likened to a foliage trilogy in Scripture: the vine, the fig tree, and the olive tree. Each one represents a distinct aspect of Israel's existence. The nation of Israel, as a political reality, is likened to a noble vine (a grape vine; Jer. 8:13), which God planted in the world (Jer. 2:21, 12:10); Israel was to be God's vineyard.

At the end of the Tribulation Period, the refined Jewish nation will receive the Holy Spirit and obtain spiritual life in Christ (Zech. 12:10). The work of the Holy Spirit in Israel is similarly depicted by the oil flowing to a lampstand from the olive tree in Zechariah's vision (Zech. 4:4-7). In this spiritually fruitful state, the Jews will be known as the olive tree which provides a testimony of God's goodness to the entire world (Hos. 14:6; Rom. 11:17-24).

When Israel is spoken of as a fig tree in Scripture, the metaphor relates to Israel's religious veracity, which often was fruitless for God (Jer. 8:13). This reality, including Judaism today, is what the Lord Jesus is addressing in this parable. The certain man who planted a fig tree in his vineyard represents Jehovah (v. 6). But after three years there was no fruit, so the owner instructed the keeper of His vineyard to cut the fig tree down (v. 7). But the keeper requested one more year to fertilize the tree and dig around its roots to try to make the tree fruitful (v. 8). If it did not bear fruit, then the tree should be cut down by its owner (v. 9).

When Christ told this parable, He had already been sharing the Kingdom message with the lost sheep of Israel about three years. But Israel was still pursuing vain religiosity instead of repenting and undergoing spiritual revival by turning to Him. Despite this fact, the Lord knew the heart of His Father (the owner) was to extend mercy to Israel, so He continued testifying of Himself in Israel (engaging in hard labor, as portrayed in *digging* about the roots) until the time of His passion.

Just a few days before His crucifixion, Christ sought fruit from a fig tree near Jerusalem and found none. He then cursed the fruitless fig tree, which immediately withered (Matt. 21:18-21). He sought spiritual fruit from the nation of Israel, and none was found. Less than forty years later, Jerusalem and the temple were destroyed, and the Jews have not sacrificed since that time. The Old Covenant was replaced by the New Covenant, sealed with Christ's blood, and God was determined not to allow the Jews to continue in what was now obsolete (Heb. 8:8-13).

One of the signs that the Tribulation Period and the Second Advent of Christ are nearing is that the fig tree (i.e., religious Israel) will again shoot forth leaves after a long winter season of deadness (21:29-31). Leaves must precede fruit, but the fig tree will bear no fruit until the spiritual rebirth of the nation occurs in the latter days of the Tribulation Period. What might the new leaves speak of? This is likely a reference to the Jews reviving the old sacrificial system during, and perhaps just prior to, the Tribulation Period.

We know from various prophecies that the Antichrist will desecrate the Jewish temple and put a stop to animal sacrifices at the midpoint of the Tribulation Period (Dan. 9:27; Matt. 24:15; 2 Thess. 2:3-7). Therefore, logically speaking, a temple will have to be erected and animal sacrifices will have to be reinstituted by that point. The generation that sees these activities will certainly see the coming of the Lord Jesus in His glory (Matt. 24:32-35). But presently, the fig tree, Israel's religious system, is leaf-less (i.e., no animal sacrifices) and fruitless (void of spiritual vitality).

A Sick Woman Healed on the Sabbath (vv. 10-17)

The legalistic traditions of the Pharisees controlled the people harshly and perverted the clear teachings of the Mosaic Law. Their oral laws had declared it wrong to serve others or to do good deeds on the Sabbath day, such as assisting a sick person to become healthier. As in the story before us, the Lord often challenged these man-made traditions that did not represent the heart of God and needlessly burdened the people. For example, the Lord also healed a withered man's hand in a synagogue on the Sabbath after the Pharisees asked Him, *"Is it lawful to heal on the Sabbath?"* (Matt. 12:10).

The Lord was teaching in one of the synagogues on the Sabbath (v. 10). There was a woman there who had been suffering for eighteen years with an infirmity that caused her to be permanently bent over (v. 11). After seeing her, the Lord called her to Himself, and she came to Him. He then said to her, *"Woman, you are loosened from your infirmity"* (v. 12). He then laid both His hands on her and she was instantly made well. She stood up straight and immediately praised God (v. 13).

The ruler of the synagogue was indignant over what Christ had done for the woman (v. 14). He turned to those gathered in the synagogue and told them that work should not be performed on the Sabbath, and therefore if they wanted to be healed, they should come back on one of the other days of the week. The ruler of the synagogue valued religious form over witnessing the power of God at work. He, as a man, would rather people continue in their sufferings, rather than have God heal them on the Sabbath.

The Lord rightly called the ruler a "hypocrite," for he thought nothing of properly caring for his animals on the Sabbath (v. 15). He would loosen his donkey to lead it to water on the Sabbath, but he did not want a daughter of Abraham that had been bound by Satan for eighteen years to be loosened from her infirmity on the Sabbath (v. 16). After hearing this rebuke, the Lord's adversaries were put to shame, but the multitude rejoiced in all the miracles they had witnessed Christ perform (v. 17).

After the Lord healed the man with the withered hand, the Lord responded to the outrage of the Pharisees by pointing out the fact that any one of them would rescue one of his sheep if it had fallen into a pit on the Sabbath day (Matt. 12:11). Yet, to God, a man is much more valuable than a sheep; so, it would be *"lawful to do good on the Sabbath"* (Matt. 12:12). Showing compassion and selfless love to others always honors God regardless of what day it is. The Lord will convey this truth again in the next chapter when He, in defiance of the Pharisees' traditions, heals a man with dropsy on the Sabbath.

The Mustard Seed (vv. 18-19)

According to Matthew, both *The Mustard Seed* and *The Leaven* parables were told during a sevenfold-parable message on *The Kingdom of Heaven* (Matt. 13). In that series, these were the third and fourth parables spoken, but Luke refers to them separately here. The kingdom of heaven is compared to a mustard seed that quickly grew into an herb and then into a tree that birds could build their nests in (vv. 18-19). The mustard seed would be the smallest seed familiar to the Lord's audience, and represents the humble beginning of the kingdom, when it was relatively small, pure, and fruitful – becoming a fruitful herb as intended. This demonstrated the power of the Holy Spirit to develop and prosper the kingdom through the preaching of the gospel message. This analogy compares well with the first three centuries of the Church Age. Roman oppression during this time had a purifying effect on the Church and resulted in believers taking the message of salvation in Christ alone throughout the empire.

However, the mustard herb continued to grow at a supernatural rate beyond this healthy and fruitful state into a sizable tree which became home to many birds. As the Lord did not explain the meaning of this parable, we must use Scripture to interpret its metaphoric language. Both Ezekiel and Daniel use a tree to depict a world power (Ezek. 17:23; Dan. 4:12). The evil birds that stole the seed (the Word of God; 13:19) in the first parable find a haven in the branches of the tree in this parable. Given these components, Warren Wiersbe discusses the parable's meaning:

> These facts suggest that the parable teaches an abnormal growth of the kingdom of heaven, one that makes it possible for Satan to work in it. Certainly "Christendom" has become a worldwide power with a complex organization of many branches. What started in a humble manner today boasts of material possessions and political influences.[35]

Thus, the parable depicts Satan's evil influences in undermining the message, order, and mission given to the Church originally by Christ. The birds picture the many erroneous religious systems that are associated with Christ's name, but not founded in biblical truth. Some have suggested that the birds in the branches speak of the kingdom's prosperity, but that is not how the Lord invokes the bird imagery in this parable series. An enemy is present in the first four parables and is opposing God's kingdom. It is not until the crowd disperses and Christ is speaking privately with His disciples that the enemy of the kingdom disappears and God's ability to establish it is declared.

The tree with its many birds represents the condition of the kingdom of heaven in the latter days of the Church Age; this reality likely refers to Christendom. Christendom has many branches and would include the true Church, but also the cults and various humanized movements that promote what is false and corrupt. In the last days, many will identify with Christ, but deny His deity, His headship (including His order for the Church), and His message of salvation. These religious establishments will deny such scriptural teachings as the Godhead (the Trinity), the eternality of the human soul, and the eternal punishment of the wicked.

Today, much of Christendom embraces false doctrine, and ignores God's expressed requirements for church leaders, roles among genders, and the Great Commission. In summary, Christendom, as pictured in the mustard tree, includes the true Church, but also many religious venues and people who are associated with Christ in name only. Christ has no fellowship with what opposes His authority and rule.

The key components of this parable are:

The mustard seed = the simple but powerful gospel message.

The mustard tree = Christendom.

The birds = Satan's corrupting influence on Christendom.

In Revelation 18:2, unclean birds are confined to a cage before being destroyed. During the Tribulation Period, Satan will work through the Antichrist and demonic deception and power to create an apostate religious system that will be ultimately destroyed. Clearly, in whatever age God's people live, they must avoid religious movements which result in unnatural spiritual unions with the world that defy Christ's headship.

The Leaven (vv. 20-21)

Three symbols – meal, leaven (yeast), and the woman – are used in this parable to depict the progressive corruption of the kingdom by the enemy through false doctrine (vv. 20-21). Warren Wiersbe summarizes the enemy's effort in this and the previous parable: "The mustard seed illustrates the false *outward* expansion of the kingdom, while the leaven illustrates the *inward* development of false doctrine and false living."[36]

Christ's divine character is typified in the meal offering of Leviticus 2. Meal (ground grain) is used to bake bread, a timeless food staple for humanity. Thus, in Scripture, bread is often likened to the receipt of and internalizing of God's Word. Scripture is God's spiritual food for us and without it there can be no spiritual growth. For example, at the end of his life, Moses admonished his countrymen: *"So He [God] humbled you, allowed you to hunger, and fed you with manna which you did not know nor did your fathers know, that He might make you know that man shall not live by bread alone; but man lives by every word that proceeds from the mouth of the Lord"* (Deut. 8:3). The Lord Jesus affirmed the necessity of internalizing God's Word to live for Him (4:4). Likewise, the apostles taught that believers must feed on God's Word to be nourished and strengthened (1 Cor. 3:1-2; Heb. 5:12-14).

Metaphorically speaking, leaven in Scripture is used to speak of sin, corruption, or evil doctrine (1 Cor. 5:8). The Lord Jesus warned His disciples against the influence of humanized traditions that oppose sound doctrine: *"Beware of the leaven of the Pharisees, which is hypocrisy"* (12:1). He also warned them concerning *"the leaven ... of the Sadducees"* (Matt. 16:6). The Sadducees were materialists who denied the existence of the supernatural, the spiritual nature of man, and the idea of a future resurrection. Lastly, the Lord Jesus warned His disciples not to be influenced by *"the leaven of Herod"* (Mark 8:15). Herod, a Jew, was in cahoots with the Roman Empire, and was, therefore, a friend of the world (Jas. 4:4).

Leaven is used to symbolize corruption in the Old Testament also. During the *Feast of Unleavened Bread*, the Jews were not to eat leavened bread, nor were they to look upon it, or even have leaven in any of their houses during the seven-day feast (Ex. 13:7).

Despite the consistent negative connotation of leaven in Scripture, some have applied an unscriptural meaning of leaven in this parable in at least two ways. First, after leaven is introduced into the meal, its influence will spread throughout the lump unhindered. This is supposed to represent the unstoppable spread of the gospel through the world. Second, the meal is said to represent all of humanity and the leaven the spread of the gospel; thus, the gospel message will spread around the world until everyone is saved. This would be the thinking of those holding a post-millennial view of the Lord's second coming. The main components in the parables must be understood with how each is consistently used in the whole of Scripture, or a wrong interpretation of the story will follow. Though these dynamics are reasonable similes of leaven, leaven is never used in Scripture to denote a positive influence.

What does the woman represent in the parable? In a prophetic vision, Zechariah saw a woman restrained in a basket having a lead lid, which was being carried back to Babylon by two winged women. In this scene, the constrained woman symbolizes the idolatry in Israel that God was removing from His people. He was returning this corrupting influence among His people to where it had originated, Babylon.

In God's original plan, woman was created to be Adam's helper and companion; however, she led Adam to disobey God in Eden (Gen. 3:1-6). Likewise, as seen throughout Israel's history, foreign women often enticed Jewish men to depart from the Lord and to embrace false gods (e.g., Num. 25:6-8). So, although women are no more inherently wicked than men, a woman is used at times in the Bible to picture an evil or seductive influence on men (e.g., Rev. 2:20). This highlights the spiritual weakness of men to be sensually seduced into error. For this reason, we observe systems of evil being assigned to expressions such as *"the daughter of Zion"* and *"the daughter of Babylon"* (Zech. 2:7; Jer. 6:2).

The key components of this parable are:

The leaven = the introduction of and spreading sway of corruption.

The meal = God's Word – God's food for His people.

The woman = wickedness or evil influence.

Learning of the opposition to the kingdom in the previous three parables and the symbolic meanings of the meal, leaven, and the woman permits us to properly understand this parable: The enemy is introducing evil into good meal to corrupt the food of God's people. By design, this parable follows the imagery of an advanced state of the kingdom, as pictured in the mustard tree – Christendom. This means that, in the latter days of the Church Age, we should expect a surge of unsound Bible translations and misleading theological frameworks. Satan will readily attack God's Word (Scripture) by perverting, changing, and diluting it. Some have suggested that the leaven represents the unstoppable growth of false professions, the evil presence within Christendom, but if this understanding were correct, the dynamic of leaven influence would corrupt all those who have identified with Christ.

Rather, the enemy knows that if he can corrupt the food of God's people, they will not thrive spiritually. Thankfully, as shown in Zechariah's vision, God is quite capable of limiting and removing wicked influences and corruption from among His people. The Lord's people need not be deceived, for God has preserved His truth for us in Scripture to live by.

Teaching While Journeying to Jerusalem (vv. 22-33)

The Lord, with His disciples (e.g., the seventy disciples who were sent out in Luke 10), had been spreading the Kingdom message throughout Judea since the Feast of Tabernacles. Since the Lord and His disciples were traveling to Jerusalem (through Herod's territory, v. 31) when this narrative occurs, it is likely that the Feast of Dedication was about to occur, as there would have been no other reason for the Lord to go to Jerusalem at this time. This meant that the Lord and His disciples had finished their Judean ministry, had made a brief trip into southern Galilee, and were now traveling to Jerusalem (v. 22). Christ taught the people as they journeyed south through various villages and cities.

Someone asked the Lord, *"Lord, are there few who are saved?"* (v. 23). The Lord had previously taught on this matter two years earlier during His Sermon on the Mount address. The Lord affirmed that the gate leading to experiencing the abundant life in Him was narrow and the way (the lifestyle) was difficult (v. 24). In contrast, the gate of living for selfish ambitions and pleasure was wide and posed an effortless pathway leading to destruction (Matt. 7:14). The wide way is the natural course of life for all that are born with Adam's nature: *"There is a way that seems right to a man, but its end is the way of death"* (Prov. 16:25). Living for self, instead of God, results in separation of some sort – which is the meaning of death in Scripture (Rom. 3:23).

Only by being born again (entering the narrow gate) and submitting to Christ's Lordship (the difficult way) can one enjoy Christ's life and please God. While entering the narrow gate may be a metaphor tied with believing the gospel message, the main idea here is that we can only have a life pleasing to our Creator by being in and following Christ. Many will try to please God their own way and attempt to earn His favor apart from Christ. These will not receive forgiveness, nor experience new birth, thus they remained condemned before God (v. 25). Many will plead their case for entering Christ's kingdom after the day of grace has passed but will not be permitted into God's presence. Those who have died will remain in their graves until the Great White Throne judgment of all the wicked (Rev. 20:11-15).

On judgment day, the Lord said many will know who He is without trusting Him for salvation and making Him Lord of their lives. Some will say that we "ate and drank" with You and listened to Your teaching (v. 26). This is a reference specifically to the Jews in Christ's Day, whom He then warns of the consequences of rejecting Him. Matthew informs us that others will say that they did things in His name (Matt. 7:22). Clearly, it is possible for people to know a lot about the Lord and even do things they believe will please Him without ever being born again (v.

23). The Lord knows those who are really His and who the counterfeits are. Having information about the Lord and doing ministry in His name does not necessarily equate to loving Him. Many identifying with Christ, even calling Him Lord, are not actually saved. The true test of knowing and serving the Lord is found in our desire to do God's will (Matt. 7:21). Consequently, the Lord says to these counterfeit believers, *"I do not know you ... depart from Me, all you workers of iniquity"* (v. 27).

There are eternal consequences of not being known by the Lord; all who are not will be cast into the Lake of Fire where there will be endless weeping and gnashing of teeth (v. 28). Even after being judged and having witnessed the patriarchs and prophets (picturing the faithful remnant of Israel), and great multitudes of Gentiles coming from every direction to enter Christ's kingdom, the rebellious disposition of the wicked will not change. Indeed, the last (those putting Christ's interests before their own) will be the first in Christ's kingdom, but the first (those who lived for themselves and not for Christ) will be last (v. 30).

While the Lord was teaching the people, one of the Pharisees warned Christ to depart from that location because Herod Antipas wanted to kill Him (v. 31). As Herod's jurisdiction was Galilee, the Lord must have been in southern Galilee at this juncture. This may have been a ploy by the Pharisees to try to scare the Lord into more quickly traveling through Herod's territory to Jerusalem, so that He could be captured there. Israel's religious leaders viewed Jesus as a threat to Judaism; the sooner He could be arrested and removed from the public scene the better.

While the Lord Jesus knew about the danger facing Him in ministry, He was not moved by this threat. Indeed, Herod was cunning and vicious, like a she-fox, but the Lord was on His own timetable in accomplishing His ministry and nothing could foil that plan (v. 32). The Lord was not declaring His travel itinerary by stating that He must travel today, tomorrow, and the day after, but rather that He had a mission to complete, and He was in full control of all that needed to be achieved. He then reminded His audience that Jerusalem had historically been the place in which God's prophets had been put to death (v. 33). This also was the place in which Abraham was to offer up his son Isaac to God (Gen. 22).

Lamenting Over Jerusalem (vv. 34-35)

Shortly after the Lord's comments concerning Herod, He and His disciples did arrive in Jerusalem. The Lord was deeply moved by the poor spiritual condition of His countrymen, as Luke records Him weeping over Jerusalem at the Feast of Dedication, and then again later, a few days before His crucifixion, four months later (19:41-44). After arriving at Jerusalem, the Lord Jesus lamented over Jerusalem: *"O Jerusalem, Jerusalem, the one who kills the prophets and stones those who are sent to her! How often I wanted to gather your children together, as a hen gathers her brood under her wings, but you were not willing!"* (v. 34).

The Lord's anguish and tears over His rebellious people were foreshadowed long ago when Joseph wept over his deceitful brothers in Egypt (Gen. 45). The tears of Joseph were both a testimony of the sorrow of his rejection and the forgiving love he desired to show in restoration. Likewise, the Lord Jesus was heartbroken over Jewish rejection and wept over His countrymen in sorrow, knowing the consequence of their rejection – the destruction of Jerusalem (19:41). Hence, He says, *"Your house is left to you desolate"* (v. 35). This is likely a reference to the temple, which had not been God's house for a long time in the same way that the feasts of Jehovah had become the *"feasts of the Jews"* (John 5:1). God was not with His people and His Messenger was leaving them.

The turtledove (the hen) likely represents mourning in Scripture (Isa. 38:14, 59:11). The Lord Jesus was grieved over Israel's rejection of Himself as their Messiah and this is symbolized by the turtledove gathering her chicks under her wing, but the chicks would not come to the place of intimacy and safety.

Speaking of the Lord Jesus, John says, *"He came to His own, and His own did not receive Him"* (John 1:11). As a result, the nation of Israel would experience war and desolation until a future day, when they would recognize Jesus as their Messiah at His second advent to the earth (Matt. 23:39; Dan. 9:26). Then when the people see Christ, they will shout, *"Blessed is He who comes in the name of the Lord"* (v. 35) and mean it!

Thankfully, there is a coming day when Israel will be restored to God. There will be great weeping on that day also, but these will be the tears of restoration and joy (Hos. 2:19-23; Zech. 12:10). The Bible does not say that there will be no tears in heaven, as some have taught. What the Bible states is that God will wipe away our tears once we are in His presence (Rev. 7:17, 21:4). What believer could possibly have a dry eye when they behold their Savior face-to-face for the first time!

Luke Chapter 14

Showing Mercy Is Appropriate Every Day (vv. 1-6)

The Lord was invited to share a meal in the home of a chief Pharisee on the Sabbath (v. 1). The Lord accepted the invitation. The situation apparently was a setup, as there was a man with dropsy (edema) present along with many other religious leaders; the latter group was closely watching Jesus to see if He would heal the man (v. 2). The verb *paratereo* rendered "watched" in verse 1 is in the middle voice, meaning that the Pharisees were watching the Lord for themselves (i.e., with evil, selfish intent), not with an open mind.

Before the Lord healed the man with a withered hand on the Sabbath previously, the Pharisees had asked Him, *"Is it lawful to heal on the Sabbath"* (Matt. 12:10). But on this occasion, the Lord asked the lawyers and Pharisees the same question (v. 3). The religious leaders said nothing, and the Lord healed the man anyway, knowing that it would infuriate them (v. 4).

Then, speaking to the religious leaders, the Lord pointed out to them that any one of them would immediately rescue his donkey or ox if it had fallen into a pit on the Sabbath day (v. 5). Yet, to God, a man is much more valuable than an animal; so, it would be "lawful to do good on the Sabbath" (Matt. 12:12). Showing compassion and selfless love to others always honors God regardless of what day it is. This logic was sound, and the leaders could not say anything against the Lord's conclusion, but certainly they were further infuriated by His actions and words (v. 6).

The Ambitious Guest (vv. 7-14)

After healing the man with dropsy in the Pharisee's home, the Lord told this parable and the Great Supper parable. During the final four months of His earthly ministry, the Lord was mainly in Perea. It is during this timeframe that the Lord's parable-telling ministry becomes prolific.

Recall that a Pharisee had invited the Lord and the esteemed and well-to-do of the community to enjoy a meal at his home (v. 1). The Lord noticed that the poor and uninfluential were not present, and that those who were attending were seeking to sit in the most honorable seats (v. 7). He responded to this dynamic by telling the story of *The Ambitious Guest.* Arriving at a wedding feast, the ambitious guest chose an honorable seat, but was later humiliated when asked by the host to sit in a less prominent place because someone more honorable than he had just arrived (vv. 8-10).

There are two main applications from this parable. First, we should not be respecters of persons. Everyone deserves kindness, but the underprivileged had not been invited to this wedding feast. Second, Paul tells us that those having the mind of Christ do not exalt themselves, but willingly take the low place and elevate the needs of others above their own (Phil. 2:2-5). We are not to follow the example of the ambitious guest in the story. He demonstrated by sitting in the best place at the wedding feast that he thought highly of himself and wanted others to esteem him as being important also. This is not the mind of Christ, and the Lord will reward those who exhibit His humility before others: *"For whoever exalts himself will be humbled, and he who humbles himself will be exalted"* (v. 11).

While social etiquette may cause us not to seek an exalted position when in the company of others, the issue that the Lord is addressing goes much deeper than just behavior. It is natural for our carnal flesh to want others to esteem us as important, and we usually feel affronted if that does not happen. For example, how do you feel when you are not recognized by others for an achievement that you labored diligently for? It is also natural for us to minimize others to make ourselves feel significant. For example, how do you respond when people treat you like a servant when you have freely shown kindness to them? If we have the mind of Christ (i.e., possess genuine humility), we would not be offended at either situation; in fact, the possibility of being offended would never enter our minds.

Believers may be recognized and honored by others for humble, diligent service, but such accolades should not be sought after. We are only on earth presently for the praise of God's glory (i.e., to make God look good; 1 Cor. 10:31; Eph. 1:12). Genuine service to others is given without thought to one's self or what others may think. This means that if we are grumbling and complaining while serving or hoping that we will be recognized by others for what we are doing, we are not really serving the Lord, but ourselves (Matt. 6:2; Phil. 2:14).

The Man and Your God

The Lord then exhorted the wealthy elite before Him not to invite friends, family, and those well-to-do to feast with them in order to be invited to their homes to feast, but rather minister to those in need, who cannot return the favor (vv. 12-13). Giving to get is selfishness, but giving with no expectation of receiving is a behavior that the Lord will reward in the resurrection of the just (v. 14).

The Great Supper (vv. 15-24)

After hearing the Lord's teaching, someone sitting at the table with Him said, *"Blessed is he who shall eat bread in the kingdom of God"* (v. 15). In response to this statement, the Lord followed His exhortation as to whom the Pharisees should be inviting to feast in their homes with a parable illustrating God's persistent desire to bless all those who desire to eat at His table, picturing the kingdom of God. *The Great Supper* parable expresses God's desire for heaven to be full of redeemed sinners, but sadly most will snub His kind offer to feast with Him. Clearly, the gospel invitation pictured in this parable could have only been heralded to the masses if Christ had completed His propitiatory work at Calvary.

A certain man (representing the Lord) sent out his servant (speaking of the Holy Spirit working through Christ's disciples) with invitations to a great feast to be held at his home (vv. 16-17). The invites first went to *the many* (i.e., the Jewish leaders; v. 17), but many made excuses for not coming (v. 18). So, the host instructed his servant to invite *the people in the streets* and *anyone in need* (i.e., the common Jews, including the poor and disabled; v. 21) to his feast. Still having plenty of available space (v. 22), the host sent his servant out to invite *the people on the highways* traveling through the land (i.e., the Gentiles; v. 23) to feast with him.

Sadly, many made excuses for not attending the great feast. Only a wealthy person buys property before looking at it first (v. 18). Materialism and wealth, speaking of self-sufficiency, are often a hindrance for considering the gospel message of Christ. The excuse of testing five yoke of oxen that had just been purchased pictures how jobs, careers, and business affairs often impede people from heeding Christ's invitation (v. 19). A husband spending time with his new wife would be a proper expectation, but no natural relationships should keep us from seeking the only One who will satisfy the longing in our souls – Christ (v. 21).

The Lord concluded the parable by stating the host's decree concerning those who rejected his kind offer to feast with him: *"none of those men who were invited shall taste of my supper"* (v. 24). The writer of Hebrews tells us that we must accept God's invitation to dine with Him, *"to taste and see,"* before we die; afterwards there will be no opportunity to receive Christ as Savior (Heb. 9:27).

The rejection of the Lord Jesus and His kingdom message by Israel's leaders is illustrated in this parable. Because they had refused Him, the poor and the outcast of the Gentiles would receive the invitation to feast with Him. As the book of Acts records, many Gentiles responded in faith to the gospel message (e.g., Acts 13:46). The supper was made ready when Christ died and rose again and sent the Holy Spirit (within His disciples) to publish the good news message. God will never force anyone to taste and see that His Son is good, but the Holy Spirit will work to convince the lost that it is most needful that they do.

The Cost of Discipleship (vv. 25-27)

Shortly after He spoke *The Great Supper* parable, a crowd began to follow Him (v. 25). Many delighted in this story, but most did not understand the repercussions of accepting His invitation to feast with Him. They just wanted a free meal, not spiritual transformation. So, the Lord stopped and turned towards them, and taught them about the cost of following Him. The Lord was much more interested in the commitment of His disciples to Him than in the crowd of people merely following Him. The Lord desired disciples who would learn of Him and be loyal to Him without reservation.

In secular movements, numbers are everything, but rarely do vast hordes of people represent God's will. This anomaly is quite evident in the modern Church movement, which equates church attendance with success. The mindset is that big church meetings are obviously evidence of divine blessing. However, it is making true disciples of Christ that is the key to Church growth and vitality (Matt. 28:19-20). May we too heed the command to "go out quickly" with the gospel message and compel anyone who will listen to consider God's offer in Christ. The various gimmicks used today in Churchianity to get the unregenerate into their buildings are a poor substitute for the message of Christ. May believers remember that what we win people with is what we win them to. Any message that steps around the gospel of Christ to gain followers will leave hungry souls dissatisfied and yearning for what is better.

The Man and Your God

The response to *The Great Supper* parable also shows us that just because a large group of people gathers after the name of Christ does not mean that they are legitimate followers. The Lord longs for the genuine disciples and both Church history and biblical history indicate that a religious majority has rarely aligned with God. Rather, crowds normally embrace doctrinal compromise and shallow spirituality, while a mere "remnant" comprises the real thing (Hag. 1:12-14; Rom. 9:27, 11:5).

The Lord Jesus demonstrated by His choice and order of parables in Luke 14 that, in spiritual matters, the mainstream rarely has God's interests at heart. The Lord was not interested in the quantity, but in the quality of those following Him. The next three parables emphasize this point – true discipleship is an all-or-nothing proposition (vv. 28-35).

Our desire to be a disciple of Christ is a direct measure of how much we truly love Christ and believe His message. The reason we hold back from being fools for Christ, and thus from seeing the mighty hand of God in our lives, is disbelief – we don't trust God. Through disbelief, the One who was offended for us becomes an offense to us. Those associating with Christ superficially will ultimately find Him offensive. The Lord Jesus didn't teach a middle ground concerning discipleship; consequently, following the Lord is an all-or-nothing venture:

> *If anyone desires to come after Me, let him deny himself, and take up his cross daily, and follow Me. For* **whoever desires to save his life will lose it***, but whoever loses his life for My sake will save it* (9:23-34).

> *If anyone comes to Me and does not hate his father and mother, wife and children, brothers and sisters, yes, and his own life also, he* **cannot be My disciple** (v. 26).

> *And whoever does not bear his cross and come after Me* **cannot be My disciple** (v. 27).

> *So likewise, whoever of you does not forsake all that he has* **cannot be My disciple** (v. 33).

A true disciple of Christ esteems Him more important than anything this world has to offer: a career, wealth, education, prestige, fame, following peers, going with the flow. The disciple's love for Christ must greatly surpass that of all natural relationships, including emotional regard for one's own life. Only profound love for Christ will enable believers to live a Christ-centered and Christ-revealing life.

Believers are called to bear their own crosses, which precludes self-ambition, self-sufficiency, self-exaltation, and self-gratification (i.e., beyond what has God's approval). William MacDonald summarizes what it means for a Christian to bear his or her cross:

> The cross is *not* some physical infirmity or mental anguish, but is a pathway of reproach, suffering, loneliness, and even death which a person voluntarily chooses for Christ's sake. Not all believers **bear** the **cross**. It is possible to avoid it by living a nominal Christian life. But if we determine to be all out for Christ, we will experience the same kind of satanic opposition which the Son of God knew when He was here on earth. *This is the cross*. The disciple must **come after** Christ.[37]

Each disciple must take up his or her cross daily. Anyone being nailed to the cross in ancient days was going to die a slow agonizing death. Those crucified had nothing on their daily planners for the following week. Dying daily means, Not my will, but Your will be done, Lord. Additionally, when one's hands were nailed to the cross, it made it impossible to grab anything. Bearing one's cross daily means that believers cannot engage in carnal appetites or get sidetracked by worldly pursuits.

> The cross of popular evangelicalism is not the cross of the NT. It is, rather, a new, bright ornament upon the bosom of a self-assured and carnal Christianity. The old cross slew men; the new cross entertains them. The old cross condemned; the new cross amuses. The old cross destroyed confidence in the flesh; the new cross encourages it.
>
> – A. W Tozer

The Lord never spoke of "becoming" His disciple, but what it meant to "be" His disciple; this implies an active, ongoing commitment. Consequently, He tells us not to call Him Lord if we are not willing to do what He commands (6:46). He must be Lord of all, or He is not Lord at all. Christianity is more than coming to the Lord for salvation; it is also going on with Him to live out His spiritual life before others. We come to His cross and leave with our own cross.

The gospel message pleads for the hell-bound sinner to embrace the cross of Christ, and no less so for the heaven-bound saint to take up his or her cross that he or she might enjoy life now. The Lord does not want us to only believe upon Him to evade judgment; He wants us to become like Him through exercising obedient faith. If we truly believe the gospel message, we will yield to Him and experience His abundant life now (John 10:10). We validate what we believe by what we do!

The Lord's message on true discipleship dispersed the people. In general, the crowds followed Him no more. Only a few loyalists were willing to make the necessary sacrifices to be His disciples. These disciples *"forsook all, and followed Him"* (5:11), including their professions and families (Mark 1:16-20).

The Unfinished Tower, the Rash War, and Salt (vv. 31-35)

These three parables were told together and have a common message – to follow Christ is an all-or-nothing venture. For example, if a king decides to take on an invasion force twice the size of his own army, it must be an all-out effort – any haphazard effort will end in defeat (v. 31). He and his soldiers must give their all in the defense of their city or capitulate and offer terms of surrender to avoid the battle. The same is true of beginning to build a tower without first assuring that one has the resources in place to finish it (v. 32). If started and abandoned because of poor planning at the onset, the builder will lose the initial investment and appear foolish to others.

After articulating these two illustrations, the Lord flatly summarized their unified meaning, *"Likewise, whoever of you does not forsake all that he has cannot be My disciple"* (v. 33). Forsaking must occur before following. Otherwise, there are too many anchors to the old life, which will hinder close exposure to the Savior. Following Christ is an all-or-nothing adventure. This is why Corrie Ten Boom could describe her FAITH as a "Fantastic Adventure In Trusting Him!"

The Lord then told a third parable concerning the cost of following Him. Salt adds flavor to what is eaten and serves as a food preservative (v. 34). But if salt loses its flavor and seasoning ability, it is worthless and must be discarded (v. 35). Paul used salt as a metaphor to speak of uncompromised truth (Col. 4:6). Salt, then, stands in contrast with leaven, which corrupts. This is why the Lord Jesus exhorts His disciples to have a "salty" testimony (e.g., Matt. 5:13). In summary, a disciple of Christ must display uncompromised truth while living in total dedication to Christ. Those who had heard His message now had no excuse; they must completely heed it if they truly desired to follow Him! True commitment is to be given over to a cause without reservation.

Luke Chapter 15

The Lost Sheep (vv. 1-7)

The parables of three lost things recorded in this chapter were spoken together by the Lord during His Perean ministry to pose a singular and crucial message to His audience. It is noteworthy that the Lord Jesus is addressing a mixed audience of those interested in listening to His message and those who were already rejecting it. Those seeking to be found (tax collectors and sinners) were positioned near to the Lord, while the murmuring religious leaders, who did not need to be found (repent), kept their distance (v. 1). Yet, they were still close enough to hear the stories, and, in fact, the parable trilogy had been crafted for their benefit.

The religious leaders complained about the Lord Jesus having close association with these sinners, even eating with them (v. 2). They believed that they had a righteous standing before God as good Law-keepers and therefore did not want to be tainted by mingling with sinners. But the Lord had come to seek and to save the lost, so He gladly spoke with sinners who were much more likely to receive Him than the self-righteous who did not need a Savior. The Pharisees had come to pick a fight with the Lord, so He included them in this parable trilogy.

The Lord begins by telling of one sheep that wandered away from the flock and the protection of the shepherd (v. 3). The shepherd, not willing to lose any of his sheep, left the ninety-nine to find the one missing (v. 4). The lost sheep that is looking for greener pastures is likened to foolish sinners who wander aimlessly pursuing their own cravings but are never satisfied. When a lost soul comes to the end of himself, a seeking Savior will be right there to pick him up and carry him home on His shoulders. Just as the shepherd rejoices when he finds his lost sheep, there is great joy in heaven when one soul repents and receives deliverance through God's divine Shepherd – Christ (vv. 6-7).

No doubt, the Pharisees listening to the parable considered themselves to be the ninety-nine good sheep who were not lost, and they were correct in their assessment! The ninety-nine sheep represented the self-righteous, who as good Law-keepers did not need to repent.

The Lost Coin (vv. 8-10)

In the second parable of the series, *The Lost Coin*, the Lord narrows the focus on the Pharisees further by decreasing the ratio from 99:1 to 9:1. It was customary for a married Jewish woman to keep part of her marriage dowry, ten silver coins, in her headdress just in case she was suddenly handed a bill of divorce. In this heart-breaking situation, the divorced wife was often put out on the street with only what she was wearing, so the silver coins in her headdress would be used to sustain herself until friends or family could assist her. All this to say that losing one of these ten silver coins was a serious matter, so with a lighted lamp, the woman would sweep the entire house looking for what was lost (v. 8). As with the lost sheep that was found, the recovered lost coin represents a repentant sinner which caused heaven to rejoice (vv. 9-10).

Whereas the sheep was lost through craving-driven wandering, the coin was lost through carelessness. A coin bears the image of the one in authority, and man was created in God's image and likeness. Humanity was to represent God's authority on earth, but all was lost in Eden through satanic deception and human rebellion. God keenly feels the loss of what He created in His own image, so when sinners repent, there is great joy in the presence of the holy angels. Just as the lost coin has value again in the finder's hand, we only have value to God through repentance and being restored to Him through Christ (John 10:28-29).

The Pharisees believed that they were the nine secure coins, who had not been carelessly lost, and they were correct in their thinking. As with the ninety-nine sheep, the nine coins represent the self-righteous who do not need to repent of anything. The Pharisees believed that they were in good standing with God because of their careful Law-keeping.

The Lost Son (vv. 11-32)

The Lord again decreased the ratio of the self-righteous souls in correlation to lost sinners coming to repentance from 9:1 to 1:1. The Lord's illustration is narrowing in on the hard-hearted, religious zealots who felt they were accepted by God without repenting of their sins.

In the story, a wealthy man has two sons (v. 11). The older son is compliant, but the younger son comes to the point of wanting his inheritance before His father died (v. 12). He desired to live his life the way he wanted to and that meant not being under his father's authority. This was an especially hurtful request to the father who loved his son.

Luke

First, it suggested that the younger son wished that his father was dead. Second, the younger son thought that he would be much happier having no contact with his father. Regardless, the father granted his son's request, and, having received his inheritance, the son went to a far country and squandered all that he had on riotous activities (v. 13).

When the prodigal son's money was spent, his supposed friends abandoned him (v. 14). His dire situation was compounded by a famine in the land which made finding work difficult, but at last he found a job feeding swine (v. 15). A Jew could stoop no lower than this occupation, as swine were unclean animals under the Law. The prodigal son became so hungry that he even thought about eating the slop he was feeding the swine (v. 16). It was then that he came to himself. He decided that it would be far better for him to return to his father, confess his sin, and just be as a servant in his father's house (vv. 17-19). But true repentance is more than good planning; the rebel son "arose and came to his father."

Apparently, day after day, the father searched the horizon for his wayward son, and one day, he spotted his son at a distance coming towards him (v. 20). The father ran to meet his son and immediately embraced him and kissed him. The son confessed his sin to his father, but he was never permitted to offer his service as a slave, for the father joyfully restored him to the status of his son (v. 21). The returning son was given the best robe to wear, a ring for his hand, and sandals for his feet (v. 22). Additionally, the father had the fatted calf slaughtered and prepared for a great feast to celebrate his lost son's return (v. 23).

Indeed, there was much joy and festivity in the father's house that day, for the son that was dead and lost had been found and made alive again! Let us remember that the wayward may be far away now, but that does not mean that they will be in a "far land" forever. After experiencing the sincere love of his father that day, there can be little doubt that the younger son wondered why he had ever forsaken his father. It did not matter that he had broken his father's heart, had wasted his money, and had engaged in wanton behavior, nor that he was filthy and smelled like swine; his father, delighted to see him, hugged and kissed him anyway.

The Pharisees readily aligned with the compliant older son who did not desert the father or engage in depraved acts and again they were correct in their assessment. But as the story continues, we will find out that though the older son was near to the father, he was just as lost as the younger son. The older son had been working in a field, but as he neared his father's house, he could hear music and sounds of merrymaking and inquired what all the hoopla was about (vv. 25-26). He became angry after learning that his troublesome brother had returned home and had been well received (v. 27). In fact, the entire party was in his honor.

It is when the father comes out to speak to his older son that we discover the wrong disposition of his heart (v. 28). The older son bemoaned that he had always been loyal to his father, but had never been given a kid of the goats so he could feast with his friends (v. 29). Yet, his father had prepared the fatted calf for his disloyal son who returned home after squandering his livelihood on frivolous and lascivious activities (v. 30).

Previously, the father departed from his place to seek and welcome his prodigal son home. Now, the father went to do the same with the older son, who was near to his house. He affirmed his love for his older son and that he had reserved an inheritance for him (v. 31). But the older son would not venture through the same door of repentance as the younger son had, even though the father begged him to do so. The older son, who had been attempting to please his father by doing good works, could not accept the same love of the father that had forgiven his younger son. The older son looked good on the outside, but was just as lost. He disdains his father's younger son because of the grace that he had received from the father (v. 32). It is for this reason that he never refers to him as "his brother," for how could he be? Only those who have experienced salvation in Christ can be called "brethren."

The Jews had the Law, which meant that they were closer to God than those without the Law, but since no one could keep the Law perfectly, even the most pious religious leaders must also humble themselves through repentance to be welcomed into God's family and dwelling place. Whether residing in a far country or in a field near the father's house, both brothers were just as lost.

Even though the father begged the older son to come into his house, he would not. The older son here represents the religious Jews that were listening to the parable. They would have readily identified themselves with the older son in the parable and they were correct. The older son boasted of his good works for the father, but he had not yet experienced the father's love, as the repentant younger son had. The Pharisees would not enter the same door of repentance as the younger son, and, hence, they were just as lost as the most wicked sinner wandering aimlessly far away from God.

Luke Chapter 16

The Shrewd Manager (vv. 1-13)

This parable was spoken during the Lord's Perean ministry just before the resurrection of His friend Lazarus. The timing would have been during the winter months, two or three months before Calvary.

The story identifies an unfaithful steward who was caught embezzling his master's wealth (v. 1). The corrupt manager knew that he would soon be required to give an account to his master, and that he could not hide his guilt (v. 2). He concluded that he was too old to dig ditches for a living and too proud to beg for mercy, so he came up with an innovative plan to ensure his livelihood after being fired by his master (v. 3).

The shrewd manager quickly went to several clients who owed his master debts and settled their accounts for much less than what was owed (vv. 5-7). He did not pocket these funds, but rather gained a good standing with those he had just helped – the idea being that these individuals would think favorably of Him and give him assistance after being fired from his job (v. 4).

It is noteworthy that the rich man in the parable did not commend his evil servant for his corrupt behavior, but for having enough foresight to look ahead to the future and plan accordingly (v. 8). He sacrificed present assets for future gain. Believers should also be future thinking and not just living for the moment. Investments into eternity are not really sacrifices because God uses these to honor His name, to further His kingdom on earth, and to reward the faithful with much more than they ever donated back to God previously.

The Lord Jesus told His disciples to use their money wisely to further His cause in the world before their money inevitably lost its value (v. 9). If they chose not to obey this command, it would indicate that they were mastered by money and not by Him. Eventually, all that is on the earth will be burned up (2 Pet. 3:10; Rev. 21:1-2), so obviously any acquired earthly wealth will be lost. The Lord's point was, "Why invest into that which will be soon destroyed?" It is better to invest one's life into what will endure forever, where neither moth, nor rust, nor thieves can diminish its value (Matt. 5:19-20). Those who choose to invest into eternity have the promise that *"their works follow them"* (Rev. 14:13).

What is the application of this parable for us then? We should use the resources that God supplies us to purchase gospel tracts, Bibles, and evangelistic tools that can be used to win souls for Christ. Additionally, we should support the Lord's servants engaged in evangelical work and strive to supply the practical needs of others in the name of Christ. By laboring to win souls for Christ, we establish friendships that will last for eternity and our heavenly reward for doing so will follow us too!

The Lord then reminded His disciples that the test of faithfulness begins in "what is least" (i.e., in what is often thought of as insignificant responsibilities; v. 10). The Lord puts value on those seemingly obscure tasks that often have no visible honor. None of us were born with discipline, but we learn discipline by doing what we know we should, even when we do not feel like it. This type of learned discipline accomplishes what good intentions cannot and continues to motivate service when difficulties arise because we want the Lord's approval in all that we do, even in the least of things. May we keep busy, even in mundane tasks of life, wherever the Lord has us in training for reigning. Relish every occasion to please the Lord and to show Him to others in what we do.

> A good many are kept out of the service of Christ, deprived of the luxury of working for God, because they are trying to do some great thing. Let us be willing to do little things. And let us remember that nothing is small in which God is the source.
>
> — D. L. Moody

The daily matters of life matter if we do everything for the Lord and for the honor of His name. The Lord provides greater opportunities for service as His people are faithful to what they have already been asked to do (vv. 11-12). But those who are not faithful with what they have been given will not be entrusted with more responsibility, and will have lost the eternal reward that would have been received for faithfulness.

There is no example in Scripture where the Lord called a lazy person to serve Him. Elisha was plowing behind twelve yoke of oxen when he received his call from Elijah. Moses and David were shepherding sheep

Luke

when God beckoned them to service. Gideon was summoned while threshing wheat. Four of the disciples were fishing when they were told by the Lord Jesus, "Follow Me."

The Lord concluded His teaching on the parable by issuing His audience a warning: *"No servant can serve two masters. ... You cannot serve God and mammon* [money]*"* (v. 13). The point being that we cannot live for what is temporal and sensual and live for the Lord. If Christ is truly the Lord of our lives, then He must have first place in our thinking; every activity, every relationship, and every conversation must have His approval. He must be Lord of all we are and have or He is not really Lord at all.

Greed Is Rebuked (vv. 14-17)

The Lord's teaching on having divided affections riled the Pharisees, for they believed that they served God, but were also "lovers of money" (v. 14). After the Lord Jesus exposed the conscience of the rich young ruler of Matthew 19 to the Law, he had to make a choice – give up His riches to follow God or continue in His affluent, pampered lifestyle – he chose the latter. Indeed, money was his god; he valued it more than treasure in heaven and following the Lord. After the rich young ruler departed, the Lord informed His disciples, *"Assuredly, I say to you that it is hard for a rich man to enter the kingdom of heaven"* (Matt. 19:23).

The disciples were astonished at the Lord's statement concerning those who value their riches above the One who gave them. They asked, *"Who then can be saved?"* (Matt. 19:25). The Lord responded, *"With men this is impossible, but with God all things are possible"* (Matt. 19:26). The Lord again emphasizes that in matters of salvation it is not merely difficult for men to earn heaven by their doings; it is impossible. The work of salvation which God brings about through humble, childlike faith in the Savior is how God ushers redeemed sinners into heaven.

The Pharisees labored hard to justify themselves before men, but God knew the wickedness in their hearts (v. 15). Humanized religion is an abomination to God because it exalts man's evaluation of what is important over what God has already revealed will please Him. The dispensation of the Law (beginning with Moses and ending with John the baptizer) was to show the Jews that they were condemned before God, as no one could keep all the precepts of the Law.

However, instead of admitting their sin before God, the Pharisees created a religion of legalism to ensure that they appeared as righteous before the people. But starting with the preaching of John, then Christ and His disciples, the era of the Law was coming to an end and the opportunity to enter the kingdom of God was now open to everyone. Many Jews had heard the kingdom gospel message and were now "pressing into it" through repentance and acknowledging Christ as Messiah (v. 16). The gate of the kingdom had been opened through the gospel of Christ, not through Law-keeping, which was an impossibility.

Many of Israel's religious leaders believed that Jesus of Nazareth was preaching a message that opposed the Law and the teachings of the prophets (Matt. 5:17). However, the Lord had come to fulfill Old Testament Scripture, not make it void, for God's Word will always be accomplished (v. 17). As prophesied by Isaiah, Jeremiah, and Ezekiel (Isa. 61:8; Jer. 31:31-34; Ezek. 36:24-28), He was going to establish a New Covenant with Israel and seal it with His own blood (Heb. 8:7-12; Luke 22:20). The New Covenant would permit God to righteously save those who realized that they were condemned by the Law (Rom. 3:20) and needed a Savior – Christ (Gal. 3:24). The Lord did not say that the Law would never pass away, but rather that God would put the Law away when it had fully served its purpose (2 Cor. 3:7-11).

Christ's Teaching on Divorce (v. 18)

In Mark's account we learn that the Pharisees were testing the Lord at this juncture, hoping to somehow catch Him in His words to accuse Him of wrongdoing. They asked Him: *"Is it lawful for a man to divorce his wife?"* (Mark 10:2). The two leading rabbis of this age, Hillel and Shammai, were rival teachers of Jewish tradition. Both lived during the reign of Herod the Great. Hillel was the liberal and taught that a man could end his marriage for any cause (Matt. 19:3). Shammai, the more conservative rabbi, stated that divorce was only permitted for the sin of adultery. All this to say that regardless how the Lord answered this question, some would not be pleased with the answer.

The Lord asked them, *"What did Moses command you?"* (Mark 10:3). They responded by saying that if a bill of divorce was written, then it was permissible to dismiss one's wife. But the Lord affirmed that such a provision was only permitted because of the hardness of their hearts. When God instituted marriage, divorce was not an option, but because

Luke

of sin, God had to put bounds on divorce to limit its destructive nature. The point being that marriage is a union established by divine charter and is not to be tampered with by human enactments such as divorce.

Matthew's Gospel contains more information as to what the Lord was specifically teaching: Unless a marriage covenant is dissolved for the case of adultery, any husband marrying another woman commits adultery with her and anyone marrying the illegally divorced wife also becomes an adulterer (Matt. 5:32, 19:9).

Because Matthew is written to a Jewish audience and the exception clause is not found in the parallel accounts in Mark and Luke, some view Matthew's statements as relating to the period of purity connected with a Jewish betrothal agreement. This timeframe is bound by the initial marriage betrothal and the physical consummation of the marriage covenant later by the bride and the groom. Mary and Joseph were in this time of purity when the Lord Jesus was conceived in her womb by the power of the Holy Spirit. While this understanding is possible, the Lord does not uphold the Mosaic Law or developed Jewish traditions, but God's design for marriage declared in Eden at the first marriage (Matt. 19:4-8; Mark 10:6-9).

The Lord affirmed God's original order for marriage, which was for one biological man and one biological woman to be bound by a marriage covenant until separated by death. Under the Law, adulterers were to be put to death if found guilty of violating the seventh of God's Ten Commandments. This would permit the innocent party to remarry if desired. In the Church Age, we do not put adulterers to death, but the act breaks the marriage covenant, nonetheless. Civil divorce for any other reason than adultery is not biblical. Those who divorce for other reasons and remarry afterwards are guilty of adultery, for the Lord views them as still married to their previous spouse.

Paul presents a high standard for Christians to follow in this matter: remain with your spouse until death ends your marriage covenant, but if living together is not possible, a husband and wife may separate and live in purity, but divorce should not be sought (1 Cor. 7:10-11). Each situation is different, and there may be safety issues or financial concerns that necessitate a civil divorce, but in God's eyes that does not free the husband and wife from their vow to each other and to God. It is important to realize that civil divorce and biblical divorce have different criterion.

Luke does not provide any of the dialogue between the Lord and the Pharisees on this topic. Rather, Luke merely summarizes the Lord's conclusion: if a divorced person has sexual relations with someone other than their spouse, both parties are guilty of adultery (v. 18). But why did the Lord interrupt His teaching on covetousness, with a short blurb on divorce and remarriage? Having just confirmed that God's moral precepts would never pass away, the Lord was challenging their thinking about the kingdom. The Pharisees could not claim a place in God's kingdom while at the same time disregarding His Law, such as His order for marriage which He established in Eden. Not only were Israel's religious leaders undermining God's standard for marriage by divorcing their wives and marrying other women, but they were also doing the same thing to God in the spiritual sense. Hence, besides coveting what they ought not, they had committed both physical and spiritual adultery.

The Rich Man and Lazarus (vv. 19-31)

The Lord now concludes His teaching on stewardship, which began with the parable of *The Shrewd Manager*, by telling His audience about the lives of two men. This is not a parable or a fictitious story, but the reality of two lives lived, two deaths, and two hereafters. This drama reminds us that God's offer to be one with Him through Christ is rescinded when physical death occurs (Heb. 9:27). The Lord's teaching in Luke 16 confirms that if someone dies apart from trusting Him for salvation, the spiritual essence of that person will await final judgment (in the Lake of Fire) in a spiritual realm of torment called Hades.

First, we are introduced to a certain rich man who lived sumptuously every day (v. 19). Next, we are introduced to a poor beggar named Lazarus, who was full of sores and had to be carried to the gate, his familiar place of begging (v. 20). Lacking food, Lazarus desired to eat the crumbs that fell from the rich man's table (v. 21). His existence was miserable; even the dogs (deemed as unclean animals) licked his sores.

Eventually, Lazarus died and was carried by angels to Abraham's bosom (v. 22). The rich man also died, and his soul was secured in Hades. Having wealth is not what condemned the rich man; rather, it was his lack of faith, for Abraham had been "very rich" (Gen. 13:2) but was in paradise because he had been justified by God for his faith (Gen. 15:6). Being in torment, the rich man begged Abraham to send the poor beggar Lazarus that was in his bosom to his aid (v. 23). Because the rich man only requested one drop of water to cool his tongue, it seems he knew his chances of obtaining any relief was not likely (v. 24).

Luke

Abraham reminded the rich man that he had enjoyed an exuberant lifestyle while alive and had ignored the needs of others, like Lazarus who had endured an insufferable existence (v. 25). The point being that greediness, gluttony, hoarding wealth, and a callous attitude towards those who are suffering when you have the means to help are indications of someone who does not know God. But now, though he was in torment, Lazarus was being comforted. The state of their disembodied spirits was a prelude to their eternal state after the resurrection of the just and wicked occurs (John 5:28-29).

Moreover, Abraham affirmed that there was an impenetrable barrier between their spiritual habitations to ensure that the wicked remain in their agonizing prison and the faithful in the realm of bliss (v. 26). These disembodied souls are completely conscious of their surroundings and are able to communicate, meaning that there is no such thing as *soul sleep* after death, nor does the human soul cease to exist after death.

The rich man, seeing his wretched state, became an instant evangelist – he did not want other family members to die and end up with him in Hades (v. 27). He pleaded with Abraham that Lazarus return to the physical realm to warn his brothers about the terrible place awaiting them after death (v. 28). Abraham explained that true faith is not based on sight, and even if his brothers witnessed someone returning from the dead to warn them, they would not believe in the miracle (vv. 29-31). The statement *"Moses and the prophets"* refers to the whole of Scripture at that time. God's Word was sufficient to show them what God expected of them. This is true today; those who trust God's Word alone for salvation do not need to fret about going to Hades.

The Lord proved the words of Abraham to the rich man to be true, *"If they do not hear Moses and the prophets, neither will they be persuaded though one rise from the dead"* (v. 31). Even though Jesus Christ was raised up from the dead, as witnessed by many, most of the religious rulers in Israel rejected the evidence and called the event a hoax. Truly, *"faith comes by hearing, and hearing by the word of God"* (Rom. 10:17). Failure to heed God's Word always has consequences!

Understanding the Difference Between Hades and Hell

Old Testament saints understood that death was unavoidable and that beyond the grave their souls would be sequestered in a spiritual abode called Sheol. The Hebrew word translated "Sheol," but sometimes rendered "grave" in the Old Testament, is the general equivalent of the

Greek *Hades*, used in the New Testament. The term *Sheol*, which is used sixty-one times in the Old Testament, may speak of the grave or the general realm of disembodied spirits (2 Sam. 22:6; Ps. 116:3), and in this sense is synonymous with *Hades* (1 Cor. 15:55).

In Luke 16, the Lord Jesus taught that this spiritual domain houses disembodied spirits in one of two compartments. Abraham's Bosom is where faithful souls consciously await resurrection unto life through Christ, and the second is a place of torment where the wicked reside until their resurrection unto final judgment in the Lake of Fire. It is the author's opinion that Christ and the repentant thief went to Abraham's bosom after dying and that this realm of disembodied spirits was emptied after Christ's resurrection (Matt. 27:52-53; Acts 2:27, 2:31).

By their evil works (including oppression of God's people; Rev. 20:11-13) and their rejection of salvation in Christ, the ungodly prove their fitness for divine judgment. These rebels will *"be punished with everlasting destruction from the presence of the Lord"* in the Lake of Fire – Hell (v. 9; Matt. 25:41-46; Rev. 20:14-15). Hell is a place where the worm never dies (it is putrid), and where the resurrected wicked wail and gnash their teeth, suffering in total darkness and unquenchable fire (3:17, Mark 9:44-46; Jude 13).

Because the KJV translates *hades* as "Hell," much confusion over proper nomenclature has occurred. The word "Hell" is found twenty-two times in the KJV, as it is derived from three different Greek words. *Gehenna* is used eleven times, *hades* is found twelve times, and *tartaroo* once. The usage of a single English word to speak of two different realities has caused much confusion. Modern Bible translations, such as the NKJV, renders *Gehenna* as "Hell," referring to the Lake of Fire (an abode of eternal judgment), and *Hades* as "Hades" (the temporary holding-cell of disembodied spirits spoken of in this chapter). There is a compartment that is associated with Hades, but distinct from the torment location, where dead believers resided before Christ's resurrection (i.e., Abraham's bosom).

Gehenna was in the valley of Hinnom, just south of Jerusalem where fires burned continually to consume the city's refuse. The Jews understood the application of the word *Gehenna* as referring to eternal divine judgment.

Luke Chapter 17

Although much of the content of this chapter seems topically disconnected, the Lord's initial remarks on the peril of offending others are linked with the story of *Lazarus and the Rich Man* from the previous chapter. William Kelly explains this connection:

> The Jewish system was judged. It was to be left entirely behind. Present favor and earthly prosperity were no tests of God's estimate. That which is unseen will entirely reverse the actual condition of things. Lazarus quits the world for Abraham's bosom; the rich man is afterwards tormented in hell [hades]; but from both the infinite moment of the Word of God is seen for every soul.[38]

Declaring Forgiveness and Real Faith (vv. 1-5)

Contemplating the future evangelical mission that He would be sending His disciples on after His departure from the earth, the Lord said, *"It is impossible that no offenses should come!"* (v. 1). Although believers should not be offensive, the content of the gospel message is offensive to the fallen human nature. There will be those who hinder its preaching and harm those sharing it. The Lord pronounced a woe on those who do such things.

The Lord had already taught His disciples that one must have childlike faith to enter the kingdom and childlike humility to advance the kingdom (Matt. 18:5-6). Anyone receiving (assisting) those who are His will receive a reward as if he or she were serving Christ Himself. Anyone who harms those who have come to Him in childlike faith will, however, be punished. Harm here speaks of robbing a believer's innocence, or seducing him or her to sin, or corrupting a believer's testimony or ministry through false doctrine. Believers can either lead others into a higher experience with God through faith, humility, and obedience or cause them to stumble in their faith through fear, pride, and rebellion.

A millstone was a heavy stone used for grinding grain and was often turned by an animal during milling operations. Having a millstone strapped to one's neck and then being thrown into the sea pictures God's zeal for punishing those who harm His children. William MacDonald surmises, "It seems clear that language as strong as this is intended to picture not only physical death but eternal condemnation as well."[39]

The Lord knew that offenses were inevitable in the work of furthering His kingdom. Having addressed those outrightly opposing His servants, the Lord turned to addressing offenses among His servants: *"If your brother sins against you, rebuke him; and if he repents, forgive him"* (v. 3). Even if this happened seven times in one day, the offended was to declare forgiveness to the offender each time if the offender acknowledged his sin and requested to be forgiven (v. 4).

Even before forgiveness is declared in words, an offended believer is to have an unconditional releasing spirit even while there is an active offense that would otherwise warrant a complaint (Col. 3:13). This does not mean we tell the offender that we forgive him, but rather that we release the matter to the Lord to deal with. That permits us to extinguish our anger over the issue and to think rationally about how to handle the situation. Could it be an opportunity for me to edify the offender by bringing the offense to his attention, or should I just let it go and say nothing? The latter choice is wise if the offense is not a pattern of behavior but an offhand comment or random act. It is foolish to declare forgiveness to someone if they have not confessed their sin; doing so would condone sin. This is why the Lord instructed us only to declare forgiveness to an offender when the offender has repented and has asked to be forgiven (v. 3).

Paul explains why believers should have a releasing spirit when wronged: *"Bearing with one another, and forgiving one another, if anyone has a complaint against another; even as Christ forgave you, so you also must do"* (Col. 3:13). Given all that we have done against the Lord and yet have been forgiven, we should be eager to show God's forgiveness to those who have repented of wrongs against us. After such an issue has been properly resolved, it should not be revisited. God is slow to anger, but quick to forgive and we should be also (Ps. 145:8). Through the Holy Spirit, Christ's love draws those who previously had nothing in common into intimate communion with each other. Therefore, believers are to be forbearing of one another and have a forgiving spirit towards each other. While forbearance is slow to take offense, when we have put on the love of Christ, forgiveness is quick to let it go.

After listening to the Lord's teaching about forgiveness, the disciples asked Him, *"Increase our faith"* (v. 5). The Law taught an "eye for an eye" concept of justice, so the idea of granting forgiveness to an offender without restitution seemed beyond their natural ability. Indeed, without the indwelling Holy Spirit, believers cannot show mercy and compassion, like God would, towards repentant offenders.

The Lord answered their request by stating that even a little faith in God, as likened to the small size of a mustard seed, can uproot a mulberry tree and plant it in the sea (v. 6). The mustard seed would be the smallest seed familiar to the disciples. Uprooting a large tree speaks of overcoming the stubborn pride which causes us to be unbroken before the Lord and to have an unforgiving spirit towards others. True faith that discerns the will of God will lay hold of the power of God to behave like Him. If the disciples simply trusted the Lord's teaching on forgiveness, they would see the Lord work powerfully through their obedience.

The Servants' Reward (vv. 7-10)

The Lord then provided an example of what true humility in a believer who is submitted to God looks like. Returning to the master's home after laboring all day in the field, a servant does not expect his master to cause him to sit down to eat a meal (v. 7). Rather, the servant puts on an apron and serves his master supper without any praise or thanks, or ill-thinking towards his master (v. 8). Only after the master is satisfied will the servant be able to eat and rest from his laboring.

Servants who have labored long in their assigned tasks do not expect special treatment by their master – they have merely done what was expected of them (v. 9). In explaining the meaning of the parable, notice that the Lord does not call His servants unprofitable when they have done all that has been requested of them. Rather, it is the disciples who refer to themselves as "unprofitable servants" even when they have done their best to please their Lord (v. 10).

This is the main point of the parable. Understanding their own unworthiness, true servants of Christ have no reason to be proud or feel self-importance. In recognizing all that Christ suffered on our behalf at Calvary to secure our redemption, we consider ourselves a bad investment. Yet, the Lord demonstrated His love for His Father and for us by suffering and dying in our place as guilty sinners. Clearly then, the Lord does consider us valuable to Him.

The Man and Your God

We realize that our salvation in Christ is an extreme display of divine grace and mercy that can never be repaid by any amount of faithful service (i.e., doing good works). In utter amazement of Christ's selfless sacrifice, true believers will want to serve the Lord out of the spirit of love, rather than being compelled by a sense of duty. Love and appreciation for Christ prompts our joyful service, while merely doing what we are obligated to do often leads to spiritual weariness and regret.

Ten Lepers Cleansed (vv. 11-19)

While journeying to Jerusalem, the Lord passed through Samaria and Galilee and met ten men in one village who were lepers (vv. 11-12). Seeing the Lord, they cried out, *"Jesus, Master, have mercy on us"* (v. 13)! After hearing their request, the Lord told them to go show themselves to the priests (v. 14). They all obeyed and as they went, they were cleansed of their leprosy. One healed leper, a Samaritan, returned to the Lord Jesus to give thanks and to glorify God for what He had done (vv. 15-16).

During Christ's earthly ministry, He healed many lepers so that the priests would have a testimony of Himself (e.g., 5:14). Each time a leper went to locate a priest to undergo the Leviticus 14 cleansing ritual, the priests were forced to acknowledge that something which had never happened before was now occurring regularly. One can only imagine the shock of the priests when the first lepers healed by Christ came knocking on their door. And then, on one day, nine came all at once to be inspected by the priests – they had all been healed by Christ.

Although the Lord physically cleansed ten lepers that day, only one thankful Samaritan received spiritual healing (vv. 17-18). The other nine were satisfied with their physically clean status and saw no need for further cleansing by the One who had healed them of leprosy. But the Lord told the thankful Samaritan to, *"Arise, go your way. Your faith has made you well"* (v. 19). Ten lepers were healed, but only one was saved.

A steady stream of ex-lepers with amazing stories of healing over a three-year period was the Lord's means of reaching the priests. Consequently, Luke records the fact that a large number of priests turned from trying to earn their salvation through religious doings to trusting Jesus Christ alone for salvation (Acts 6:7). The priests thoroughly knew the Law; they had copied it and taught it to their brethren. The miraculous healing of so many lepers by one man awakened them to the fact that the

Healer was the One the Law was calling their attention to – their Messiah had arrived and was fulfilling Scripture before their eyes.

The Faithless Do Not Observe the Kingdom (vv. 20-21)

Matthew wrote of the "kingdom of heaven" thirty-three times in his Gospel, while only referring to the "kingdom of God" five times. Luke is nearly opposite this representation with thirty-three occurrences of the "kingdom of God" and no mention of the "kingdom of heaven." Certainly, the hierarchical presentation of Christ as king, versus a man, cascades into the decision of submission. The "kingdom of heaven" presents a choice, whereas the "kingdom of God" more closely acknowledges man's dependence upon a sovereign God. The Lord told the Jews that the "kingdom of God" was in their midst, but they did not recognize it; therefore, it would not come visibly but would continue in its invisible, spiritual form until Christ's second advent (vv. 20-21).

Christ's Second Coming (vv. 22-37)

Next, the Lord told His disciples that after His departure, they would long for even one of the days they were enjoying together now (v. 22). While the kingdom is in its spiritual phase on the earth (i.e., the Church Age), there will be much anticipation and much deception about when Christ's second coming will occur. The Lord warned His disciples not to be fooled by such talk (v. 23).

The Lord's second advent to the earth will be like lightning which suddenly appears in one place but illuminates the whole sky (v. 24). Likewise, He will suddenly appear on the earth and will be visible to everyone. But before He could ever return to establish His earthly kingdom, He first must complete the propitiatory work that had been assigned to Him at Calvary (v. 25).

When the Lord does return to the earth, the world will be surprised by His coming to judge the wicked. At that time, the behavior of man will be like that of Noah's day (vv. 26-27) and of Lot's Day (vv. 28-29) when sexual perversion and unceasing wickedness characterized man's behavior prior to divine judgment. Man will be living for all the pleasure life can offer and have no remorse for the Creator's grieving heart.

Noah's contemporaries lived as if they had flood insurance, but the only insurance was the ark. Likewise, today, in our post-Christian society, man lives for the day, not realizing that judgment is coming, and that the good news of Jesus Christ is the only means of escape. Much of the world will be suffering from stubborn spiritual blindness when Christ returns to judge them (v. 30). When Christ appears, there will be no time to repent and receive God's peace; Christ's judgment of the nations will immediately occur. Those who followed the Antichrist, the goats, will be put to death, but those who lived through the Tribulation Period and worshiped God, the sheep, will be permitted to enter Christ's kingdom (Matt. 25:31-46).

It was at this juncture that the Lord warned, *"Remember Lot's wife. Whoever seeks to save his life will lose it, and whoever loses his life will preserve it"* (vv. 32-33). Abraham's nephew, Lot, and his family lived in the wicked city of Sodom, which pictures worldliness of a sensual nature in Scripture. He and his family had become so infatuated with worldliness that the two angels God sent to rescue them literally had to lay hold of them to pry them from the city, so God could destroy it (Gen. 19:16).

Even after Lot understood that righteous souls must be separated from ungodly living, he still longed to have a bit of the world in his life. The angel told him to separate and to flee to the mountains for safety, but Lot begged him to allow him to dwell in a "little" city (Zoar) that he not die. This was clearly the issue: Lot was not willing to die to self and live for God. It is a testimony of God's grace that the selfish request of carnal Lot saved the city of Zoar from God's wrath! Lot, a ruined man, eventually found out that the world offered nothing substantial. He was estranged from God, and in the end, he was deserted by the world also. The world had exacted its price and proven its hatred for all that have been declared righteous; thus, Lot is driven by his own fears into further isolation.

The angels had commanded that they not look back towards Sodom – they were to make a "clean break" from the world. But, the heart of Lot's wife was still in Sodom, and as God rained down fire and brimstone upon the city, she either stole a glance at her old life or was lagging far enough behind that she instantly experienced the judgment of God. She either instantaneously became a pillar of salt or perhaps was buried by tons of salt when the catastrophic upheaval destroyed the cities of the plain. The Hebrew word translated "looked back" is *nabat* which means "to look intently" or "to regard with pleasure." Christian discipleship requires forsaking the pleasures of the world and following Christ unhindered.

Lot's wife was used as an example by the Lord to warn those listening not to think lightly about His offer of salvation. During His entire ministry, the Lord told His listeners to remember only two people – Himself and

Lot's wife. The choice He gave to His listeners was Himself or the world; the consequences of this choice would be life or death, blessing or judgment. We are given the same choice!

At His second advent, the wicked will be suddenly removed in judgment from the earth, while the faithful will be welcomed into His kingdom (vv. 34-36). Two men will be sleeping in a bed or working in a field together and one of them will suddenly disappear. Likewise, two women will be grinding grain and one will be taken away while the other will enter the kingdom. As part of judging the nations, all those who took the mark of the Antichrist will perish in judgment and not be permitted to enter Christ's kingdom (Rev. 13:11-18, 19:21). This analogy does not refer to the rapture of the Church to Heaven but is a judgment of the wicked occurring at Christ's second advent. On this point, Louis A. Barbieri, Jr. writes:

> Clearly the church, the body of Christ, cannot be in view in these statements. The Lord was not describing the Rapture, for the removal of the Church will not be a judgment on the Church. If this were the Rapture, as some commentators affirm, the Rapture would have to be posttribulational, for this event occurs immediately before the Lord's return in glory. But that would conflict with a number of Scriptures and present other problems that cannot be elaborated on here (e.g., 1 Thess. 4:13-18 and Rev. 3:10). The Lord's warning emphasized the need to be prepared, for judgment will come at a time when people least expect it.[40]

Regrettably, many commentators insert the Church into this Jewish-focused text because of the sudden taking of people from the earth. In the Rapture of the Church, that occurs before the Tribulation Period commences, redeemed saints are removed from the earth to be with the Lord in heaven, but in the event that Christ is describing here, it is the wicked that are removed from the earth in judgment. In this former situation, being left behind is a bad thing, but in the latter, to "be left behind" is a good thing as these believers will enter Christ's kingdom.

After hearing about people being suddenly removed from the earth, the Lord's audience asked Him about where they went. He provided a cryptic reply to their question: *"Where the body is, there the eagles will be gathered together"* (v. 37). The idea being that when vultures are flying overhead, it meant that there was impending doom. The point being that judgment could suddenly fall wherever unbelief was found.

Luke Chapter 18

The Unjust Judge (vv. 1-8)

Christ told this parable to emphasize His statement, *"Men always ought to pray and not lose heart"* (v. 1). The parable was apparently told just after Christ raised Lazarus from the dead, but just prior to his final journey to Jerusalem. Though this parable was told during the Lord's Perean ministry, the location at which it was uttered may have been in Samaria (17:11). F. B. Hole explains the contextual tie between this chapter and the last:

> In speaking the parable, with which this chapter opens, the Lord was continuing the same line of thought, as is shown by His application of the parable in verses 7 and 8. When the kingdom arrives, it will mean judgment for the evildoers, but the days just before its arrival will mean tribulation for saints. Their resource will be prayer.[41]

The unrighteous judge in the story did not fear God (v. 2). An oppressed widow petitioned the judge to obtain justice for her, but he was not motivated to pursue the case or rule against the widow's adversary (vv. 3-4). Moreover, the magistrate displayed no compassion for her plight. So why did the unjust, atheistic, cold-hearted judge finally rule in the widow's favor? The answer is, because of her persistent pleading (v. 5). She would not be swayed to drop her just cause because of the judge's inactivity.

The point of the parable is this: If the unrighteous, unsympathetic judge will rule on the behalf of the widow, how much more willing will God the Father, who is righteous and caring, be to act in favor of His suffering children (vv. 6-7)? God is never inactive on righteous matters!

Given the context of the preceding passage and verse 8, the specific group being spoken of, "the elect," is likely the Tribulation saints or even more specific, the faithful remnant of Jews suffering during the Tribulation Period. Regardless, God desires to abundantly care for all His people in any age by answering their prayers (e.g., Rev. 6:9-11).

Luke

The idea is that we do not force God to give us what we want because we petition Him often. Rather, we plead with Him often in prayer because we realize that He is our only hope in any hardship. The widow had no one else to turn to for help and neither do we. We trust our Heavenly Father to sustain us through sorrowful times and that He will bring good out of our suffering for His honor and glory (1 Cor. 10:13).

The Pharisee and the Tax Collector (vv. 9-14)

The Lord was speaking directly to the Pharisees when He uttered this parable. It was spoken just after the *Unjust Judge* parable, and the tie between the two stories is evident, as Norman Crawford explains:

> There is a link between this parable and the preceding one about the unjust judge. The lesson of that parable was to trust in God; this parable was spoken to those who trusted in themselves. They believed in their own self-righteousness, and the corollary was contempt of others. These two characteristics were so obvious in the Pharisees.[42]

The Lord included a Pharisee in His story to confront the proud, self-justifying attitude that characterized many religious leaders at that time (v. 9). They arrogantly elevated their own spiritual eminence before God by comparing their devout status and pious deeds to those from the general populace (vv. 11-12). In their minds, they were closer to God because they were spiritually superior to those beneath them, and thus, far more deserving of God's favor. However, the tax collector knew his proper place before a holy God and "stood afar off" (v. 13). But the Pharisees were wrong; God is not impressed with a pompous, religious facade, but rather assists those, like the tax collector, who exhibit genuine brokenness, humility, submission, and repentance (v. 14).

Indeed, the Pharisee in the story prayed and did good deeds, but not to or for God. He prayed to be heard, to be appreciated, and to be honored by others. Previously the Lord warned His audience, *"Therefore, when you do a charitable deed, do not sound a trumpet before you as the hypocrites do in the synagogues and in the streets, that they may have glory from men. Assuredly, I say to you, they have their reward"* (Matt. 6:2). The frequent occurrence of the pronoun "I" in the Pharisee's prayer is indicative of someone suffering from self-sufficiency and pride.

The Pharisee engaged in two prayer activities that should never mark the believers' petitions to a holy God: First, we should not boast to God about what we have done for Him. He knows what we have done, the value of it, and what motivated us to do it. When considering the tremendous cost of our salvation at Calvary, all that we do for God is nothing more than our duty to Him as His redeemed people (17:10).

Second, we should not boast to God about our spiritual fortitude. This is especially offensive to God when we seek to establish our own spiritual supremacy by comparing ourselves to others. As Paul confirms, anyone with such an attitude will receive God's condemnation (Rom. 2:1-4). God is an omniscient and just Judge. He holds humanity accountable to His standard of righteousness (i.e., His perfection). Naturally speaking, we all fall short of moral perfection (Rom. 3:23). It is only through being justified in Christ that anyone can be accepted by a holy God into heaven (Rom. 4:2-4). In Christ, we have a positional perfection that can never be lost. Consequently, no one has anything to brag about before God. Paul knew his flesh was biased, so he was hesitant to even judge the value of his own ministry (1 Cor. 4:3-4).

The tax collector exhibits the type of prayer that God appreciates: a spirit of honesty, self-defamation, and humility culminating in genuine repentance. The tax collector did not exalt himself before God, but rather pleaded for mercy, which he received. Ironically, the self-justified Pharisee had the honor of men and the condemnation of God, but the self-defacing tax collector, though disdained by men, was justified by God.

Little Children Are Blessed (vv. 15-17)

Little children (infants) were being brought to the Lord that He might touch them and pray over them (v. 15). The disciples saw this activity as a waste of time and tried to stop it. However, the Lord never turned away genuine seekers, no matter how much they irritated His disciples. The Lord responded to their angst by providing an object lesson as to how one may enter into His kingdom, that is, by exercising childlike faith in Him: *"Let the little children come to Me, and do not forbid them; for of such is the kingdom of God"* (v. 16). Children do not need to become adults to be saved, but adults must become childlike in faith to become God's children (v. 17).

Accordingly, the Lord continued to lay His hands on the children and bless them. The Lord is not granting these little children access to heaven by touching them and praying for them. Those old enough to understand that they have an inherent sin problem and need for a Savior could then exercise faith in Christ and be saved by Him (John 3:18). Those too young to understand this were blessed by Christ's presence and may have received His healing and gained further protection from evil, which would permit them a later opportunity to believe the truth and be saved.

The Rich Young Ruler (vv. 18-27)

Matthew and Mark also record the dialogue of a rich young man who wanted to be justified before God and thereby be assured of heaven. Their conversation began when the young man asked the Lord Jesus, *"Good Teacher, what shall I do to inherit eternal life?"* (v. 18). Many think that they are good by their own standards of evaluation, but since only God is *good*, the Lord Jesus challenged the young man to think of goodness according to *divine standards* (v. 19).

The Lord then used God's Commandments to bypass the intellect to speak to the inquirer's conscience (v. 20). He referred to the last six of the Ten Commandments (which are manward in application). However, He placed the fifth commandment concerning honoring one's parents behind the ninth, and then represented the tenth concerning not coveting by its application of loving one's neighbor as yourself. If you truly love your neighbor, you will selflessly give to your neighbor, not lust for what he has for yourself.

Why did the Lord order the commandments in this way? The purpose of the Law is to show us our sin and that we might understand that only God is good (Rom. 3:9-12). The Lord knew all about the sin of this young man, so He placed the most applicable commands last to convict him of what the Lord knew that he had failed to do.

Sadly, the Law did not achieve its intended purpose in the rich young ruler's heart. Instead of feeling guilt and impending judgment, he pompously declared that he had kept all of the Law, which he ironically broke by that false assertion (v. 21). Our gracious Lord did not rebuke the young man for his audacious statement, but instead set about to show him who his god really was. After being told that he needed to sell his possessions, give the proceeds to the poor, and follow Him, the young man departed in sorrow, for he was wealthy (vv. 22-23). Money was his god; he valued it more than treasure in heaven and following the Lord.

For those of us who have reckoned ourselves as needy sinners and have received the Savior, we can exclaim with David: *"O taste and see that the Lord is good: blessed is the man that trusts in Him"* (Ps. 34:8). Truly, God is good and does good (Ps. 119:68).

After the rich young ruler departed, the Lord informed His disciples, *"How hard it is for those who have riches to enter the kingdom of God"* (v. 24). He then supplied a hyperbolic illustration to accentuate His point: *"For it is easier for a camel to go through the eye of a needle than for a rich man to enter the kingdom of God"* (v. 24). Some have suggested that this analogy references the act of camels walking on their knees to get under a low archway. However, the Lord's point is not one of difficulty, but impossibility. The Greek word *rhaphidos* rendered "needle" speaks of a sewing or surgical needle. The idea of a large camel fitting through the eye of a surgical needle was impossible. Likewise, anyone trusting in their riches for security or esteeming what they have as more important than pleasing God by doing His will cannot gain heaven. Eternal life and entrance into God's kingdom cannot be earned; these are gifts from Him in response to sincere faith founded in His Word.

The disciples were astonished at the Lord's statement concerning those who value their riches above the One who gave them (Matt. 19:25). They asked, *"Who then can be saved?"* (v. 26). The Lord responded, *"The things which are impossible with men are possible with God"* (v. 27). The Lord again emphasizes that in matters of salvation it is not merely difficult for men to earn heaven by their doings; it is impossible. The work of salvation which God brings about through humble, childlike faith in the Savior is how God ushers redeemed sinners into heaven.

Sacrifice Will Be Rewarded (vv. 28-30)

The rich young ruler had departed the Lord's presence sorrowfully because he was not willing to part with his wealth to follow Christ. This was the opposite response of the disciples, who had identified with Christ and had forsaken all to follow Him. Peter felt that he and the other disciples were doing much better than the rich young ruler, so he asked the Lord, *"See, we have left all and followed you. Therefore, what shall we have?"* (v. 28; Matt. 19:27). Later, Peter would learn that what *we get* for following Christ was not as important as *having* the crucified life so that He can live within us and work through us (Gal. 2:20).

The Lord could have responded to Peter's not so humble inquiry with a mild rebuke, "How do you know you will have anything in the kingdom?" But He did not. Rather, the Lord affirmed that they, and all

Luke

who had suffered the loss of home and family for the sake of the kingdom of God, would be highly honored and rewarded in the age to come (v. 29). Additionally, they would possess eternal life and even now could expect a hundredfold increase for every relationship severed by the gospel (Matt. 19:29).

It is the same for believers today. For every person who persecutes a believer, there will be a hundred more believers to extend him or her a helping hand. Christian love is a powerful weapon against the enemy, for it conveys the reality of the gospel message to the lost. May we all give thanks to the Lord for all the gracious benefits of a loving community of saints during our earthly sojourn. Indeed, rewards will be received at the *Judgment Seat of Christ*, but we can assist each other to be faithful to Christ until that day. Hence, believers should consider that any personal sacrifices for Christ now are merely privileged investments for eternity.

Christ Foretells of His Death Again (vv. 31-34)

The Lord Jesus had concluded His Perean ministry and was beginning His westerly journey to Jerusalem through Jericho (v. 31). Matthew informs us that after concluding the parable of *The Workers in the Vineyard*, He paused with His disciples to speak of His forthcoming suffering in Jerusalem. According to Matthew's account, this is the fourth time that Christ had foretold His upcoming death and resurrection.

He knew that He would be betrayed into the hands of Israel's religious leaders, who would condemn Him to death. Because the Jews did not have the authority to judicially execute the condemned, the Lord knew that He would be given over to the Gentiles (the Romans), who would spit on, mock, scourge, and crucify Him (v. 32). But on the third day, He would rise again from the grave (v. 33). Matthew does not record the Lord's words concerning being spit on, but Mark and Luke do. Luke refers to the offense at the conclusion of what Christ would suffer at Calvary, to highlight the disgust and shame that He would be enduring as God's Lamb of sacrifice. Instead of kissing the Son, to declare their love and loyalty to God's Son, the Jews spat on Him to show their utter disgust of Him (Ps. 2:12). Consequently, God is still chastening His covenant people unto this day for their gross disdain of His Son.

Although the Lord clearly informed His disciples what would happen to Him in Jerusalem, they were not able to comprehend the meaning of His words. Although the prophets and the Lord Jesus, Himself, had expressed God's plan of propitiation for human sin, none of them, nor Satan, would have fully understood what God was accomplishing in Christ, for this was an unrevealed truth before Calvary (1 Cor. 2:8-9).

Blind Bartimeus Receives Sight (vv. 35-43)

A great multitude of people followed the Lord and His disciples out of Jericho as they journeyed towards Jerusalem (Matt. 20:29). Although both Mark and Luke record a blind man being healed near Jericho, neither mentioned that two blind men were actually healed, but Matthew does to uphold his Jewish vantage point of two witnesses. Mark states that a blind man was healed when the Lord departed Jericho, but Luke indicates that the miracle happened just before the Lord entered the city. It is possible that there were two separate miracles, but it seems more likely that Matthew and Mark are speaking of the old city Jericho and Luke the new Jericho; both were on the Lord's route. If this is one incident, then one of the two blind men healed would be Bartimaeus as identified by Mark. His name was mentioned because of his personal dialogue with the Lord.

Two blind men were sitting on the road near Jericho and engaged in begging when they heard the commotion (v. 35). Although Luke does not provide his name, Bartimaeus is the blind man interacting with the Lord in this story. After learning that Jesus of Nazareth was nearing his position, he cried out as loudly as he could even after being warned by the crowd to be quiet, *"Jesus, Son of David, have mercy on me"* (vv. 36-39). The Lord Jesus heard his cries for help and paused to speak to him. He commanded that the blind man be brought to Him.

Mark informs us that after hearing the Lord's command, Bartimaeus threw aside the cloak identifying him as a blind man and immediately stood up and was led to the Lord (Mark 10:50). After he arrived, the Lord asked him, *"What do you want Me to do for you?"* (vv. 40-41). The blind man responded that he might gain his sight. The Lord had compassion on him and said, *"Receive your sight; your faith has made you well"* (v. 42). Matthew records the Lord touched his eyes, and immediately he gained his sight and followed Jesus, glorifying God (v. 43). The people who witnessed the miracle also gave praise to God.

What a blind person needs is not a teacher but another self.

– Helen Keller

Luke Chapter 19

Zacchaeus Is Converted (vv. 1-10)

To preface the account of Zacchaeus's conversion, let us remember the words of the Lord Jesus after the wealthy young ruler departed from Him unconverted, *"The things which are impossible with men are possible with God"* (18:27). Zacchaeus was a rich man, but after hearing the Lord's message, he was willing to part with his wealth to have a relationship with his God. Indeed, God can save all those who will humble themselves before Him, whether wealthy or poor.

A multitude of people was with the Lord as He passed through Jericho while en route to Jerusalem with His disciples (v. 1). A chief tax collector and wealthy man named Zacchaeus wanted to see Jesus, but because he was vertically challenged, he knew that would not be possible (v. 2). Therefore, he ran ahead, climbed up in a sycamore tree, so that he could get a view of Jesus when He passed by (vv. 3-4).

When the Lord arrived at his location, He paused and looked up at Zacchaeus perched in the tree and said, *"Zacchaeus, make haste and come down, for today I must stay at your house"* (v. 5). The man of short stature eagerly and joyfully responded to the Lord's statement, which caused others in the crowd to bemoan the idea that Jesus would want to spend time in the home of a tax collector, a sinner (vv. 6-7). Those in this profession typically took more from the people than Rome required to line their own pockets with money.

After spending some time with the Lord and hearing His teaching, Zacchaeus stood up and publicly said that he would give half of his wealth to the poor and that he would restore fourfold to those whom he had previously taken advantage of (v. 8). After hearing His host's declaration, Jesus said, *"Today, salvation has come to this house, because he also is a son of Abraham; for the Son of Man has come to seek and to save that which was lost"* (vv. 9-10). Faith without works is dead by itself (Jas. 2:17) and Zacchaeus's radical deed of parting with his wealth proved that He believed that Jesus Christ was the Messiah. For this reason, the Lord refers to him as a "son of Abraham."

Both the unregenerate and believers are described as children (sons) in Scripture. Believers in Christ are sons of God waiting to receive their full inheritance. The unregenerate are called the "sons of disobedience" (Eph. 2:2), the "children of the devil" (1 Jn. 3:10) and the "children of wrath" (Col. 3:6). In contrast, believers are called "children (sons) of God" (Rom. 8:16), "children of light" (Eph. 5:8), "children of obedience" (1 Pet. 1:14), and "children of Abraham" (Gal. 3:7). The former list of names describes those who follow the devil in rebellion against God, while the latter list speaks of those who honor God by exercising faith in the truth and thus abide in Christ. Zacchaeus had followed Abraham's example of simply trusting in God's word without any signs to verify it; thus, he was "a son of Abraham."

The Ten Minas (Pounds) (vv. 11-27)

The Lord had spoken *The Workers in the Vineyard* parable just prior to meeting with Zacchaeus on the outskirts of Jericho. This parable was spoken a short time afterwards as He and His disciples were nearing Jerusalem (v. 11).

In the parable of *The Ten Minas*, the master gave each of his ten servants one mina (worth about 100 denarii) to invest while he was on a long journey. The disciples believed that Christ's earthly kingdom would be soon, but this parable was to teach them that there would be a long interim between His first and second advents (v. 12). During this time, believers in the Church Age would have the opportunity to invest into Christ's kingdom. When He does return, each servant will give an account of their stewardship to Him. This will occur at the *Judgment Seat of Christ* directly after the rapture of the Church, but before the Tribulation Period and Christ's second coming to the earth.

In the story, all ten servants were given one mina (a pound) to invest during the interim that the master was away (v. 13). Yet, the servants had varying success depending on their degree of faithfulness. In the Church Age, all believers receive differing spiritual gifts and abilities, and prospects to serve, but this parable deals with those things we are all given equal *availability* to. For example, all believers are given the gospel message to share, the same amount of time each day to work, mutual access to God through prayer, and the same access to God's Word. However, not all believers will use what God has made available to them for serving Him in the same way. As an example, many

Christians have homes, but few use what God has given them to show hospitality to others, though we are expected to do so (1 Pet. 4:9-10).

One servant earned ten pounds and was rewarded with ten cities to rule, while a second servant made five pounds and was given five cities (vv. 15-19). The slothful servant, who did not appreciate the true character of his master, lost the mina given him and received no reward (vv. 20-24). A person may be a Christian but still choose to waste his or her life – living a life without any concern for what God wants. Such unfaithful believers will lose what they were given, which will be given to the faithful person with proven devotion. This is how a Christian may lose the crown they could have received at the *Judgment Seat of Christ* (Rev. 3:11). Let us be found faithful to what the Lord has graciously entrusted us with. If we are unsure how to invest what the Lord has given us, may we entrust it to those who do, so both we and those investing can be rewarded for the profitable outcome.

As this parable relates to the Church Age, the dispensation of grace between Christ's two earthly advents, it is suggested that the individuals who did not want Christ to rule over them represent the religious Jews at that time (v. 14). In 70 A.D. the obsolete religious system under the Law was abruptly put away by the destruction of much of Jerusalem and the temple by the Romans (v. 27). Judaism today continues to be an affront to God's message of salvation in Jesus Christ; thus, the Jewish people will continue to suffer in spiritual blindness until a national remnant is refined and revived during the Tribulation Period.

The Lord has given each believer different abilities and opportunities to serve, but we have all been given equal availability to a variety of things: twenty-four hours each day to use, the Word of God to study, the gospel message to share, access to the throne of grace to pray, and food, clothing, and homes to share. Some will take greater advantage of the Throne of Grace than others will, and some will use their time more frugally than others and thus receive a greater reward. How available are you to serve?

The King's Triumphant Entry Into Jerusalem (vv. 28-44)

The Lord and His disciples traveled towards Jerusalem (v. 28). John informs us that after departing Perea, the Lord had briefly gone to Jerusalem and then to the wilderness near the city of Ephraim to escape

The Man and Your God

hostility (John 11:54). Now the Lord is returning to Jerusalem for the final time of His earthly ministry, just a few days before His passion.

As the Lord and His disciples drew near the village of Bethphage on the eastern side of Mount Olivet, the Lord sent two of His disciples on a mission (v. 29). The Lord again shows the importance of the two-by-two principle in ministry for the benefit of encouragement and accountability (10:1; Mark 6:7). The two disciples were to go into the nearby village where they would immediately find a tied-up donkey with her unbroken colt (v. 30). The disciples were to loosen the donkey and bring both animals to Him (Matt. 21:3). If anyone confronted them for taking the animals, they were to reply, *"The Lord has need of them"* (v. 31; Matt. 21:3). After hearing this, there would not be an objection. Everything occurred just as the Lord said (v. 32). Although Matthew does not record the protest of the owner, Luke does, but the owner immediately released the animals into the care of the disciples after hearing that the Lord had need of them (vv. 33-34). As noted by the "them" in Matthew 21:3 and 7, both the donkey and her colt were brought to the Lord. The other Gospels do not mention that detail.

Both Bethphage, meaning "a place of young figs," and Bethany, meaning "house of figs," were villages on the eastern slope of Olivet. The Lord and His disciples often resided with beloved friends in Bethany (John 11:18, 12:1). Luke mentions both villages (v. 29), but we are not informed which village supplied what the Savior was looking for, the colt of a donkey. These villages stand in stark contrast to the barren fig tree that the Lord cursed en route to Jerusalem to illustrate His sorrow over Israel's barren spiritual state (Matt. 21:19).

On the Sunday prior to His crucifixion (John 12:1,12), the Lord Jesus descended the Mount of Olives and entered Jerusalem on the colt of a donkey (v. 35). The people cut down palm branches and put articles of their clothing on the road before Him (v. 36; John 12:13). Christendom often refers to this event as *Palm Sunday*, but this scene has little to do with the palm branches being placed on the road ahead of the Lord. This was the triumphant entry of Christ into His kingdom's capital.

This scene fulfilled Zechariah's prophecy four centuries earlier (Zech. 9:9). Zechariah says for Israel to "rejoice greatly." Matthew informs us that most of this crowd did not know who Jesus was, but some did believe that He was a prophet from Nazareth (Matt. 21:10-12). Regardless, the entire crowd was caught up in the frenzy of the moment as a host of Christ's disciples was rejoicing and praising God (v. 37).

Luke

Kings usually mounted horses in time of war (Rev. 19:11) but rode donkeys in time of peace. At this juncture, the Lord Jesus was offering genuine peace to the nation of Israel, but they must receive it on His terms through repentance and submission to His Father's will.

Palm branches were tokens of victory and of peace (Rev. 7:9) and a display of righteousness (Ps. 92:12). According to Matthew, the multitude, referring to Psalm 118:25-26, shouted, *"Hosanna to the Son of David!"* (Matt. 21:9). Luke records that they also said, *"'Blessed is the King who comes in the name of the Lord!' Peace in heaven and glory in the highest"* (v. 38). For a fleeting moment, the Lord was rightfully declared to be the long-awaited Jewish Messiah.

Psalm 118:25 reads, *"Save now, I pray, O Lord; O Lord, I pray send now prosperity."* The Greek form of the Hebrew *yasha na* (meaning "save now") is "Hosanna." In John's account of this event, he notes that the people called the Lord Jesus, "the King of Israel." This is also how Zechariah identified the one riding a foal of a donkey. Mark states that the people said, *"Blessed is the kingdom of our father David that comes in the name of the Lord"* (Mark 11:10). All this highlights the intense desire of the Jewish people to be freed from Gentile oppression. They clearly wanted to be immediately liberated from Rome, but not to be saved from their sins. Many shouting "Hosanna" were merely curious seekers who got caught up in the fanfare of the moment without truly believing in Christ (John 12:18).

Matthew states that the entire city was moved with wonder and curiosity concerning the One who rode on the colt of the donkey. *"Who is this?"* (Matt. 21:10). Could this be the One prophesied by Zechariah four centuries earlier? Yet, even after three years of preaching the Kingdom Gospel message throughout Israel, there was still much confusion concerning who Jesus really was.

The Pharisees were greatly agitated by the immense crowd that was shouting "Hosanna" to the One they believed was threatening Judaism (John 12:19). Luke tells us that the Pharisees demanded that Jesus should rebuke His disciples for making such a declaration (v. 39). But the Lord said to them, *"I tell you that if these should keep silent, the stones would immediately cry out"* (v. 40). John later notes that he and the other disciples did not understand the significance of Christ's entry into Jerusalem until after His resurrection (John 12:16). For three years Jesus' identity as Israel's Messiah had been kept secret, but now, five days before His crucifixion, His grandeur was to be emphatically publicized.

What had been considered dangerous to state earlier was now necessary to boldly publish. Ironically, however, only the Lord Jesus fully understood the significance of the incident.

The Lord Laments Over Jerusalem (vv. 41-44)

Luke states that as Christ entered Jerusalem, He was moved to lament over her rejection of Himself (v. 41). The Lord may have been moved to tears a second time that same week, for Matthew records the Lord's anguish two days later while looking over the city just before ascending Mount Olivet on Tuesday with His disciples (Matt. 23:37).

The Lord's anguish and tears over His rebellious people were foretold long ago when Joseph wept over his deceitful brothers in Egypt (Gen. 45). The tears of Joseph were both a testimony of the sorrow of his rejection and the forgiving love he desired to show in restoration. Likewise, the Lord Jesus was heartbroken over Jewish rejection and wept over His countrymen in sorrow, knowing the consequence of their rejection – spiritual blindness and the destruction of Jerusalem (vv. 42-44). Hence, He says, *"Your house is left to you desolate"* (Matt. 23:38). Luke tells us that this is a reference to the temple, which would soon be destroyed and not one stone would be left sitting on another (v. 44). The temple had not been God's house for a long time in the same way that the feasts of Jehovah had become the "feasts of the Jews" (John 5:1). The Lord was telling His audience that God was not with His covenant people and His Messenger was leaving them.

Speaking of the Lord Jesus, John says, *"He came to His own, and His own did not receive Him"* (John 1:11). This is what the Lord meant by the statement that Israel *"did not know the time of your visitation"* (v. 44). Their Messiah had visited them, but they had not received Him. As a result, the nation of Israel would experience war and desolation until a future day, when they would recognize Jesus as their Messiah at His second advent to the earth (Dan. 9:26). Then when the people see Christ, they will shout, *"Blessed is He who comes in the name of the Lord"* (Matt. 23:39) and mean it!

Thankfully, there is a coming day when Israel will be restored to God. There will be great weeping on that day also, but these will be the tears of restoration and joy (Hos. 2:19-23; Zech. 12:10). In a coming day, once we are in His blissful presence, God will wipe away all of our tears and erase our sorrows (Rev. 7:17, 21:4).

Christ Cleanses the Temple Again (vv. 45-48)

Mark records that the Lord and His disciples departed from Jerusalem to Bethany after Christ's triumphant entry into Jerusalem and then they returned to Jerusalem the next day, on Monday (Mark 11:11-12). Mark refers to Christ cleansing the temple on Monday (Mark 11:15), while Matthew and Luke indicate that it was on Sunday. Perhaps, the Gospel writers are referring to a single event, but it is plausible that when the Lord returned to the temple on Monday, the merchants and moneychangers had not learned the lesson from the previous day and the Lord had to cleanse the temple again.

Although the Lord Jesus is rarely spoken of in Scripture as being angry, it is evident that His righteous anger, His holy zeal for God, flared up on some occasions. After arriving at the temple, He made a scourge to drive the animals and their masters from the temple and He threw over the tables of the moneychangers (v. 45; Matt. 21:12). Besides the inappropriate business activities that were occurring in the temple, the money changers were engaging in fraudulent practices that robbed the people and made God's house into a den of thieves. Norman Crawford explains the business dynamic:

> Only Tyrian coins were acceptable as a temple offering, for they had a high level of silver purity, better than the standard Roman coinage. When offerers came to the temple, the moneychangers, for a surcharge, sold Tyrian coins for other kinds. The practice gave room for dishonesty and at the Passover time the trade was unusually brisk, so the Lord upset the business of the moneychangers at the busiest time of the year (I. B. D. Tyndale).[43]

These racketeers had turned the temple, God's house, into a place of commerce and thievery, but the Lord restored it to a house of prayer (v. 46). The moneychangers were corrupting the intended purpose of God's house. The very atmosphere of the temple was to be one of prayer and worship. The sweet aroma that refreshes the heart of God is that of open hearts that are genuinely engaged in worship and prayer.

The Lord Jesus cleansed the temple twice, once at the beginning of His earthly ministry (John 2:14-17), and then again a few days before His death. Throughout the ages, whether a physical or a spiritual temple, the Lord demands that holiness and spiritual sincerity characterize His dwelling place.

The Man and Your God

Previously, while confronting the Pharisees, the Lord healed a man on the Sabbath day to challenge their shallow spirituality (Mark 3:5). With utter contempt, He later warned them of impending judgment (Matt. 23:13-36). At other times, the Lord's anger did not result in direct action; instead, He relinquished the offense into His Father's care (3:34). The Lord shows us that there are times to defer from righteous anger to accomplish a greater good: *"The discretion of a man makes him slow to anger, and his glory is to overlook a transgression"* (Prov. 19:11).

After cleansing the temple, the Lord resumed His ministry there (v. 47). The blind and the lame were healed by Him (Matt. 21:14). However, when the chief priests and scribes saw the wonderful things that He was doing and how the people intently listened to Him, they became indignant towards Him. It would be difficult to imagine a more spiritually repulsive situation than what we have here – religious leaders moved to envy against the Lord Jesus because those in their care are "attentive to hear" His words. Israel's religious leaders sought how they might destroy Him but were afraid to take any action against Him because they feared how the common people might respond if they did (v. 48).

The religious pride of Israel's leaders had now brought them to the point of justifying the murder of an innocent man. When the fear of God rules the human heart, integrity and charitable deeds will follow, but when governed by the fear of man, any act of cowardice, immorality, or pompous piety is possible. Fearing what God controls stems from an erroneous view of God apart from faith. In short, we will not revere, nor trust a God that we do not accurately know through His revealed truth.

> If I am afraid to speak the truth lest I lose affection, or lest the one concerned should say, "You do not understand," or because I fear to lose my reputation for kindness; if I put my own good name before the other's highest good, then I know nothing of Calvary love.
>
> – Amy Carmichael

The Lord was destined to suffer for human sin at a particular time in God's sovereign calendar and no one, no religious agency, nor circumstances could change that. The envy and fears of Israel's religious leaders concerning Jesus Christ was foreknown by God and incorporated into His sovereign purposes to accomplish His proprietary work for humanity at Calvary.

Luke Chapter 20

Jesus Christ's Authority Is Challenged (vv. 1-8)

During the final week of His earthly sojourn, the Lord Jesus taught the people daily in the temple, so conflict with Israel's leaders was unavoidable; He was on their religious turf, so to speak. How could a Jewish carpenter, with no formal training and no religious credentials, publicly speak for God? Who gave Jesus of Nazareth authority to cleanse the temple and to do miracles? The Herodians, the Sadducees, the Pharisees, and various scribes and lawyers now take turns challenging the Lord's authority as He taught the people in the temple on the Tuesday before His crucifixion (v. 1).

On this day, the Lord would silence multiple challengers, speak three parables to the multitudes, deliver a *woe* message to the Pharisees, and privately teach His disciples about things to come on the Mount of Olives.

The chief priests and Jewish elders were the first to confront the Lord with two questions: *"By what authority are You doing these things?" "Who is he who gave You this authority?"* (v. 2). The Lord chose to answer their two-part question with a question of His own, which, if they answered, then He promised that He would answer their inquiry concerning the origin of His authority (v. 3). So, the Lord asked them, *"The baptism of John – was it from heaven or from men?"* (v. 4).

The priests discussed the matter and decided that there was no safe answer to the Lord's question. If they said that John's authority came from heaven, then they would be guilty of ignoring His message as the Messiah's forerunner (v. 5). However, if they said that John was not from God, then they feared that the people would revolt against them, because they believed that John was a true prophet of God (v. 6). So, they declined to answer the Lord's question, but their silence rather affirmed the answer to their own questions to Him (v. 7).

Therefore, the Lord was neither obligated to nor did He need to answer their challenge with a response (v. 8).

The Man and Your God

The Landowner and the Wicked Vinedressers (vv. 9-18)

This is the second of three parables spoken together in the temple on the Tuesday before Christ's Crucifixion. Luke does not record the parable of *The Two Sons* (Matt. 21:28-32) spoken just before this parable or that of *The Marriage Feast* uttered directly afterwards (Matt. 22:1-14). To summarize, a landowner planted a vineyard and leased it to tenants, who would not render to him its fruit and, in fact, the tenants injured or killed the owner's messengers, including his only son, who came to collect what was owed to the landowner (vv. 9-14). The tenants, therefore, would receive the wrath of the landowner, who afterwards would lease the vineyard to others (vv. 15-16).

The nation of Israel, as a political reality, is likened to a noble vine (a grape vine; Jer. 8:13), which God planted in the world (Jer. 2:21, 12:10). In fact, several Old Testament prophets refer to Israel as God's special vine that He had planted (e.g., Isa. 5:1-7; Ezek. 15:2-4).

The prophet Hosea rebuked Israel because, though it (as a vine) had lush foliage, its fruit was worthless because it was self-produced for itself, and was not from God or for God: *"Israel empties his vine; he brings forth fruit for himself"* (Hos. 10:1). Two centuries later, the prophet Jeremiah told his fellow countrymen that God had planted a beautiful vineyard (speaking of the Jewish nation), but Israel's shepherds had made it desolate (Jer. 12:10). Israel was God's vineyard, but even in Christ's day, corrupt leaders were keeping it from being fruitful to God.

God repeatedly attempted to restore the vine to a fruitful condition by sending prophets to rebuke Israel's wayward and carnal leaders, but to no avail. Finally, God sent His beloved Son to plead with Israel to repent and be restored to God, but the Jewish nation rejected Him and had Him put to death. As Paul explains to the Ephesians, the offer of grace in Christ has been presented to the Gentiles, who through faith have been brought into the commonwealth of the blessing promised to Israel (Eph. 3:2-12). Gentile believers in the "dispensation of the grace of God" (Eph. 3:2) are now bearing spiritual fruit to God. This is what God wanted from Israel, but having rejected Christ, the opportunity was given to those who were not God's covenant people (Rom. 9:25).

The key components of this parable are as follows:
The certain man or landowner = God.

The vineyard = Israel.

The vinedressers by lease = Israel's leaders.

The servants = the former prophets and John the baptizer.

The Son = the Lord Jesus.

The other vinedressers = Gentiles trusting Christ in the Church Age.

Paul's analogy of the olive tree in Romans 11 parallels Christ's teaching in this parable. In this analogy, the root of the tree is the Abrahamic covenant, and the olive tree is Christ; through Him the promises of God will bless Israel, the natural branches. Yet, disbelief leads to rebellion and the loss of God's blessings and fellowship. Willful sin and rebellion will always invoke God's chastening hand. God did to Israel exactly what He told them He would do if His people erred from the Law and abandoned Him (Deut. 28); thus, the natural branches (the Jewish people) were removed from the opportunity to be nationally blessed by God through Christ.

Yet, the analogy shows us that God will restore Israel to Himself. The fact that the Jews (the natural branches) could be, and indeed will be, grafted back into the olive tree indicates that the focus of the illustration is not eternal salvation per se, but rather the blessings that God desires to share with those who exercise faith in Christ. Gentile believers (the wild branch) are a second benefactor of the New Covenant and thus are permitted to share in the blessings promised Israel (Eph. 2:11-3:7). Gentiles are grafted into the olive tree, indicating the blessings of Christ rooted in God's covenant with Abraham. The New Covenant permits individual Jews to be saved now and the Jewish nation to be reconciled to God after the Church Age ends.

However, when Christ spoke this parable, proud Israel was in rebellion against God, His prophets, and His Son, whom they put to death. The tenants wanted the inheritance (to control the people and receive their honor and praise) instead of giving it to the rightful owner – God. The scribes and Pharisees condemned themselves when they answered the Lord's question as to what should be done with the rebellious tenants (Matt. 21:40-41). They adamantly stated that the tenants should be killed for their brutal insolence and the vineyard should be leased to others who would render to the owner the fruit of his vineyard.

After answering Christ's question correctly, the Lord quoted Psalm 118:22 to affirm that God would provide the Gentiles an opportunity to be tenants of His vineyard to receive the desired fruit He longed for (vv. 17-18). At that time, the Jewish nation had no place for Christ; He was the rejected Stone that they tripped over and were thus broken up. God then used Christ, the rejected cornerstone, to create and build the Church (i.e., a Gentile bride for His Son). Those who repent and receive Christ alone for salvation in the Church Age (i.e., become broken on the Stone) will be saved and have the opportunity to bear fruit to God. But those who reject Christ will be eternally judged by Christ at His second advent to the earth (i.e., they will be crushed to powder by the Stone from heaven; Dan. 2:45).

Matthew informs us that the scribes and Pharisees were infuriated by this conclusion because it was obvious that Christ was likening them to the proud, murderous tenants who would be destroyed (Matt. 21:45). These religious leaders would have arrested the Lord Jesus but declined to do so for fear of how the crowd listening to Him might respond (Matt. 21:46).

The Challenge of the Herodians (vv. 19-26)

Previously, the Lord Jesus warned His disciples not to be influenced by *"the leaven of Herod"* and by implication, others with the same ideology (Mark 8:15). Herod Antipas the tetrarch, the infamous son of Herod the Great, was a ruling Jew in cahoots with the Romans to preserve his power. James would refer to him as "a friend of the world" (Jas. 4:4). In the case of Herod, and those like him, love for God and His Word had been supplanted by the love for materialism, fame, and political ambition. Such individuals are prone to skepticism, immorality, and worldliness and thus close association with them was to be avoided.

On the Tuesday before Christ's crucifixion, the Pharisees, the Sadducees, and the Herodians all challenged Christ's authority. Luke does not record the Pharisees' questions to Christ at this juncture, but he did chronicle the Lord's challenge to them. By articulating divine wisdom, the Lord not only stopped the mouths of His objectors, but He also denounced them as corrupt leaders of God's covenant people. These shepherds had not cared for God's sheep in Israel, but rather had led them away from the Lord into a miserable spiritual condition.

After the Lord spoke *The Marriage Feast* parable, the religious leaders began plotting how they might entangle Jesus in His words to formally charge Him with wrongdoing before the Roman governor (vv.

19-20; Matt. 22:15-16). After they devised what they thought would be foolproof questions to accomplish this goal, the Pharisees came with the Herodians to pose their inquiry. These two parties were bitter foes, but they had a common enemy, the Lord Jesus, which temporarily caused them to work together. The objective was to dupe Jesus into uttering a political statement against Rome that would then force the Roman authorities to act against Him.

In the true form of politicians, the Herodians first complimented the Lord before moving to spring their trap (v. 21). They claimed that He was a true teacher who taught the way of God accurately despite what men might say about what He taught. Their mistake was thinking that wicked men could ever appeal to the ego of a righteous man. Their praise would not entice the Lord to say something that they wanted to hear; rather, their empty praise just revealed the deceit harboring in their hearts.

The question was then posed to the Lord, *"Is it lawful to pay taxes to Caesar, or not?"* (v. 22). If He said "yes," then He would be viewed as affirming Gentile oppression over Israel, and many of His countrymen would refuse to listen to His message. This position would oppose the Abrahamic covenant which promised Gentile liberation. This would be ultimately achieved by the coming Jewish Messiah. Certainly then, if Christ was the Jewish Messiah, He would not endorse paying taxes to Rome. If the Lord said "no" to the question, then He would certainly be arrested by Roman authorities for leading a rebellion against the empire.

But the Lord perceived their wickedness and addressed them as hypocrites for testing Him with such an inquiry (v. 23). How did the Lord answer their question? He said, *"Show Me a denarius"* (v. 24). Matthew refers to this coin specifically as *"tax money"* (Matt. 22:19). He was shown a denarius and asked His audience, *"Whose image and inscription does it have?"* They responded by saying that it was Caesar's image and inscription on the coin. The Lord then said, *"Render therefore to Caesar the things that are Caesar's, and to God the things that are God's"* (v. 25).

If they were using Roman coinage, then they were admitting that they were under Roman rule. But given the warnings of Moses (e.g., Deut. 28:47-48), Israel would only be under Gentile rule because they had rebelled against Jehovah. So, the Lord was reminding them that they were paying taxes to Rome because they were under the chastening hand of God. When the Lord's oppressors heard His response, they marveled at His wisdom and departed from Him without asking any more questions (v. 26). He had thwarted their best attempt to hoodwink Him into saying something that would be viewed as controversial or dangerous.

The Challenge of the Sadducees (vv. 27-40)

The next group to challenge the Lord's authority were the supernatural-denying Sadducees. This religious sect formed part of the Jewish judicial court called the Sanhedrin. They did not believe in the angels, miracles, or resurrection (v. 27). These were the liberal theologians of Christ's day and touted ideologies such as higher-criticism and skepticism that negated the proper interpretation of Scripture.

The Sadducees asked the Lord Jesus about a woman who had been married to seven different men (she was widowed seven times and never married to more than one man at once; vv. 28-32). As the Sadducees did not believe in a bodily resurrection, their question to the Lord was clearly a test: *"In the resurrection, whose wife does she become? For all seven had her as wife"* (v. 33). The Lord's rebuke of the Sadducees was threefold: they were mistaken, they did not know the Scriptures, and they did not know the power of God (vv. 34-38).

They were mistaken, because in the resurrection, people would not be given to marriage, in the same way angels were not given to marriage (vv. 35-36). Rather than reiterating what they had already rejected, the Lord used the opportunity to affirm the truth of resurrection. The Sadducees did not know the Scripture, for Jehovah was the God of the living (v. 37). They also did not know the power of God, for God was the God of the living, not the dead (v. 38). How could God keep His unconditional covenants with Abraham, Isaac, and Jacob, all of whom had died, unless their souls were eternal, and they each would experience bodily resurrection in the future?

Contrary to the Mormon and Islamic views of heaven, people in heaven will neither be male nor female, at least in the way we understand the genders to exist today. There will be no marriages (save the Lamb with His saints) or sexual activities in heaven as some world religions tout. Those listening to His teaching on this matter were astonished at His wisdom and dared not ask Him any more questions (vv. 39-40; Matt. 22:33).

Those who experience resurrection will not be gender-significant in eternity, but will be like the angels, who do not reproduce. Angels are neither male nor female, although when they deliver God's messages to humans, they always appeared as men when taking a human form (e.g., Gen. 18). Male and female genders were God's design to provide complementing companionship in marriage and for the purpose of procreation (Gen. 1:28, 2:18).

In heaven, the need for reproduction will be eliminated as everyone will be eternal. Moreover, our communion with God in heaven will far exceed anything we could have ever experienced in an earthly relationship. Accordingly, we will be completely satisfied with being in fellowship with God and desire nothing else, including marital relationships. One of the clear warning signs of a false teaching is the notion that fleshly desires will be satisfied in heaven, or even worse, that such things are a part of some supreme deity's reward system.

The Lord Challenges the Pharisees (vv. 41-44)

While the Pharisees were still gathered before Him, the Lord asked them some questions, *"How can they say that the Christ is the Son of David?"* (v. 41) and *"Whose Son is He?"* (Matt. 22:42). Matthew notes that the Pharisees answered correctly, *"The Son of David."* Then the Lord asked them how it was possible for David, speaking by the Holy Spirit, to call His descendant "Lord" (Matt. 22:43). The Lord then quoted David (Ps. 110:1) to validate His question: *"The Lord said to my Lord, Sit at My right hand, till I make Your enemies Your footstool"* (v. 43).

In Psalm 110, as the writer of Hebrews proclaims (Heb. 1:13), God the Father is speaking to God the Son, whom David calls his "Lord." Given this understanding, the Lord Jesus poses His final question to the Pharisees, *"Therefore David calls Him 'Lord'; how is He his Son?"* (v. 44). The only logical answer to this question is that David's Son, the future Jewish Messiah, must be both God and a descendant of David.

But the Pharisees would not answer this question, for to do so would validate the Lord Jesus' claims as being God's Son and the rightful heir to the throne of David. Because they refused to reply, the Pharisees showed that they understood the point of the Lord's question. The Lord Jesus is God incarnate – the Word of God became flesh (John 1:14). He is the Son of God and the Son of David.

Through wisely conveying the truth, the Lord soundly defeated all those who had come to test Him. Afterwards, no one challenged Him with further questions (Matt. 22:46).

Beware of the Scribes (vv. 45-47)

Having silenced the Pharisees by His questions concerning David's Son also being his Lord, the Lord Jesus spoke to the multitude (including His disciples) about the hypocrisy of the scribes and the Pharisees (v. 45). F. B. Hole suggests that all that remained for the Lord to do was to unmask these evil men, and this He did in verses 46-47:

> They were hypocrites of the most desperate type, using religion as a cloak to cover their self-seeking and rapacity. He unmasked them, and pronounced their doom. He did not speak of a *longer* damnation, as though judgment were bounded by time and not eternal. But He did speak of *greater* damnation, showing that judgment will differ as to its severity. They suffer "more abundant judgment" (Textus Receptus).[44]

He mentions several of their negative behaviors to show why they had been rejected by God as His shepherds in Israel. The people would be wise to beware of their teaching, for they were prone to self-seeking and self-exalting behavior. Matthew's list of ill behaviors is more extensive than Mark's or Luke's record.

First, the scribes wore long robes in public to appear pious before the people. They desired others to take note of their outward religiosity and praise them for it (v. 46).

Second, the scribes sought the best seats in the synagogues and at feasts to convey their pompous superiority over the people. What they wore and did in public was for the appreciation of men, rather than by an inward compulsion to please God. To appear spiritual to others, they developed practices that went beyond what the Law required.

Third, instead of caring for the poor, the scribes robbed defenseless widows of what little they had and then attempted to cover up their evil by uttering long prayers (v. 47). Because the scribes had used their authority to undermine God's Word and character, to exalt themselves among the people and to take advantage of them, they would have great accountability on Judgment Day.

Luke Chapter 21

The Widow's Mites (vv. 1-4)

The story of the widow's two mites follows on the heels of the Lord's rebuke of Israel's spiritual leaders for using their authority to gain prosperity, while callously ignoring the needs of the poor, or worse, abusing them for profit.

Voluntary gifts were collected at *the women's court* located on the east side of the temple and were stored there in the temple treasury (v. 1). Offering boxes had trumpet-shaped funnels to receive coins and each box was labeled as to how the gifts collected were to be used. As the Lord was observing individuals putting their gifts into the treasury, He was mindful of the stark contrast between the hearts of those who gave.

The rich had not given sacrificially to the Lord, but out of their abundance – what they did not need (v. 4). He called His disciples' attention to a poor widow who had put two mites into the collection; this was the smallest offering that could legally be accepted at the temple (v. 2). Although the rich had contributed more monetarily, the Lord declared that she had given more from God's perspective because her contribution was from her livelihood. The poor widow had sacrificed from what she could not spare, not from any excess, like so many others did (v. 3).

In the Lord's day, it was common for boys to go out and catch sparrows and then sell them to the poor who would then make a little pie out of them. Two sparrows were sold for a farthing (Matt. 10:29), which was the equivalent of the two mites. This is the amount that the poor widow cast into the temple treasury (Mark 12:42). She basically gave her last meal to the Lord and was trusting in Him to supply her needs. God puts a premium on such sacrifices because such show the giver's faith and confidence in His character.

Likewise, when we give to God and share with others what we have and leave the implications with God, He blesses our generosity and causes us to flourish: *"The generous soul will be made rich, and he who waters will also be watered himself"* (Prov. 11:25). *"Cast your bread upon the waters, for you will find it after many days"* (Eccl. 11:1). We can have great confidence in our generous, omniscient God to rightly examine our hearts and to reward us for properly motivated giving (ministry), for He *"is not unjust to forget your work and labor of love which you have shown toward His name"* (Heb. 6:10).

Because God controls all things, He alone can satisfy all our needs, even after we have been His instrument to bless others. The more God enables us to help others, the more we will be blessed. If someone really has a heart to give to the Lord, He will provide a way for that person to do so. Not desiring to give back to the Lord what He has freely bestowed is the evidence of a spiritual problem. The widow had limited finances, but she still gave all that she had to the Lord in faith and was blessed by Him for doing so.

The Temple to Be Destroyed (vv. 5-6)

The Tuesday before Calvary was an incredibly busy day for the Lord Jesus. Besides mastering the verbal challenges of the Herodians, the Sadducees, the Pharisees, the scribes, and a lawyer, He also spoke the "Woe" message to the Pharisees and conveyed several parables. After these events, the Lord departed with His disciples to the Mount of Olives for a time of private ministry. At this time, He proclaimed to them important details concerning the future of Israel and the time of His Second Advent to the earth. Because this teaching was privately given on the Mount of Olives, it is often referred to as "The Olivet Discourse."

As with the "Sermon on the Mount," Matthew records the specific details of this incident more prominently than the other evangelists (Matthew 24 and 25). Both Mark and Luke devote one chapter each to the narration (Mark 13 and Luke 21), while John does not mention the discourse at all. Much of the detail contained in Matthew 25 is completely unique to Matthew.

The Olivet Discourse is *strictly* Jewish, for the Church will already be in heaven before the events of the Tribulation Period begin to unfold. The Olivet Discourse provides escalating signs of the coming Tribulation Period and describes events in the first half, mid, and last half of this horrendous time on earth. Then the Lord spoke of His Second Coming to the earth to judge the wicked.

After departing the temple and arriving on the Mount of Olives, one of the disciples called the Lord's attention to the grandeur of the temple directly west of them across the Kidron Valley (v. 5). The Lord told His disciples that this temple would be destroyed; not one stone would remain on another (v. 66). This prophecy was fulfilled when Roman armies under Titus's command destroyed the temple and much of Jerusalem with fire in 70 A.D. The extreme heat crumbled the stones of the temple, but also melted the gold band around the top of the temple. After the rubble cooled down, Roman soldiers then removed each stone to retrieve the precious metal.

Signs of the Coming Age (vv. 7-11)

Having sat down opposite the temple on the Mount of Olives, Christ began to teach His disciples. Peter, James, John, and Andrew asked Him to explain in more detail about the future events He had just alluded to (v. 7; Matt. 24:3). They especially wanted to know, *"What will be the sign of Your coming, and of the end of the age?"*

In response to their inquiry, the Lord identified many signs associated with the coming of the Tribulation Period, the first half of the Tribulation Period, the Abomination of Desolation in the middle of the Tribulation Period, then the Great Tribulation (i.e., the last half of the Tribulation Period), and His second Advent. He desires that Christians in the Church Age, as indicated by the phrase *"the end of the age,"* would not be deceived by false prophets or false Christs.

He first speaks of the Beginning of Sorrows (vv. 9-11). This would be an era marked by specific prophetic fulfillment which would alert the Jews to the forthcoming Tribulation Period. These troubling events are of an escalating nature and are meant primarily to be signs to Israel that the time of *Jacob's Trouble* is nearing. But as the Church will be removed from the earth prior to this seven-year period of Israel's final chastening, believers in the Church Age can be excited about these signs also. However, Christians should remember that there are no signs given to the Church for Christ's imminent return. The rapture of the Church is the next eschatological event on God's calendar.

First, the Lord explains that in the era just prior to the Tribulation Period there would be a dramatic increase in those claiming to be sent from God, especially claiming some type of Messianic authority (v. 8). Many false prophets will rise at this time to confuse and deceive the inhabitants of the earth from believing the truth.

Second, there will be wars and rumors of wars before the Tribulation period (v. 9). The twentieth century saw the first two wars that were worldwide, which ushered in the Nuclear Age and the resulting Cold War – the constant threat of nuclear annihilation. It is not likely that there will be another world war until the Tribulation Period.

Third, nation will rise against nation, and kingdom against kingdom (v. 10). The Greek word rendered "nation" in this verse is *ethnos*, which is the root word for our English word "ethnic." As the Tribulation Period nears, there will be a dramatic increase in ethnic violence. A shift from large numbers of soldiers perishing in warfare to ethnic genocide is likely indicated by this prophecy (this scenario has been observed during the last century of human history).

Fourth, there will be a dramatic increase in famines, pestilences, and earthquakes in various locations throughout the planet (v. 11; Matt. 24:8).

The previous, escalating signs prior to the commencement of the Tribulation Period were referred to by the Lord as "the beginning of sorrows" (Matt. 24:8). The eschatology timeline presented in Matthew 24, Mark 13, and Luke 21 is chronological with the Tribulation Period beginning in Matthew 24:9, Mark 13:9, and Luke 12 and ending with the second advent of Christ to the earth to judge the wicked.

The Tribulation Period (vv. 12-24)

The Lord then informed His Jewish brothers that when the time of Jacob's Trouble began, the Jews (the "you") would be hated by the Gentiles (the "they") and be delivered up to tribulation, including imprisonment and death (v. 12, Mark 13:12). During the first half of the Tribulation Period, many will be offended by the gospel of the kingdom being preached throughout the world (Matt. 24:14). This message will cause much division, betrayal, oppression, and hatred among those living on the earth (v. 17). There will even be a loss of trust in and love for one's own family members (v. 16).

While the context of the passage pertains to the refined remnant of Israel during the Tribulation Period, it is also true that believers during the Church Age will suffer for preaching the gospel message of grace. Thus, the Lord's instructions to His disciples then concerning a future day are equally applicable to our present day.

Previously, the Lord told His disciples that they would have the opportunity to testify of His name before kings (Matt. 10:18). When a believer chooses to obey God's calling for his or her life, God will equip and enable that individual to successfully answer every difficulty associated with fulfilling that call. The disciples did not need to worry about what to say or how to say it; the Holy Spirit would enable them to speak the truth that God wanted them to convey (Matt. 10:19-20). Likewise, Jewish evangelists during the Tribulation Period would have the opportunity to share the Kingdom Gospel message with the world and God would enable them to do so (vv. 14-15).

The Lord told His disciples that their message would cause great social division, such that even family members would betray each other because of it (v. 16). He warned them that they would be hated for identifying with Him (v. 17). If suffering rejection and persecution in one city, they were to flee to the next, but to keep preaching, for the Lord was with them and not even a hair on their heads would be lost until their work was complete (v. 18). All cities must hear the good news message, and evidence of possessing the truth is faithfulness to the Lord until He calls His servants home (Matt. 10:23). The Lord's command will be ultimately fulfilled during the Tribulation Period, when 144,000 Jewish evangelists will be preaching the Kingdom message again throughout the world (Matt. 24:14; Rev. 7:1-8).

There will be 144,000 divinely chosen and sealed Jewish evangelists that will be preaching the kingdom message throughout the earth at this time (Rev. 7:3-8, 14:1-5). The kingdom message is what Christ preached to Israel initially but was rejected; she was offered a literal, earthly, political kingdom (Matt. 4:17). Today, the Church preaches the gospel of grace: Christ crucified and raised from the dead for our justification. Only believers are tasked by the Lord with sharing this message with the lost (Matt. 28:19-20). There is no example in Scripture of even angels intruding on this responsibility. After the Church Age has concluded, the kingdom message will be preached again in Israel and indeed throughout the world. John foretold that angels would then fly over the earth to publicly declare its validity – the true King is coming to judge; do not worship the Antichrist (Rev. 14:6-12). These gospel distinctions show that Christ's plans for His Church and for restoring Israel are different. The Church has a heavenly citizenship, calling, and inheritance, while Israel has earthly promises and inheritance.

All those who endure through the Tribulation Period and believe that Christ will come to the earth to avenge His name and set up His kingdom will be delivered by Him at His second advent. These individuals will not worship the Antichrist or take his mark (Rev. 13:11-18, 19:20). In fact, a great multitude will not identify with the Antichrist and will be put to death during the Tribulation Period (Rev. 7:9-15). Using the example of the Tribulation saints, the Lord reminded His disciples that the reality of true faith is proven by endurance, thus the adage, *"by your patience possess your souls"* (v. 19). These Tribulation saints will be resurrected to rule and reign with Christ in His earthly kingdom (Rev. 20:4).

Unlike Matthew, Luke does not mention the abomination of desolation by the Antichrist in the temple that marks the middle of the Tribulation Period (Matt. 24:18). Rather, he describes the social upheaval to the Jewish people at that time as the *Times of the Gentiles* conclude (vv. 20-24).

When the abomination of desolation occurs at the midway point in the Tribulation Period, there will also be war in heaven. The archangel Michael, along with his angels, will war against the devil and his fallen angels to constrain evil to the earth (Dan. 12:1; Rev. 12:7-10). Satan, knowing that his time is short, will be enraged and seek to exterminate the Jewish people (Rev. 12:12-15). Jerusalem will be invaded and conquered by the armies of the Antichrist (Zech. 14:1-3). However, the Lord will preserve and protect a remnant of His covenant people from harm (Rev. 12:16-17). The slaughter will be so severe and widespread that the Lord warns His countrymen not to tarry for any reason but to journey to places of hiding in the mountains as quickly as possible (vv. 21-22). The Lord then acknowledged the difficulties of accomplishing this in wintertime, or for those who were pregnant or were caring for young children (vv. 23-24).

Christ's Second Coming (vv. 25-28)

While speaking of signs associated with the Great Tribulation (Matt. 24:21), the time when the Antichrist will be gaining followers on the earth and slaughtering those who will not take His mark (Rev. 13:15-18), the Lord gave a warning concerning the powerful signs of the Antichrist to deceive the masses (Matt. 24:23-24). The Lord then stated that during this time the slaughter on the earth would be so great that no one would survive the Great Tribulation if it lasted longer than three and a half years (Matt. 24:20). But for "the elect's sake" (speaking of the refined Jewish remnant to survive the Tribulation Period), this terrible time would not be permitted to go beyond the appointed time.

The Tribulation Period concludes with the second advent of Christ to the earth to destroy the Antichrist and liberate surviving Jews in Jerusalem (Zech. 14). This will be a time of great upheaval in heaven and on earth (vv. 25-26). Christ's return will be a visible coming in which the entire world will see the glory of Christ (v. 27). Like lightning that flashes across the sky, the Lord's coming will be sudden and visible to all (Matt. 24:27).

When the Jews see Jesus Christ returning to the earth in glory and power, they will mourn as a family would if they had lost their firstborn son or their only son (Zech. 12:10). With Christ's Second Advent to earth, the spiritual blindness of the Jewish nation will come to an end. They will trust in the Lord Jesus Christ, their Messiah, the One they had pierced two thousand years earlier (Zech. 12:10). Although we see that individual Jews in the Old Testament were filled by the Holy Spirit to speak for God or to serve Him (e.g., Ex. 35:30-35; 1 Sam. 10:10), the nation has never been indwelt by the Spirit of God (Zech. 4:4-7). This will not happen until Christ's second coming to the earth (Isa. 59:21). When the surviving Jews lift their heads to see Christ's coming to the earth, then they can rejoice, for their *"redemption draws near"* (v. 28).

Immediately after Christ's arrival to the earth, there will be a blast of a trumpet and the angels will gather all of God's covenant people remaining in the world back to the land of Israel (Matt. 24:27). The prophet Ezekiel states that the Lord will not leave one Jew anywhere in the world; all should be brought back to Israel to witness the complete fulfillment of the Abrahamic covenant (Ezek. 39:28-29).

The Parable of the Fig Tree (vv. 29-33)

The Lord spoke a prophetic parable concerning the fig tree, which also mentioned other "trees" (v. 29). The generation that sees the fig tree bud and shoot forth leaves again after being dormant over the winter will see all the things that Christ has just foretold about the Tribulation Period and His second coming to the earth (vv. 30-32). The Lord reminded His disciples that though heaven and earth will pass away, His words were eternal and would come about (v. 33).

What is symbolized by leaves (not fruit) appearing on the fig tree? As explained in the Luke 13 discussion, the Jewish nation is allegorically likened to a foliage trilogy: the vine, the fig tree, and the olive tree. Each one represents a distinct aspect of the nation's existence. For example, the prophet Jeremiah told his fellow countrymen that God had planted a beautiful vineyard (Israel), but Israel's shepherds had made it desolate (Jer. 12:10). The nation of Israel, as a political reality, is likened to a noble vine (a grape vine; Jer. 8:13), which God planted in the world (Jer. 2:21); Israel was God's vineyard. Jeremiah explains that the destruction of Israel in his day would be like livestock moving freely through God's vineyard and trampling the vines. It would consequently have no productivity, bearing only the fruit of sowing to sin, that is, the thorns of affliction and a harvest of shame (Jer. 12:11-13).

When Israel is spoken of as a fig tree in Scripture, the metaphor relates to the religious element of Israel, which often was fruitless for God (21:19-21; Jer. 8:13). This reality, Judaism today, was identified during one of the events in the life of the Lord Jesus (13:6-9). After preaching three years to the lost nation of Israel, Christ cursed the fruitless fig tree just before His death at Calvary. Less than forty years later, Jerusalem and the temple were destroyed, and the Jews have not sacrificed since then. The Old Covenant was replaced by the New Covenant, sealed with Christ's blood, and God was determined not to allow the Jews to continue in what was now obsolete.

One of the signs that the Tribulation Period and the second advent of Christ are nearing is that the fig tree (i.e., religious Israel) will again shoot forth leaves after a long, winter season of deadness (vv. 29-31). Leaves must precede fruit, but the fig tree will bear no fruit until the rebirth of the nation occurs in the latter days of the Tribulation Period. What might the new leaves speak of? This is likely a reference to the Jews reviving the old sacrificial system during, and perhaps just prior to, the Tribulation Period.

It was Gentile rule under the Romans that destroyed the temple and stopped the Jewish sacrifices, thus, Israel must regain political status among the nations ("all the trees") to achieve religious freedom again. Politically speaking, Israel was recognized as one of the trees among many in May of 1948. The next step then in this prophecy would be for Israel to begin sacrificing again – the fig tree shoots forth leaves again after a long winter of no activity. This may happen shortly before or after the rapture of the Church, but the generation that witnesses the Jews sacrificing again in Jerusalem to God will see Christ's second advent to the earth.

We know from various prophecies that the Antichrist will desecrate the Jewish temple and put a stop to animal sacrifices at the midpoint of the Tribulation Period (Dan. 9:27; Matt. 24:15; 2 Thess. 2:3-7). Therefore, logically speaking, a temple will have to be erected and animal sacrifices will have to be reinstituted by that point.

Therefore, we see that, during the Tribulation Period, the Jews will again offer sacrifices under the Levitical system. The Lord Jesus said that the generation permitted to witness this event would also visibly see His coming to the earth in glory (v. 32).

Watchfulness Is Required (vv. 34-37)

Speaking of Christ's second advent and establishing His kingdom on earth, the Lord states that no one knows the day and hour in which that will occur (Matt. 24:36). Not even the angels in heaven are let in on this secret. Meanwhile, all the Lord's servants are to be alert while faithfully laboring for Him until He returns (v. 34). The Jews waiting for the coming of Christ's kingdom were not to allow their own hearts to be weighed down with secular activities such as carousing, drunkenness, or worldly affairs that would rob them of precious time and resources.

Those living for temporal things will be surprised by Christ's second advent; they will not be expecting divine judgment for their carelessness (v. 35). But Jews loyal to Christ would be watching and praying at this time, while eagerly waiting for the Son of Man to return to establish His kingdom (v. 36).

Although the context of this passage is addressing the Jewish remnant in the Tribulation Period, the aspiration equally applies for believers in the Church Age who are to anticipate Christ's imminent return to the air for them (1 Thess. 4:13-18). This mindset has a purifying effect on how one lives his or her life for Christ (1 Jn. 3:2-3).

Although the Lord had just revealed escalating signs of the coming Tribulation Period and His future return to the earth, these were for Israel, not for the Church. There are no specific prophetic signs given to the Church concerning Christ's coming to the air to snatch His Bride to heaven. The signs that Christ had just mentioned to His disciples would be of great encouragement to the Jewish people suffering under the Antichrist during the Tribulation Period. However, the Church does not know when Christ is returning. His imminent return means that faithful believers should be constantly watching for Him while faithfully serving Him.

Luke Chapter 22

Judas Agrees to Betray the Lord (vv. 1-6)

According to both Matthew and Mark, directly after Mary's anointing of the Lord Jesus in the house of Simon (Matt. 26:6-13), Satan entered into Judas, who then *"conferred with the chief priests and captains"* to negotiate Christ's betrayal (vv. 3-4). The chief priests and scribes desired to put Jesus to death but feared the response of the people if they did so (v. 2). Judas offered them a private way of arresting Jesus without instigating a public revolt. This betrayal agreement was likely reached on Wednesday evening, the day before the Passover, which began the eight-day feast of Unleavened Bread (v. 1).

No doubt that Judas, who pilfered the ministry money box (John 12:6), was put out by the terrible waste of the spikenard oil, as he could have secretly profited from its sale. Although Luke did not record the exact amount of the betrayal money, Matthew does, thirty pieces of silver, the price of an injured slave (Ex. 21:32; Matt. 26:15).

During the next two days, two symbols of redemption in Scripture will be used to signify what Christ would be securing on our behalf at Calvary. Both silver and barley symbolize redemption (Ex. 30:12-16; Lev. 23:9-14, 25:9). The Lord Jesus was betrayed for thirty pieces of silver, which was later referred to by the Pharisees as "blood money" and indeed it was (Matt. 27:3-9). Additionally, in keeping with the Passover meal, the Lord broke unleavened barley bread the night before His crucifixion (vv. 14-20).

The prophet Zechariah uttered a messianic prophecy stating that the Lord would be betrayed for thirty pieces of silver. This prophecy was inserted between the breaking of the first and second staffs by the prophet to ensure that the meaning of both acts would be associated with the rejection of God's Shepherd by the Jewish nation:

> *Then I said to them, "If it is agreeable to you, give me my wages; and if not, refrain." So they weighed out for my wages thirty pieces of silver. And the Lord said to me, "Throw it to the potter" – that princely price*

they set on me. So I took the thirty pieces of silver and threw them into the house of the Lord for the potter (Zech. 11:12-13).

Indeed, the chief priests decided that it would be worth thirty pieces of silver to get rid of Jesus, and Judas also agreed that this would be a fair price (v. 5). From that moment on, Judas would be looking for an opportunity to betray Christ to the priests in the absence of a crowd (v. 6). But the betrayal price is only one part of Zechariah's prophecy. Not only would the Jewish Messiah be betrayed for thirty pieces of silver, but this money would also be returned to the temple and be used to buy a potter's field. Matthew confirms that Judas and the Pharisees fulfilled every detail of this prophecy (Matt. 27:3-10).

The phrase *"a princely price they set on me"* in the prophecy reveals how deeply the Lord felt this scornful denunciation by His own people – those whom He came to deliver. David foretells the Lord's anguish over His betrayal and desertion:

> *Reproach has broken my heart, and I am full of heaviness; I looked for someone to take pity, but there was none; and for comforters, but I found none. They also gave me gall for my food, and for my thirst they gave me vinegar to drink* (Ps. 69:20-21).

Judas' betrayal indicated just how much he valued the Lord, who had abandoned the supreme glory of Heaven to be the incarnate man born of a virgin, to live in a sin-cursed world, to endure the contradiction of sinners for thirty-three-plus years, to endlessly serve those in need to the point of exhaustion, to lay down His life and to be cursed of God to save others from Hell that they might enjoy the abundant life of God. What an insult for Judas, who had been with the Lord for more than three years, to value Christ for a mere thirty pieces of silver.

Preparation for the Passover Feast (vv. 7-13)

The next day was the first day of the Feast of Unleavened Bread, the day that the Passover lambs were slaughtered (v. 7). The Lord instructed Peter and John to *"prepare the Passover for us, that we may eat"* (v. 8). They asked the Lord, *"Where do You want us to prepare?"* (v. 9). The disciples understood that the Lord would be hosting the Passover for them and wanted to get everything ready for the meal later that evening.

The Lord answered their question by instructing them to go into the city and when they saw a man carrying a pitcher, they were to follow him (v. 10). Then they were to say to the master of the house in which the man entered, *"The Teacher says to you, 'Where is the guest room where I may eat the Passover with My disciples'"* (v. 11). Luke and Mark provide the most details concerning the interchange, and both writers tell us that the master of the house showed the disciples a large, furnished, upper room that he would make available for the Lord to eat the Passover with His disciples (v. 12).

Typically, women retrieved water for the household, so it would be an unusual sight to see a man carrying a pitcher of water. But this would be how the disciples would meet their contact, who then would show them where the Lord wanted to host the Passover meal for His disciples. All was accomplished just as the Lord foretold them (v. 13).

The Last Passover Feast (vv. 14-18)

Around sundown on Nisan the fourteenth, the Lord gathered with His disciples to keep the Passover in a large, furnished, upper room (v. 14). Its size meant that anyone who wanted to enjoy Christ's presence would be welcome. It was a furnished room, meaning that all that was needed to enjoy Christ's presence was available. Furthermore, because it was an upper room, the disciples could enjoy Christ's presence without any distractions from the hustle and bustle in the street below. Moreover, John informs us that the Lord girded Himself as a slave, poured water in a basin, picked up a towel, and washed the dirty feet of His disciples before instituting the Lord's Supper (John 13:4-13). Christ's provision of cleansing through the confession of sin is vitally important, as believers cannot enjoy His presence with unconfessed sin (1 Jn. 1:7-9).

The Lord informed His disciples that He had a fervent desire to eat the Passover meal with them before He, as God's Passover Lamb, suffered for humanity (v. 15). On God's calendar, there would be no more Passovers to keep until the Kingdom was established, for God would be putting away the entire Levitical system after Christ's work at Calvary was finished (Heb. 8:13). Hence, the Lord (Who ate this Passover with His disciples) would not be celebrating the deliverance of the Israelites from Egypt by eating the Passover again as required by the Law (v. 16). He knew that He was going to die on the next day and then, after His resurrection, return to heaven. But He would feast with His Jewish countrymen again in a future day, after He had established His kingdom and delivered them from the Antichrist and all Gentile oppression forever.

After informing the disciples that this would be His last Passover with them, the Lord gave thanks for the cup and told the disciples to divide it among themselves (v. 17). There were four cups incorporated into the Jewish Seder. Being the initial reference, this cup was likely the first one passed during the Passover meal after "the blessing" was spoken over it. It is doubtful that the Lord spoke the second part of the traditional blessing over this cup, which related to Israel's national admiration and righteousness (which did not characterize the nation's present state). It also seems unlikely that the Lord drank from this or any of the other cups associated with the Seder. On this point, William Kelly writes:

> The Lord said unto them, "With desire I have desired to eat this Passover with you before I suffer: for I say unto you, I will not any more eat thereof, until it be fulfilled in the kingdom of God" (vv. 14-16). It was the last act of communion of Christ with them. He eats with them: He will not drink. Another cup was before Him. As for this cup, they were to take it, and divide it among themselves. It was not the Lord's Supper, but the paschal cup. He was about to drink of a far different cup, which His Father would give Him – the anti-type of the Passover, and the basis of the Lord's Supper. But as to the cup before them, He says, "I will not drink of the fruit of the vine, until the kingdom of God shall come."[45]

F. B. Hole agrees with Kelly's conclusion:

> As to the cup (v. 17), this does not appear to have been any part of the Passover as instituted through Moses, and the Lord apparently did not drink of it. Instead, He indicated that His day of joy, which the fruit of the vine symbolized, would only be reached in the coming kingdom.[46]

Rabbinical tradition informs us that the wine shared at the Passover was one part wine and two parts water to avoid any intoxicating effects of the wine during the memorial feast.[47] After this first cup was passed, there was a ceremonial washing of hands, which also occurred again after supper with the pouring of the third cup. This Jewish tradition of washing hands after the first cup was passed correlates to when the Lord Jesus washed the feet of the disciples (John 13).

The Lord's Supper Is Instituted (vv. 19-20)

Towards the end of the Passover feast, the Lord did something that did not follow the Seder tradition: *"He took bread, gave thanks and broke it, and gave it to them, saying, 'This is My body which is given for you; do this in remembrance of Me'"* (v. 19). *"Likewise, He also took the cup after supper, saying, 'This cup is the new covenant in My blood, which is shed for you'"* (v. 20). It seems likely that the Lord used the third cup of wine in the Jewish Seder, known as "the cup of blessing," which was tied with Israel's redemption from Egypt (Paul likely refers to this cup in 1 Cor. 10:10) to institute the Lord's Supper. This cup was poured at the close of the meal and after Judas had departed. Likewise, He used some of the unleavened bread that had been blessed and broken at the start of supper and then put aside to express a new memorial feast which was to be kept in His absence. As the cup of wine and the bread were being used in a new way, for those following Him to remember His sacrifice for them, it seems unlikely that the Lord partook of either.

It is noted that the fourth cup of wine, "the cup of Praise," passed in the Seder, symbolized the joy and blessing that Israel would have after being restored to God in a future day. In the good sense, wine symbolizes joy in Scripture, and during the Kingdom Age, the Jewish nation would again enjoy God's presence and praise His name. The Lord would wait to drink this cup with His Jewish countrymen when they were restored to God in the Kingdom Age (v. 18; Ezek. 45:21). The Lord symbolically drank of all four cups presented during the Passover at Calvary to extend to Israel (and to Gentiles also as a second benefactor of the New Covenant) the opportunity to be sanctified, delivered, redeemed, and restored to a praiseworthy God (Matt. 26:39, 42). After the disciples drank from the fourth cup, the Lord and His disciples sang the remainder of the Jewish Hallel (Pss. 115-118) and then departed the upper room (Matt. 26:30).

In instituting the Lord's Supper, the Lord Jesus provided two symbols for believers to regularly use to remember Him and His sacrifice: the broken bread representing His battered and torn body at Calvary and the blood of the grape, wine, to picture His blood shed from the cross for our redemption. Paul later reiterates the words of the Lord on this occasion to the Corinthians: *"'Take, eat; this is My body which is broken for you; do this in remembrance of Me.' In the same manner He also took the cup after supper, saying, 'This cup is the new covenant*

Luke

in My blood. This do, as often as you drink it, in remembrance of Me'" (1 Cor. 11:24-25). "As often as" means every time it is kept. Believers are to keep the Lord's Supper often, in the way specified, but no specific regularity was stated. The first Lord's Supper was not held in a church building; in fact, the Church did not exist at that time. The first Christians obeyed the Lord's command by continuing steadfastly in the breaking of the bread (Acts 2:42), and they did so often from house to house (Acts 2:46). Christians were meeting informally and often to remember the Lord (not just on Sundays or as a local assembly).

Years later, the practice of the local church gathering on Sundays to break bread became the pattern of the Church. For example, on one occasion, Paul waited a week in Troas to break bread with the saints there on Sunday (Acts 20:7). Yet, because Paul preached long, they did not break bread until early Monday morning and that was acceptable.

To summarize, *the commands* for the Lord's Supper are to do it often and to preserve its protocol and purpose. The *developed pattern* of the Church was that saints gathered in local assemblies each Sunday to break bread together. The latter point is a scriptural observation, which means there is no prohibition in Scripture preventing saints from remembering the Lord on other days of the week or in smaller groups. While following the scriptural pattern is safe for guiding our behavior, not following what is observed should never negate what is commanded. So, no matter what our circumstances might be, let us follow the Lord's command and remember Him the best possible way that we can!

The Lord Jesus did not drink from the cup that He passed to the disciples, but He promised to drink it with His disciples at a future day of God's kingdom (v. 18). By drinking the contents of the cup, the disciples were accepting the full test to be faithful to Christ. They were following Christ's example of drinking down to the dregs the cup of wrath to be received from His Father at Calvary.

The disciples partook of the Lord's Supper which anticipated the sealing of a New Covenant between God and His covenant people that would provide redemption. This scene was prefigured long ago at Mount Sinai. After the Jews were made aware of God's awesome holiness and their own sinfulness, having received God's Law through Moses, they were sprinkled with atoning blood from the burnt sacrifices put on the altar built by Moses (Ex. 24:1-8). After the people were sprinkled with blood, Moses, Aaron, Nadab and Abihu (who were the oldest sons of Aaron), and the seventy elders of Israel (the elders represented all the people) ascended partway up the mountain to eat a meal before God (Ex. 24:9-11). They could not approach God's holy mountain previously, but now that atonement had been made, they were able to come into God's presence without fear. Although the Jews could not come intimately into God's presence, they were permitted to come safely near to Him through blood atonement, and they saw the base of God's sapphire throne.

The mutual acceptance of the covenant was signified by the eating of a meal before God, though He did not eat with them. The eating of a meal was a customary way for two parties to show their agreement to a covenant (Gen. 26:30, 31:54). This circumstance is similar to the upper room scene in which the Lord's disciples, the future leaders of the Church, ate the Lord's Supper in Christ's presence, though He Himself did not partake of it.

The upper room meal occurred on the eve of the ratification of the New Covenant, which would be sealed by Christ's own blood (v. 20). The New Covenant, which was made with the house of Judah and Israel (Heb. 8:8), would end the dispensation of the Law and usher in the age of grace – the Church Age. Thankfully, the Gentiles would be a second benefactor of this covenant (Eph. 2:11-3:6). The events on Mount Sinai in Moses' day all pointed to a future incredible event on Mount Calvary in Christ's day. There, God's supreme Altar and Sacrifice would once and for all satisfy the righteous claims of God's throne in relationship to human wickedness.

Christ Foretells of His Betrayal (vv. 21-23)

The discussions in verses 21-27 likely occurred before the Lord Jesus instituted His remembrance feast. John informs us that the discussion about a betrayer occurred after the Passover feast had commenced and then Judas departed the upper room (John 13:21-30). After they began eating the Passover feast, the Lord stated that one of them would betray Him (v. 21; Matt. 26:21), and it would have been better if that man had never been born rather than to suffer God's wrath for his evil deed (v. 22; Matt. 26:24). The disciples became sorrowful and began asking Him which of them could do such a thing (v. 23).

On the previous night, Judas had agreed to betray Christ to the chief priests for thirty pieces of silver. The realization that a betrayer sat with Him at the table troubled the Lord's spirit (John 11:33). It was customary for the host to dip a piece of bread in gravy or vinegar and give it to the honored guest (sitting to his left) during the feast. It is likely, given Christ's private charge to Judas, that he occupied this place of honor (John 13:27, 30). Christ gave Judas the sop and thus identified him as the betrayer (John 13:26). John says that Satan entered Judas after he received the sop (John 13:27). Judas then asked the Lord, deceitfully, *"Rabbi, is it I?"* (Matt. 26:25). The Lord confirmed that it was and told Judas, *"What you do, do quickly"* (John 13:27). Judas then departed the upper room; the other disciples did not discern what Christ meant by these words. They assumed that Judas, having the purse, was taking care of feast-related matters or giving a gift to the poor (John 13:28-29).

Renewed Strife Over Greatness (vv. 24-27)

As just mentioned, it seems unlikely that the disciples would be arguing about their position in the kingdom after just learning that one of them was a faker (v. 24). Rather, the discussion of greatness likely occurred before the Passover and was related to who would have the seat of honor on Christ's lefthand at the Passover. Given the discussion around the table later, it appears that Judas sat in this place of honor.

The Lord then told His disciples that true greatness from God's perspective was using authority to humbly serve others (vv. 25-26). The disciples were not to follow the example of Gentile rulers who lorded their authority and status over others. Rather, they were to follow His example of exercising authority – sacrificially giving to serve others (v. 27). Greatness is not obtained by having position and power, but by revealing the character of Christ in what we do.

What the Lord taught in word and deed was counter to the world's philosophies of success. Worldlings will say, "save your life at all costs," but the Lord taught, "lose your life to gain one worth living." The world exclaims, "live for the moment," but Christians are to "live for eternity." Worldlings want to be served by others, but Christ taught His disciples to humble themselves and serve others, for that was the true path to greatness in His kingdom.

Biblical leadership is not one of lordship or heavy-handed tactics of control, but rather is a style that serves God's sheep and upholds them so that they flourish. The Gentile kings were often dictators, who oppressed their subjects, but those who would lead God's people must not do so. Those who love Christ must follow His sacrificial example. Christ stated that He had not come into the world to be served, but rather to die – to give His life as a ransom for those who did not deserve God's favor in any way, shape, or form. If the Lord of Glory can do that for others, should not we be able to serve those who are difficult to serve?

One must be a submitted servant before he or she can be a true leader of others. The Lord Jesus humbled Himself to serve and develop others into profitable leaders. He devoted three-plus years of His life to train twelve men, one of which was a traitor. A true mark of Christlike leadership is the ability to develop greatness in others by serving them.

The Apostles Reward in the Kingdom Age (vv. 28-30)

Verse 28 was probably spoken after Judas had departed the upper room, as those who were still sitting with Christ at the table were marked by faithfulness. Some have concluded that Judas was not present at the Lord's Supper by referring to Paul's specific use of the imperfect verb tense in the expression, *"on the same night in which he was betrayed"* (1 Cor. 11:23). While this conclusion is possible, all that can be categorically said is that Judas engaged in the activity of betrayal on *the same night* as the Lord's Supper was instituted, not necessarily *at the same time*.

The eleven disciples had continued with Christ despite hardship and persecution. God rewards faithfulness, and just as His Father had honored Him for faithfulness by giving Him the kingdom, He would also reward His dedicated followers in His kingdom (v. 29). Not only would there be feasting and joy at that time, but the disciples would have authority to judge the nation of Israel during the Kingdom Age (v. 30).

At this time, the Church will rule and reign with Christ in glorified bodies (Rom. 8:17; 2 Tim. 2:12; Rev. 20:4), while the nation of Israel will enjoy the fulfillment of God's covenant promises. At this time each tribe of Israel (excluding Levi) will receive a land allotment as an earthly inheritance (Ezek. 47-48). The Levites will dwell around the Lord's gigantic millennial temple and the sons of Zadok will minister before Him on behalf of the Jewish nation (Ezek. 40:46, 43:19, 44:15, 48:11).

Christ Foretells of Peter's Denials (vv. 31-34)

According to John, after the Lord Jesus instituted His remembrance feast, the Lord informed His disciples that He would soon be leaving them (John 13:36-38). Matthew, who repeatedly referred his Jewish audience to the Old Testament prophecies concerning the Messiah throughout his gospel account, states that the Lord quoted Zechariah 13:7 to inform His disciples that they would all scatter from Him that night.

Luke

God was about to strike His Shepherd with a sword at Calvary and all the disciples would stumble before the Lord because of it. But the Lord then promised that after His resurrection, He would see them again in Galilee (Matt. 26:32).

Peter specifically asked where the Lord was going (John 13:36). The Lord answered his question by saying that where He was going Peter could not follow Him then, but implied that he would later. Christ was going to the cross and then on to heaven. Peter would do the same in about thirty-five years.

Peter then declared his allegiance to the Lord and that he would follow Him now even if all others stumbled at Him (Matt. 26:33). It is at this juncture that Luke records the Lord's words to Peter: *"Simon, Simon! Indeed, Satan has asked for you, that he may sift you as wheat. But I have prayed for you, that your faith should not fail; and when you have returned to Me, strengthen your brethren"* (vv. 31-32). The Lord foretold that Peter would soon deny Him. Peter immediately rejected this statement and replied, *"Lord, I am ready to go with You, both to prison and to death"* (v. 33). But the Lord informed Peter that before the early morning watch was over (known by the cock's crowing), he will have denied him three times (v. 34; John 13:38). Peter responded to this statement, *"Even if I have to die with You, I will not deny You!"* (Matt. 26:35). The other disciples also affirmed the same allegiance to the Lord.

Luke also records Peter's willingness to die with the Lord (vv. 49-50). John states that the Lord then warned Peter with a question, *"Will you lay down your life for My sake?"* (John 13:38). In a few hours, Peter would learn just how impossible it was to serve Christ in the strength of the flesh.

Indeed, the Lord warned Peter that Satan had already asked that he might sift all the disciples as wheat (i.e., the "you" in verse 31 is plural). As the Lord was speaking to Peter, He addresses him as a representative of all the disciples. The satanic testing would be permitted, but the Lord wanted Peter to know that He had already prayed for him (and by implication, the other disciples also). The devil wanted to remove Peter's faith and cause him to fail the Lord, but the Lord wanted to use the experience to rid the chaff of self-confidence from Peter's character.

Any of us would be stunned to learn that Satan, perhaps the most powerful being ever created and the arch-enemy of God, desired to bring us down in defeat. What a comfort for Peter to also be informed that the Lord had already prayed for him: *"that your faith should not fail."* As

Paul explains, we have the same provision of mercy from the Lord Jesus: *"Who is he who condemns? It is Christ who died, and furthermore is also risen, who is even at the right hand of God, who also makes intercession for us"* (Rom. 8:34).

Peter's courage did fail him, for a few hours later he did deny the Lord three times, exactly as the Lord said he would. But thankfully his faith was refined and strengthened through the failure. This is the tenacious nature of true faith – what is not perfect is not destroyed but made stronger through suffering and hardships. We are to learn from our mistakes, rise up in grace, and go on with the Lord.

Through Peter's refining process, he would gain a greater capacity to encourage and bless others. Foreknowing this, the Lord Jesus instructed him that after he was restored to Him again, he was to strengthen his brethren. The Lord was speaking of a future day when Peter would repent of his failure (sin) and be brought back into fellowship with Him. Our fellowship with Christ is based on our behavior, but our position in Christ is based on His ability to secure what is His.

Suffering and Persecution Are Coming (vv. 35-38)

Verses 35-38 contain Luke's summary of what the Lord taught His disciples in John chapters 14 through 16. For example, the Lord told His disciples that because they had identified with Him, the world would hate them and persecute them (John 15:18-20).

When He had previously commissioned them to go two by two throughout Galilee to preach the kingdom message, they had lacked nothing (v. 35). He had labored alongside them to reach the lost sheep of Israel and they had received all that was needed to complete that task. But a new age was coming, the Church Age, in which He would continue to labor with them, but He, Himself, would be in heaven (Mark 16:20).

After His resurrection He would be commissioning them again, with new authority, and a new message which would spread throughout the world. But this meant that they would experience a new hatred in the world also. While He was with them in Israel, He protected them from harm, but after His departure, they would be required to rely on Him in new ways as they faced opposition. This is the idea behind taking a money bag, a knapsack and selling one's garment to purchase a sword. Although the Lord would continue to supply and protect them, they also would be challenged to rely on Him in faith in a different way than when He was physically with them (v. 36).

He was to be numbered with the transgressors and be put to death, which meant that He was leaving them (v. 37). The disciples did not understand the Lord's allegorical teaching pertaining to the Church Age, so they volunteered, *"Lord, look, here are two swords"* (v. 38). The Lord did not correct their misunderstanding, but simply said, *"It is enough."* He already knew that He must be arrested, that His disciples must not fight for Him (John 18:11, 36), and that He must be abandoned by them (Mark 14:27). It was His time to die for them, not theirs to die for Him!

Christ in the Garden of Gethsemane (vv. 39-46)

After leaving the upper room, the Lord and His disciples meandered through the streets of Jerusalem, trekked eastward across the Kidron brook and up the Mount of Olives to the Garden of Gethsemane, a place the Lord often resided with His disciples (v. 39). He asked His disciples to sit in a particular place and then exhorted them to watch and pray lest they be given over to temptation (i.e., solicitations to do evil; v. 40). The Lord was informing His disciples what Paul would later confirm as true in his own life: None of us can do what pleases God in the power of the flesh (Rom. 7:15-18). Peter had claimed to be the tough guy that would never deny the Lord, but when the Lord needed him most, he was sleepy.

It is unclear whether the Lord's charge was to all the disciples or just Peter, James, and John who went a bit further into the garden with the Lord (Matt. 26:36-37). The Lord then informed the three disciples with Him that His soul was *"exceedingly sorrowful"* (Matt. 26:38). He then asked them to stay with Him and watch with Him while He prayed.

The Lord then departed from them about the distance of a stone's throw to engage in private prayer (v. 41). He knelt and prayed, *"Father, if it is Your will, take this cup away from Me; nevertheless, not My will, but Yours, be done"* (v. 42). There is no evidence in Scripture that the Lord slept at all the night before His passion. His human soul was "exceedingly sorrowful," and He spent the night preparing His disciples for what was coming and in prayer. Luke, who upholds the humanity of Christ in his gospel account, informs us that an angel ministered to Christ in the garden (v. 43). As His disciples were sleeping, this angelic companion was most encouraging.

Luke then informs us that Christ, *"being in agony, He prayed more earnestly"* (v. 44). A similar scene is recorded in Mark, but not in John, who presents Christ in His deity. Thus, there is not one word in John's account about Christ's anguish of soul or perspiration while praying in Gethsemane, but Luke writes, *"Then His sweat became like great drops of blood falling down to the ground"* (v. 44). Commenting to this statement Warren Wiersbe writes:

> Dr. Luke is the only Gospel writer who mentions "sweat … like great drops of blood." His use of the word *like* may suggest that the sweat merely fell to the ground like clots of blood. But there is a rare physical phenomenon known as *hematidrosis*, in which, under great emotional stress, the tiny blood vessels rupture in the sweat glands and produce a mixture of blood and sweat.[48]

These statements describe the Son of Man as the Man of Sorrows. John is the only one to present the heavenly view of Christ that night; thus, he highlights Christ's great expectation of being received into heaven, regaining His glory, and being with His Father forevermore (John 13:1, 17:1-5).

The Lord returned to find Peter, James, and John sleeping. At the most critical moment in the Lord's ministry, even His closest friends were not there for Him (v. 45). Luke does not record that the Lord Jesus returned three times to find His disciples sleeping, but rather only mentions the final moment, just before His arrest. He said to them, *"Why do you sleep? Rise and pray, lest you enter into temptation"* (v. 46).

The hour had now come for Him to be betrayed "into the hands of sinners" (Matt. 26:45). But prayer had accomplished its work, despite His previously expressed distress; the Lord declared that He would continue to please His Father no matter the personal cost to Himself: *"Rise, let us be going. See, My betrayer is at hand"* (Matt. 26:46).

In comparing Luke's and John's accounts of the events in the Garden of Gethsemane the night Christ was arrested, you might think the writers were speaking of two different instances. John describes a band of men approaching the Garden with *"lanterns and torches and weapons"* to seek out and arrest Jesus. In John, the Lord is shown to be the great I AM by referring to Himself by that name three times in response to His arresters, who fell backwards at Christ's first declaration of that title. John declares once again that the Savior is God in flesh, the Great I AM who is in full control of the situation. Conversely, Luke upholds the Lord's humanity in Gethsemane. In Luke alone do we read of the Lord's anguish in prayer; *"His sweat was, as it were, great drops of blood falling"* (v. 44). Only in Luke do we read of an angel ministering to Christ in the garden and that the Lord healed Malchus' ear after Peter severed it. The same event from two perspectives!

Christ's Betrayal and Arrest (vv. 47-53)

While the Lord was speaking, His betrayer arrived in Gethsemane. Judas knew the place that the Lord often resided with His disciples, and he had led a great multitude having clubs, torches, and swords to that location, with the Jewish leaders also (Matt. 26:47).

Why so many people to arrest someone that had never hurt anyone? Apparently, Christ's arrestors thought that He would be hiding, and they would have to search him out. The moon would have been full at the Paschal Feast, so there would have been plenty of light to find a hiding Jesus. But John states that seeing His arrestors approaching Him, He stepped forward and asked them who they were looking for (John 18:4). The Lord Jesus already knew what was going to happen to Him at Calvary and did not resist being arrested, though He had the power to do so.

Judas had told the mob that he was leading, *"Whomever I kiss, He is the one; seize Him"* (Matt. 26:48). He then went up to the Lord and said, *"Greetings, Rabbi!"* and kissed Him (v. 47). The Greek verb for "greetings" in Matthew 26:48 is in the present tense, indicating that Judas likely spoke to the Lord more than once (and likely kissed Him repeatedly) to ensure that everyone knew who should be arrested. Kenneth Wuest's *Expanded Translation of the New Testament* renders what Judas did in Matthew 26:49 this way: "He [Judas] embraced Him and kissed him tenderly and again and again."

How did the Lord respond to such blatant betrayal? He said to Judas, *"Friend, why have you come?"* (Matt. 26:50). Fully knowing what Judas was doing, our Savior still extended kindness and compassion to Judas. Although under Satan's control, the Lord still felt it was necessary to appeal to Judas' conscience one last time, *"Judas, are you betraying the Son of Man with a kiss?"* (v. 48). When it seems like everything around you is dark and evil, remember individual souls still need to be reached by compassion and with the truth. But Judas did not respond to the Lord's tenderness, and He had to be arrested. The disciples, seeing what was happening asked Jesus, *"Lord, shall we strike with the sword?"* (v. 49).

As Christ's arrestors stepped forward, Peter drew his sword without Christ's approval and was ready to face down a band of soldiers to protect his Lord. Peter struck one of the high priest's servants named Malchus and sliced off his ear (v. 50; John 18:10). The Lord Jesus told Peter to put his sword away, lest he perish by it, and then He repaired the damage that Peter's sword did to Malchus' ear (v. 51; John 18:10-11). Peter needed to learn that the Lord did not want Peter to die once to serve Him, but to die daily to self to live for Him. It is easy to swing a sword when one is ignorant of God's will and make a mess of things. It is entirely another matter to fully rest in the Lord to witness God accomplish what only He can.

The Lord's response to those arresting Him was noteworthy (vv. 52-53). He clearly states the facts to appeal directly to the consciences of those arresting Him: "I was with you daily in the temple without any expression of hostility; why then are you coming against Me now with clubs and swords?" "What have I done that now justifies you treating Me like a robber?" The Lord does not try to escape what He knows is necessary, but He still has a compassionate heart towards those under the enemy's control. He chooses to reason with them, not attack or retaliate against them in any way.

Indeed, the situation was being incited by wickedness in high places, yet the Lord's compassion for those individuals under its influence is paramount. Additionally, He told His arrestors that all that was happening was to fulfill what the prophets had foretold, as recorded in Scripture (Matt. 26:56). Then, as the Lord had previously predicted in the upper room, all His disciples forsook Him and fled.

This is one of many examples in Scripture where Satan attacks proper authority (God-ordained authority) and tries to replace it with weaker authority (those under Satan's authority). Absalom's revolt against the rightful king of Judah – David – is a good example of this tactic. The Pharisees were now directly attacking the Lord's authority and message to replace it with human traditions and legalism.

Peter Denies the Lord (vv. 54-62)

As William MacDonald summarizes, given all four gospel accounts, there are six different examples of Peter denying the Lord:

Luke

1. A young woman (Matt. 26:69, 70; Mark 14:66–68).
2. Another young woman (Matt. 26:71, 72).
3. The crowd that stood by (Matt. 26:73, 74; Mark 14:70, 71).
4. A man (Luke 22:58).
5. Another man (Luke 22:59, 60).
6. A servant of the high priest (John 18:26, 27). This man is probably different from the others because of what he said – "Did I not see you in the garden with Him?" (v. 26).[49]

The Lord stated that Peter would deny Him thrice before the cock's crowing (likely referring to the early morning watch). It should be understood that in almost all these accounts there were multiple people present and it is doubtful that only one person would have questioned Peter in such a situation. Hence, different writers would have been later highlighting different aspects of Peter's own testimony.

Peter followed the Lord at a distance, but after arriving at the high priest's courtyard, he sat down to see what would happen and warmed himself by a fire with Caiaphas' servants (vv. 54-55). John tells us that because he was known by the Jewish officials, he spoke on Peter's behalf so that he would be permitted into the courtyard.

While Peter was sitting outside in the courtyard with others by a fire, a servant girl saw him and said, *"This man was also with Him"* (v. 56). Peter utterly denied this assertion in front of everyone, *"Woman, I do not know Him"* (v. 57). Strike one. Whether or not Peter heard the warning, we do not know, but Mark states that a rooster crowed after his first denial. Apparently, Peter became uncomfortable with his surroundings and ventured towards the porch by the courtyard gateway (Mark 14:68).

A little later, another man (apparently with another girl present also) said to Peter, *"You also are of them"* (v. 58; Matt. 26:72). Peter promptly denied knowing Jesus Christ. Strike two. About an hour later, a relative of Malchus recognized Peter as having been in the garden with Jesus and said, *"Surely this fellow also was with Him, for he is a Galilean"* (v. 59; Matt. 26:72-73). Matthew states that Peter, while cursing and swearing, adamantly declared, *"I do not know the Man!"* (v. 60; Matt. 26:74). Strike three.

No sooner had the words departed Peter's lips, when he heard the rooster crow (all four Gospel writers record that event). It was normal for roosters to crow in the fourth watch (3 a.m. to 6 a.m.). Mark notes that the rooster had sounded his warning previously, but only now did Peter recognize it and remember the Lord's prediction, *"Before the rooster crows, you will deny Me three times"* (Mark 14:72). Luke states that at this moment Peter's eyes and the Lord's eyes briefly met (v. 61). It was a sorrowful look that Peter would never forget. The defeated fisherman directly went out of the courtyard and wept bitterly (v. 62).

Christ's Religious Trials (vv. 63-71)

The Lord would endure three religious trials and three civil trials in less than nine hours. Quirinius, the governor of Syria, appointed Annas as the Jewish high priest in 6 A.D. However, the Romans did not want a long-standing high priest. Limiting the high priest's tenure would reduce the priest's sway among the people. So Annas had been replaced in 15 A.D. by Valerius Gratus, procurator of Judea and then each of his five sons were appointed the high priest and then Caiaphas, his son-in-law.[50] Luke confirms that both Annas and Caiaphas were high priests currently (3:2). From the Jewish perspective, Annas was the true high priest, though Caiaphas was the acknowledged leader to pacify Roman rule.

John states that Christ first appeared before Annas and then was interrogated by a larger gathering of Jewish leaders with Caiaphas present (Matt. 26:57; John 18:13). Interestingly, night gatherings of the Sanhedrin for a capital trial were illegal.[51] The introduction of false witnesses at the trial and the declaring of a verdict before the trial commenced were also forbidden (John 7:51). As F. B. Hole observes, the worst part was not the presence of false witnesses, but that Israel's leaders, who were to represent God's justice, sought false witnesses:

> The mob delivered Him to the leaders of Israel, and these men, who claimed to represent God, had thrown away any pretense of seeking righteousness. We are not told that they were *misled* into accepting false evidence, nor that they were *tempted* into receiving it because it was thrust upon them. No, it says, they *"sought* false witness against Jesus, to put Him to death." They SOUGHT it. Has there ever, we wonder, been another trial upon this earth where the judges started by hunting for liars, that they might condemn the accused? Thus, it was here; and in the presence of it, Jesus held His peace. Judgment being utterly divorced from righteousness, He met them with a dignity that was Divine, and He only spoke to affirm His Christhood, His Sonship, and to affirm His coming glory as the Son of Man.[52]

Luke

Moreover, the Defendant was not permitted any time to prepare His case. This was a sham trial from start to finish, and one that violated Sanhedrin protocol on several points.

Caiaphas, being the high priest, put Christ under oath to implore Him to answer whether He was the Christ, the Son of God (Matt. 26:63)! Under the Mosaic Law, the Lord Jesus would bear guilt if He did not answer the high priest who put Him under oath (Lev. 5:1). The Lord's response affirmed that He was the Christ, the Son of God. Speaking to Caiaphas who had put Him under oath (the first "you" in verse 64 is singular), the Lord said he would not see Him again. However, all Israel (the second and the third "you" are plural) would see Him when He returned from heaven in power and glory to establish His kingdom (Matt. 26:64). The Lord was claiming Daniel's prophecy for Himself (Dan. 7:13); He was "the Son of Man" returning from heaven in glory and the high priest understood the connection (Dan. 7:13).

Caiaphas responded by tearing his priestly apparel, which was forbidden, for such was considered holy before the Lord (Matt. 26:65; Lev. 10:6, 21:10). Caiaphas declared that the Lord Jesus spoke blasphemy and that there was no need of further witnesses, for they had heard the offense themselves. His constituents agreed saying, *"He is deserving of death"* (Matt. 26:66). In a fit of rage, they spit in Christ's face and struck Him with their fists.

As the Lord was being beaten, they mocked His testimony by saying, *"Prophesy! Who is the one who struck You?"* (vv. 63-64). Considering that He could have quickly ended all their lives, the Lord demonstrated incredible restraint in not swiftly judging His oppressors, who were also uttering many blasphemous insults (v. 65).

At first light, the Lord was brought before the full Sanhedrin to determine how He should be put to death (v. 66). They questioned Him again concerning His identity, *"If you are the Christ, tell us"* (v. 67). But the Lord knew that they would not believe Him, if He told them the truth, nor would they let Him go, no matter how He answered, so He merely confirmed that soon He would be sitting on the right hand of the power of God (vv. 68-69). Only God can sit on His throne, so they candidly asked Him, *"Are You the Son of God?"* and the Lord Jesus affirmed that He was (v. 70). The Sanhedrin viewed Jesus' statement as blasphemy and thus He deserved to be put to death; no more witnesses were needed; the trial was over and the verdict sealed (v. 71).

Luke Chapter 23

Christ's First Civil Trial: Before Pilate (vv. 1-7)

A large gathering from the Sanhedrin then brought Jesus to the Roman Governor of Judea, Pilate, to be examined (v. 1). It did not take the Sanhedrin long to decide Jesus' fate, for when He arrived at the Praetorium, it was still early morning (John 18:28). The chief priests and elders informed Pilate that Jesus was subverting the nation by denying that the Jews should pay Caesar tribute and by claiming Himself to be King instead of Caesar (v. 2). Pontius Pilate then interrogated the Lord to discern if these charges of sedition were legitimate.

Pontius Pilate asked Jesus if He was *"the King of the Jews"* (v. 3). The Lord affirmed that what he had asked was correct. John records a lengthier dialogue between Pilate and the Lord Jesus. John tells us that Pilate was also told by Jesus Christ that though He was a king, His kingdom was not of this world; if it were, His servants would have fought for Him, and the Jews would not have arrested Him (John 18:36).

While before Pilate, the chief priests and Jewish elders accused Jesus of many things, but Christ did not defend Himself, even when Pilate extended an opportunity for Him to do so (Mark 15:3-5). Pilate marveled greatly at the Lord Jesus' restraint, and Luke tells us that he told the Jewish leaders, *"I find no fault in this Man"* (v. 4). This may have been the first time that Pilate had an accused offender at his judgment seat who made no effort to defend himself.

Mark does not refer to Christ's second civil trial before Herod, but Matthew and Luke do. According to Luke, after Pilate proclaimed Christ's innocence, the Jewish elders became fiercer in their accusations of Jesus, saying that He was a Galilean and had incited trouble from Galilee to Judea (v. 5). After learning that Jesus was from Galilee, Pilate sent Jesus to Herod to be examined (v. 6). Galilee was Herod's jurisdiction as a tetrarch, and he was in Jerusalem at that time for the feast (v. 7). This would be Christ's second civil trial.

Christ's Second Civil Trial: Before Herod (vv. 8-12)

Herod was exceedingly glad to have the opportunity to question Jesus of Nazareth, about whom he had heard so much. The tetrarch was hoping that Jesus might perform a miracle for him (v. 8). Although Herod asked Jesus many questions, the Lord answered him nothing (v. 9). However, the chief priests and scribes were not silent before Herod; rather they continued to vehemently accuse the Lord of much wrongdoing (v. 10). After Herod's soldiers had mocked and abused the Lord Jesus, Herod sent Him back to Pilate (v. 11). Previously, there had been animosity between Pilate and Herod, but Pilate's gesture of sending Christ to Herod forged a friendship between the two leaders (v. 12).

Christ's Third Civil Trial: Before Pilate Again (vv. 13-25)

Pilate, a Roman who had no desire to be involved with Jewish affairs, was hoping that Herod would deal with the Jewish leaders and their religious accusations against Jesus. Pilate called the priests and rulers before him and stated that he had found no evidence that Jesus of Nazareth was misleading the people against Rome. According to Roman Law, Pilate found Jesus to be innocent of their charges against Him (v. 14). He had done nothing worthy of death, and he and Herod agreed on the matter (v. 15).

To try to appease the Jewish leaders and perhaps spare Jesus from death, Pilate stated that he would *"chastise Him and release Him"* (v. 16). The Greek verb *paideuo* is rendered "chastise" in this verse. While addressing the importance of raising children for the Lord, Paul uses the noun form of this Greek word, *paideia*, which means "to train by disciplinary punishment" (Eph. 6:4). *Nurture* (KJV) or *training* (NKJV) comprises a broad range of educational methods, which also includes the provision "to train by pain." It is this idea that Pilate is invoking. Perhaps Pilate thought that if Christ were severely scourged, the hostile crowd might then show Him sympathy and His life would be spared. But Pilate would soon learn that the Jewish crowd had no sympathy for Jesus Christ; they wanted Him dead, not just whipped and released.

There were likely 150,000 to 300,000 people in Jerusalem for the Passover Feast. The potential for a riot was high and Pilate wanted to avoid that scenario, lest he be called to Rome and questioned by Caesar for the uprising. To encourage a peaceful situation, it was Pilate's custom to pardon a Jewish prisoner of the people's choosing during the feast (v.

17). As an attempt to release Jesus, Pilate offered the Jewish assembly a choice of whom he would pardon. They could choose to free Jesus of Nazareth or a notorious prisoner, Barabbas, who had been found guilty of inciting rebellion in Jerusalem and of murder (v. 19; Matt. 27:16-17).

The Roman governor chose to contrast the worst convicted criminal available to him with an accused Man that, in his judgment, was completely innocent, to expose the envy of the Jewish leaders in indicting Jesus (Matt. 27:18). However, Pilate was unable to persuade the Jews to turn from their bloodthirsty intentions. They wanted Barabbas released and Christ crucified (vv. 18, 20-21). Pilate, for a third time, asserted that Jesus had done nothing worthy of death, but the crowd, as prompted by their religious leaders, cried out the more, *"Crucify, crucify Him!"* (vv. 21, 23).

Fearing a riot, Pilate washed his hands in a basin and proclaimed, *"I am innocent of the blood of this just Person. You see to it"* (Matt. 27:24). The Jewish crowd answered, *"His blood be on us and on our children"* (Matt. 27:25). In effect, they had put themselves under a blood curse for condemning a righteous man to death (Acts 2:23, 3:14-15, 5:28). The Jewish nation had no idea the centuries of pain and sorrow that would result from this proclamation. But the consequences of cutting off their Messiah were foretold by the prophet Daniel long ago: War and desolations would be determined against them until the end of the Tribulation Period, when, by grace, the blood of expiation will erase the blood of the curse (Dan. 9:24-27). The Jews crucified God's incarnate Son and their Messiah.

Pilate then released the notable murderer Barabbas, while Christ was to be scourged and then crucified (vv. 24-25). The Roman whip did much more than put stripes on the condemned; it was designed to rip the flesh wide open. A Roman flogging resulted in deep lacerations which exposed muscles and caused excessive bleeding. Church historian Eusebius of Caesarea recounts the horror of a Roman scourging: "For they say that the bystanders were struck with amazement when they saw them lacerated with scourges even to the innermost veins and arteries, so that the hidden inward parts of the body, both their bowels and their members, were exposed to view."[53] The term "half-dead" was commonly associated with a Roman scourging, as many who endured its wrath died afterwards. Yet, the idea of scourging was to stop the beating before death resulted to ensure that the victim was still able to undergo the humiliation of a public crucifixion.

In the previous hours, the Lord Jesus had been abused by the servants of the chief priests and by Herod's men. He had already received many blows from human fists. After being scourged, Matthew informs us that the Lord was taken into the Roman Praetorium, and an entire garrison of soldiers (typically comprised of 200 to 300 men) gathered to have sport with Him (Matt. 27:27-28). They stripped Him of His clothes and put a scarlet robe or cloak on Him, which likely being of a short nature, revealed His nakedness. Scarlet and purple were colors of royalty. They also twisted a crown of thorns and placed it on His head and put a hollow reed in his right hand. Thorns resulted after God cursed the ground (i.e., the earth; Rom. 8:20-22) because of Adam's sin (Gen. 3:17-18). Now the Creator was bearing on His brow the very curse He levied on humanity in Eden.

Being adorned with a mock robe, crown, and scepter, the Roman soldiers then bowed the knee to Jesus in mock worship, *"Hail, king of the Jews!"* (Matt. 27:29). The Lord had been rejected and abused by the Jewish authorities; now the Gentiles also were guilty of disdaining the Savior. They spat on Him and took the reed out of His hand and beat the crown of thorns into His brow with it (Matt. 27:30). Afterwards, the soldiers put His own clothes on the Lord and led Him away to be crucified (Matt. 27:31).

Verse 25 states that Pilate *"delivered Jesus to their will."* The Greek verb rendered "delivered" is in the imperfect tense, meaning that the Jewish nation would only have their evil way with Christ for a short duration; then Christ would bring about His sovereign way with them!

On the Way to Calvary (vv. 26-31)

In the Lord's physically weakened state, He was not able to bear his own cross (bar or beam) on His shoulder. Such a beam typically weighed between 75 and 125 pounds. The Romans compelled Simon from Cyrene (a city in northern Africa with a significant Jewish population) to bear Christ's cross to the place of public execution (v. 26). A great multitude, including many lamenting women, followed the grotesque procession to Golgotha (v. 27).

Observing the weeping women following Him, the Lord Jesus told them not to weep for Him, but rather for themselves and their children (v. 28). The Jewish nation had rejected God's Son and their Messiah and maliciously consented to His death; therefore, God's judgment upon

Israel would be horrendous and prolonged (vv. 29-30). There was a coming day when barrenness and death would be more advantageous than enduring God's judicial wrath, especially during the Tribulation Period. If the Jewish people could be this rebellious and cruel "in the green wood" (with their Messiah present), how outrageous would they become in the dry season (without Him; v. 31).

Jesus Christ Is Crucified (vv. 32-43)

The Lord Jesus, with two others (who were criminals), was led to *Calvary* to be publicly executed (v. 32). Before the nails were driven through the Lord's wrists to the cross bar, He was offered wine mingled with gall (a narcotic to numb the senses to reduce pain), but after tasting the mixture, He would not drink it, to fulfill the Messianic prophecy of Psalm 69:21 (v. 36; Matt. 26:34).

The Roman soldiers then stripped the Lord of His clothes and crucified Him. They cast lots for His outer garment that was woven without seam and tore his inner garment into four pieces, so that each soldier would receive a portion (v. 34; Matt. 27:35). After the soldiers had crucified two condemned men on either side of the Lord, they placed a placard over the Lord's head that read, *"This is the King of the Jews,"* and then they sat down to watch over the pitiful sight (vv. 33, 38; Matt. 26:36-38). Both Luke and John document that the superscription hanging above the Lord's head was written in Greek, Latin, and Hebrew. As Luke is an appeal to humanity and John is writing to the whole world, it makes sense that the use of all three languages was recorded by these two evangelists.

The place of execution was called *Golgotha*, the "Place of the Skull" (Matt. 27:33). John Heading describes the meaning of Golgotha (or its Roman equivalent "Calvary") and what it symbolized:

> Golgotha and the corresponding Roman name Calvary (Luke 23:33) both mean "skull" – hence Matthew's interpretation "a place of a skull." Various reasons have been suggested why the place had this name – for example, because the shape of the place resembled a skull. Typically, however, the name speaks of the apex of human wisdom, for those who crucified the Lord of glory possessed this wisdom, the opposite to the wisdom of God (1 Cor. 2:6–8). It speaks of the unsanctified intelligence of men who still reject Christ in unbelief.[54]

Luke

Luke records three statements that Christ uttered from the cross, but the first one was uttered several times, *"Father, forgive them, for they do not know what they do"* (v. 34). As the people looked on, the rulers *sneered*, the soldiers *mocked*, one of the condemned thieves *blasphemed*, and the crowd *rebuked* Jesus. All four Greek verbs translated "sneered," "mocked," "blasphemed," and "rebuked" are in the imperfect tense, meaning that these activities continued for a duration of time and then ceased. The Greek verb *aphiemi* rendered "forgive" in verse 34 means to "release and let it be" (see Matt. 27:49). This verb is also in the imperfect tense, which means Christ repeatedly pleaded with His Father for a certain timeframe not to take action against the sneering rulers, the mocking soldiers, the blasphemous criminal, and the rebuking crowd (vv. 35-40).

Although these were profane crimes, the Lord was abdicating His lawful claim for justice to achieve a greater good: "Father, do not judge this now – let it be." As the insults came up to Him while suffering on our behalf, the Savior relinquished the offenses and asked His Father to take no immediate action to right the wrongs. The Lord shows us that there are times to defer from righteous anger to accomplish a greater good: *"The discretion of a man makes him slow to anger, and his glory is to overlook a transgression"* (Prov. 19:11).

Those passing by blasphemed Him, the chief priests mocked Him, and even both robbers initially reviled Him (Matt. 27:39-44). His oppressors quoted back to the Lord Jesus His own words to cast doubt on their validity, given His situation. Let us see you build the temple in three days now (Matt. 27:40). If you are the Son of God and the King of Israel, prove it by saving yourself (v. 37)! If God was really your Father, He would deliver you (Matt. 27:43). *"If you are the Christ, save Yourself and us"* (v. 39).

Although both condemned criminals reviled the Lord in the beginning, one thief, after observing Christ's merciful behavior while suffering, changed his mind about Jesus. No normal man offers intercession to God for those who are abusing him. As a result, the repentant thief began to rebuke the other condemned man, saying that they were getting what they deserved for their crimes, but that Jesus had done nothing wrong (vv. 40-41).

Additionally, the repentant thief asked the Lord to remember him when He came into His kingdom (v. 42). The Lord responded, *"Assuredly, I say to you, today you will be with Me in Paradise"* (v. 43).

The verbs rendered "answering" (v. 40) and "said" (v. 42) are in the imperfect tense meaning that the repentant thief continued rebuking the other thief for a while and repeatedly asking the Lord to remember Him until the Lord responded to his request. The verb translated "said" in verse 43 is in the aorist tense, meaning that the Lord only said it once, which is all that He needed to do to validate the surety of His promise.

Only Luke describes the Lord's conversations with the dying thief during the crucifixion account and then the thief's conversion prior to the Lord's death. The thief, quite familiar with suffering for wrongdoing, saw in the Lord's sufferings a purity and righteousness that both convicted him of his sinful state and caused him to look to the Savior for salvation. This man accepted his just punishment, while also acknowledging that though Jesus was about to die, He would also be coming into His kingdom. The only way that this could occur is if Christ was raised from the dead. This was extraordinary faith based on only what the thief had heard and witnessed over a few hours.

The Hebrew word translated "Sheol," but sometimes rendered "grave" in the Old Testament, is the general equivalent of the Greek *Hades*, used in the New Testament. The Lord Jesus taught that this spiritual domain houses disembodied spirits in one of two compartments (16:19-31). Abraham's Bosom is where faithful souls consciously await resurrection unto life through Christ, and the second is a place of torment where the wicked reside until their resurrection unto final judgment in the Lake of Fire. It is the author's opinion that Christ and the repentant thief went to Abraham's bosom after dying and that this realm of disembodied spirits was emptied after Christ's resurrection and joined Him in heaven (Matt. 27:52-53). Apparently, at least some of these saints experienced the First Resurrection after Christ's own glorification (Rev. 20:6). In the Church Age, the souls of departed saints join Christ in heaven immediately after death (2 Cor. 5:8).

Victory in Death (vv. 44-49)

Mark informs us that Christ was crucified at the third hour (9 a.m.; Mark 15:25). Matthew does not record any of the Lord's statements or intercession during His first three hours on the cross. Both Matthew and Luke state that at the sixth hour (noon in Roman time) until the ninth hour (3 p.m.) there was an intense darkness "over all the earth" (v. 44). Luke says that the sun "was darkened" (v. 45). The Greek verb is in the passive voice meaning that the sun did not darken itself, but God acted on the Sun to diminish its light or to block its light from reaching the earth. The judgment of human sin was a private matter between the Son and the Father; nothing would be permitted to intrude into the work of eternal propitiation.

After suffering for three hours in darkness, the Lord cried out with a loud voice, saying, *"Eli, Eli, lama, sabachthani?"* meaning, *"My God, My God, why have You forsaken Me?"* (Matt. 27:46). This quotation of Psalm 22:1 was declared just prior to His death at 3:00 p.m. The Lord affirmed that while He was being our Sin-bearer, fellowship with His Father was severed. The Lord also wanted to ensure that Psalm 22 would be associated with His redemptive work. The English expression "loud voice" is derived from the Greek *megas phone*. A megaphone effectively amplifies sound for all to hear. While the Lord Jesus was hanging from a cross, He was fully aware and in complete control of His situation. He astutely fulfilled every Old Testament prophecy so there would be no question that He was Israel's promised Messiah.

After finishing the required suffering for all human sin (Heb. 2:9; 1 Jn. 2:2), the Lord Jesus cried out again with a loud voice twice before expiring. "Loud voice" in both statements is again derived from the Greek phrase *megas phone*. Matthew and John refer to the first expression (Matt. 27:50), but only John tells us what the Lord said, before commending His spirit into His Father's care: *"It is finished!"* (John 19:30). John uses the perfect tense verb *teleo* to declare that what Christ had just accomplished at Calvary could never be undone – it was an eternal propitiatory and redemptive work. Afterwards, there would never be another offering for the offense or damages of human sin (Heb. 9:28, 10:12-14). Luke records the second, and final statement by Christ from the cross, *"Father, into Your hands I commit My spirit"* (v. 46). After this statement, Christ "breathed His last" – at least for three days!

When the centurion who was overseeing Christ's crucifixion saw all that had happened, he and those with him feared greatly, saying, *"Certainly this was a righteous Man"* (v. 47) and *"Truly this was the Son of God"* (Matt. 27:54)! The three hours of intense darkness, the Savior uttering gracious intercession for His oppressors, and the great earthquake convinced them that Christ was who He proclaimed Himself to be (Matt. 27:51). The evil deed was done and all they could do was beat their breasts and return to their homes (v. 48).

Luke then notes that many of the women who had served Christ during His three-plus-year ministry were watching from afar (v. 49). Among these were Mary Magdalene, Mary the mother of James the less, and Salome, the mother of James and John (Matt. 27:56; Mark 15:40).

The Body of Christ Is Buried (vv. 50-56)

A rich man named Joseph, a secret disciple of Christ from Arimathea, went to Pilate and requested the body of Jesus (v. 52). He was a just man, a member of the Sanhedrin, but had not consented to the Lord's death (vv. 50-51). Pilate was surprised that Jesus had already expired and asked the centurion in charge of His execution to confirm the matter (Mark 15:44). Learning that the claim was true, Pilate granted Joseph's request (Matt. 27:58).

There was not much time to bury the body as the Sabbath was at hand (v. 54). As the Lord's death was at 3:00 p.m. and the dialogue between Pilate, Joseph, and the centurion occurred afterwards, there was likely less than 90 minutes to take the body off the cross, transport it to the tomb, wrap it in linen, and seal it in the tomb (v. 53). Nicodemus, another secret disciple of Christ, joined Joseph in the task. He brought a hundred pounds of myrrh and aloes to the tomb (John 19:39).

Joseph and Nicodemus quickly wrapped Jesus' body with the spices in strips of clean linen (John 19:40). Then both men placed the Lord's body in Joseph's own tomb hewn out of rock (John 19:42). This new tomb was in a garden near the crucifixion site (John 19:41). Luke informs us that *"no one had ever lain before"* in this tomb (vv. 55), which directly fulfilled Isaiah's prophecy concerning the burial place of the Jewish Messiah (Isa. 53:9).

After the body was placed in the tomb, the men sealed it with a large rolling stone (Matt. 27:60). Women from Galilee who had been serving and traveling with Jesus and His disciples observed the location where Christ was buried. Afterwards they returned to their homes to prepare spices and fragrant oils to properly bury Jesus' body after the Sabbath day had passed. The aforementioned women who had observed where Christ's body had been placed planned to return to the tomb Sunday morning with others to properly prepare the Lord's body for burial.

Luke Chapter 24

Resurrection Morning Activities (vv. 1-12)
Now that the Sabbath had passed, various women were going to the tomb with spices and oils at the earliest possible moment to properly prepare the Lord's body for burial (v. 1). How these women were going to get past the Roman guard, open a tomb that had been officially sealed, and move the large rolling stone to gain access to the tomb is unknown; regardless, they came to show their love and respect for the Savior.

Matthew states that the Marys were en route to the tomb at the starting of dawn. Mark's account has three women (Salome is included with the Marys) arriving at the tomb near sunrise (Mark 16:1). John states that Mary Magdalene came to the tomb when it was yet dark (John 20:1). Luke mentions at least five women that came early to the tomb that morning (v. 10). Putting the accounts together, we have various women coming from various locations and arriving at the tomb early Sunday morning at various times. Some arrived while it was still dark, while others arrived at sunrise.

We then learn what happened just prior to the women arriving at Christ's tomb; an angel descended from heaven and rolled away the stone that sealed the tomb and then sat on it (Matt. 28:2). This feat was accompanied by, but not caused by, an earthquake. A great earthquake had occurred at Christ's death and now another announced His resurrection. The countenance of the angel was like lightning and his clothing as white as snow (Matt. 28:3). The guards were terrified at the angel's presence and fell to the ground like dead men (Matt. 28:4).

When the women arrived at the tomb, they found that the stone had already been rolled away from the entrance and that the body of Christ was missing (vv. 2-3). As the women came forward to peer into the tomb, they saw two angels, which frightened them and caused them to bow down to the earth (vv. 4-5). Matthew and Mark describe one angel speaking to the women, while Luke and John state that two angels were in the tomb. We may conclude that, indeed, there were two angels at the tomb, but only one served as the primary spokesman, though Luke indicates that both angels spoke to the women.

The angels asked the women, *"Why do you seek the living among the dead? He is not here, but is risen!"* (v. 6). Then they reminded them that while Jesus spoke to them in Galilee, He had foretold how He would suffer at the hands of sinners, be crucified, and then rise from the grave on the third day (v. 7). The women then remembered what Christ had previously said (v. 8).

The women (five are listed in verse 10) then departed the tomb and told all that had happened to "the eleven" (the twelve disciples less Judas) and others that were also with them (v. 9). But the disciples were under the influence of things seen instead of anticipating in faith the fulfillment of Christ's words. Consequently, they did not believe the testimony of the women, which they consider to be a concocted story by a group of distraught women (v. 11).

After noticing that the rolling stone had been removed from the tomb's entrance, John informs us that Mary ran to tell Peter and John that the Lord's body was not in the tomb. She said, *"We do not know where they have laid Him"* (John 20:2). The "we" indicates that there were likely other women who had arrived at the tomb, before Mary had departed to inform the disciples of the news.

After hearing Mary's observation, Peter and John ran to the tomb, but John arrived ahead of Peter to find that indeed the stone had been rolled away from the entrance and no longer contained a corpse (John 20:3-4). Luke only records that Peter ran to the tomb. After Peter arrived, He went directly into the tomb and discovered that the head wrap had been folded and was lying in a different location than the linens used to wrap the Lord's body (John 20:6-7). Peter marveled at the sight with great amazement (v. 12).

Christ Appears to Disciples on Emmaus Road (vv. 13-32)

It is important to realize that each Gospel writer presents Christ from a different perspective. If all the writers gave the same story, same order, same details, we would immediately become suspicious that the records were the copies of a single account. But because some events are recorded in some Gospels and not others, we have proof of multiple accounts and not one story repeated. For example, only Matthew records Christ's first appearance to the women, while only Luke records the

Luke

events transpiring on the Emmaus Road. Luke does not record Mary Magdalene's visit to the tomb. Only John and Luke record Christ's appearance in the upper room on resurrection day. Given all the information recorded in the Gospels, there is a reasonable construction of all that took place on resurrection morning without contradiction.

New Testament Scripture confirms at least ten separate post-resurrection appearances of Christ prior to His ascension. Five of these incidents occurred on the day of Christ's resurrection. None of the Gospel writers mentions all of these appearances (see John 20 comments for a listing of these appearances). In summary, the Lord Jesus remained on earth to encourage and instruct His disciples for forty days after His resurrection, then He ascended back to Heaven (Acts 1).

Two of the Lord's disciples (but not of the eleven) were traveling to the town of Emmaus, which was located seven miles northwest of Jerusalem (v. 13). It was Sunday, the day after the Sabbath. They were talking together about all that had transpired in recent days when the Lord joined their company (vv. 14-15). The two disciples did not recognize the Lord, for *"their eyes were restrained so that they did not know Him"* (v. 16). The Lord inquired about what they were discussing and why they looked forlorn (v. 17). One of them, Cleopas, voiced his surprise that their new companion was not informed about how the priests and rulers had crucified Jesus of Nazareth (v. 18). This implied that the entire nation was familiar with Christ's ministry.

The Lord did not affirm Cleopas's conclusion, but simply asked, *"What things?"* (v. 19). As they walked along together, both men explained about *"Jesus of Nazareth, who was a Prophet mighty in deed and word before God and the people"* (vv. 19-20). The two dismayed travelers had believed that Jesus was a Prophet of God and perhaps the Messiah, but now doubts filled their minds (v. 21). Furthermore, that very morning (the third day after Jesus' death) certain women visited His tomb and found it empty (v. 22). The women also saw angels who affirmed that Jesus was alive (v. 23). Some of the Lord's disciples then went to the tomb to investigate this report and found the tomb empty, just as the women had said (v. 24)!

The Lord chided them for not believing what the Old Testament had revealed about Messiah's coming and how He must first suffer before entering into His glory (vv. 25-26). Beginning with Moses (speaking of the Pentateuch) and ending with the prophetic books of the Old Testament, the Lord supplied His walking companions a panoramic view of what Christ would accomplish for Israel and when. No doubt this Old Testament Survey included aspects of both His advents to the earth: *"He expounded to them in all the Scriptures the things concerning Himself"* (v. 27). Good pulpit preaching occurs when Scripture is accurately expounded to exalt Christ, for He is the central message of the Bible.

As they drew near to Emmaus, the Lord made as if He would walk on, but His walking companions invited Him to stay with them for the night, as the day was far spent (v. 28). The Lord Jesus is a perfect Gentleman; He does not force Himself on anyone, but He is also quite happy to spend time with those who desire to know Him further, so the Lord accepted the invitation (v. 29). At the evening meal, the Lord took bread, blessed it, and then broke it and gave to His disciples (v. 30). It was at this moment that their eyes were opened, and they knew who was in their midst – the Lord Jesus and He was alive (v. 31)! It seems likely that when the Lord held the bread up to break it and then passed it to His companions, they saw the fresh wounds in His wrists. The divine intervention that had kept them from recognizing Jesus Christ was taken away at that moment and the Lord instantly vanished from their presence (v. 31).

The disciples told each other how their hearts burned within them as the Lord had expounded the Scriptures to them as they journeyed (v. 32). What these men experienced is what believers can enjoy today also: the more we receive God's Word, the more fellowship with Christ we will desire! It is impossible to breathe the atmosphere of the risen Savior and remain in an isolated or independent condition – these men had to return to Jerusalem to tell Christ's disciples – Israel's Messiah is alive!

Christ Appears to His Disciples in Jerusalem (vv. 33-43)

The two disciples who had walked with the Lord on the road to Emmaus immediately returned to Jerusalem with the good tidings that Jesus Christ was alive (v. 33). They found the eleven, who were secretly sequestered behind locked doors for fear of the Jews and informed them of all that had happened on the road to Emmaus, and how they found out that their companion was the Lord Jesus Christ "in the breaking of the bread" (v. 35; John 20:19). The eleven and others informed the men from Emmaus that the Lord had also appeared to Simon Peter (v. 34). All were rejoicing and saying to each other, *"The Lord is risen indeed."*

At that moment, Jesus appeared in their midst and said to them, *"Peace to you"* (v. 36). The disciples were terrified and supposed that they were only seeing Jesus' spirit (v. 37). Not only could He pass through solid objects (like closed doors and walls) prior to His appearance, but He also knew right where the disciples were. The Lord told them not to be troubled, nor to be doubting, but to feel Him, for a spirit does not have flesh and bones (vv. 38-39). Notice that the Lord did not say that He was flesh and blood; His blood had been shed at Calvary – His risen body did not need blood flow to maintain it.

After examining the Lord's hands and His side, and watching Him eat a piece of broiled fish and some honeycomb, the disciples were completely convinced that the One before them was He that had been crucified three days earlier (vv. 40-43). This was one of five separate eye-witness accounts on the very day He was raised from the dead.

The Lord Jesus prophesied His own resurrection (John 2:19-21; Acts 2:26-27) and now showed His disciples His resurrected body. By showing the nail prints in His body to the disciples, the Lord Jesus demonstrated that the body He now had was the same body which had been nailed to a cross.

While it is true that the Lord kept some of His disciples from immediately recognizing Him after His resurrection (this was for teaching purposes), most of them recognized Him immediately. This meant that the Lord's glorified body was much like His pre-resurrection body in appearance, though it was flesh and bone without blood. His resurrected body could taste food, could be touched, and could be seen and heard; it also could instantly vanish and reappear elsewhere. So, while His body exhibited some properties of natural law, it also had supernatural qualities. Same body, but different.

The Lord's body was flesh and bone. His glorified body did not require natural metabolic operations to sustain it as our bodies do. In fact, Paul says *"that flesh and blood cannot inherit the kingdom of God"* (1 Cor. 15:50). Obviously, we too need resurrected bodies because our present ones are not fit for heaven.

The Commissioning of the Disciples (vv. 44-48)

Throughout Old Testament Scripture, Jehovah provided His covenant people with a detailed prophetic portrait of their coming Messiah. God wanted His covenant people to recognize the true Messiah when He appeared to them. The Lord Jesus not only confirmed that the Law and prophets foretold of Himself, but that the book of Psalms prophetically spoke of Him as well (v. 44). The difficulty of evaluating potentially messianic psalms is distinguishing the personal and spiritual experiences of the writer from those which are a prophetic reference to Christ. The latter is affirmed by New Testament quotations of the psalm being prophetically fulfilled. For instance, both Peter and Paul quoted Psalm 16, which relates to the resurrection of the Jewish Messiah, and affirmed that the Lord Jesus Christ had fulfilled that prophecy (Acts 2:25-28, 13:35).

Luke informs us that Christ opened the understanding of the disciples to comprehend Scripture, especially how God's Word related to Him (v. 45). John tells us that the Lord breathed on His disciples after His resurrection and that they received the Holy Spirit (John 20:22). This ministry of the Holy Spirit seems to have equipped the disciples with the understanding of Scripture for their apostolic ministry of proclaiming the gospel message.

Old Testament passages such as Isaiah 53 and Psalm 22 clearly proclaimed that Christ must suffer, be put to death, and be raised from the grave. Shadows and types of Christ abound in the Old Testament; even the Lord used Jonah's three days in the belly of a large fish before he preached God's message to warn Nineveh of judgment as a picture of His three days in the grave before rising from the dead to commission His disciples to preach the gospel throughout the world (v. 46).

The apostles were to warn worldlings that a holy God must judge sin, and only through Christ could they receive repentance and the remission of sin (v. 47). They were now His witnesses to the world (v. 48). Witnesses are to testify of what they know to be true wherever they are. The Lord specifically instructed His apostles to begin their evangelical ministry in Jerusalem, then begin spreading out to Judea and Samaria, and then to the end of the earth (v. 47; Acts 1:8).

Christ's Ascension (vv. 49-53)

The Lord reminded His disciples what He had told them in the upper room the night before His crucifixion: He would pray to the Father to send the Comforter, the Spirit of Truth, to them after He departed (John 14:16-18). They were to tarry in Jerusalem until the Holy Spirit came upon them and they received "power from on high" (v. 49). We learn from the book of Acts that this event occurred ten days later at the Feast of Pentecost to fulfill the typological meaning of that feast – that is, the

Luke

creation of the wave wheat loaves (the Church) from the sourdough lump derived from the wave barley sheaf (Christ) at Passover fifty days earlier.

The barley wave sheaf (represented Christ) was presented before the God at Calvary as a representative of the harvest of souls to follow. But at Pentecost, believers in Christ were united with Him (as pictured in the wave wheat loaves) to present acceptable spiritual and living sacrifices to God through Him. Although there was still leaven present in these loaves, the invisible heat of the oven nullified its corrupting effect. This pictures the power of the Holy Spirit in the life of believers. Only being in Christ and through the power of the Holy Spirit can we please God!

The Lord then led His disciples to the southeastern slopes of Mount Olivet, near Bethany (v. 50). Luke began his account with people praying at the temple, for they were longing for Messiah's coming. He closes his record with Messiah praying for His people, who would be His newly created temple – the Church.

The Lord lifted His hands to bless His disciples before returning to heaven, thereby identifying with them, and showing His divine care of them. In Luke's Gospel, the hands of the Lord are repeatedly touching and blessing those in need. Luke often refers to the Lord's prayer-life, which is in keeping with his presentation of Christ's humanity. Especially in Luke's Gospel, the Lord shows us the importance of prayer from the beginning to the end of our ambassadorship for Christ.

Each Gospel writer concludes his account in a unique manner to climax his theme of Christ's glory. Matthew presents Christ in His kingdom on earth, while Mark records the ascension of Christ, then notes that He is still working with His disciples. Luke concludes his Gospel in no less a remarkable manner: *"He was parted from them and **carried up into heaven"*** (v. 51). The Son of Man did not ascend back to heaven, but was "carried up" to heaven. The choice of words conveys a connotation of human frailty and the consequential necessity of God's helping hand.

The disciples looked on in amazement and worshiped Him. After the Lord's ascension, they returned to Jerusalem with great joy and continued praising and blessing God in the temple (vv. 52-53). Besides obeying what the Lord said to do (i.e., wait in Jerusalem until the Holy Spirit came upon them), the apostles teach us by their example that proper worship of Christ must precede any service for Him. Only work resulting from genuine worship of Christ will have eternal value.

Throughout his Gospel, Luke focuses his audience's attention to human events surrounding Christ's life, the humanity of the Lord Jesus,

The Man and Your God

and the human appeal of His ministry. Luke presents a touchable Savior who is more than willing to demonstrate the love of God by touching and blessing all that will come to Him.

Man of Sorrows

Man of sorrows, what a name
for the Son of God, who came
ruined sinners to reclaim:
Hallelujah, what a Savior!

Bearing shame and scoffing rude,
in my place condemned He stood,
sealed my pardon with His blood:
Hallelujah, what a Savior!

Guilty, helpless, lost were we;
blameless Lamb of God was He,
sacrificed to set us free:
Hallelujah, what a Savior!

He was lifted up to die;
"It is finished" was His cry;
now in heaven exalted high:
Hallelujah, what a Savior!

When He comes, our glorious King,
all His ransomed home to bring,
then anew this song we'll sing:
Hallelujah, what a Savior!

– P. P. Bliss

John

John

Introduction

Each Gospel writer conveys a unique perspective of the Lord Jesus Christ to a different audience to enhance our appreciation of our Savior. Matthew affirms Christ's royal authority, Mark presents Christ as the lowly Servant of God, Luke highlights Christ's sinless humanity, and John uphold the Savior's deity. Why was John entrusted with the privilege of presenting Christ as the Son of God incarnate?

John seems to answer this quandary in John 14:21: *"He who has My commandments and keeps them, it is he who loves Me. And he who loves Me will be loved by My Father, and **I will love him and manifest Myself to him**."* Five times the night before the Lord was crucified, He told His disciples of the intimate tie between their love for Him and practical obedience: *"If you love Me, keep My commandments"* (14:15). He would demonstrate this truth Himself the next day: *"But that the world may know that I love the Father, and as the Father gave Me commandment, so I do. Arise, let us go from here"* (14:31). There was no question of the love of the Father for the Son, or of the Son for the Father, but the Son was going to show the world how much He loved the Father through obedience.

John 14:21 contains a promise for all those who will likewise demonstrate love for God by simply obeying His Word: The Lord said He would *"manifest [Himself] to him."* John was the beloved disciple and, apparently, the least inhibited in expressing his love for the Lord – it was to him, the disciple who loved much, that a fuller manifestation of Christ was granted. It was John, and only John, who was an eyewitness to the Apocalypse, *"the Revelation of Jesus Christ"* (Rev. 1:1). The divine disclosure of Christ's glory to John is a direct testimony of the immensity of John's love for the Lord Jesus. Those who have been forgiven much love Christ more, those who love much obey Christ more, and those who obey Christ are enabled to comprehend Him more. Thus, our highest aspiration each day should be to be drawn more deeply into the secret recesses of infinite love through obedience.

During Christ's ministry on earth, the seventy disciples were empowered and sent forth to preach (Luke 10). Twelve disciples received specialized ministry. Three (Peter, James, and John) were permitted to see a maiden's resurrection, to witness the Lord's transfiguration, and invited to pray with the Lord at Gethsemane. But then there was the one: John, the beloved disciple, who laid his head on the Lord's breast just hours before His death. Others could have done the same, but only John was willing to express his affection for the Lord. Each of us is as near to the Lord Jesus as we desire to be!

The Author

As in *Matthew*, *Mark*, and *Luke*, the writer of *John* does not identify himself within his literary work. However, the writer clearly was a Jew living in Israel, was an eyewitness to what he writes, was an apostle sent by Christ and had intimate knowledge of things privy to the twelve disciples or only to Peter, James, and John (19:35). The author was with Christ from the beginning of His ministry on earth and witnessed His resurrection (1:14, 21:24). The writer also identifies most of the twelve disciples: Andrew, Simon Peter, Philip, Nathanael, Thomas, Judas (not Iscariot), the sons of Zebedee (i.e., James and John), Judas, son of Simon Iscariot (6:71, 14:22, 20:24, 21:2). Rather than referring to himself by name, he identifies himself, with his brother James, as "sons of Zebedee." The evidence supplied in the final verses of John (21:20-24) confirm that the writer was indeed John, the brother of James, "the beloved disciple." He was the one sitting next to the Lord at the Last Supper, and the one to whom Peter beckoned to ask the Lord about who would betray Him.

The writer assumes a humble writing style that rarely employs first-person language, but rather identifies Christ's disciples as "they" instead of "we" and refers to himself as the disciple that Christ loved (13:23, 20:2). The Lord entrusted the care of His mother into the hands of this beloved disciple (19:26). Church history records that John took Mary to Ephesus and there cared for her until her death. John shows his esteem for Mary by never referring to her by name in his account, but only in regard to her unique relationship to her Son. With high confidence, we may assert that John, the son of Zebedee, is the writer of this gospel account.

The Date
Polycarp, a second-century Christian father and martyr who knew John personally, told Irenaeus that John wrote this Gospel while serving the church in Ephesus. Irenaeus, who claimed to be the spiritual grandson of John, also identified John as the "beloved disciple" (13:23).[55] This would mean that the earliest possible date for this literary work would be about 70 A.D. Irenaeus also states that John lived until the reign of Emperor Trajan, or about the turn of the first century A.D.[56] If John was writing from Ephesus, as Irenaeus states, then a date of 85 to 90 A.D. (before John's exile to the Isle of Patmos) would be reasonable.

The Audience
Matthew's audience was Jewish; Mark wrote to the Romans, and Luke addressed the Greeks. Who is left? Anybody and everybody. John's audience is the whole world (e.g., world is mentioned four times in 3:16-17). John refers to the world eighty times in his Gospel, compared to eighteen references in Matthew, five in Mark and ten in Luke. John has over twice as many references as the other three Gospels have combined.

Unlike the synoptic Gospels, John uses the Roman reference of time in lieu of Jewish reckoning. This difference is important to understand; otherwise, there would appear to be serious disagreement between the Gospel writers on major events in the Lord's life. For example, Matthew states that, while Christ was on the cross, darkness covered the land at the sixth hour, but John records Christ was in the judgment hall before Pilate at the sixth hour. The sixth hour by Roman reckoning would be six o'clock, but the Jews would understand it to be twelve o'clock.

The "Only Begotten Son"
The term "begotten" in Scripture usually conveys the idea of a father producing a child, while "only" expresses an aspect of uniqueness. The Greek word *monogenes*, rendered "only begotten" in John 3:16 is used to combine these two thoughts as pertaining to the Son of God in John's Gospel. Luke uses this word to indicate an "only son" or "only daughter" family situation, but John, who is advocating Christ's deity, only uses *monogenes* to speak of Christ's unique and divine sonship. Accordingly, the term "begotten" in Scripture is connected with the Lord Jesus in various ways to declare His "uniqueness" as God's Son. He is the only

begotten of the Father (1:14, 1:18, 3:16, 3:18), which speaks of the Son's unique position and eternal relationship as the Son of God, the One who was with the Father in glory from the beginning (1:1, 17:5).

"Begotten" is also used to speak of Christ's unique resurrection and ascension back to glory in Hebrews 1:5 and Acts 13:33. Additionally, the writer of Hebrews (quoting Deut. 32:43), states that God will "again" bring His begotten Son as *"the firstborn into the world"* and that all the angels shall worship Him (Heb. 1:6-7). Although God's Son took a position lower than the angels, God commands the angels to worship Christ, for He has a position over all creation as declared by the title "firstborn." The expression firstborn when used metaphorically may speak of first in point of time (e.g., Luke 2:7) or to speak of position and rank over something (Ps. 89.27). The latter view is advanced here with Christ's second coming to the earth to rule and to reign in view.

Some commentators believe that Hebrews 1:5 is speaking of the incarnation of God's only begotten Son, instead of His second advent to the earth. J. N. Darby suggests that the divine glories of this verse are associated with Christ's incarnation:

> *"Thou art My Son, this day have I begotten Thee."* It is this character of Sonship, proper to the Messiah, which, as a real relationship, distinguishes Him. He was from eternity the Son of the Father, but it is not precisely in this point of view that He is here considered. The name expresses the same relationship, but it is to the Messiah born on earth that this title is here applied.[57]

The "only begotten" Son of God is "unique" in His eternality, incarnation, resurrection, and exalted position.

John is bestowed with the honor of presenting the Lord Jesus as the "Son of God." It is a divine title appearing more times in John than in any of the other Gospels. John does not introduce "a son of God," but *"the only begotten Son"* and *"the only begotten of the Father."* These expressions are found nowhere else in all of Scripture, save the one time John also declares this divine solidarity in his first epistle (1 Jn. 4:9). Hence, John proclaims Jesus Christ as the unique Son of God to the whole world. In response, the world should "honor the Son," an exhortation found six times in John's Gospel. In fact, of the twenty-two times the word "honor" is found in the four Gospels, thirteen reside in

John. "Honor" is a key word pertaining to the fourth gospel account. The Son of God is to be respected, revered, and worshiped.

The special relationship of the Eternal Son of God with God the Father is exhibited in the Lord's frequent use of the expression "My Father." The phrase is found in John thirty-two times, compared to fifteen times in Matthew, not at all in Mark, and five in Luke. The Jews understood perfectly what the Lord was implying by the use of the term: *"Therefore the Jews sought all the more to kill Him, because He not only broke the Sabbath, but also said that God was His Father, making Himself equal with God"* (5:18). The Jews sought to kill Jesus for claiming equality with God, a fact that He repeatedly stated.

By using the expression "My Father," Christ was claiming a unique relationship with God that no one else possessed and enjoyed. It is ironic that the religious Jews of Christ's day perfectly understood the Lord's claim of deity, but the skeptics of our day allow their heads to swell with intellectual reasoning to avoid the clear facts of the matter. The discussion boils down to this: either Christ is who He said He was, the Son of God and the Savior of the world, or a lunatic, or the most notable liar that ever lived. The latter options are impossible, for the Lamb of God would not have been a sacrifice without blemish; consequently, we would still be dead in our trespasses and sin. There is absolutely no middle ground on this matter – Jesus Christ is God incarnate. He claimed to be God and that was the blasphemous charge that the Sanhedrin determined He deserved death for (Mark 14:63-64; Luke 22:66-71). Each person must decide if the Lord spoke the truth and then exercise faith in Him to be saved.

John's Omissions

No parables in John. Parables both revealed and concealed divine truth. For the seeker, the parable presented an opportunity to learn more, but for those who were rejecting Christ, the fuller truth would never be known (Matt. 13:10-13). The word "parable" is found thirty-two times in the Gospels, but only once in John. The Greek word rendered "parable" in John 10:6 is *paroimia*, literally meaning "a proverb" or a "figure of speech." The normal Greek word used thirty-one times in the synoptic Gospels is *parabole*, meaning "a similitude implied by a fictitious narrative." The Lord articulated the importance of Himself as the Good Shepherd in John 10; the passage is not an application-enriched story aimed at the listener.

No genealogies. In keeping with the priestly type of Christ presented in Melchizedek, the Lord is *"without descent, having neither beginning of days, nor end of life"* (Heb. 7:3). Because God is eternal, there just is no genealogy that could establish "The Ancient of Days."

No details of Christ's baptism. From the synoptic Gospels we learn that John the Baptist did not want to baptize Christ, for he understood that he was unholy and that the Messiah needed no repentance. Christ, however, insisted that John baptize Him, for in His baptism Christ demonstrated His condescension to identify with those He came to save. John records none of these details, but does highlight God's own emblematic recognition of Christ as the Son of God. John (the baptizer) states the matter plainly just after Christ's baptism:

And John bore witness, saying, "I saw the Spirit descending from heaven like a dove, and He remained upon Him. I did not know Him, but He who sent me to baptize with water said to me, 'Upon whom you see the Spirit descending, and remaining on Him, this is He who baptizes with the Holy Spirit.' And I have seen and testified that this is the Son of God" (1:32-34).

No record of the temptation. John presents Christ as God made flesh (John 1:14), and as James insists, *"God cannot be tempted"* (Jas. 1:13). This fact should put to death any degrading doctrines that pertain to the Lord's ability to sin or to His members having the capacity to be enticed to sin.

No transfiguration. This omission may seem puzzling, for didn't the transfiguration declare the inherent glory of Christ? Doesn't this fit John's theme? Yes, but where did the glory of Christ shine forth? On earth. John presents Christ from the heavenly view, not in an earthly relationship. Matthew gave prominence to Christ's kingly glory on earth; John speaks of the embedded glory that only heaven has witnessed and can fully comprehend. In the transfiguration, it is not the man who is God that is paramount, but that God became an earthly man. Samuel Ridout comments on the practical side of this truth:

Our Lord is transfigured throughout the entire Gospel of John, but it is only to faith: *"We beheld His glory, the glory as of the Only Begotten of the Father."* No need for Him to manifest that glory visibly. His one great object throughout the Gospel is to bear witness to the truth of who He was and who had sent Him.[58]

John

No appointed apostles. In John, all ministry and work are designated for the hands of the Son of God (see 2:23-25 as an example). In this way, Christ is ensured the preeminence among all those with whom He comes in contact. No sharing of ministry or glory is seen in John's Gospel; that would come after Christ's resurrection (17:22).

No "repent" or "forgive." Matthew proclaims the earthly kingdom message of repentance and acceptance of the Messiah. Matthew, three times, applies the term "believe" in association with Christ's interaction with individuals. This term is never publicly proclaimed as part of the gospel of the kingdom; repentance is stressed instead. John, however, stresses the heavenly perspective of mankind's spiritual condition and the ultimate solution – rebirth. In God is all life, and apart from God is death. John reckons all men spiritually dead and, thus, needing to be spiritually reborn (3:7) and quickened or made alive (5:21). It is necessary to repent to truly believe, but only by believing the gospel can one be made alive.

No "prayers" by Jesus. The most common Greek word associated with "praying" in the Gospels is *proseuchomai*, which means "to pray to God either in supplication or worship." It is found forty-seven times in Matthew, Mark, and Luke but not once in John. The root word *proseuche,* also translated "prayer," occurs eight times in the synoptic Gospels but not at all in John. Another Greek word *deomai*, translated "beseech," "pray," or "make request," is found nine times in the synoptic accounts, but again not in John. One more Greek word that is translated as "prayer," *erotao,* when added with the preceding three Greek words, accounts for nearly all references to prayer in the Gospels. *Erotao*, a verb that denotes "to ask from an equal," is translated "pray" or "prayed" only four times in Matthew, Mark, and Luke and is used to show equality in human speech, not to petition the throne of heaven for help. If we were enjoying a meal together at our dining room table, I might ask you to "please pass the salt." I am speaking to you as an equal (*erotao*); it would be unbefitting for me to drop to my knees and beg you for the salt.

Erotao is associated with prayer seven times in John. Once it is used to illustrate the literal meaning of "asking" in John 4:31: *"In the meantime His disciples urged ["prayed" in KJV] Him, saying, "Rabbi, eat."* This was clearly not a petition to God for something, but an expression of their concern for their leader. The remaining six occurrences are related to Christ "praying" to His Father or, literally,

The Man and Your God

"talking to His Father as an equal." In all, *erotao* is translated "pray" six times in John (seven in the KJV). Why is this significant?

The Lord Jesus explained the answer publicly, *"I and My Father are one"* (10:30). The response of the Jews in the next verse showed that they understood that He was asserting divine equality: *"Then the Jews took up stones **again** to stone Him"* (10:31). Christ, being self-existing Himself, "spoke with" the Father as an equal, not as a subordinate. John employs *erotao* to show the Lord's equality with His Father in normal speech. In essence, they are equal and speak as equals. In the other Gospels, the Lord prays to His Father as a subordinate, because as the Son of Man, He took on the form of a servant and, thus, lowered Himself in "position," but not in essence.

No apprehensions of the Cross. As the "Son of God," Christ stood above His sorrow and grief, whereas the other Gospels record His apprehensions of the cross. What Luke records would be completely out of place in John: *"Father, if Thou be willing, remove this cup from Me,"* or *"being in an agony, He prayed more earnestly."* Not one word in John describes Christ's perspiration while praying in Gethsemane, but Luke writes, *"His sweat was, as it were, great drops of blood falling down to the ground."* These statements describe the "Son of Man" as the "man of sorrows." John is the only one to present the heavenly view that night and, thus, highlights Christ's great expectation of being received into heaven, obtaining His glory again and being with His Father forevermore:

> *When Jesus knew that His hour had come **that He should depart from this world to the Father**, having loved His own who were in the world, He loved them to the end* (13:1).

> *Jesus spoke these words, lifted up His eyes to heaven, and said: "Father, the hour has come. **Glorify Your Son, that Your Son also may glorify You**"* (17:1).

> *I have glorified You on the earth. **I have finished the work which You have given Me to do. And now, O Father, glorify Me together with Yourself**, with the glory which I had with You before the world was* (17:4-5).

No ascension. Each Gospel writer superbly concluded their account in a means which crescendoed their presentation of the Lord Jesus. In concluding his Gospel, John upholds the theme of the Lord's deity through the omission of the ascension of Christ to heaven. Why? Because the Son of God is omnipresent. The Lord avowed: *"No one has ascended to heaven but He who came down from heaven, that is, the Son of Man who is in heaven"* (John 3:13). God the Father and the Holy Spirit are visibly seen in God's heavenly throne room (Rev. 4:2-3, 5, 5:1), but yet are omnipresent. The Lord Jesus throughout eternity will be viewed in human form, but likewise is omnipresent. Hence, there was no need for John to record His bodily ascension to heaven.

Light, Love, and Life

John abounds with key words and phrases that distinctly highlight his theme of the Lord's deity. These would include: "Son of God," "My Father," "I AM," "world," "believe," "eternal life," "honor," "verily, verily," "love(d)," "light," and "life." John stresses that when one believes in the light of God, they experience the love of God and receive eternal life. Note the distribution of these gospel-related words (in their various forms of speech) among the four writers:

Key Words	Matthew	Mark	Luke	John
Light	14	1	13	24
Love	13	7	15	57
Life, Live	17	9	19	54
Believe	10	17	11	99

Whereas Matthew stresses "righteousness" in association with the kingdom, John focuses on "eternal life." Both are connected and form one divine truth: Without life in Christ, one cannot display the righteousness of God. Why will the kingdom of God be full of righteousness? Righteousness is what emanates from a Holy God. All those who are born of God will radiate His righteous and holy life.

The words "repent" and "forgive" are not found in John because John conveys the gospel message from a precise heavenly perspective. Spiritually speaking, the plain truth is shrouded in a sincere warning that is often introduced by the phrase "truly, truly." This phrase is not found in the other Gospels. From the onset, John wants his audience to understand the basics of spiritual life and death. There is nothing like death to bring life into focus. *"All things were made through Him, and without Him nothing was made that was made. In Him was life, and the life was the light of men"* (John 1:3-4).

To Nicodemus, the inquisitive Pharisee, the Lord invited and warned: *"He who believes in the Son has everlasting life; and he who does not believe the Son shall not see life, but the wrath of God abides on him"* (3:36). To beloved Martha, the Lord Jesus inquired, *"I am the resurrection and the life. He who believes in Me, though he may die, he shall live. And whoever lives and believes in Me shall never die.* ***Do you believe this?"*** (11:25-26).

Sent

One of the many words that John profusely uses as compared to the synoptic accounts is the word "sent." August Van Ryn explains:

> Twenty-five times we find the word "sent" (Greek *pempo*) in connection with the Father sending the Son. Seventeen times we find the word *apostello* in the same sense. Twenty times more we read of Christ sending the Spirit, sending us [disciples], or others. This word is found almost as many times in John as in the other three Gospels together.[59]

John's Sevens

The number seven is God's number throughout the Bible. Seven represents perfection and completeness; it is God's holy number. For this purpose, the number seven is employed at least twenty times in John's gospel account.

Seven titles of Christ are found in John 1: "the Word" (v. 1), "the Light" (v. 7), "the Lamb of God" (v. 29), "the Christ" (v. 41), "the Son of God" (v. 49), "the King of Israel" (v. 49), "the Son of Man" (v. 51).

Seven different people confess the Deity of Christ: John the Baptist, Nathanael, the Samaritan woman, Peter, the healed blind man, Martha, and Thomas.

Seven "I AM" titles are ascribed by Christ to Himself: "The Bread of Life," "The Light of the World," "The Door," "The Good Shepherd," "The Resurrection and the Life," "The Way, the Truth, and the Life," and "The True Vine."

Seven public miracles are recorded: He turned water to wine; He healed a nobleman's son who was near death; He healed the

John

impotent man at the Pool of Bethesda; He fed 5000 men, plus women and children, from a boy's sack lunch; He calmed a raging storm while in the midst of it; He healed the man born blind; and He raised Lazarus from the dead.

Seven private manifestations of His deity: He knew Nathanael while he was still under the fig tree, He did not commit Himself to the people because He knew the thoughts of all men, He knew the sins of the Samaritan woman, He moved the disciples' boat instantaneously to Capernaum, He knew of Lazarus' sickness and death without being told, He declared the details of Calvary to His disciples beforehand; and He provided a catch of 153 fish for His disciples.

Seven times *"These things have I spoken unto you"* appears in John.

Seven times Christ references His Father's "will."

Seven times Christ addressed the woman at the well (John 4).

Seven times Christ spoke of Himself as *"The Bread of Life"* (John 6).

Seven things the *Good Shepherd* does (John 10).

Seven times Christ made reference to "the hour" in which He would accomplish His Father's work.

Seven discourses: The New Birth (3:1-36), The Water of Life (4:1-42), The Divine Son (5:19-47), The Bread of Life (6:22-66), The Life-Giving Spirit (7:1-52), The Light of the World (8:12-59), and The Good Shepherd (10:1-42).

Seven feasts or holy convocations: First Passover (2:13, 23), Feast of the Jews – Second Passover (5:1), Third Passover (6:4), Tabernacles (7:2), The Great Day of Convocation (7:37; Lev. 23:36), Dedication (10:22), and Fourth Passover (11:55).

Seven witnesses of Christ's deity: John the baptizer (1:29-34), Nathaniel (1:43-51), Peter (6:66-69), the Lord Jesus (10:22-30), Martha (11:27), Thomas (20:28), and John (1:14, 20:30-31).

Seven times Christ instructed His disciples to pray in His name.

Seven times the word "hate" is found in John 15.

Seven ministries of the Holy Spirit to the believer are noted (John 16).

Seven times Christ referred to believers as the Father's "gift" to Him (John 17).

Seven times John recorded that Christ spoke only the Word of the Father.

Seven times the writer of John (John) referred to himself but not by name.

Seven important events pertaining to Christ's ministry appear in all four Gospels: The ministry of John the Baptist as the forerunner of Christ, the feeding of the 5000, Peter's confession of Jesus being the Christ, the Triumphal Entry presentation of Messiah, and the crucifixion, burial and resurrection of the Lord.

The Divinity of Christ

Christ is Holy; the following are the divine attributes of Christ which John upholds to his audience:

Creator: *"All things were made through Him, and without Him nothing was made that was made"* (John 1:3). Paul declares: *"For by Him all things were created that are in heaven and that are on earth, visible and invisible, whether thrones or dominions or principalities or powers. All things were created through Him and for Him. And He is before all things, and in Him all things consist"* (Col. 1:16-17). The Lord Jesus is the Creator and the Sustainer of all. He then must be Lord and sovereign over all; thus, Paul refers to Him as the "firstborn" of creation to speak of His preeminence and authority over all things. He is not Michael the archangel, as some cults teach, or any created being, for that matter, for how can one create themselves, be before themselves or maintain themselves – He created all things, and nothing was made without Him.

Omnipresent: John spoke of the Lord Jesus, while He walked upon the earth: *"The only begotten Son,* **who is in the bosom of the Father***, He has declared Him"* (John 1:18). The Lord Himself declared, *"No one has ascended to heaven but He who came down from heaven, that is,* **the Son of Man who is in heaven**" (3:13). Some Christians have a problem with the thought of the Lord being omnipresent and human. How can I see God in one place, and yet He dwells everywhere? It is simply beyond human comprehension but not human observation. John wrote of the visible manifestation of all three persons of the Godhead in Revelation 4 and 5. He described the brilliant and majestic glory of the Father (Rev. 4:2-3) and then of the Father's hand (Rev. 5:1). He noted the representation of the Holy Spirit in seven fires before the throne of God (Rev. 4:5) and of the Lamb (the Lord Jesus) standing in the midst of the heavenly multitude (Rev. 5:6). All three persons of the Godhead are omnipresent but may choose to display their divine glory in just one particular location. The visible manifestation of Christ is fixed – glorified humanity forever. This attribute allows Christ to literally fulfill His promise to believers, *"I will never leave you nor forsake you"* (Heb. 13:5).

Omniscience: The Lord said to Nathanael, *"Before Philip called you, when you were under the fig tree, I saw you"* (1:48). Though many people sought Christ, most were half-hearted followers or just interested in a good story or seeing a supernatural wonder. Speaking of these, John writes, *"But Jesus did not commit Himself to them, because **He knew all men**, and had no need that anyone should testify of man, for **He knew what was in man**"* (2:24). How astounded the Samaritan woman at the well must have been to hear the Lord's response to her denial of having a husband: *"You have well said, 'I have no husband,' for you have had five husbands, and the one whom you now have is not your husband; in that you spoke truly"* (4:18). How is it possible for the Lord to know and to do anything that we ask in His name (14:14)? We understand that the asking is in accordance to His will (1 Jn. 5:14), but how is He to know our needs and hear our requests if He is not omniscient?

Omnipotent: The Lord, referring to Himself, said, *"Destroy this temple, and in three days I will raise it up"* (2:19). In Himself He had the power to lay down His life and raise it up again (10:17-18). He demonstrated His sovereign authority and power over creation by walking upon water, calming storms, feeding multitudes from a boy's sack lunch, moving a boat instantaneously across the Sea of Galilee, and raising the dead. The demons feared His presence and yielded to His instruction (Luke 4:41, 8:28). Satan was rebuked by Christ and submitted to His command (Matt. 4:10-11).

Eternal: *"In the beginning was the Word, and the Word was with God, and the Word was God. **He was in the beginning with God**"* (1:1-2). *"**Before** Abraham was I Am"* (8:58). The fact that He created all things is solid evidence that He is God, the pre-existent One (1:3-4). *"And now, O Father, glorify Me together with Yourself, with the glory which I had with You before the world was"* (17:5). The Lord Jesus is the eternal Son of God, the *"Alpha and Omega, the first and the last"* (Rev. 1:11).

Equality with the Father: *"I and My Father **are one**"* (10:30). The Jews fully understood the Lord's claim: *"Therefore the Jews sought all* *the more to kill Him, because He not only broke the Sabbath, but also said that God was His Father, making Himself equal with God"* (5:18).

True: *"Jesus said to him, 'I am the way, the truth, and the life. No one comes to the Father except through Me'"* (14:6). There is no other way to enjoy eternal paradise with God than through the Lord Jesus Christ. Thomas A. Kempis wrote of the Lord Jesus: "I am the Way unchangeable; the Truth infallible; the Life everlasting."[60] His blood alone washes away sin, and only through His sacrifice can a repentant, believing sinner be justified – receive a righteous standing before God.

Just: *"My judgment is righteous [or, just; KJV]"* (5:30). *"For the Father judges no one, but has committed all judgment to the Son"* (5:22). Speaking of the just Judge, Paul declares: *"For it is written: 'As I live, says the Lord, every knee shall bow to Me, and every tongue shall confess to God.' So then each of us shall give account of himself to God"* (Rom. 14:11-12). *"Therefore God also has highly exalted Him and given Him the name which is above every name, that at the name of Jesus every knee should bow, of those in heaven, and of those on earth, and of those under the earth"* (Phil. 2:9-10).

Holy and Sinless: When the Lord Jesus asked, *"Which of you convicts Me of sin?"* (8:46), no one could reply; not a word! Albert Barnes comments to the significance of the Lord's question:

> The word sin here evidently means error, falsehood, or imposture. It stands opposed to truth. The argument of the Savior is this: A doctrine might be rejected if it could be proved that he that delivered it was an impostor, but as you cannot prove this of Me, you are bound to receive My words.[61]

Perfect Love: *"Greater love has no one than this, than to lay down one's life for his friends"* (15:13). The Lord is love, displayed sacrificial love for others, and exhorted His disciples to do the same:

> *Beloved, let us love one another, for love is of God; and everyone who loves is born of God and knows God. He who does not love does not know God, for God is love. In this the love of God was manifested toward us, that God has sent His only begotten Son into the world, that we might live through Him. In this is love, not that we loved God, but that He loved us and sent His Son to be the propitiation for our sins"* (1 Jn. 4:7-10).

Grace: *"And the Word became flesh and dwelt among us, and we beheld His glory, the glory as of the only begotten of the Father, **full of grace** and truth"* (1:14). The Lord's example should be followed by all those who name Him as Savior – let us not be just balanced, but full of both grace and truth. Paul puts it this way: *"Let your speech always be with grace, seasoned with salt, that you may know how you ought to answer each one"* (Col. 4:6). If it was not necessary to say, could not be said in love, and was not true, the Lord Jesus did not say it. May the Lord's people follow the same threefold rule before speaking to others.

Unique Son of God: Concerning Christ, God the Father revealed to John the Baptist, *"This is the Son of God"* (1:34), and *"The only begotten of the Father"* (1:14). The Lord affirmed: *"He who has seen Me has seen the Father"* (14:9). Only the Lord has such a special relationship with the Eternal Father as evidenced by the frequent use of the phrase "My Father," which is found in John thirty-two times. The Jews understood perfectly what the Lord was implying by the use of the term and sought to kill him for *"making Himself equal with God"* (5:18). Even though the Jews desired to kill Him for this assertion, the Lord Jesus continued to proclaim that He was the unique, eternal Son of God.

Controls Time and Events: *"Therefore they sought to take Him; but no one laid a hand on Him, because His hour had not yet come"* (7:30). In the Garden of Gethsemane, the Lord commanded the very soldiers that were arresting Him to take only Him and let His disciples go – this after Peter tried to kill a man (18:8-12). And let us recall the dignity of our Lord's words about being in control of His own death:

> *Therefore My Father loves Me, because I lay down My life that I may take it again. No one takes it* [speaking of His own life] *from Me, but I lay it down of Myself. I have power to lay it down, and I have power to take it again. This command I have received from My Father* (10:17-18).

Laid Aside His Glory: While speaking to His Father, the Lord Jesus said: *"I have glorified You on the earth. I have finished the work which You have given Me to do. And now, O Father, glorify Me together with Yourself, with the glory which I had with You before the world was"* (17:4-5). Paul explains in Philippians 2:5-11 that the Son of God willingly set aside the honor and glory associated with His high station in heaven to become a lowly human servant to be sacrificed to provide propitiation for humanity's sin. The Lord's utter humility and sacrificial behavior in serving others is an example for all to follow.

The Man and Your God

To the extent that He was despised and disgraced by mankind, God has highly exalted Him above all power and principalities, to be esteemed, worshiped, and appreciated. Presently, the Lord Jesus sits at the right hand of the Majesty on high (Heb. 1:13), on His Father's throne (Rev. 3:21). This is a position of highest honor and privilege and acknowledges that the Lord perfectly completed the work of redemption that the Father gave Him to accomplish. Sitting at the right hand of God symbolizes a position of power (Matt. 26:24) and identifies who God delights in (Ps. 16:11). The outcome of Christ's selflessness is majestic honor and glory!

The Light of the World: *"Then Jesus spoke to them again, saying, 'I am the light of the world. He who follows Me shall not walk in darkness, but have the light of life'"* (8:12). He was God's Light from heaven so that all on the earth could witness real and eternal life. *"In Him was life, and the life was the light of men. And the light shines in the darkness, and the darkness did not comprehend it"* (1:4-5). Concerning this truth, Andrew Jukes notes:

> There stood One, in a servant's form, in the likeness of sinful flesh, whose life, even while others judged Him, was judging everything, and showing, by its holy contrast, what was in men and what was not, according to God's mind. "The Life was the light."[62]

The first Adam was originally created in the "likeness" and "image" of God, but, after the fall, moral "likeness" was lost, and man would bear God's "image" with diminished capacity. Man was still God's representative on earth, but not a very good one. Genesis 5:3 states that Adam begot children *"in his own likeness, after his image."* Image is not likeness; these are distinctly different ideas. Likeness is similitude, being like; image is representation, whether alike or not. The Lord Jesus, *the last Adam,* is never spoken of as "being in the likeness of God." He cannot be "like" God since He is God. Adam's descendants, though still representing God, would be like their father Adam in moral likeness.

The Lord Jesus Christ, being fully God, revealed the glory of God on earth as only a Holy God could. Though the first Adam failed to represent God and show forth God's moral glory, the last Adam displayed perfect representation. *"And the Word became flesh and dwelt among us,* **and we beheld His glory, the glory as of the only begotten of the Father***, full of grace and truth"* (1:14).

John Chapter 1

The Eternal and Living Word of God (vv. 1-5)

Just as Luke presents the life of Christ more uniquely than any other Gospel, John acclaims the deity of Christ like no other. Only God is perfect, self-sufficient, and self-existing – there is none like Him! *"For I am the Lord your God, the Holy One of Israel, your Savior"* (Isa. 43:3). *"I, even I, am the Lord, and besides Me there is no savior"* (Isa. 43:11). *"For I am God, and there is no other; I am God, and there is none like Me"* (Isa. 46:9). The prophet Isaiah clearly teaches that the Savior of mankind is none other than Holy God Himself. As God is triune, Isaiah highlights the roles of God the Father, God the Son, and of the Holy Spirit in His salvation plan for humanity (Isa. 48:16-17). These truths are then expounded in the New Testament.

F. B. Hole explains the dangerous tide of secular Gnosticism that was prevalent in John's day which attempted to undermine what Scripture had revealed concerning Christ's deity and humanity.

> The early Christians were much troubled by the so-called "Gnostics"; that is, the "Knowing-ones." We have been made familiar with agnostics, that is, people who deny that any certain knowledge of God and His things is possible. The Gnostics were at the opposite pole: they claimed to be initiated and have the superior knowledge, but their theories denied both the essential Godhead and the true humanity of Jesus. Then there were those who separated Jesus from the Christ. The Christ was to them an ideal, a state into which man might graduate; whereas Jesus was the historic Man who appeared at Nazareth. The Gospel that John wrote meets these errors and was designed to do so.[63]

John uses plain language, Old Testament types and symbols, and numerical imagery to show that Jesus Christ is God in flesh – *holy humanity*, the Creator, in the opening verses of his account:

> *In the beginning was the Word, and the Word was with God, and* ***the Word was God****. He was* ***in the beginning with God****.* ***All things were***

> ***made through Him***, *and without Him nothing was made that was made.* ***In Him was life****, and the life was the light of men. And the light shines in the darkness, and the darkness did not comprehend it* (vv. 1-5).

Even before there was anything created the Word existed and was God (v. 1). Peter states that He, Christ preincarnate, was *"before the foundation of the world"* (1 Pet. 1:20). The Son of God describes His eternal Personage as being *"before the world was"* and *"before the foundation of the world"* (17:5, 24). The Greek word *pros* rendered "with" in verse 1 means "in company with." The verb that is rendered "was" four times in verses 1 and 2 is in the imperfect tense. This means that God's Messenger and Message, His Son, the living Word (v. 14), "already was" in company with God the Father and "always was" God, even when only God existed.

The phrase "with God" has a definite article in the Greek text, but the phrase "was God" does not. This has led some to erroneously add an indefinite article before "God" and to translate the full phrase as "the Word was a God." However, the absence of a definite article before a noun does not necessarily render it indefinite. For example, there is no article before "king" in John 1:49, but clearly "the" and not "a" before "king" is what Nathaniel meant. When a predicate noun, like *theos*, precedes the verb and lacks a definite article, then it is best to see it as either qualitative or definite, rather than indefinite. Hence, rendering *theos* as "a god" twists the grammatical structure of the text and promotes a polytheistic teaching. Furthermore, as John Heading summarizes, there are other passages that include a definite article to acknowledge Christ's deity.

> In Matthew 1:23, we read "Emmanuel ... God with us," literally "the God with us" since the definite article is present in Greek. And also, in John 20:28, Thomas said, "My Lord and my God" (*ho kurios mou kai ho theos mou*), literally, "The Lord of me and the God of me," namely with the definite article "the" attached to "God." These two examples prove conclusively the absolute Deity of Christ and reduce the heretics' claims to nothing.[64]

John then states that the Word created all things which now exist. The Greek verb in verse 3 translated *"were made"* is in the aorist tense, meaning that "all things became through Him." The living Word is the source of all life. This clearly includes physical life, but more

John

importantly the Word is God's source of revealed truth (light) to men that they might receive eternal, spiritual life in Him (1 Jn. 5:20). No darkness (i.e., evil) can suppress God's light of truth to the world in His Son, the living Word. Nor can what is not of God, darkness, comprehend what is of God. Literally, the darkness, what is evil, did not take hold of the light. Just as darkness cannot exist when light appears, evil cannot resist or control God's light (truth) declared by His Word, the Lord Jesus.

The Witness of John the Baptizer (vv. 6-9)

Centuries earlier, the prophet Isaiah was a voice crying in the spiritual wilderness of Israel's apostasy, so God used him to speak of one that would come in a future day in the same spirit of ministry to announce the Lord's coming: *"Prepare the way of the Lord; make straight in the desert a highway for our God"* (Isa. 40:3). All four of the Gospel writers apply this verse to John the baptizer (1:23, Matt. 3:1-4; Mark 1:1-4; Luke 1:76-78). John was sent by God to be a witness to others of the Light that God was shining into the world through His Son, the living Word (vv. 6-8). Though John dwelt in the desert, his preaching formed a highway for the Lord Jesus through the spiritual wilderness of Israel.

God desired that those in Israel would be drawn to God's Light from heaven, Christ, through John's witness (v. 9). The Creator, in person, came into the world to declare God's message of salvation, but generally speaking, *"the world did not know Him."* Yet, initially, many in Israel were moved by John's ministry. Some even believed John's message and followed Christ, but the majority did not (v. 11). The Lord Jesus, speaking to the Pharisees, said that John *"was the burning and shining lamp, and you were willing for a time to rejoice in his light"* (5:35). Later, the Lord reminded the Pharisees of their rejection of John's message: *"For John came to you in the way of righteousness, and you did not believe him"* (Matt. 21:32).

God's Light Can Be Received or Rejected (vv. 10-13)

The majority of the Jewish nation rejected John's introduction of their Messiah: *"He was in the world, and the world was made through Him, and the world did not know Him. He came to His own, and His own did not receive Him"* (vv. 10-11). *Kosmos* is the Greek word rendered "world" in this verse three times and elsewhere in the book nearly eighty times. While *kosmos* does speak of God's design and order for physical creation, as *"the world was made through Him,"* it more amply speaks of the realm of humanity, for *"the world did not know Him."*

The phrase "His own" is found three times (twice in verse 11) in John's Gospel and marks a spiritual divide within Israel. The first "His own" in verse 11 is neuter plural, and the second "His own" is masculine plural to indicate a more restrictive group of focus than all of humanity. Initially, Christ came to "His own" (the Jewish nation, v. 11), but His countrymen largely did not receive Him. However, some, like the disciples, did believe on Him. Of these John says, *"having loved His own who were in the world, He loved them to the end"* (13:1). The transition of initial ministry to the lost sheep of Israel to those Jews responding to the Good Shepherd's call and receiving salvation in Him is thus marked in the text by the words "His own" in John's account.

Salvation itself is a three-part reality consisting of a process of God that is sandwiched between two acts of God. Salvation begins when an individual believes the gospel of Jesus Christ and is, consequently, regenerated (born again) by the Holy Spirit (vv. 12-13; Tit. 3:5). The soul is saved at this time and receives God's eternal life (3:3). After this act of God, the long process of sanctification begins. This process morally transforms us to act and think as Christ does (Rom. 8:29). Salvation concludes with glorification, an act of God which transforms the believer's body and makes it holy and fit for Heaven (1 Cor. 15:51-52).

John tells us that if we are only born once, then we will die twice, speaking of physical death and eternal spiritual separation from God (Heb. 9:27). But if we are born twice (physical and spiritual birth), then, at the most, we will die once (speaking of physical death). The Lord told Nicodemus that we cannot get to heaven without being born again (3:3) and John tells us that we cannot be born again, unless we "receive Him," which he clarifies to mean that one must personally believe in Christ alone for salvation (v. 12). Therefore, becoming a child of God has nothing to do with "blood" (i.e., human ethnicity, e.g., being a Jew), or "the will of the flesh" (i.e., the ceremonial rites of humanized religion), or "of the will of man" (i.e., human efforts, such as good works and morality; v. 13). Speaking of "blood," since all humans are joined by a common bloodline back to Adam (Acts 17:26), no one can lay claim to God's salvation based on human ethnicity. God promised Abraham that all families of the earth would be blessed through one of his descendants, speaking of the Messiah (Gen. 12:3).

Indeed, many witnessed the glory of God in Christ during His first advent, but the entire world did not see it, for Christ, as foretold, first sought "His own," the lost sheep of Israel (Matt. 15:24). But the Jews rejected Jesus Christ as their Messiah. The Jewish nation will need to embrace the Lord in faith and in truth before the glory and the blessings of the Lord will be witnessed by all men. The process will begin when Israel exercises genuine faith in revealed truth, and it will be completed in the Kingdom Age when Israel receives the Holy Spirit and is able to exhibit the character of Christ. In the Kingdom Age, Isaiah's prophecy of all flesh seeing the glory of God will then be fulfilled (Isa. 40:5).

The Word Became Flesh (v. 14)

Long ago, the fine flour of the *meal* offering (Lev. 2) symbolized our Lord's perfect moral character – His sinless perfection in all His doings. John wrote of Christ's demonstration of the perfect character of God in all that He did: *"And the Word became flesh and dwelt among us, and we beheld His glory, the glory as of the only begotten of the Father, **full of grace and truth**"* (v. 14). *"Of the only begotten"* is derived from the Greek *monogenous*. Edwin A. Blum explains what this word means in the Son's association with His Father: "Jesus is the Son of God in a sense totally different from a human who believes and becomes a child of God. Jesus' sonship is unique, for He is eternal and is of the same essence of the Father."[65]

The Lord's flesh concealed the outshining glory of God (the same glory that His Father possesses) but allowed His divine moral excellence to be viewed by all. Of all the men who have ever walked on this earth, only the Lord Jesus Christ could say:

My judgment is righteous, because I do not seek My own will but the will of the Father who sent Me (5:30).

I always do those things that please Him [His Father] (8:29).

Whatever I speak, just as the Father has told Me, so I speak (12:50).

If you had known Me, you would have known My Father also (14:7).

I have manifested Your name to the men (17:6).

In every respect of moral nature and divine character, the Son was a perfect representation of the Father: *"The Son can do nothing of Himself, but what He sees the Father do; for whatever He does, the Son also does in like manner"* (5:19). This is why the Lord Jesus could adamantly declare to Philip on the eve of His death: *"He that has seen Me has seen the Father"* (14:9). He was perfect in all His doings, in every circumstance, in each word spoken, and in every thought mentally conceived – all to the glory of God and thus achieving in His life the full appreciation of His Father. In application, the Lord's pattern of behavior should be followed by all those who name Him as Savior – let us not be just balanced in what we do, but strive to be full of grace and truth, that we too can manifest His name among men.

John the Baptizer Bears Witness of the Word (vv. 15-28)

John's forerunning ministry of pointing his countrymen to Christ began prior to the anointing of Christ by the Holy Spirit. For several months, perhaps even a year or two, John proclaimed the necessity of repenting of one's sins to receive the One coming after him, the One that existed before him and was preferred before Him (v. 15). Interestingly, John states that he knew of the Person he was speaking of but did not know him personally at this time (vv. 31-32). Regardless, John taught the people that by believing on Him that was soon coming, the One full of grace and truth, forgiveness of sins could be received and His advocacy for sin after conversion would then follow; this is the idea of the expression "grace for grace" (v. 16).

Being shown mercy by being released from our just punishment is wonderful, but then to receive forgiveness that conveys a high status (Eph. 2:6) and ensures we experience the riches of God's grace is just incredible (Eph. 1:7). Priestly intercession results in the forgiveness of sin and Christ, as our High Priest and Advocate, is ever making intercession on our behalf (Rom. 8:34; Heb. 7:25; 1 Jn. 2:2). In Scripture, the number *five* symbolizes grace, the number *twenty* pictures redemption, and the number *twenty-five* relates to forgiveness. In God's mathematics, the *forgiveness of sin* (*twenty-five*) is the outcome of *five*, symbolizing *grace*, and *twenty* representing *redemption*. Just as the Levitical priests could not serve in the tabernacle until they were *twenty-five* years old (Num. 8:24), we cannot serve God as believer-priests until our sins have been forgiven.

The Law given through Moses condemned, but grace and truth came through Christ to offer man the forgiveness of sins, or grace for grace (v.

17). Grace for (or upon) grace (*five* times *five*) equals *twenty-five*, the forgiveness of sins. In the Christian life, believers experience one wave of God's grace followed by another and another!

John then refers to a statement that God made to Moses, asserting that no human in their earthly state could see God's glory and survive (Ex. 33:20). Yet, the "only begotten" Son of God, incarnate, though still spiritually one with His Father in heaven, had come into the world to show the glory of His Father (v. 18). The term "begotten" is used frequently in Scripture to refer to the relationship of a father to his son in the ancestral sense. The word "only" refers to uniqueness. The Greek word *monogenes*, rendered "only begotten" here is used to combine these two thoughts as pertaining to the Son of God (i.e., Christ has a unique relationship with His heavenly Father). Hebrews 11:17 refers to Isaac as Abraham's "only begotten" son, yet Abraham had several other sons, including Ishmael, who was born before Isaac; here the term clearly expresses uniqueness (i.e., Isaac was the son of promise and Ishmael was not). God's Son is also unique; Jesus Christ is His Son of promise (3:16).

Sometimes, the word "begotten" is used alone to express the unique relationship between God the Father and God the Son. For example, Hebrews 1:5 speaks of the Lord being "begotten again" – referring to the Lord's unique resurrection, which the Father initiated (Eph. 1:17-21). Obviously, this verse is not implying that the Lord Jesus was born again, so "begotten" must have a wider meaning than mere physical birth.

There are many other Scriptures which address the eternal sonship of the Lord Jesus Christ. For example, John 16:28 teaches that Christ came forth from the Father, while John 17:5 and 24 indicate that there was a Father-Son relationship in the Godhead even before the creation of the world. Hebrews 1:2 also states that the Son created all things. God gave His Son (3:16), implying that Christ was God's Son before He was given – He did not give one that would become His Son, but was already His Son. Isaiah 48:16-17, Psalm 40:6-8, and Hebrews 10:6-9 also confirm this same understanding. There are many passages which speak of the Father "sending" the Son; these all imply that Christ existed as God's Son prior to His mission (John 20:21; Gal. 4:4; 1 Jn. 4:10, 14). Clearly, the Son eternally existed in the bosom of the Father (v. 18) and He alone enjoyed that nearness and the fellowship of that relationship prior to His incarnation.

Proverbs 30:4 and Psalm 2:7-12 indicate that the Father had a Son prior to the Lord's incarnation. In Proverbs 30:4, Solomon implies that the Son has the same characteristics that God has; God who is the Creator has a Son of the same nature.

Some have argued that because the Lord Jesus referred to His Father as "God" while suffering on the cross, a Father-Son relationship could not have existed at that point. They say that if such a relationship existed, the Lord would have surely said, *"Father, Father,* why have You forsaken Me." The fact that Christ called His Father "God" does not undermine His continuing relationship with His Father as His Son. At that moment, Christ had become the sin-bearer for humanity (Heb. 2:9). He was being punished by a Holy God for all human sin and was doing so in complete subjection to His Father (1 Cor. 11:3). Communion, but not relationship, was lost temporarily at Calvary. The Lord Jesus was still the Son when He referred to His Father as "God," both from the cross and later when speaking to Mary in the garden after His resurrection. The Lord Jesus said that He was the Son of God and that He had been sent into the world by His Father (10:36-37).

Because many were venturing into the wilderness to hear John's message, various priests and Levites were dispatched from Jerusalem to investigate him and his ministry (v. 19). Their inquiry was twofold: "Who are you?" (vv. 20-23) and "Why are you baptizing?" (vv. 26-27, 31). First, they asked John, *"Who are you?"* After John confessed that he was not the Christ, the religious leaders asked if he was Elijah (v. 20). They were contemplating Malachi's prophecy that Elijah would return to Israel before the kingdom would be established (Mal. 4:5-6). John answered the priests and Levites, "I am not." Then they asked him if he was the prophet that Moses foretold would come to speak for God and lead Israel into the promised kingdom (Deut. 18:15-16). John replied to this question with a concise, "no" (v. 21).

Although John was not "the Prophet" (speaking of Christ), Matthew explains that the Jews were speaking to a true prophet of God at that very moment (Matt. 11:9). John was a prophet, and in fact the greatest of the prophets because He was Christ's chosen forerunner as prophesied in Isaiah 40:3 (vv. 22-23). Unlike the synoptic writers, John quotes Isaiah's prophecy about his ministry as Christ's forerunner in first person, *"I am the voice."* Indeed, John was a prophet and the voice that announced Christ's coming. It was not that John was greater in character or eloquence than those preaching before him, but his task of being the Messiah-King's herald was greater in grandeur than the assigned duties of previous prophets (Matt. 11:10).

John

The Lord Jesus confirmed that "all the prophets and the Law" foretold of the coming kingdom, but when John arrived to announce that Christ had arrived, Israel rejected Him and His literal offer of an earthly, political kingdom (Matt. 11:13). The prophet Elijah labored to call the hearts of his idolatrous countrymen back to Jehovah, but the people rejected his ministry. If Israel would have received John's message, who was preaching in the spirit and power of Elijah (Mal. 4:5-6), then Elijah's ministry would have been fulfilled, but it was not to be (Matt. 11:14).

Moses' prophecy of a coming, powerful Prophet to the nation of Israel also spoke of Christ's first advent. After seeing Jehovah's awesome display of power on Mount Sinai, the Israelites asked Moses to be their mediator (Ex. 20:19). The Lord was pleased with their understanding of His holiness and their need of an intercessor to approach Him. Moses then uttered this prophecy to them:

The Lord your God will raise up for you a Prophet like me from your midst, from your brethren. Him you shall hear, according to all you desired of the Lord your God in Horeb in the day of the assembly, saying, "Let me not hear again the voice of the Lord my God, nor let me see this great fire anymore, lest I die" (Deut. 18:15-16).

This meant that Moses would serve as Jehovah's prophet to communicate crucial messages to His people. Though God would send a long line of prophets to converse with Israel in the unfolding centuries, Moses' prophetic ministry was unique in comparison (Deut. 34:10). He had enjoyed extended, intimate fellowship with God, he spoke for God to the people, and he was a mediator representing the people to God. In this sense, Moses pictured the special Prophet (speaking of Christ) that God would send in a future day to bring His ultimate message of hope to Israel. Those not heeding His Prophet's message would be judged appropriately by God (Deut. 18:18-19).

The role of a prophet was an important ministry in Israel; the prophet had to bravely stand before the people and be a mouthpiece for God. Prophetic exercise occurred mostly when there was spiritual decline among God's people. At such times, God sent prophets to make people aware of their sin, to call them to repentance, and to warn them of forthcoming judgment if they did not repent. Such was the situation in Israel when the Lord Jesus, the Living Word of God (1:1-2), was sent to the earth and was born of a virgin to testify for God.

During the Lord's first advent to the earth, He entered into the office of prophet after being anointed by the Holy Spirit at thirty years of age (Luke 3:21-23). After being tested forty days in the wilderness by Satan, the Lord Jesus began His prophetic ministry of declaring God's message to the nation of Israel, the gospel of the kingdom (Matt. 4:17). Luke declares that the words of Moses pertaining to the special prophet were fulfilled by Christ (Acts 3:22-26). Christ came to be the Great Revealer of the mind of God to the lost sheep of Israel. He continued this prophetic ministry among the Jews for over three years before giving Himself as a ransom for humanity at Calvary. The Lord ended His prophetic ministry on earth when He ascended into heaven.

After John affirmed that he was not the Christ, not Elijah, and not the foretold Prophet, the priests asked him why he was baptizing people, since there was nothing in the Law about water baptism (vv. 24-25). John replied that he had been sent by God to point the Jewish nation to Christ through the necessity of repentance. They would not recognize Him without repentance (v. 26). After Christ was revealed in Israel, John's ministry would be complete. He then would willingly diminish in preference to the one who was highly preferred before Him and indeed existed before Him (3:30). Before Christ, John would gladly take the position of a lowly slave tasked with washing the dirty feet of house guests (v. 27). John the baptizer was performing his preaching and baptismal ministry in the most southern portion of the Jordan River at Bethabara (v. 28).

God's Lamb Is Anointed (vv. 29-34)

The next day John saw the Lord Jesus walking towards him and said of the Lord Jesus in the hearing of all those with him, *"Behold! The Lamb of God who takes away the sin of the world!"* (v. 29). This was the very One that John spoke of the previous day as being preferred before himself and indeed existed before him (v. 30). Since John the baptizer was born about six months before Jesus, this statement refers to His eternal essence as the Son of God – a matter that God the Father will also testify of shortly, after Christ's baptism.

From the synoptic Gospels we learn that John the baptizer did not want to baptize Christ, for he understood that He was holy, and that the Messiah needed no repentance. Jesus Christ, however, insisted that John baptize Him, for in His baptism Christ declared His condescension to identify with those He came to save. John does not mention Christ's baptism in his Gospel, but he does highlight God's own emblematic recognition of Christ as His Son, Israel's Messiah. God had already revealed to John that the Holy Spirit would come down from heaven in the form of a dove and remain on Israel's Messiah and that He would be the one that would baptize the repentant with the Holy Spirit (vv. 31-33).

After Christ was baptized by John, the baptizer witnessed the anointing of Christ by the Holy Spirit in the form of a dove (Mark 1:10). It had been accomplished, as revealed to him by God, to verify that Jesus of Nazareth was the Son of God, and Israel's Messiah. Luke affirms the fact that Christ was anointed by the Holy Spirit (Acts 10:38). Just as Israel's kings, prophets, and priests were previously anointed with oil at their consecration, the Holy Spirit anointed the Lord Jesus to initiate and enable His ministry to the lost sheep of Israel.

Christ's Public Ministry Begins (vv. 35-51)

Directly after Christ's baptism, Matthew tells us that God the Father declared His love and pleasure in His Son: *"This is My beloved Son, in whom I am well pleased"* (Matt. 3:17). Every thought, word, and deed of Christ pleased His Father; there was no sin or any kind of defilement within Him. John had already declared that the Lord Jesus *was*, not that He might be, *"the Lamb of God who takes away the sin of the world!"* (v. 29). The Father never questioned the impeccability of Christ – only Satan and men do that. Christ was blameless and perfect, the only acceptable substitutionary sacrifice for man's sin. This is the reason why John does not record the forty days of the devil's testing of our Savior directly after His baptism. Christ, God who became flesh (John 1:14), cannot be tempted to sin (Jas. 1:13).

The synoptic Gospels report that Christ immediately went into the wilderness to be tested by the devil for forty days. Afterwards, a gap exists in the synoptic accounts until the Lord is ready to begin His two-year Galilean ministry. This activity began shortly after Christ attended the Passover feast in Jerusalem (2:13) and about the time John the baptizer was put in prison by Herod (Mark 6:17). Details of what happened after Christ's baptism, mainly in Judea, but before His Galilean ministry, are provided in John 1:35-3:30.

John is presenting Christ in His deity, so Christ's 40-day wilderness testing does not interrupt his record of events that occurred directly after his baptism. On the next day, two disciples of John were with him, when the Lord Jesus walked nearby, one of which was Andrew, Simon Peter's brother (vv. 35, 40). The other unnamed disciple is likely John, the brother of James. John the baptizer said to his disciples, *"Behold the Lamb of God!"* (v. 36). After hearing this statement, both disciples left John to follow Christ (v. 37). This marks the beginning of an important transition of John's disciples becoming the Lord's disciples, for John knew that Christ must increase, and he must decrease (3:30). John had many disciples before Christ was revealed as the Lamb of God, but afterwards and throughout the Church Age, believers became Christ's disciples only, not the disciples of other men.

Noticing the two men following Him, the Lord stopped and turned towards them and asked, *"What do you seek?"* (v. 38). This question seems to have been designed to cause them to ponder what they were really desiring in life, for following Him would not be an easy lifestyle. They replied *"Teacher, where are You staying?"* (v. 39). The Lord said to them, *"Come and see."* It was about 10 a.m. and the disciples followed the Lord to his lodging and spent the remainder of the day with Him (v. 39) and perhaps even the night (v. 43).

Afterwards, Andrew immediately found his brother Simon and told him that he had found the promised Jewish Messiah, the Christ (v. 41). He then brought his brother to meet Jesus. When the Lord saw him, He said, *"You are Simon the son of Jonah. You shall be called Cephas"* (v. 42). *Cephas* is Aramaic for a stone or a rock. *Petros* or "Peter" is the Greek equivalent. Thus, Simon became Simon Peter.

We are not told if Philip was one of John's disciples or not, but the Lord knew all about Philip, and while journeying to Galilee, He found Philip, and said to him, *"Follow Me"* (v. 43). Philip, Andrew, and Simon Peter were all from Bethsaida and likely knew each other (v. 44). If John is referred to in verse 37, Philip became the fifth disciple of Christ.

After meeting the Lord, Philip informed an acquaintance named Nathanel that he had found the One that Moses and the prophets had foretold would come to deliver Israel (v. 45). His name was Jesus, the son of Joseph, who was from Nazareth. After hearing where Jesus lived, Nathanel said, *"Can anything good come out of Nazareth?"* (v. 46). Philip did not waste any time arguing about the matter; he simply said, *"Come and see,"* and Nathanael agreed to do so. Nathanael's name means "gift of God" and is only mentioned by name here and in John 21:2, but evidently Nathanael went by the name of Bartholomew also

John

(e.g., Luke 6:14). When listed in the Synoptic Gospels, Bartholomew is placed next to Philip's name, the one who led him to the Lord.

As Nathanael was approaching the Lord, He said, *"An Israelite indeed, in whom is no deceit!"* (v. 47). Nathanael was surprised by this statement concerning his character and wondered how this Stranger knew him. The Lord said, *"Before Philip called you, when you were under the fig tree, I saw you"* (v. 48). This was obviously a detail that no mortal man could have known unless he had been nearby, so Nathanael quickly concluded that he was talking to the Son of God and the King of Israel (v. 49). The Lord used the opportunity to inform Nathanael that he would see much more astounding things than this if he would agree to follow Him (v. 50). He would even see the greatness of His kingdom on earth, in which angels themselves would be ascending to heaven and descending to earth in acknowledgement of His authority (v. 51).

This scene was foreshadowed nearly two thousand years earlier, when Jacob had a prophetic dream while journeying north to Padan Aram to flee Esau's wrath (Gen. 28). While dreaming, Jacob observed holy angels ascending and descending on a broad and extensive ladder reaching from the earth to the canopy of heaven with God Himself positioned at the top.

In the dream, God spoke to Jacob and reconfirmed the covenant He had made with Abraham and Isaac. Jacob was the promised seed that would be as the dust of the earth. Isaac was promised descendants as numerous as the stars of heaven (26:4). Abraham, in whom the covenant was established, was promised both (22:17). Why the difference? Because Isaac represents the resurrected Christ who has inherited a heavenly land, and Jacob represents the expansion of the nation of Israel, which will inherit an earthly land during the Kingdom Age.

The Lord told Jacob, now a homeless wanderer, that He was with him. God promised to return him to the land that He had promised as an inheritance to his descendants. What Nathanael was told by Christ was that He was the fulfillment of the prophetic dream that Jacob had received long ago. He was the One who would deliver Israel and establish an earthly kingdom that would fulfill all the promises made to the Patriarchs.

The first chapter of John declares seven titles of Christ. He is ... "the Word" (v. 1), "the Light" (v. 7), "the Lamb of God" (v. 29), "the Christ" (v. 41), "the Son of God" (v. 49), "the King of Israel" (v. 49), and "the Son of Man" (v. 51). This is the first of many sets of seven in his Gospel.

John Chapter 2

The First Miracle – Water Turned to Wine at Cana (vv. 1-12)

We were informed in the last chapter that the Lord was traveling north to Galilee when He called Philip to follow Him (1:43). He apparently had planned to attend a wedding of a relative or friend in Cana (vv. 1-2). Cana was a village situated about five miles north of Nazareth. As Mary, the Lord's mother, was also attending, and would later direct the servants, the wedding of a relative is inferred.

At this time, the Lord had not named His twelve disciples, but there were already at least five disciples traveling with Him. The reference to *"on the third day"* in verse 1 likely connects with the "next day" statements in John 1:29 and 35. If so, that would mean that three days had passed since John's conversation with the Pharisees about who he was and was not. Or the phrase may mean that it was the third day since the calling of Philip and Nathanael, and that Christ had been traveling north since that time (1:45).

After a Jewish bride and groom had enjoyed seven days of intimacy together, a marriage feast, typically at the groom's home, was held for family and friends (Matt. 22:1-10). During the festivities, the Lord was informed by His mother that the hosts had run out of wine. This was an embarrassing situation, which Mary hoped that her Son would remedy, although she did not ask Him specifically to do so. Mary had been called a fornicator for over thirty years because of the unique conception and birth of Israel's Messiah, the holy One of Israel. No doubt, she was hoping that Jesus would use this situation to reveal Himself and remove the shame that she had been enduring.

The Lord then said to her, *"Woman, what does your concern have to do with Me? My hour has not yet come"* (v. 4). The title "woman" was not an unkind expression (e.g., 19:26), but what followed was more direct; Christ affirmed that His ministry was bigger than resolving a shortage of wine and that His affairs were on His Father's timetable, not hers. However, Mary still hoped that her Son would act on her request, so she instructed the servants to do whatever her Son requested (v. 5).

There were six empty stone waterpots nearby that had been earlier used for the ceremonial washing of hands commanded by rabbinical law. Each pot held between twenty and thirty gallons, and the Lord commanded the servants to fill all the pots (v. 6). To draw about 1,500 pounds of water from a well would have taken some time and required a lot of work, but the servants *filled* all the pots to the brim (v. 7).

Afterwards, the Lord told the servants to draw out some of the contents of the pots and take it to the master of the feast, which they did (v. 8). After tasting the water, that was now a delicious wine, the master of the feast called out the bridegroom and complimented him on saving the best wine for last (v. 9). The normal practice was to serve the best vintage first, as later the guests would not be as discerning about the quality of the wine being served (v. 10). The servants knew from where this high-quality wine had come, from waterpots full of water, but they did not reveal the secret at that time. It had apparently turned to wine after being drawn out of a pot, but before it was tasted. This was the beginning of miracles that Christ would perform, which not only manifested His intrinsic glory, but affirmed in His disciples' minds that indeed He was the Christ (v. 11).

The behavior of the servants at the marriage feast is noteworthy and a good pattern for us to follow also in serving the Lord. First, they were willing to serve (v. 5). Second, they were available to serve (i.e., they were present; v. 6). Third, they obeyed the command of the Lord (v. 7). Fourth, they were willing to work (v. 8). Fifth, they remained under authority, even when it seemed unreasonable to do so, and consequently saw the power of God working through their service.

From an allegorical perspective, the miracle at Cana had significant ramifications. As pictured in the empty waterpots, religious legalism offered God's covenant people nothing. The Mosaic Law only condemned them, and Rabbinical tradition put them under further bondage. But God intended for His Law to cause His people to acknowledge His holiness and their unworthiness before Him and then to receive His solution for their sin – Christ (Rom. 3:20; Gal. 5:24). Christ was now in their presence, and He was declaring the glory of God before their eyes and offering them satisfaction and joy for their souls, as pictured in the pots full of wine. Although drunkenness is always forbidden in Scripture, in the good sense wine speaks of joy (Ps. 104:15). All true satisfaction and joy in life are found in Christ.

The Man and Your God

The water being turned to wine at Cana is the first of thirty-five miracles recorded in the Gospels. Of these thirty-five miracles, only seven are found in *John*. Five of these seven miracles are found *only* in John's account: Turning the water into wine (ch. 2), healing the nobleman's son (ch. 4), healing a man with an infirmity at the pool of Bethesda (ch. 5), healing a man born blind (ch. 9), and raising Lazarus from the dead (ch. 11).

After turning the water into wine at Cana, the Lord traveled to Capernaum, but did not stay there many days (v. 12). He was accompanied by His mother, His half-brothers (their names are listed in Matt. 13:55 and Mark 6:3), and His disciples. It is likely that His half-sisters were with Him also.

The First Passover (vv. 13-25)

When the seven feasts were first commanded by Jehovah through Moses, they were called "The feasts of Jehovah" or "The feasts of the Lord" (Lev. 23:2). The first feast on the fourteenth day of the first month was referred to as "the Lord's Passover" (Lev. 23:5). But man invariably works to replace what is of God and for His pleasure with what is of man to please himself. Hence, when Christ was on the earth, the Passover was referred to as "the Passover of the Jews." Despite what it was now called, the Lord obeyed the dictates of the Law, that all Jewish males should attend the feast of unleavened bread, the feast of weeks, and the feast of booths each year in Jerusalem (Ex. 23:17). Because John correlates his narrative with the feasts of Jehovah, we know that the Lord would be crucified three years from the Passover mentioned in John 2.

Although the Lord Jesus is rarely spoken of in Scripture as being angry, it is evident that His holy anger blazed up on this occasion. After arriving at the temple, He made a scourge to drive the animals and their masters from the temple and He threw over the tables of the moneychangers (vv. 14-15; Matt. 21:12). The court of the Gentiles surrounded the temple and its sacred enclosure (i.e., the temple and the court of the priests where the bronze altar was located), the court of Israel (where Jewish men could worship), and then further east, the women's court (the location of the treasury and where Jewish women could worship). Harold Paisley addresses the error that Christ was correcting:

> The high priest had permitted a market in the court of the Gentiles, for sale of items used in the temple ritual, such as wine, salt, oil, and birds

and animals. There were also moneychangers who produced large revenues, often by fraud. There were those also who carried baggage merchandise from the markets through the sacred temple area, as a shortcut home. Mark is the only writer who records this added act of irreverence.[66]

These merchants and racketeers had turned the temple, God's house, into a place of commerce and thievery, but the Lord restored it to a house of prayer (v. 16). Matthew tells us that the Lord then quoted Jeremiah to affirm Israel's offense against God concerning appropriate behavior in the temple, God's house: *"My house shall be called a house of prayer for all nations. But you have made it a den of thieves"* (Matt. 21:17). The Lord Jesus cleansed the temple twice, once at the beginning of His earthly ministry (vv. 14-17), and then again a few days before His death (Matt. 21:12). In both situations, His righteous anger prompted behavior that honored His Father.

Having witnessed the Lord's boldness in the temple, the disciples immediately remembered the Messianic prophecy from Psalm 69:9: *"Zeal for Your house has eaten Me up"* (v. 17). Man had turned God's house of prayer into a place of commerce and corruption and the Lord keenly felt the offense and responded to remove the filth from His Father's house.

Given the Lord's audacious actions in the temple, the Jews demanded evidence of a sign to legitimize His actions as being under God's authority. The Lord Jesus responded, *"Destroy this temple, and in three days I will raise it up"* (v. 19). This statement confused His audience, because, historically speaking, it had taken 46 years for Herod to refurbish the temple that had been built under Zerubbabel's leadership almost six centuries earlier (v. 20).

The New Testament speaks of several types of temples that were important to God. Besides Jehovah's temple in Jerusalem, and the spiritual temple of the Church on earth (1 Tim. 3:15; 1 Pet. 2:5), there was also the temple of the Lord Jesus' body. The latter was what Christ was speaking of in verse 21. The Lord's body is referred to as a temple seven times in the Gospels, mostly by sarcastic witnesses at His crucifixion. In Himself, Christ had the authority and power to lay down His life and raise it up again (10:17-18). After Jesus Christ had raised Himself up from the dead after three days, His disciples remembered His statement issued early in His ministry and believed it to have come true (v. 22).

Many who observed the Lord's speech and doings during the Passover feast believed that He was indeed the Messiah (v. 23). Yet, the Lord knew what was in their hearts, so He did not commit Himself to them (vv. 24-25). The Jews wanted deliverance from Gentile rule and oppression that the promised Messiah would bring, but not the spiritual ramifications of brokenness before God as shown through repentance. Their confession of Christ was sight-based faith, and their thoughts and motives were not genuine.

It is doubtful that anyone, at this juncture, hearing Christ speaking figuratively about His resurrection, understood what He meant, yet the works which He accomplished did have a positive effect in the minds of many. Many Jews had subscribed to the dictum that "Seeing is believing." But as shown in the conclusion of chapter 6, faith based on sight is shallow and prone to waver when things change – this kind of faith does not please God, nor will it save anyone (Heb. 11:6).

Previously, the Lord said to Nathanael, *"Before Philip called you, when you were under the fig tree, I saw you"* (1:48). Frequently throughout the Gospels we read that Jesus Christ knew what was in people's hearts and minds, as well as being familiar with other facts that He could not have otherwise known unless He was omniscient. How astounded the Samaritan woman at the well must have been to hear the Lord reply to her denial of having a husband with these words: *"For you have had five husbands, and the one whom you now have is not your husband"* (4:18). How is it possible for the Lord to know and to do anything that we ask in His name (14:14)? We understand that the asking is in accordance to His will (1 Jn. 5:14), but how is He to know our needs and hear our requests if He is not omniscient? For the Lord Jesus to be our Great High Priest, He must be omniscient, otherwise He could not make intercession for all believers at the throne of grace.

In John's gospel account, all ministry is designated for the hands of the Son of God until His redemptive mission is completed (e.g., vv. 24-25). In this way, Christ is ensured the preeminence among all those with whom He comes in contact. In John, prior to His resurrection, we see neither the sharing of ministry nor glory (17:22). After His resurrection, the Lord commissioned His disciples to spread the gospel message and to disciple those trusting in Him for salvation (20:21-23, 21:15-25).

John Chapter 3

New Birth Is Explained to Nicodemus (vv. 1-21)

John now introduces us to a Pharisee named Nicodemus, who was one of the seventy elders composing the Sanhedrin, the Jewish judicial body (v. 1). The Pharisees numbered about 6,000 at this time and were an influential sect within the Sanhedrin. They held a strict interpretation of the Law and embraced many oral traditions. After the Jewish war against Rome (66-70 A.D.), their teachings formed the basis for Talmudic Judaism.[67]

Nicodemus visited Jesus at night as to not arouse suspicion against himself (v. 2). He respectfully referred to Jesus as "Rabbi" (a polite title given to a teacher) and knew that God was with Him because of the signs that He had performed. Although lacking in knowledge to whom he spoke, Nicodemus was a genuine seeker, so the Lord answered the question that was most on his mind, *"When the kingdom of God would come?"* (Luke 17:20). However, in the Pharisee's mind, this pertained to Israel receiving her full land allotment promised to Abraham and being liberated from Gentile oppression.

Although such blessings would characterize Christ's kingdom, this was not what the kingdom of God was about. From God's perspective, it had to do with His rule in the hearts and lives of His covenant people, such that they displayed His morality and authority to all nations. This meant that God must be living within His people, but how was that possible? The Lord Jesus tells Nicodemus the answer: *"Most assuredly, I say to you, unless one is born again, he cannot see the kingdom of God"* (v. 3). John Heading explains that the English word rendered "again" in this verse does not represent the best meaning of the Greek word *anothen* from which it is derived:

> The doctrine of being "born again" is of fundamental importance. The word "again" (*anōthen*) is not the usual word for "again" (*palin*). Strictly, it means "from above" as when the veil was rent from "the top" to the bottom (Matt. 27:51). John quotes the word five times, as

"He that *cometh from above*" (John 3:31); "except it were given thee *from above*" (19:11). In other words, this birth is entirely distinct from ordinary human reproductive processes.[68]

Hence, the Lord Jesus, who had come down from above, likened the receiving of His life to being born again. No one can live for God or reside with God in heaven without receiving spiritual life in Christ. Through rebirth, those who have trusted Christ for salvation become God's spiritual children (1:12-13). The only way to avoid eternal death is to receive eternal life in Christ. While those in Christ may experience physical death, they will never experience spiritual death (11:25-26).

Through being born again, the Christian can enjoy the resurrection life of Christ now (Phil. 3:10) and have the hope of bodily resurrection into His presence later (1 Cor. 15:51-52). God's personal offer to be one with Him is rescinded when physical death occurs (Heb. 9:27). If a person dies without Christ, he or she will spend eternity without Him in a spiritual abode called the Lake of Fire, commonly referred to as Hell (Rev. 20:13-15).

Christ's statement was confusing to Nicodemus, who asked how a man could reenter his mother's womb again to experience physical birth (v. 4). Obviously, this was an unreasonable meaning of what the Lord had said, but an even more impossible scenario was an individual gaining heaven without being spiritually born from above. Hence, the Lord answered Nicodemus' inquiry by saying that unless an individual is born of water and the Spirit, he or she cannot enter the kingdom of God (v. 5).

There are four possible understandings of what the Lord meant by this statement, with the last three being the most reasonable. First, born of water may speak of natural birth and being born of the Spirit, spiritual birth. This interpretation is awkward and without Scriptural basis, but it is true that a person must be physically born (i.e., the embryonic sac surrounding an infant with water in the womb must be broken) before he or she can be spiritually born again by trusting Christ. Second, to be cleansed by the water of the Word (15:3; Eph. 5:26) is necessary before an individual can experience spiritual regeneration by the Holy Spirit (1 Pet. 1:23). Scripture reveals our sin to us and our need to be cleansed by the Savior before God can reside within us. Thus, both God's Word and His Spirit are necessary to receive salvation. Third, the reference to water may be alluding to eternal life itself (4:14), which comes through the work of the Holy Spirit, who is also typified as moving water (7:38-39).

Fourth, the connective word *kai* between water and the Spirit can be translated as "even." Hence, the text would read "water, *even* the Spirit."

This author favors the second explanation as it follows the Old Testament's pattern of God first cleansing what He chooses to indwell. L. M. Grant further explains why this understanding has merit:

> Natural birth is "of blood," not "water": "the life of the flesh is in the blood." But as well as being by the Spirit of God, the new birth is "of water." Certainly, this is not mere natural water, but explained in Ephesians 5:26, where water symbolizes the word of God. Therefore, we may say that the life of the Spirit is in the word (compare John 5:24; Jas. 1:18; 1 Pet. 1:23). The word of God and the Spirit of God work in perfect concord in this marvelous miracle of new birth: it is absolutely a divine work, for no one's will or work has anything to do with his birth: it is of God.[69]

F. B. Hole suggests that Christ was referring to Israel's future cleansing and indwelling by the Holy Spirit as foretold by Ezekiel. The Lord was implying that Nicodemus as a religious leader should have been expecting the fulfillment of this prophecy:

> The Lord's words in verse 5 are clearly a reference to the prophecy of Ezekiel 36:24-32, which foretells the deep and fundamental cleansing which will reach Israel in the beginning of the millennial age, when God will "sprinkle clean water" upon them, giving them "a new heart," and putting within them "a new spirit," and then putting His Spirit within them. As a result of this, they will be so cleansed in their very being that they will loathe themselves as in their former corruptions, and then they will be blessed of God. This passage does not give us the full truth of the matter, but it gives so much that Nicodemus ought to have felt no surprise at the things he had just heard.[70]

What is not suggested by this text is that someone is born again through undergoing the rite of water baptism. The Lord makes it clear that a repentant sinner is born again by the Holy Spirit; there is no power in the water (vv. 6-8). Later, Paul would teach that believing the gospel and not water baptism was necessary for salvation (1 Cor. 1:17).

Types of Christ in the Old Testament are usually represented by people or objects: the ark, the rock, the rod, the door, the arm, the shepherd, the veil, etc. These are used to accomplish a work and to picture Christ performing the Father's will. The Holy Spirit, however, is generally depicted as an active fluid, such as flowing olive oil (Zech. 4), blowing wind (John 3), rushing water from a rock (John 7) or seven flames of fire (Rev. 4). The Holy Spirit, in these types, is not visibly seen doing the Father's will (as in the types representing Christ), but rather He enables and accomplishes the task at hand in a powerful and invisible fashion. Thus, individuals must receive Christ's message and come under the power of the Holy Spirit to be born from above (v. 8).

Nicodemus did not understand what the Lord was saying (v. 9). While Old Testament Scripture foretold of the New Covenant that Messiah would secure on behalf of the Jewish nation (Heb. 8:8), the ramifications of how one came into the good of that were obscure. As the Lord pointed out to Nicodemus, he was a religious teacher in Israel and yet did not know what the Lord was saying about the only means of entering the kingdom of God (and being with God in heaven; v. 10).

Verse 11 contains the first of twenty-five "Most assuredly" statements (also rendered "truly truly" or "verily verily") in the Gospel of John. The expression means "listen up," for what I am going to tell you now is vitally important. This phrase is not found in the other Gospels. The Lord Jesus said to Nicodemus, *"Most assuredly, I say to you, We speak what We know and testify what We have seen, and you do not receive Our witness"* (v. 11). But who is the "we" in this verse? Is the Lord including the testimony of John or His disciples with that of Himself to form the "we" in His statement? The fact that the Lord explains that He is expressing heavenly things, which only those from Heaven would understand, indicates that He is likely speaking of His Father (v. 12, 5:17, 37-38). It is possible that the Lord may also be including deceased prophets that God had expressed heavenly things to, yet none of them would have fully understood what God was accomplishing in Christ, for this was an unrevealed truth before Calvary (1 Cor. 2:8-9).

The writer of Hebrews informs us that God the Father *"has spoken unto us by His Son"* (Heb. 1:2). The Lord Jesus perfectly reflected the character and will of His Father in everything that He spoke and did, thus the gospel message declared by Jesus Christ was fully endorsed by the Godhead. The Lord Jesus had told the Jewish leaders about His coming earthly kingdom which God's Word had foretold, but they had not believed Their testimony. The first "you" in verse 12 is singular and relates to Nicodemus, but the last three occurrences of "you" are plural, speaking of the Jewish nation and particularly Israel's leadership. The "you" in "how will you believe" is relating to the verb in the active voice, meaning *"how will you believe on your own?"* Without heeding the testimony of Christ and His heavenly Father and coming under the enlightening power of the Holy Spirit, they could not understand heavenly things and be saved.

The Lord told Nicodemus that "no one has ascended to heaven" then returned to the earth to teach heaven's wisdom. The exception being that He had been in heaven and had come to earth (by His incarnation) to be the Son of Man, God's Messenger and Message to Israel (v. 13). Yet, because He was still omnipresent, He, in the spiritual sense, was still in heaven, though appearing visibly as the Son of Man on earth. The Lord Jesus referred to Himself much more often by the title "Son of Man" than by the title "Son of God." In so doing, He was not calling attention to His divine essence but to His lowly position and ministry on earth.

To further speak of His earthly mission, the Lord reminded Nicodemus of a story recorded in Numbers 21 that wonderfully typified His message of salvation. The Israelites had become completely dissatisfied with God's provision of manna for them. Jehovah brought fiery serpents among the people of Israel because of their murmuring and disbelief; those bitten died (Num. 21:4-6). The serpent's bite resulted in death! The correlation the Israelites were to learn was that the root of sin in them also had repercussions – death. C. A. Coates explains that God cannot bring us into what His love proposes to give us without first teaching us this profound truth:

> This visitation of God [the fiery serpents] brought home in a sharp and terrible way that the naughtiness of the flesh is really satanic in origin. It is a poison introduced by Satan himself. … Can we wonder that it is directly and positively adverse to God? It is a terrible thing to contemplate, but there is no full conviction of sin until this is brought home to one experimentally. The bite of the fiery serpent is the divine conviction of what the flesh truly is in the very source of its being. … We shall never understand what life is as the gift of God until we realize that we are death-stricken, and deservedly so, and we can do absolutely nothing to extricate ourselves from that state or its consequences.[71]

Understanding their desperate need, the Israelites came to Moses and acknowledged: *"We have sinned, for we have spoken against the Lord and against you; pray to the Lord that He take away the serpents from us"* (Num. 21:7). Moses immediately interceded on behalf of the people and God responded with a solution to avoid death: *"Make a fiery serpent, and set it on a pole; and it shall be that everyone who is bitten, when he looks at it, shall live"* (Num. 21:8). Moses did as the Lord said and explained the "look and live" provision to the people. No one forced anyone to take advantage of this lifesaving provision. Those bitten, who wanted to live, looked by faith at the bronze serpent and those who refused were responsible for their own demise.

In Scripture, bronze speaks of "fiery" judgments, while the serpent itself is a symbol of sin and rebellion (Rev. 12:9), and the lofty pole prefigures Christ's cross. The typological imagery is astounding, and the Lord Jesus wanted to ensure that Nicodemus understood the pattern put in place centuries before: *"And as Moses lifted up the serpent in the wilderness, even so must the Son of Man be lifted up, that whoever believes in Him should not perish but have eternal life"* (3:14-15). At Calvary, Christ became sin for us and took our place. Everyone who looks by faith to the Savior's completed work on the cross shall not experience spiritual death but shall live forever with Christ. Because Christ rose from the grave, those trusting in Him receive eternal life in Him. All of us were born snake-bitten (i.e., we are spiritually dead in Adam; Rom. 5:12), meaning that we too must look to Christ to live!

Verse 16 is one of the most popular verses in the Bible and poses the central context of all Scripture: *"For God so loved the world that He gave His only begotten Son, that whoever believes in Him should not perish but have everlasting life."* Because of God's love for condemned humanity, God sent His *monogene* (one and only one) Son into the world that by believing in Him (i.e., that He is the sole means of divine reconciliation), individuals would not perish in eternal judgment.

Verse 17 is the first of thirty-nine occurrences in John to state that God the Father sent His Son into the world. Those who believe in Christ, God's only begotten Son, alone for salvation gain everlasting life in Him, but those who do not believe in Him remain in their sin, for they are *"condemned already"* (v. 18). When Adam sinned in Eden, it was the sin of the people (for all were in Adam), so all are born dead in sin and condemned before God (Rom. 5:12-14). It is observed that the Greek word *krino* occurs three times in verses 17-18 and is best rendered "judged" (referring to the process of a trial). When the preposition *kata* is added to *krino*, the connotation changes to "condemnation" (i.e., the sentencing of the guilty). For Adam, the trial is over, and although those born in Adam have been found guilty in him (literally "judged already") and deserve death (condemnation), but the final sentencing will not occur until the Great White Throne judgment. This means that until individuals die, they can have their sin and guilt cleansed away by Christ's blood and escape the final sentence of eternal judgment (Heb. 9:14, 27).

Paul says that God will take flaming vengeance on all those who do not obey the gospel message of Christ (1 Cor. 15:3-4; 2 Thess. 1:8). The idea of disobedience means that some first heard the gospel message and then made a conscious decision to reject it. So those who believe the gospel of Christ are eternally saved, those who do not are still condemned in Adam, and those who reject the gospel will be eternally punished. This means that God can still apply the blood of His Son in grace to those born condemned who by faith later obeyed the revelation that they had received without hearing the gospel message. Examples would be those who trusted in creation's testimony of a Creator (Rom. 1:19-20), or believed that they could not ease their own guilty conscience by doing good works (Rom. 2:15), or by heeding the warning of Angels not to worship the Antichrist during the Tribulation Period (Rev. 14), or those who were too young to morally understand their sinful condition and need for a Savior. For example, Jeremiah refers to the young children being sacrificed by the Jews at Tophet as "the innocents" (Jer. 19:4).

The Son of God had come to the earth incarnate to be God's light (revelation of divine truth) to the world. Natural man loves darkness (the absence of light, that which is not of God), for he thinks that his sin will not be noticed and that he will not be punished for it (vv. 19-20). On the contrary, those obeying the light walk with God and do those things which He approves of (v. 21). In his first epistle, John affirms that if believers (those born again) want to have fellowship with God, we must depart from darkness, confess our sin, and yield to His will for our lives (1 Jn. 1:6-9). God will not walk in darkness with us; we must walk with Him in the light of divine truth.

John the Baptizer's Ministry Concludes (vv. 22-36)

The Lord with His disciples journeyed south into Judea and continued preaching the kingdom gospel message to the lost sheep of Israel and His disciples baptized (under His supervision) those responding in repentance and faith to His message (v. 22, 4:1-2). John, who had not been imprisoned by Herod yet, also continued his preaching ministry, as Christ's forerunner, and was baptizing in Aenon near Salim,

The Man and Your God

for there was much water there (vv. 23-24). This site is unknown today but is generally thought to be on the Jordan River about halfway between the Sea of Galilee and the Dead Sea.

An argument occurred between some of John's disciples and the Jewish elite over purification required by rabbinical law (v. 25). The dispute quickly transitioned into a comparison of John's ministry with that of Christ and His disciples. The Jewish leaders (4:1) were apparently trying to make John jealous by calling his attention to the fact that his disciples were leaving him to follow Jesus Christ (v. 26). Yet, John turned their words around on them, by declaring that this dynamic was proof that his ministry was approved by God (v. 27). As he had told them when they were beyond the Jordan River previously, He was Christ's forerunner, and his divinely appointed mission was to call his countrymen to repentance and point them to the Savior – Jesus Christ.

We pause to consider two applications from John's ministry. First, if a so-called Christian minister or preacher is gathering people to themselves and not pointing those they are influencing to Christ, then that activity or person must be rejected. Disciples of Christ should not seek the praise of men, high positions, or honorable titles – all epithets and all praise are reserved for the Lord Jesus Christ. Second, John always knew that he had been sent by God to preach Christ (1:6, 33). All of God's servants must realize that none can preach Christ except that they are sent by God (Rom. 10:15). If preachers send themselves or are commissioned by men into ministry without God sending them, the end result will be worse than if they had not gone at all.

John had already told the Pharisees that he was not the Christ, that he was not Elijah, and that he was not the esteemed prophet foretold by Moses (v. 28, 1:20-21). John was merely the friend of the Bridegroom who rejoiced greatly because the Bridegroom was nearby and John could still hear His voice (v. 29). John's declaration should be the motto of every servant of Christ: *"He* [the Lord Jesus] *must increase, but I must decrease"* (v. 30).

> Until self-effacing men return again to spiritual leadership, we may expect a progressive deterioration in the quality of popular Christianity year after year till we reach the point where the grieved Holy Spirit withdraws – like the Shekinah from the Temple.
>
> — A. W. Tozer

An earthly man (like John) speaks of earthly things, but the One coming from heaven, Christ, speaks of heavenly things and is above all that is on the earth. Christ had accurately testified of the heavenly things that He knew to be true, but His testimony had been generally rejected (vv. 32-33). Christ had been sent by His heavenly Father and anointed by the Holy Spirit, which meant His ministry was under the full authority and power of God (vv. 34-35). John reminds His audience that the Holy Spirit cannot be received in measure; He indwells and fully empowers those who choose to walk in God's light (truth).

Verse 36 is a nice summary of what the Lord had early conveyed to Nicodemus and especially resounds the message of verses 15-18. Those believing on Christ have eternal life, but those who do not believe shall not receive eternal life, and in fact the wrath of God abides on them. The two Greek words rendered "believes" and "does not believe" in verse 36 are different; the second occurrence means "to disobey," which as mentioned earlier infers that someone has heard and rejected the truth. The verb translated "wrath" is in the present tense, which agrees with verse 18; all in Adam are born judged (guilty) with God's judicial anger looming over us. The only means of escaping final sentencing (eternal condemnation) is to receive a pardon in Christ through faith.

Whereas Matthew's gospel account stresses "righteousness" in association with the kingdom, John focuses on "eternal life." Both are connected and form one divine truth: Without life in Christ, one cannot display the righteousness of God. Why will the kingdom of God be full of righteousness? Righteousness is what emanates from the eternal God of the universe. All those who are born of God will radiate His righteous and holy life.

The words "repent" and "forgive" are not found in John's gospel account because John conveys the gospel message from a precise heavenly perspective. Spiritually speaking, the plain truth is shrouded in a sincere warning that is often introduced by the phrase "verily, verily." One prevalent message in John is that in God is life, and apart from God is death. Man chose to be independent from God in the Garden of Eden and, consequently, brought death upon the entire race. In reality, the Lord Jesus was the first spiritually alive human to walk upon the planet since that dreadful day in which our first parents died. One cannot turn to Christ without repenting first (Luke 13:3, 5), but that is not John's emphasis. He speaks of death and life and of believing and not believing.

John Chapter 4

Christ Departs Judea for Galilee (vv. 1-4)

After hearing that the Pharisees were concerned about the growing number of new converts being baptized by the Lord's disciples, the Lord decided it was time to leave Judea and take the Kingdom Gospel message to Galilee (vv. 1-2). Normally, Jews traveling north and south through Israel trekked through the Jordan Valley to avoid the Samaritans in central Palestine. However, at this juncture the Lord Jesus was determined to travel north through Samaria back to Galilee (v. 4).

Understanding the history of Samaria is needful to fully appreciate the events occurring in this chapter. Because of Israel's stubborn idolatry, God chastened His covenant people through the Assyrians who invaded and conquered northern Israel in eighth century B.C. Many Jews died and many more were enslaved and removed from their homeland; then the Assyrians repopulated the area of Israel with Gentiles from various places (2 Kgs. 17:1-24). The Law prohibited Jews from intermarrying with Gentiles, but given the oppressed situation, this became commonplace, and the people of Samaria became of mixed ethnicity.

This meant that the Samaritans could not engage in worship in Jerusalem. Under the leadership of a rogue Levitical priest, a new type of paganism was developed, and Mount Gerizim, with its own temple, became the sacred place of worship for the Samaritans (2 Kgs. 17:27). Thus, the Jews in Galilee and Judea despised the Samaritans and had no dealing with them (v. 9).

Christ and the Samaritan Woman (vv. 5-38)

The Lord and his disciples came to the city of Sychar in Samaria which was near Jacob's well. The area and the well were steeped in Jewish history and nostalgia. Jacob's well is a biblical site that exists to this day.

John

Near Sychar was a parcel of ground that was first purchased by Jacob (Gen. 33:18-20) and then was given to Joseph by Jacob (Gen. 48:22). Later, Joseph's bones were buried in this location after the liberated Israelites returned to the promised land from Egypt (Josh. 24:32). In this way, the death of Joseph was connected to the life-sustaining water from Jacob's well. This relationship prefaces Christ's teaching in this chapter: through His death, Christ would provide living water to guilty sinners coming to Him for eternal life.

Being wearied by the journey, the Lord remained at the well to rest while His disciples went into town to buy supplies (v. 8). The Lord's weariness and thirst indicate that He was subject to human frailty as we are; He was not divinely immune from the limitations and experiences of the human body. The Lord clearly orchestrated this situation to create the perfect opportunity to dialog with a particular Samaritan woman, whom He was waiting to meet at the well.

Symbolically speaking, water is often connected with God's rest and blessing (Gen. 2:10; Rev. 22:1) – He is the fountainhead of both. This concept is first demonstrated in Genesis 16, when the Lord met with a runaway bondservant named Hagar in the wilderness by *"a fountain of water"* (Gen. 16:7) also referred to as *"a well"* (Gen. 16:14). This is the first mention of a well in Scripture. How fitting for the all-sustaining Lord to meet a distressed woman in a life-threatening situation by a well in a desert place!

Interestingly, the first occurrence of a well in the New Testament is the scene before us; the Lord went out of His way to meet a Samaritan woman with a sin-devastated life at Jacob's well. The Lord's dialogue with this woman is fascinating and it is His longest personal conversation recorded in Scripture. Because of her ignoble reputation, she came to the well at about 6:00 p.m. to avoid other women drawing water later at dusk; no one wanted to talk to her, but the Lord Jesus did (vv. 5-6). (Although the Synoptic Gospels reference time by Jewish reckoning, John adopts the Roman standard throughout his account.) Just as Rebekah, centuries earlier, had arrived at a well at the most opportune time to draw water for Abraham's servant (who had just prayed for this sign; Gen. 24:13-20), the Samaritan woman came to the well at the most appropriate time to also enter into God's purposes.

There can hardly be a stronger contrast in Scripture between the Lord's interview with Nicodemus in the previous chapter to the Samaritan woman in this chapter: Nicodemus, a respected Jewish man, a pious Pharisee, was seeking answers from Christ, but this immoral Samaritan woman, an outcast of society, was indifferent to Christ. However, the well-educated religious man was just as lost as this ignorant woman of the world.

In the social prejudices of that day, men and women did not engage in public conversations, especially if strangers, and Jews and Samaritans did not converse unless for legitimate reasons, such as business dealings. Ignoring the ethnic bias of that day, the Lord, being thirsty, asked her to draw water for Him (v. 7). The Samaritan woman was surprised that a Jew would speak to her, let alone ask her for something (v. 9). As the Lord talks with this woman, her understanding of who He is progresses from "a Jew," to "a prophet," and then to "the Christ" (vv. 9, 19, 29).

The Savior used His own human need to introduce Himself as God's gift to her that would satisfy her soul's desperate need. He said to her, *"If you knew the gift of God, and who it is who says to you, 'Give Me a drink,' you would have asked Him, and He would have given you living water"* (v. 10). He offered her "living water" (Himself) to satisfy her spiritually-parched life. Scripture often portrays God, Himself, as the "living water" (the spiritual agency) that will satisfy the deepest need of the human soul (Jer. 2:13; Zech. 14:8).

But the woman did not understand the analogy. She did not see how the Lord could provide her with living water from a deep well when He had nothing to draw water with (v. 11). Accordingly, she asked Him how the living water He spoke of was to be obtained. She also inquired if He thought He was greater than their father Jacob who initially dug the well centuries earlier (v. 12). In other words, "If you have something better, why are you asking me for a drink." But what the Lord offered her was "the gift of God," which could only be received in grace, not by human works. Physically speaking, those who drank mere water would need to drink again to live (v. 13). But spiritually speaking, anyone drinking the living water that He provided in Himself would never thirst again (v. 14). The human soul finds full satisfaction in Christ alone!

Peter mentions a well, for the final time in Scripture, when he warns against false teachers: *"These are wells without water, clouds carried by a tempest, for whom is reserved the blackness of darkness forever"* (2 Pet. 2:17). False teachers offer falsehoods, which culminate in false hopes. No bubbling fountain of refreshment is there; only a deep, dry hole waiting for its next victim to fall into it. In contrast, the Lord Jesus is God's messenger of truth, and offers an abundant life of joy despite circumstances (10:10). When one embraces the Savior, a jubilant fountain of refreshing spiritual drink is enjoyed and blessings of the abundant life are obtained. Like Israel in the wilderness, we too can sing to the Fountain of Life, *"Spring up, O well"* (Num. 21:17).

The idea of never being thirsty and not having to draw water from the well again appealed to the Samaritan woman who asked the Lord for His living water (v. 15). It was at this juncture that the Lord asked her to get her husband, but she replied by saying that she was not married (vv. 16-17). Clearly, she had no desire to open her heart to a stranger. Although her statement was true, it was not the whole truth, and her past was completely known to the Lord Jesus. He affirmed that she had superficially told the truth, then filled in the details of her life's story: she had been married five times and was now living with a man (i.e., in fornication) that was not her husband (v. 18). This affirms that God does not recognize "living together" as a state of matrimony, as there is no marital covenant with Him (Prov. 2:17). The woman was living in sin, and the Lord could not give her living water until she confessed her sin.

The woman knew that there was no way for a Jewish stranger to have known her past; so, she responded by saying, *"Sir, I perceive that You are a prophet"* (v. 19). Being uneasy about her past sins being exposed, she abruptly changed the subject to their differing customs in worshiping God (v. 20). Pointing to Mount Gerizim, she informed the Lord that *"our fathers worshiped on this mountain"* (v. 20). The Samaritans believed that they stemmed from Ephraim and Manasseh, thus her reference to Jacob as "our father" (v. 12) and those who had worshiped on Ebal and Gerizim in Joshua's day as "our fathers" (v. 20). As previously mentioned, because of their mixed pedigree, the Samaritans were not permitted access to the temple in Jerusalem and a harsh disdain for Samaritans by the Jews became the cultural norm.

Over time, the Samaritans developed their own religious system of worship on Mount Gerizim near Jacob's well. Regrettably, their esteemed place of worship had displaced the proper Object of worship. This same religious pride keeps many religious people today from properly worshiping the Lord Jesus Christ. When places of worship or pious formality have replaced the One to be worshiped, man ignorantly honors himself and disdains the Lord.

The Lord did not ignore her diversion tactic but responded to it to teach her of Himself. In fact, there was a day coming when neither Mount

Gerizim nor Jerusalem would be the place of worship (speaking of the Church Age):

> *Woman, believe Me, the hour is coming when you will neither on this mountain, nor in Jerusalem, worship the Father. You worship what you do not know; we know what we worship, for salvation is of the Jews. The hour is coming, and now is, when the true worshipers will worship the Father in spirit and truth* (vv. 21-23).

The erroneous religion that the Samaritans practiced would never provide them salvation, for God had chosen to extend wonderful privileges to Israel, including the promised Messiah who would be born of the Jewish nation (Rom. 9:4-5). Only through Him would individuals become true worshipers of God. The human spirit is God-conscious and once spiritual regeneration occurs, individual believers will be able to spiritually commune with God, that is, as he or she abides in the truth. Thus, God's salvation to the world (through His Messiah) would come from "the Jews," not the Samaritans. The woman replied, *"I know that Messiah is coming (who is called Christ). When He comes, He will tell us all things"* (v. 25). The Hebrew word for God's *Anointed One* is "Messiah" and the Greek equivalent is "Christ." The Lord's answer was concise, *"I who speak to you am He"* (v. 26). The One offering eternal, living water to her was none other than the promised Jewish Messiah.

The Lord informed the Samaritan woman that there was a time coming in which those who would worship God would be able to do so in spirit and truth. The Lord was speaking of the Church Age. Those who had been born from above through the gospel message would have the Holy Spirit within them and be able to worship God through their human spirit in scriptural truth. Like Hagar, she believed and obeyed the Lord, and received a great blessing from Him. The prophet Isaiah writes, *"Therefore with joy you will draw water from the wells of salvation"* (Isa. 12:3). A fountain of lasting joy springs up from the believer's spirit when Christ dwells within. Thankfully, the woman found a seventh man that day, the perfect Man, who gave her eternal life and she responded by gladly telling others that the awaited Messiah had come.

As promised, today the Holy Spirit guides believers into a deeper understanding of truth concerning the Lord Jesus and the overall greatness and goodness of God (16:13-14). Only through Spirit-led worship, which will be completely founded in divine truth, can the

John

believer offer any acceptable sacrifice of praise to God. Thus, the words of John the baptizer ring true: *"A man can receive nothing, except it be given him from heaven"* (3:27). Many continue this practice today by identifying with Christ through religious rote without knowing Him personally as Savior (Matt. 7:21-23). Worship that pleases God must emerge from a willing heart that is illuminated by the Holy Spirit in accordance with revealed truth: *"God is Spirit, and those who worship Him must worship in spirit and truth."* God is a holy spiritual being. If what we say or do in worship is not true or Spirit-led, it cannot honor God; it is mere form, religious fanfare, and has no eternal value.

The disciples returned from obtaining supplies about the time the Lord identified Himself to the Samaritan woman as the promised Messiah (v. 27). Though the disciples marveled that their Master was talking to her, none of them said a word about it. Additionally, the Lord's example of proper motive in gospel ministry is noteworthy: He put aside His own need for water (for He was thirsty) to meet the more pressing need of satisfying the woman's spiritual thirst. There is no indication that the woman ever drew water from the well to provide the Lord Jesus a drink. Effective gospel outreach will cost believers their time, resources, creature comforts, and in some cases their very lives, but all believers are to be faithful witnesses for Christ wherever He has placed them in the world (Acts 1:8).

The woman then departed the well, without her waterpot, to tell others of the One who knew about her degenerate past but still offered Himself to her (v. 28)! She posed the question to her fellow Samaritans, *"Could this be the Christ?"* (v. 29). This was an effective question, for many came out of the city to determine whether Jesus of Nazareth was the promised Messiah (v. 30). The Lord had spoken to the Samaritan woman seven times during their dialogue. The woman had also spoken seven times, six times to the Lord and then once to the men of Sychar. Her testimony reminds us that those who speak often with the Lord will also yearn to speak to others about Him.

After the woman departed from them, the disciples urge the Lord to eat something (v. 31). The Lord replied to them, *"I have food to eat of which you do not know"* (v. 32). The disciples were confused by this statement and wondered if someone else had given Him something to eat while they were in town securing supplies (v. 33). Therefore, the Lord Jesus clarified His statement: His "food" was to do His Father's will and finish the work that His Father had tasked Him with (v. 34). Food is necessary to sustain physical life, but in comparison, the spiritual life that He was providing to others was much more important.

The Lord then caused His disciples to look out over the fields in the valley – they were *"already white for harvest"* though harvest time was still four months away (v. 35). Normally wheat was planted in December and harvested in mid-Spring. As the wheat seed sprouts and grows, it appears green, then as the heads of grain ripen, the wheat fields appear yellow in color and then white, signaling that the crop is ready to harvest. But in the Lord's estimation, though it was seeding time for wheat, the fields were already ripe for harvesting souls. The Lord's statement provides a clue to the timing of his encounter with the Samaritan woman: likely, at or near the Feast of Dedication in mid-December (10:22). (This feast is known as Hanukkah today.) During their religious feasts, the Samaritans typically wore white robes, and this may have been what triggered the Lord's request that the disciples look out over the countryside to see the ripened fields of souls needing to be harvested.

The Lord then likened the difficult work of evangelism to that of sowing and reaping (v. 36). Rarely, is someone led to the Savior through one person's efforts, but rather there is a cooperative laboring among God's servants to achieve the final ingathering of souls into God's barn (heaven; vv. 37-38). Believers labor together with God in their assigned callings and wherever He places them in His field of harvest (1 Cor. 3:6-9).

The Lord and the Samaritans (vv. 39-45)

Many believed the testimony of the Samaritan woman and came to hear Christ's message for themselves (v. 39). After hearing His message, the Samaritans urged the Lord to stay longer (v. 40). The Lord remained with the Samaritans for two days and many trusted in Him after listening to His message (vv. 41-42). In only seven brief statements the Lord masterfully led a poor destitute sinner to salvation, who then brought others to the Savior also.

After spending two days with the Samaritans, the Lord continued His journey northward to Galilee. As the Lord was from Nazareth of Galilee, He knew that the people in this region would be less likely to heed His message, *"for a prophet has no honor in his own country"* (v. 44). This ill disposition was later proven to be true, for the citizens of Nazareth sought to throw Him over a cliff after hearing His teaching (Luke 4:28-

30). Months later, after returning to Nazareth, He would repeat the saying in verse 44, for He was hindered from performing many miracles because of their rejection of Him (Matt. 13:57).

Regardless of Jewish disbelief in various places, it was needful for the Lord to preach the kingdom message throughout Israel. John states that many Galileans did receive Him, because they had been at Jerusalem during the Passover feast and heard Christ's words and witnessed His signs (v. 45). But a social recognition of Jesus' fame was not the same as accepting Him as the Son of God.

The Lord Heals the Nobleman's Son (vv. 46-54)

The Lord returned to Cana, where He had previously turned water into wine at a wedding feast (v. 46). There was a certain nobleman from Capernaum, who after hearing that Jesus had come to Galilee, went looking for Him, to seek help for his sick son who was at the point of death (v. 47). The Lord used the man's request to publicly rebuke the idea that witnessing signs and wonders would somehow boost true faith (v. 48). The "you" in verse 48 is plural and does not refer to the nobleman, but to the Jewish people in general. The type of faith that pleases God rises above what the human senses can verify or what the human intellect can rationalize to trust that what God has said is true. Even after the Lord had used the man's request to rebuke sign seekers, the distraught father continued to plead for Him to help his son. This is the kind of persistent faith that pleases the Lord!

The Nobleman felt that Jesus Christ was his only hope, so he implored the Lord to show his son mercy (v. 49). The Lord longs to honor this kind of faith, so the Lord told the distressed father not to worry, for his son lived and the man believed the Lord's declaration and returned home (v. 50). Even before he arrived at his home, his servants informed him that his son was well (v. 51). When the man inquired at what time his son improved, his servants told him that it was at the seventh hour on the previous day (v. 52). Then the man knew that it had been the Lord who had healed him and not just a coincidence.

The nobleman then testified of Jesus to his family and friends and all in his household believed that Jesus of Nazareth was their promised Messiah (v. 53). The healing of the nobleman's son was the second of seven miracles that John recorded in his gospel account (v. 54).

John Chapter 5

Healing of a Crippled Man at the Pool of Bethesda (vv. 1-16)

John informs us that there was a feast of the Jews and that the Lord Jesus went to Jerusalem for this feast. The feast is unnamed but was likely the first feast in the Jewish calendar, the Passover. If this was the case, then this event would mark the end of the first year of the Lord's ministry, as a previous Passover feast was mentioned in John 2.

Another possibility is that the reference relates to the human-instituted feast of *Purim*, which commenced after God delivered His people from Haman's evil plot in the days of Esther. This was a popular feast occurring on the fourteenth day of Adar (typically in March) and would thus have preceded the Passover feast on the fourteenth day of Nisan, by one month. Hence, the timing of Christ's third miracle recorded by John would have likely been in early spring, near the conclusion of the Lord's first year of ministry.

The miracle takes place at the pool of Bethesda located on the northeast side of Jerusalem near the Sheep Gate (v. 2). Bethesda means "house of mercy." L. M. Grant suggests that the proximity of the pool with its five porches to the sheep gate has typological meaning:

> The pool of Bethesda (meaning "house of mercy") by the sheep gate would remind us that though God is indeed a God of mercy, and the water (the word of God) does have healing power, yet under law the availability of this was practically nil. This was true despite its nearness to the sheep gate, which typifies the entrance of the sheep (the people of God) into the city. The five porches adjacent to the pool would speak of the responsibility which, under law, man had assumed (v. 2). But rather than producing active work and blessing, they were filled with impotent people. The responsibility imposed by law only found mankind helpless and without strength.[72]

Indeed, Israel was a spiritually sick nation to the point of death, and this miracle shows that though they had the Law, it had no power to heal them. In the five books of the Law (pictured by the porches), God reveals man's failure (Genesis) and His remedy, substitutional death of a perfect sacrifice for the guilty (Exodus to Deuteronomy). The number *five* is usually obtained in Scripture by combining the numbers *one* and *four* together. *One* speaks of our all-sufficient God, while *four* declares His creative work as pertaining to man (i.e., earthly order). Through the all-sufficient God's redemptive work, He is able to offer *grace* to man, though humanity corrupted His creative work by sin in Eden. Therefore, from a numerological meaning, the number *five* symbolizes *grace*, and as seen in Christ's third miracle, He came to Israel to supply what the Law could not.

There were many sick or disabled Jews gathered at this pool waiting for a stirring in the water, which Jewish tradition taught was an angel who had come to heal the first person who could enter the water (vv. 3-4). It is noted that the earliest Greek manuscripts do not contain the last half of verse 3 or verse 4. There is nothing in Scripture that would substantiate this scenario, so it is possible that a scribe later added these words to the text to explain why the water was "stirred." John Heading further explains this point of view:

> The descent of an angel to heal the first one who steps into the moving waters is a strange concept, and quite out of keeping with the way God acts in both OT and NT, and would even appear to be a rival to the Lord Jesus in His divine capacity to heal. Faith is not unintelligent when it has to weigh up such a strange concept whose absence from the text is supported by many manuscripts. In fact, it was an intermittent natural spring whose waters had healing properties. The Jews, who were much concerned with angels, interpreted this phenomenon as angelic in character, since they had no knowledge of any scientific explanation of such healing waters.[73]

Regardless of the custom's validity, the people believed it to be true. However, those most needing to be healed would be unable to enter the water before others in better physical condition could. This meant that the disabled man of thirty-eight years who laid beside the pool was completely dependent on someone else to put him in the water (v. 5).

The Lord Jesus knew all about the man's physical condition and how long he had suffered because of it. He asked the disabled man, *"Do you want to be made well?"* (v. 6). The correct answer should have been an emphatic "yes," but instead the man offered an excuse for his condition:

How could he get well when there was no one to help him enter the pool before others did (v. 7)? Human reasoning had caused the man to only seek a natural solution for his problem, but the Lord was going to show him a supernatural remedy for his hopeless condition – faith in Christ!

The Lord said to the invalid man, *"Rise, take up your bed and walk"* (v. 8). Immediately, the man was made well, obeyed the Lord, and he rolled up his bed and walked away (v. 9). The adverb "immediately" relates to the man exercising faith in the Lord's words, although the Lord has not yet identified Himself to the man (e.g., Matt. 9:2).

John informs us that it was the Sabbath day. Rabbinical Law prohibited carrying one's bed (doing work) on the Sabbath and the Jewish leaders quickly noted the healed man's offense and challenged him (v. 10). Clearly, the Lord had performed the miracle on the Sabbath to challenge the coldhearted, legalistic teachings of the scribes and Pharisees.

The healed man informed his Jewish accusers that he was obeying the one who had healed him (v. 11). The Jews then asked the man to identify the man who had told him to carry his bed on the Sabbath (v. 12). But because Jesus has not identified Himself and quickly withdrew from the pool after performing the miracle, the healed man did not know His name (v. 13). However, later the Lord found the man in the temple and said to him, *"See, you have been made well. Sin no more, lest a worse thing come upon you"* (v. 14).

Notice that the Lord had healed the man, but had not forgiven him of his sins, as he had not confessed his sin, nor received Christ as Lord. Therefore, the Lord warned him of the danger of continuing in sin, without true repentance and being forgiven. This same warning is given to the woman caught in adultery in John 8. The Lord came to seek and to save the lost; therefore, He neither condemned the woman nor forgave her of her sin, but rather warns her not to continue in sin.

After the healed man learned who it was that healed him, he informed the Jews that it was Jesus (v. 15). Why he did this we do not know. Perhaps he was offered a reward for the information, or he had been threatened with excommunication if he willingly withheld information from them (e.g., the healed blind man in John 9 was excommunicated for siding with Jesus, instead of the Pharisees; 9:35). Although an incredible miracle had undeniably occurred, the Jewish leaders sought to persecute Jesus for His good deed. They were infuriated that He had undermined their authority by performing the miracle on the Sabbath day and therefore they sought to kill Him from that day forward (v. 16). Humanized religion rejects God's efforts to reveal its erroneous teachings and corruption.

The Son's Equality With the Father (vv. 17-30)

After being confronted by the Jews as to why He healed the disabled man on the Sabbath day, the Lord Jesus replied, *"My Father has been working until now, and I have been working"* (v. 17). This response further enraged the Jewish leaders for two reasons. First, by employing the phrase "My Father" instead of "Our Father," Christ was claiming a unique relationship with God that they did not have. The special relationship between the Eternal Son of God and the Everlasting Father is exhibited in the Lord's frequent use of the expression "My Father." The phrase is found thirty-two times in John, compared to fifteen times in Matthew, five occurrences in Luke, and none in Mark.

Second, Christ claimed to be cooperatively working with God the Father in a unique way that they could not. Not only did they feel that Jesus had dishonored God by performing a miracle on the Sabbath, but now He was claiming to be equal with God (v. 18). Later, the Lord would put the matter plainly; He and His Father were One (10:30). The Jews clearly understood the Lord Jesus' self-declaration of deity because they sought to kill Him for His supposed blasphemy (v. 18, 8:59). Through the remainder of this chapter the Lord affirms His divine unity with the Father (vv. 19-30) and provides several witnesses to His divine personage (vv. 31-47).

The Lord perfectly reflected the character and will of His Father in everything that He spoke and did, thus the gospel message declared by Jesus Christ was fully endorsed by the Godhead. All of His speech, gestures, and actions perfectly represented the character of God (8:29, 14:6, 17:6). The Lord could only do what He saw the Father do (v. 19). He could only declare the doctrine of the Father (7:16). The Lord Jesus did only what the Father had taught Him to do (8:28). The Son and the Father are unified in all activities.

The Father loves the Son and works all things through the Son to manifest the glory of God (v. 20). This includes raising the dead back to life. The Father and Son are unified in the giving of life.

Furthermore, the Father and the Son are unified in judicial matters. The Father has trusted the Son with overseeing all judicial affairs concerning moral beings, that is, angels and humans (vv. 21-22). In this way, the Father ensures that everyone will honor His Son. Those who will not honor the Son also dishonor the Father and will be judged appropriately by the Son (v. 23).

However, those who believe that the Father sent the Son heed the Son's message of life. Those trusting the Son will immediately receive everlasting life in Him and will never come under condemnation for sin – they have once for all time *"passed from death into life"* (v. 24). Christ must be the object of our faith to believe in God and receive salvation from Him. The Father and the Son are unified in granting eternal life.

The Lord then stated that the time had now come for those who were spiritually dead to hear His word and receive everlasting life in Him (v. 25). Just as the Father is the source of life, so is the Son the essence of life. The Father had sent the Son into the world that He might share His life with those who would believe His message (v. 26). Furthermore, the Father had entrusted the Son to judge all those rejecting the Son's offer of life (v. 27).

The Lord's audience was stunned by these words, but the Lord reminded them that all those who had already died would be resurrected from their graves in a future day (v. 28). Those who were physically dead will come back to life to be with Christ in His kingdom or to suffer everlasting condemnation without Him in the Lake of Fire (v. 29). Without Christ, God's Son, there is no life. Just as those who were dead will come back to life, those who were spiritually dead (all born in Adam), could receive spiritual life immediately by trusting in the Son. The Father and the Son are in unity concerning the eternal condemnation of the wicked.

Though Job is one of the oldest books in our Bibles, ironically it is the first to speak of resurrection (Job 19:25-27). The prophets Isaiah, Ezekiel, and Daniel also looked forward to the day that they would be resurrected from death (Isa. 26:19; Ezek. 37:11-14; Dan. 12:2-3). Whether one spends eternity in heaven or in hell, everyone will undergo a bodily resurrection. This ensures that all individuals will have a body suited for their final destination.

The Lord Jesus taught that He, as the Son of God, had life within Himself and created all life (1:3-4). Accordingly, at His command all the deceased would be resurrected (i.e., every disembodied soul would be joined to an immortal body). Two types of resurrections are identified in Scripture. First, there is the resurrection of the just to enjoy eternity with

God in heaven; this is called *the first resurrection* (Rev. 20:5). This resurrection occurs in stages beginning with Christ, then the Church, Old Testament saints, those of refined Israel, and martyred Tribulation saints. Second, the resurrection of the wicked to be punished forever in the Lake of Fire occurs all at once; this is called *the second death* (Rev. 20:10-15). The Lord Jesus has received authority from His Father to initiate both resurrections and He will be honored by both the faithful and the wicked through these events (Phil. 2:9-11).

Extending life to those who would receive Him and condemnation to those who rejected His offer of life was the will of His Father. The Lord did not seek His own will and could do nothing outside of the Father's will (v. 30, 6:38). Hence, the Father and the Son are unified in their just assessment of the wicked.

Witnesses to Confirm Christ's Validity (vv. 31-47)

Under the constraints of the Mosaic Law, there had to be at least two witnesses to validate a matter as true, thus the Lord says, *"If I bear witness of Myself, My witness is not true"* (v. 31). To address this legitimate point of the Law, the Lord Jesus supplies five witnesses that could authenticate His Messianic credentials (vv. 32-47). But before hearing from these other witnesses, we pause to consider the Lord's statement in John 8:14, *"Even if I bear witness of Myself, My witness is true..."* as compared to what He said in John 5:31. As August Van Ryn explains, there is no disagreement between these statements:

> These two passages might seem contradictory, but they are not. In John 5:31 our Lord simply means that, however true His witness was in itself, yet as a legal matter it was not sufficient. One's personal testimony must be substantiated to be valid, so our Lord furnished the corroborating evidence of the witness of John the Baptist, His Father, the Scriptures and His own mighty works.[74]

The first of five witnesses is mentioned in verse 32, *"There is another who bears witness of Me."* The Greek adjective *allos* is rendered "another" and means "another of the same kind." In the previous verses, the Lord spoke of the Father and the Son having life in themselves; the additional witness of the same kind then must be the Holy Spirit. The Son states that the testimony of this witness is positively true. Indeed, as

The Man and Your God

God, the Holy Spirit always states what is true, for He is the Spirit of Truth (14:17).

The second witness was Christ's forerunner, John the baptizer (vv. 33-35). The people believed that John was a prophet sent by God, a perception that the Pharisees were quite aware of (Luke 20:6). John had declared that Jesus was the Messiah, *"the Lamb of God who takes away the sin of the world"* (1:29). Why would anyone want to reject what a prophet of God had declared to them?

The third witness was the works that He had done (v. 36). Though the Lord knew that the Jews would not believe in Him through signs alone, He understood the need to fulfill Scripture and work wonders before them to prove He was the Messiah. Later, He pled with those who had rejected His claims: *"If I do not do the works of My Father, do not believe Me; but if I do, though you do not believe Me, believe the works, that you may know and believe that the Father is in Me, and I in Him"* (10:37-38). Only God could cleanse lepers, cure diseases, heal blindness, and raise the dead, and if He was only pretending to be God, why would God do such miracles through Him?

The fourth witness was God the Father (vv. 37-38) who on three separate occasions had spoken from heaven to express His pleasure in His Son, Israel's Messiah. The first was directly after Christ's baptism, *"This is My beloved Son, in whom I am well pleased"* (Matt. 3:17). A similar statement was uttered from heaven at Christ's transfiguration (Matt. 17:5). The third time is after the Lord foretold His death and asked His Father to glorify His name. God affirmed that He would do so again through Christ's work at Calvary (12:28).

The fifth witness was Old Testament Scripture, which provided hundreds of predictive prophecies concerning both His first and second advents (vv. 39-47). He suggested that if they believed in the Law of Moses, then they should believe His message, for Moses foretold of His coming: *"But if you do not believe his writings, how will you believe My words?"* (v. 47). To reject Christ is to reject Scripture! To reject the truth means that men will embrace a lie and follow false teachers (v. 43).

What hindered the Jews from heeding the testimony of these five witnesses? They sought the honor (literally "the glory") of men, instead of being honored (glorified) by God (v. 44). Yet, Christ desired to be honored by His Father. The Lord was not motivated by the honor that men bestow (v. 41), but rather, His main ambition in life was to do the will of His Father, knowing that He would be honored by Him (4:34).

John Chapter 6

John mentions another Passover in verse 4, which means the setting for this chapter is in the spring of 29 A.D. About a year had elapsed between the narratives of John 5 and 6. Matthew and Mark primarily fill in the details of what happened during this timeframe. The Lord Jesus and His disciples have spent two years mainly in Galilee, but it is now time to take an excursion northward to Sidon and then back south and east to the region of Decapolis.

The Lord has begun His final year of earthly ministry and will spend about six months in the north and in Decapolis before journeying to Judea for the feast of tabernacles in the fall. John largely passes over this period in his gospel account.

Five Thousand Fed (vv. 1-14)

On two different occasions, the Lord Jesus performed miracles to feed the multitudes that had gathered in remote locations to hear His message. The first event, the feeding of the five thousand, is the only miracle recorded in all four Gospels and signals the close of Christ's two-year Galilean ministry. After this, Christ will travel to Phoenicia, Decapolis, Caesarea-Philippi, Judea, Perea, and then back to Jerusalem for His final days of ministry culminating with His death, burial, and resurrection.

The first miracle of feeding the masses occurred in "a deserted place" (Matt. 14:15) that was remotely near Bethsaida according to Luke (Luke 9:10). However, John refers to the location being near Tiberias, a city on the western shore of the Sea of Galilee (v. 23). Bethsaida, on the northern side of the sea, was the hometown of Peter, Andrew, and Philip (1:44). But there were two towns that went by this name: Bethsaida Galilee (Tabgha) on the northwest side of the Sea of Galilee and a Bethsaida Julias on the north-northeast side of the sea. Some commentators believe that the miracle occurred on the northern side of the Sea of Galilee, near Bethsaida Julias, but this viewpoint does not agree with some of the details recorded in the Gospels.

Luke apparently refers to Bethsaida Galilee as the location of the miracle, which is just north of the area that John identifies for the event. Two towns named Bethsaida are mentioned: Luke says that the miracle occurred near Bethsaida and Mark states that the Lord told His disciples afterwards to cross the sea to Bethsaida. Although the information in the Gospels is not conclusive to identify the exact location of this miracle, we can speculate its most probable location.

John, an eyewitness of these events, states that the feeding of the 5,000 occurred near the city of Tiberias (v. 23). The disciples departed from this location in a boat without the Lord and were told by Him to go to Bethsaida (Mark 6:45). If Bethsaida Julias was meant, that would be an eight-mile journey to the northeast of Magdala directly across the sea, which would be a risky venture at night. John records that the disciples rowed towards Capernaum, which would be in the direction of Bethsaida Galilee (v. 17). This would be a safer trek northward as the shoreline would remain in sight.

However, a windstorm throughout the night hindered their progress northward until the Lord came to them walking on the sea in the fourth watch. After He entered the boat, He calmed the sea, and instantly moved the boat to a location just southwest of Capernaum (v. 24), which allowed them to do ministry in Gennesaret the next day (Matt. 14:34; Mark 6:53). This agrees with John's statement that people came in boats from Tiberias to Capernaum looking for Jesus the next day and found Him (vv. 23-24). If the miracle occurred at Magdala (about four miles south of Bethsaida Galilee and three miles northwest of Tiberias), it would have been possible for the news to have spread down to the people from Tiberias overnight, but it seems more likely that these seekers from Tiberias had witnessed the miracle themselves and sought Jesus in the most likely place they might find him, Capernaum. Capernaum was the Lord's home base, so to speak, during His Galilean ministry.

Returning to the text, we read that the Lord and His disciples crossed the Sea of Galilee (also called the Sea of Tiberias) from east to west in a boat (v. 1). A great multitude followed them mainly on land because of the signs and miracles that the Lord Jesus was performing (v. 2). After arriving on the western shoreline north of Tiberias, the Lord took His disciples privately up on a mountain; this may have been Mount Arbel (v. 3). John notes that this event occurred just prior to the Passover (v. 4). However, it did not take the multitudes long to find the Lord (v. 5).

John

Matthew and Mark inform us that the Lord ministered to the people throughout the day. Towards evening, the disciples came to the Lord and asked Him to send the people away, so that they could journey to surrounding villages and purchase food for themselves before nightfall overtook them (Matt. 14:15). The Lord, having compassion for the people, informed His disciples that there was no need to send the people away, but rather they should feed them (Matt. 14:16). The Lord then asked Philip, "Where shall we buy bread, that these may eat?" (v. 5). John adds that the question was to test Philip's faith, for He already knew what He was about to do (v. 6). Philip said that even two hundred denarii worth of bread was not enough to even give the people a small portion of food (v. 7). Furthermore, because it was a deserted place, there was nowhere to purchase bread anyway. John's account affirms that there were neither sufficient funds available nor nearby resources to feed a crowd of this size.

In fact, the only food that the disciples had found was a boy's sack lunch of two fish and five loaves which Andrew had spied out (v. 9; Matt. 14:17). The Lord told His disciples to cause the people (numbering 5,000 men plus women and children) to sit down in the grass and to bring him the fish and the loaves (v. 10). After receiving what was available, the Lord gave thanks for the fish and the bread, broke the bread, and gave the fragments to the disciples to be passed out to the people (v. 11). After everyone had eaten their fill, there were twelve baskets full of fragments that remained (vv. 12-13).

The Greek word *kophinos* (translated "basket") is found six times in the Gospels and all references pertain to the feeding of the 5,000. *Kophinos* is a handbasket which one person could carry. The Greek word *spuris* is rendered "basket" in Matthew's and Mark's accounts of the feeding of the 4,000 and refers to a larger basket, such as the one in which Paul was let down from the Damascus city wall in to escape capture (Acts 9:25).

Those observing the miracle that Jesus performed concluded, *"This is truly the Prophet who is to come into the world"* (v. 14). The people alluded to Moses' prophecy of a coming powerful Prophet to the nation of Israel, which pertained to Christ's first advent. After seeing Jehovah's awesome display of power on Mount Sinai, the Israelites asked Moses to be their mediator (Ex. 20:19). The Lord was pleased with their acknowledgment of His holiness and their need of an intercessor to approach Him. Moses then uttered a prophecy that in a coming day there would be a Prophet sent to Israel that would enjoy communion with God and explain the message of God to the Jewish nation (Deut. 18:15-16).

Though God would send a long line of prophets to converse with Israel in the unfolding centuries, Moses' prophetic ministry was unique in comparison (Deut. 34:10). He had enjoyed extended intimate fellowship with God, he spoke for God to the people, and he was a mediator representing the people to God. In this sense, Moses pictured the special Prophet (speaking of Christ) that God would send in a future day to bring His ultimate message of hope to Israel.

Those not heeding His Prophet's message would be judged appropriately by God (Deut. 18:18-19). Those who had witnessed the miracle of the feeding of the 5,000 believed that Jesus of Nazareth was the Prophet that Moses spoke of. While this understanding was correct, the Lord Jesus was more than just the foretold Prophet; He was the Savior of the world, God incarnate. The lost sheep of Israel must come into a deeper understanding of His message and His full identity to experience the power of His life.

Three helpful applications are suggested from this story. First, serving will always precede the reward for service, and the reward will be far more than we deserve! There was a basket for each serving disciple, and each received an abundant portion after their service was completed.

Second, everyone was completely satisfied with the Lord's provision. He fed an estimated 20,000 people (5,000 men, plus women and children). The Lord Jesus satisfies all genuine need when we rest in Him. Help may not always come the way we expect it to or when we think it should, but the Lord's provision will never leave us disappointed!

Third, the pattern of service in this story is a good one for us to follow: Understand what the Lord has given each of us, be willing to give it back to the Lord, obey how He says to use it, and then preserve the blessing that God supplies afterwards as a testimony of His goodness.

Walking on Water and Calming a Storm (vv. 15-21)

After witnessing the miracle, the people concluded that Jesus was the long-awaited Prophet that Moses had foretold would come to Israel (v. 14). The Lord knew what the people wanted – deliverance from Rome; therefore, before they could rally to make Him their king, the Lord dispersed the crowd (v. 15). By the end of this chapter, many followers of Christ deserted Him on their own (v. 66).

The Lord desired to be alone with His Father, so He instructed His disciples to enter into a boat and cross the sea towards Capernaum (specifically Bethsaida per Mark 6:35) without Him (vv. 16-17). At dusk, the Lord saw His disciples in the sea and struggling to row against a contrary wind (v. 18; Mark 6:48). The Lord continued praying throughout the night and in the early dawn hours (i.e., the fourth watch was between 3 and 6 a.m.) the Lord came towards them walking on the rough sea (Matt. 14:24-25). John says that they had rowed only three to four miles since entering the boat (v. 19).

Although it was not the Lord's intention, it seemed to the disciples that the Lord was going to pass them by, so they cried out to Him (Mark 6:48). At first, they were terrified by His presence, thinking He was a ghost, but He comforted them with these words, *"It is I; do not be afraid"* (v. 20). Although Peter briefly walked on the water at this juncture, John does not record that detail in his account.

The Lord then entered the boat and the impeding wind ceased and the boat was instantly moved across the sea to a place near Capernaum, its intended destination (v. 21; Matt. 14:32). The Lord and His disciples engaged in ministry in Gennesaret immediately thereafter (Mark 6:53). The disciples' half-day arduous trial was over. Mark notes that the disciples were *"greatly amazed ... beyond measure, and marveled"* at this feat. Although they were exhausted from hours of rowing, they humbled themselves before the Lord and worshiped Him, *"Truly You are the Son of God"* (Matt. 14:33).

This text reminds us that the Lord is completely cognizant of where we are and what we are going through. The disciples were safer in that boat in a raging sea than anywhere else on earth because they were in the will of God. In fact, what they feared most, the sea, is what brought the Lord nearer to them. This is often the case in our own difficulties. The Lord did not force Himself into their hardship until they called out for Him; when they did, they were comforted by His presence and their grueling trial was over. The Lord longs to show Himself strong in our lives, but He will wait to be invited to do so.

The following map is a possible scenario derived from the gospel accounts as to the disciples' boat journey.

The Man and Your God

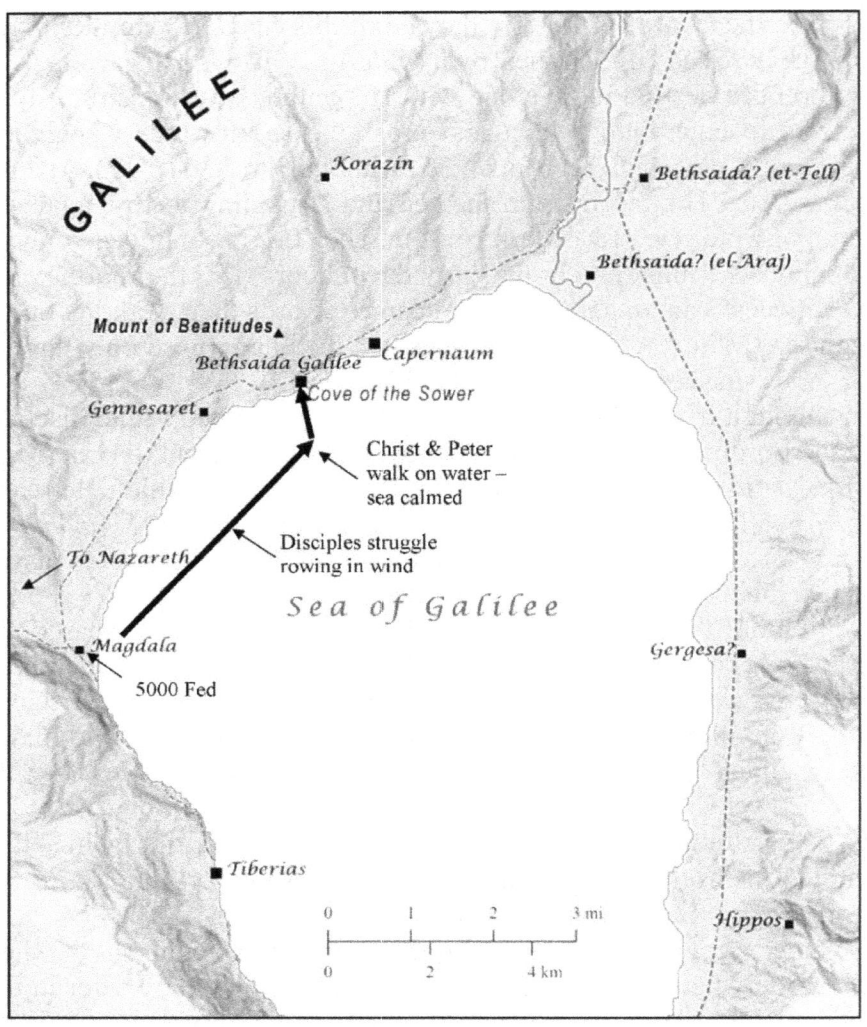

Jesus Christ Is the Bread of Life (vv. 22-29)

The next morning there was quite a stir at the location in which Christ had fed the multitude. Apparently, many spent the night in that area after Christ dispersed them the evening before. The prior evening, the people had watched the Lord's disciples depart in the only boat available without their Master, yet Jesus was nowhere to be found (v. 22). People from Tiberius arrived in boats at the site of the previous day's miracle also looking for Jesus (v. 23). These departed for that location in their boats and came northward to Capernaum to search for the Lord (v. 24).

When they had found Him, they were puzzled, *"Rabbi, when did You come here?"* (v. 25). This is the first of four questions posed to the Lord Jesus by these sign-seekers which prompted His Bread of Life declaration. His audience will generally have a deteriorating response to His message, complaining (vv. 41-51), quarreling (vv. 52-59), and then departing from Christ (vv. 60-71).

Rather than explaining that He had walked across the Sea of Galilee during a windstorm, the Lord addressed their real motive in searching for Him – they had received a free meal the day before and wanted to benefit again from His generosity (v. 26). There was no interest in the spiritual significance of the sign He had performed, but rather in the temporary physical benefit of being fed by Him.

Food has a brief benefit in preserving physical life, but they should be pursuing what would result in everlasting life, that is, trusting in the One the Father had sent to them with His words of life (v. 27). This caused the people to ask the Lord a second question, *"What shall we do, that we may work the works of God?"* (v. 28). Having misunderstood the Lord's exhortation about laboring for what abides unto eternal life, they inferred that they had the capacity to do something to please God. The Lord then explained that eternal life could not be worked for, as one labored for food to preserve physical life, but must be received by believing in Him for salvation (v. 29). Hence, other than trusting in Him, there was nothing they could do to receive God's approval.

The Bread of Life Came Down From Heaven (vv. 30-59)

Although it is unclear as to where the following dialogue took place, most of the Lord's teaching about the bread of life from heaven occurred in the synagogue at Capernaum (v. 59).

After finding Christ, those who had witnessed the miracle performed by Him the previous day asked Him two more questions: *"What sign will You perform then, that we may see it and believe You? What work will You do?"* (v. 30). Their request begs the question, "How many miracles must be witnessed before someone should trust in the one performing them?" Five? Ten? Fifty? What is enough evidence to satisfy human reasoning? We conclude that signs apart from the biblical message that they affirm will never lead someone to believe the truth; only faith in God's Word will result in knowing the truth and being set free from sin.

The Man and Your God

These sign seekers went on to say that Moses had given their forefathers such a sign by providing them bread from heaven (v. 31). In other words, "If You are greater than Moses, as You say, then do more than Moses did – feed us again, for Moses fed our forefathers forty years in the wilderness." They were hoping the Lord would repeat the miracle He had done the day before. The natural man wants to confirm with his senses some supernatural work in the natural world (i.e., a sign or a miracle) to believe that God exists (i.e., that He is beyond natural order). However, the spiritual man understands that it is through exercising faith in God's revealed Word that people understand spiritual things and know God. They *believe and know* the truth, instead of wanting *to see to believe* what God says (vv. 66-69). While in the wilderness, the nation of Israel witnessed daily miracles for forty years, yet seeing the spectacular did not stimulate their faith in God, for they constantly complained and murmured against God. What is important is not the magnitude of the miracle itself, but how one perceives its significance.

The Lord then corrects the statement of the sign-seekers; it was not Moses that gave their forefathers bread, but His Father, who again was now offering them "the true bread from heaven" (v. 32). What their forefathers received in the wilderness to sustain life was only a foreshadow of the true bread from heaven that would provide those partaking of it eternal life. The true bread of God was Himself, who had come down from heaven to give His life for the world (v. 33).

Eating bread that would give eternal life sounded too good to be true; therefore, the Lord's audience said, *"Give us this bread always"* (v. 34). Commenting to verse 34, William Kelly writes:

> This is their last effort to get what they sought – bread for this world, bread evermore .... But unbelief is every way wrong. It is life that God is giving, and nothing less meets the true need of man; and this life is in Christ, not from Him. Apart from Him, given out of Him, and thus, so as to be independent of Him, it exists not. In Him was life; in Him only is life found. He is the Bread of life.[75]

The Lord responded to their carnal request for endless food by identifying Himself as the bread of life that had come down from heaven (v. 35). One eats physical bread to avoid physical hunger, but to receive the bread of life which would satisfy spiritual hunger and thirst of the soul, one must believe His message. The Bread of Life must be appropriated by faith, not by physically eating Him. The Lord stated in

John

verse 63 that He was not speaking in literal terms but was teaching them spiritual truth by applying an analogy that they could understand.

The Lord said, *"I am the bread of life"* (v. 35). Jehovah identified Himself to Moses at the burning bush as the great *I AM* (Ex. 3:13-15). The Hebrew word *hayah* is used to mean "I will be," and is a wordplay on *Yahweh* (Jehovah) in Exodus 3:15, which means "to be." Moses was to tell the children of Israel that I AM, the self-existing One, had sent him to deliver them from bondage and out of Egypt. It is of no surprise then that the New Testament reveals the Lord Jesus Christ as the great I AM of Exodus; He is the only One who can satisfy all human need.

Seven is the number of perfection and completeness and John presents in his gospel account the seven I AM statements of Christ: "The Bread of Life," "The Light of the World," "The Door," "The Good Shepherd," "The Resurrection and the Life," "The Way, the Truth, and the Life," and "The True Vine." The self-existent One declared in His own words the fullness of I AM. John combines three "wilderness images" that the Lord used to speak of Himself as the only way of salvation: The manna from heaven (John 6), the water from a rock (John 7), and the pillar of fire at night (John 8). Specific Jewish rituals during the Feast of Tabernacles celebrated the latter two.

Seven times in this chapter, the Lord Jesus refers to Himself as the "Bread of Life" which came down from heaven. He likens the Israelites feeding upon the manna in the wilderness to live to a believer feeding on Him now to obtain eternal life and to be able to live for Him.

Eating of the Bread of Life from Heaven confers eternal salvation, and continuing to feed on Him is the only spiritual food which satisfies the human soul and strengthens the inner man for spiritual conflict. The Lord Jesus said, *"He who comes to Me shall never hunger, and he who believes in Me shall never thirst"* (v. 35). Just as the Israelites had to eat manna in the wilderness to live, the believer in the Church Age will be destitute of spiritual vigor unless he or she consistently feeds on the Bread of Life. The manna of Exodus and the Bread of Life of John 6 have a number of specific typological correlations. Both the manna to the Israelites and Christ to those trusting Him:

1. Were a supernatural gift from God (rained down from heaven vs. directly from heaven's throne).
2. Were supplied where the people were (in the wilderness vs. in the world).

3. Were to be eaten (to sustain physical life vs. to gain spiritual life).
4. Were to be gathered daily (each morning vs. throughout each day).
5. Were obtained by labor (going out to gather vs. meditation on God's Word).
6. Were not to be neglected (turned to worms vs. lost opportunities to know and serve).
7. Were incomprehensible to the natural man (not natural vs. obviously supernatural).
8. Were despised by the mixed multitude (hated by the Egyptians vs. despised by the world).
9. Were preserved for future generations (placed in the ark vs. the eternal Word).
10. Were supplied until the destination was reached (ceased at Canaan vs. grace received by faith no longer needed in heaven).

The Lord told His audience that they only wanted to have their belly filled by Him, rather than receiving Him and having their souls eternally refreshed (v. 36). However, the Lord Jesus was not discouraged by their unbelief, for He knew that many others would believe in Him and be saved, for He had divine authority to preserve them forever: *"All that the Father gives Me will come to Me, and the one who comes to Me I will by no means cast out"* (v. 37). While the full meaning of this statement is difficult for the human mind to grasp, we can be certain that a sovereign God foreknows who will believe on His Son and be saved by Him.

The Lord may only be referring to His disciples at this juncture as in His prayer to His Father in John 17:2, *"You have given Him authority over all flesh, that He should give eternal life to as many as You have given Him"* (in conjunction with 17:20 and 18:9). If He is speaking of all that would be saved, then, as Warren Wiersbe suggests, the Lord is speaking of the process of personal salvation:

> The Lord explained that salvation involves both divine sovereignty and human responsibility. The Father *gives* men and women to the Son (John 6:37, 39; 17:2, 6, 9, 11-12, 24), but these men and women must *come* to Him, that is, *believe* on Him. He assured them that nobody who came to Him would ever be lost but would be raised at the last day. Even death cannot rob us of salvation! (In regard to the "last day," see John 6:40, 44, 54. Jesus was referring to His return and the final events that climax God's program for mankind.)[76]

The agency of human responsibility is quite apparent in the previous chapter when Christ told His obstinate Jewish audience, *"But you are not willing to come to Me that you may have life"* (5:40). Later, the Lord again pleaded with His Jewish countrymen, *"Though you do not believe in Me, believe in the works, that you may know and believe that the Father is in Me, and I in Him"* (10:38). If God chooses some people to be saved and condemns everyone else to Hell, why does Christ plead with those who are rejecting Him? On this point, John Phillips writes:

> Whatever is to be said about the sovereignty of God in human salvation, God never sets up arbitrary, impossible, and wholly unobtainable terms for our coming to Christ. Nor does He violate our moral accountability by ravishing anyone's human will in certain cases (by so-called "irresistible grace"). The solution to the problem suggested by some, built around such tests as John 6:37, lies in the omniscience of God and in the timelessness of His mode for being. God knows all those who will accept Christ and He knows them because He knows everything.[77]

Indeed, the Father sent His Son into the world to seek and to eternally save lost souls (vv. 38-39). It was the Father's will that all those believing in the Son will receive everlasting life and be resurrected in a future day to be with God forever (v. 40). Thus, if anyone is saved, it is by faith in God's Word to receive God's grace in Christ (Eph. 2:8). All those perishing will receive what is deserved for their own wickedness (Rev. 20:13-14). Rebellious men secure for themselves God's wrath, but God prepares those seeking His mercy for glory (Rom. 9:22-23).

The Jews listening to the Lord's declaration rejected the idea that He was the bread which came down from heaven, because they knew His earthly parents, Mary and Joseph (vv. 41-42). How could someone arrive from heaven whom they had watched grow up in a normal way in Nazareth? The Lord responded to their murmuring by stating that only those that the Father was drawing to Himself through the Son would be saved and raised up in the last day (vv. 43-44). Additionally, no one could be drawn to the Father unless they had first been taught by God's Word (v. 45). This highlights the process of both hearing and learning from Scripture to understand the truth. The truth is presented to all men, but only those responding to God's Word will be drawn to the Father through the Son.

Only the Son intimately knew the Father; therefore an individual must first believe in the Son to know the Father and receive everlasting life (v. 46). Just as their forefathers chose to eat the manna that God provided for them in the wilderness to live, they must now choose to eat of the Bread of Life that had come down from God to gain eternal life with God (vv. 47-48). Although the manna preserved individuals in the wilderness until they physically died (v. 49), it typified the Bread from Heaven that God would provide later through His Son to provide eternal life (v. 50). One eats the Bread of Life by appropriating by faith the work that Christ would accomplish at the cross when He gave His own flesh (body) as a sacrifice for sin for humanity (v. 51).

The Jews did not understand the spiritual meaning of His words, and they were appalled by the idea that they had to eat human flesh to gain eternal life (v. 52). They quarreled and strove among themselves while trying to ascertain the meaning of Christ's words. The Lord reiterated the reality of His sacrificial message in verse 53: He was going to permit His body to be nailed to a tree that His own blood would be shed to secure God's propitiation for sin (Rom. 3:24) and means of redeeming the condemned (Rom. 3:23). Therefore, individuals must believe in the value of His broken body and shed blood to gain salvation through Him; this was allegorically likened to eating his body and drinking His blood (vv. 54-56, 35-36, 40, 47). The Lord was not promoting cannibalism or the drinking of blood which the Law prohibited. Rather, He was emphatically stating that outside of exercising faith in His finished work at Calvary there was no salvation. Those who would eat this bread, trust in Christ alone, would live forever (vv. 57-58).

The verb tense and mood for both "eating" and "drinking" in verses 50-51 and 53 is aorist subjunctive to convey the idea that there must be an initial once-and-for-all-time act of trusting the gospel of Christ to receive eternal life. Clearly then, the Lord is not speaking of humanly devised sacraments (drawn from the Lord's Supper) that must be repeatedly consumed to maintain spiritual life. An individual is either in Christ and has His life or he or she does not; there is no middle ground, and eternal life in Christ is not contingent on human doings (5:24).

However, the verb tense and mood for the same words "eating" and "drinking" in verses 54 and 56 is present participle. This usage implies that ongoing "eating" and "drinking" is necessary to ensure spiritual growth and maturity in Christ.

Accordingly, the finished work of Christ applied to one's account by faith is the only means of receiving eternal life and applying His Words for life is the only way to live for Him. Just as the manna was God's food

John

to sustain Israel for forty years in the wilderness, His Word in Christ is our spiritual food to sustain us and equip us today to serve Him! The Israelites quickly learned that though the manna was God's provision for them, it had to be personally gathered in the morning or it spoiled by the afternoon.

Likewise, believers today must continually feed on the Lord Jesus (i.e., to meditate on His Word) to receive help and guidance for each day. His Word is our spiritual food for each day! No believer can gather another's manna; each one must personally meditate on the Word of God to obtain his or her provision of grace for each day. Starving our spiritual man of what God provides to maintain our spiritual vitality can only end badly for the believer. Christ speaks to us in the quietness of His presence and provides all that we need. We need a fresh, daily portion of manna because we cannot live on yesterday's enjoyment of Christ!

The Lord had been teaching publicly in a synagogue in Capernaum (v. 59). The Lord knew their hearts and that they could not accept the spiritual meaning associated with His allegorical teaching about eating His body and drinking His blood (v. 60), so He asked them, *"Does this offend you?"* (v. 61). The English word "scandalous" is derived from the Greek word *skandalizo* rendered "offend" in this verse. The Lord was asking His audience, "Do you think that my teaching will cause you to stumble into sin or apostasy?"

The Lord then asked them if they would believe His words if He were to ascend back to where He was before, heaven (vv. 61-62). Spiritual life could only be gained through the Holy Spirit by heeding the spiritual words of life that He had spoken to them (v. 63). By saying, *"the flesh profits nothing,"* the Lord was affirming that His words concerning His "body" and "blood" were not literal, but figurative and spiritual in meaning.

The plural form of the Greek word *rhema* is rendered "words" in verse 63 and means exactly what is spoken. However, the word "saying" in verse 60 expressed by the Jews is *logos* and refers to the revelation of an overall concept or thought. In other words, the Lord told them exactly what they must believe to have eternal life; He was not speaking of a complex concept that they could not understand.

Because He knew the hearts of everyone before Him, He knew that many did not believe in Him, and that one of them, Judas, would betray Him (v. 64). With this realization stated, the Lord reiterated what He had already said in verses 37 and 44: only those who the Father drew to Himself through the Son would be saved (v. 65).

The Lord's statements were offensive to many Jews, and many who had been following the Lord turned away from Him at this juncture (v. 66). The Lord Jesus then turned to the twelve and asked them if they would also be turning away from Him (v. 67).

Previously, the Lord Jesus stated that it was the unrighteous who wanted to see a "sign or a wonder" in order to believe in Him. He called these "sign seekers" an evil generation (Matt. 12:38-39). Even those people who had witnessed the miracle of the feeding of the 5,000 were pestering the Lord the very next day: *"What sign will You perform then, that we **may see it and believe** You?"* (v. 30).

In contrast, Peter shows us that true faith opens our eyes to understand the spiritual things of God. When the Lord asked His twelve disciples if they, too, would turn away from Him, as many had done, Peter responded, *"Lord, to whom shall we go? You have the words of eternal life. Also we have come **to believe and know** that You are the Christ, the Son of the living God"* (vv. 68-69). The unrighteous want a sign to believe, but the righteous believe to understand. Until we exercise faith, we will not understand from where we came and to where we journey. *"By faith we understand that the worlds were framed by the word of God, so that the things which are seen were not made of things which are visible"* (Heb. 11:3). Oswald Chambers puts the matter this way: "I must know Jesus Christ as Savior before His teaching has any meaning for me other than that of an ideal which leads to despair."[78]

Indeed, Christ had chosen all His disciples with divine purpose in accordance with sovereign timing (v. 70). Based on their faith or lack of it, the Lord would use each of them to bring about God's plan of salvation. Eleven of the disciples would serve the Lord by powerfully proclaiming the gospel message during the Church Age, and all but John would suffer martyrdom for doing so. Judas Iscariot went his own way, instead of following the Way. The Lord foreknew His betrayal (17:12). God would honor his choice to fulfill Scripture as the prophesied betrayer of Christ (13:26; Ps. 41:9). God's plan orchestrated before creation to son-place redeemed sinners into all the blessings and inheritance association with being one in Christ would not be foiled by anyone. Ultimately, everyone, both the faithful and the wicked, will honor God, the former through their willful submission and service, and the latter by receiving God's righteous judgment for their rebellion.

John Chapter 7

John does not address Christ's ministry in Decapolis, but rather focuses on His Judean ministry in chapters 7 to 10. His record transitions from the events occurring at the Passover (6:4) to those at the Feast of Tabernacles about six months later (7:2). Thus, John does not mention the Lord's transfiguration on a Galilean mountain because it occurred during this interval, and His transfiguration was merely an outward manifestation of His intrinsic glory that was limited to an earthly venue.

John presents Christ from the heavenly view, not in an earthly relationship. John speaks of the embedded glory of deity that only heaven has witnessed and can fully comprehend. In the transfiguration of Christ, it is not the man who is God that is paramount, but that God became an earthly man.

Christ Is Pressured by Family to Go to Jerusalem (vv. 1-9)

The Lord returned to Galilee after completing His ministry in Decapolis, for He knew that the Jews in Judea sought to kill Him (v. 1). As the Lord's brothers (named in Matt. 13:55) did not believe in Him (v. 5), they asked Jesus to go to the Feast of Tabernacles in Jerusalem to work public signs before the people and His disciples (vv. 2-3). Why did the Lord's half-brothers encourage Him to go to Jerusalem? We are not told why, but two possibilities seem most likely.

First, Jesus' family had probably heard about His diminishing number of disciples (6:66). But, if He went to where a great multitude of people would be gathered for several days, that would be an opportune place to gain more followers.

Second, previously His brothers thought that Jesus was *"out of His mind"* (Mark 3:21), but now their concern had turned to animosity, so they encouraged Jesus to not stay hidden in Galilee, but to declare Himself before the multitudes that would be in Jerusalem at that time (v. 4). Perhaps they were hoping that their brother would be arrested and the ongoing shame that He was bringing on the family would come to an end.

The Lord responded to their charge by stating that it was not yet time for His ministry to conclude; in fact, He would be sending seventy of His disciples to preach the kingdom message throughout Judea in the following months (v. 6; Luke 10:1). Therefore, it was their time to hear and to heed His message of life, not His time to cease declaring it. The world hated His message because it exposed the evil in the world and the inherent sinfulness of man (v. 7). His brothers did not believe that He was Israel's Messiah; thus, they were of the world.

The Lord's ministry would not be manipulated by His unbelieving family members. All His doings were in accordance with His Father's will and it was not yet time for Him to be arrested and to suffer death (v. 8). Although it was customary for Jewish families to travel together in large companies to Jerusalem to celebrate the feasts (Luke 2:44), the Lord told His brothers to journey south without Him. He implied that He would come to Jerusalem later to celebrate the Feast of Tabernacles (v. 9).

Christ Attends the Feast of Tabernacles (vv. 10-36)

The Lord Jesus, in keeping with the dictates of the Law (Ex. 34:22-23), did journey to Jerusalem afterwards, but initially kept Himself out of the public eye, though many were looking for Him (vv. 10-11). John notes that there was much controversy in Jerusalem concerning Jesus of Nazareth; some thought Him to be legitimate, but others believed Him to be a deceiver (v. 12). Yet, because the people feared the Jewish leaders, who generally despised Jesus, they did not discuss Him openly (v. 13).

The Feast of Tabernacles was an eight-day celebration beginning on the fifteenth day of the seventh month in the Jewish calendar (Lev. 23:34-36). This feast generally occurs in late September or early October in our Gregorian calendar. Midway through the feast the Lord began to teach publicly at the temple and the people marveled at His wisdom and skill (vv. 14-15). Before He revealed Himself in the temple, most people were discussing His character (vv. 11-13), but after He began to teach, His doctrine quickly became the talk of the town (vv. 14-19).

The Lord's main audience at this juncture was the common people who were gathering at the temple daily (Luke 21:37-38). The priests and Pharisees were privately discussing what the people were saying about Jesus and what should be done about Him (vv. 32, 45-52). They were clearly not at the temple, as they sent officers to arrest Jesus there and later the officers returned to their Jewish leaders emptyhanded.

The Jewish authorities thought that someone must have either attended a Rabbinic school or be self-taught to have enough education to speak in the manner that the Lord did. However, the Lord informed His audience that what He was teaching them did not come from men but was from His Father in heaven who had sent Him (v. 16).

Those wanting to do the will of God would understand that His doctrine was not His own; it had been received from God and represented His Father's authority (v. 17). The Lord is not proposing, "Give Me a try to see if I am telling the truth." Rather, He is saying that anyone genuinely seeking and then committing to the truth will gain spiritual understanding of Himself. This meant, as F. B. Hole explains, that any difficulty that His questioners felt sprang from their own attitudes:

> If only they had a real desire to do the will of God, they would have recognized that His teaching was of God. If we desire to do God's will, we are of necessity marked by *sincerity* and *subjection,* and our convictions become clear and correct. The mists of doubt shroud the minds of those who are merely triflers or curious.[79]

Next, the Lord Jesus affirms that someone must be under authority to represent the interests of that authority; otherwise, he is seeking his own glory (v. 18). But Jesus Christ was not seeking His own glory, but to honor His heavenly Father; therefore, His testimony was true and undefiled. But the same could not be said of the Jewish populace. They were under God's Law given to them by Moses, yet they did not seek to honor God by obeying it; if they did, they would not be seeking to kill Him. The act of murder violated the sixth of the Ten Commandments (v. 19). The Lord was speaking directly to the priests and the Pharisees who had been plotting His death for some time; the common people were not of such a dastardly mindset at this juncture.

Rather than admitting the truth, those in His audience denied that they were seeking to put Him to death. They even claimed that the Lord must be possessed by a demonic spirit to assert such an outlandish claim (v. 20). The Lord Jesus then verified that their hatred towards Him began a year and a half earlier after He had healed a crippled man on the Sabbath (v. 21, 5:1-16). But why did they despise Him for doing good on the Sabbath? The Lord uses the example of male circumcision to show that their response was inappropriate, for it was acceptable to God and to them to circumcise an infant boy on the Sabbath.

Even before the Mosaic Law legalized the procedure, God had commanded Abraham to circumcise himself, those males in his household, and then all those descending from him (through Isaac) on the eighth day after birth (v. 22; Gen. 17:12). Obviously, the eighth day after the birth of a male baby would sometimes fall on the Sabbath; thus, per the Law, circumcision must be performed on that day. Performing the ceremonial rite was work, but this was acceptable to God, for it was a labor in accordance with God's will. The Lord had likewise done a good deed in the will of God by healing the crippled man on the Sabbath (v. 23). If caring for one part of the body was acceptable to God on the Sabbath, would not healing of the whole body be permissible also? The Lord then implied that their judgment was biased because they were not accurately discerning the matter according to righteousness (i.e., with true spiritual discernment; v. 24).

We might be quick to condemn the Lord's audience, but we all tend to judge matters after hearing or seeing only part of the story (especially if presented by a friend or loved one). Yet, Scripture warns us not to permit our feelings or a superficial examination of the facts to guide our decisions. For example, King Solomon warns:

He who answers a matter before he hears it, it is folly and shame to him (Prov. 18:13).

The first one to plead his cause seems right, until his neighbor comes and examines him (Prov. 18:17).

If someone is asking us for counsel, or to help resolve an offense, it behooves us to listen carefully to what is said, to ask questions, and to gather available information before rendering a decision. Moreover, we must realize that it would be normal for those in sin to try to deceive us by providing inaccurate information or by spinning the truth. Someone desiring to hide the truth from us will flavor the events of what really happened in order to win us to their side. But in such matters, there is only one side that matters – that the Lord is honored by the truth.

Furthermore, the first appearance of things is usually not the reality of the matter, and a wise person does not grip a one-sided story. If the first party does not want us to talk to the other party in a disagreement, that is usually a good indication of some level of guilt. A believer should always desire that the truth be revealed in a situation, which will require investigating the facts, praying for wisdom, and maintaining an unbiased perspective.

James reminds us that if we lack wisdom, we have an opportunity to receive what we need: *"If any of you lacks wisdom, let him ask of God, who gives to all liberally and without reproach, and it will be given to him"* (Jas. 1:5). Paul encourages believers to go to wise brethren in the Church for judgments on unresolved personal disagreements (1 Cor. 6:5). May we all remember that deception is of the devil and that God's nature is truth.

Many in the crowd were stunned to see Jesus speaking publicly, as they knew their religious leaders had rejected Him and were plotting His death (v. 25). However, because they took no action against Jesus, this caused some to wonder if their leaders had changed their minds about Him and were now thinking that He was the Christ (v. 26). Yet, others said that He could not be the Christ, because they knew where Jesus was from (i.e., He was born to Mary and Joseph who lived in Nazareth), but no one knew from where Christ would come when He did appear (v. 27). This reasoning was not entirely correct because Scripture supplied both the birthplace of Christ, Bethlehem of Judea, and from where He would be raised, Galilee (Micah 5:2; Isa. 9:1-2, 11:1). In essence, the Jews were not expecting Christ to appear in Israel as a baby born to a lowly couple in Nazareth. But the Lord confirmed that this was how His holy Father, whom He intimately knew, had sent Him into the world (vv. 28-29).

After claiming to be under God's authority and to enjoy a special relationship with Him that others did not have, many sought to lay hold of Him (v. 30). But the specific hour of His arrest and passion had not yet come, so the hostile Jewish crowd was not able to seize Him. This is the first of seven references in John to a specific "hour" relating to the Lord's abuses, crucifixion, and death to accomplish the Father's work of propitiation. Christ was in complete control of this *hour*. Evil men would not be able to arrest Him before the appropriate time as determined by the counsel of God. Even in the Garden of Gethsemane, the Lord commanded the same soldiers that were arresting Him to take only Him and let His disciples go – this was after Peter tried to kill a man (18:8-12). The Lord Jesus was in complete control of His own death!

Many in the Lord's audience did believe that He was the Christ because of the many signs that He had worked (v. 31). They asserted, *"When the Christ comes, will He do more signs than these which this*

Man has done?" After the Pharisees heard these murmurings from the crowd, they and the chief priests sent officers to arrest Jesus (v. 32). Although it was not time for Him to be arrested, the Lord did inform His audience that He was leaving them to return to Him that had sent Him into the world (v. 33). After He departed, they would seek Him, but would not find Him, for they could not venture to where He would be (i.e., in heaven with His Father; v. 34). The Jews did not understand what He meant and speculated that Jesus was going to lead His disciples to a foreign land to do ministry among the Greeks (vv. 35-36).

The Holy Spirit Shall Come in Power (vv. 37-39)

The eighth day of the Feast of Tabernacles was to be a holy convocation to the Lord (i.e., a high day, a Sabbath day). It was on this day that the Lord stood up and proclaimed with a loud voice, *"If anyone thirsts, let him come to Me and drink. He who believes in Me, as the Scripture has said, out of his heart will flow rivers of living waters"* (vv. 37-38). To better understand the metaphoric language of this declaration, we first must review its historical introduction.

After delivering the Israelites from their bondage in Egypt, the Lord brought them to Rephidim, but there was no water in that desolate place (Ex. 17:1-7). It was not long before the people complained to Moses, and Moses brought the matter to the Lord. God's solution was an unusual one; he was to strike a specific rock at Horeb with the rod of God. Moses did so, and an abundant flow of water came gushing out of the rock. Though the Israelites strove with God at Rephidim, they were not chastened, for God's judgment fell on the Rock in one stroke. The Rock, of course, pictures Christ, who was crucified and suffered divine wrath for our sin (1 Cor. 10:4). Because of Christ's work at Calvary, the blessings of God can freely flow out to humanity through Christ.

Forty years after this, Moses received the rebuke of God for striking another rock in the same manner when he had been instructed to speak to the rock to receive God's provision of water (Num. 20:7-13). Moses' disobedience mattered to God, because it broke the "type" of Christ that He wanted to present to Israel. Christ was to suffer only once for sin, and then the blessing of His priestly work would be received through speaking to Him as High Priest (Heb. 10:10-18).

The Lord often used Jewish traditions to speak of Himself, and He did so twice at this Feast of Tabernacles (vv. 37-39; 8:12). The first tradition related to celebrating water from the rock in the wilderness to sustain the Israelites (vv. 37-39) and the second the pillar of fire in the camp of the Israelites (8:12).

What was the Jewish ritual practiced at the Feast of Tabernacles that celebrated God's provision of water in the wilderness? Each day for seven days, a solemn procession of priests traveled from the temple to the spring of Gihon to fill a gold pitcher with water. They then returned to the temple and poured out the water before the Bronze Altar to symbolize the water gushing from the rock Moses struck in the wilderness.[80] This was not done on the last day of the feast, so the Lord substituted Himself as the Source of water that anyone could drink. J. G. Bellett summarizes the message that the Lord Jesus was declaring to the nation of Israel:

> He tells Israel that they had now no title to the rest and glory which it pledged to them – that they were not really in Canaan, and had never yet drawn water out of the wells of salvation; that their land, instead of being watered by the river of God, was but a barren and thirsty portion of the accursed earth; that they had forsaken the fountain of living waters, and all their own cisterns were but broken. And, accordingly, as the feast was closing, Jesus puts the living water into other vessels, and dries up the wells which were in Jerusalem. He turns the fruitful land into barrenness, for the wickedness of them that dwelt therein, and opens the river of God in other places.[81]

Without endorsing their feast or its practices, the Lord extended an invitation to come to Him and drink abundantly. He was the Rock that would be struck, and the blessings of the Holy Spirit would be enjoyed by all who drank of Him. "Rivers" is plural in verse 38 to indicate the abundant flow of blessing to others that the Holy Spirit can produce within obedient believers in Christ. This realization would occur after Christ's death, resurrection, and glorification in heaven (i.e., in the Church Age; v. 39).

Division Concerning Jesus Christ (vv. 40-53)

After listening to His words, there was much division concerning who the people thought Jesus was (v. 43). Some thought He was the Christ, while others believed that He was the Prophet foretold by Moses (vv. 40-41; Deut. 18:15-18). The people knew that Messiah must come from the seed of David whose hometown was Bethlehem in Judea, but Jesus was from Nazareth in Galilee, so how could He be the Messiah?

Although the Pharisees wanted to arrest Jesus, the officers that they had sent to do so returned to them empty handed; Christ had arrested them instead (vv. 44-45). When the Pharisees asked the officers why they did not arrest Jesus, they answered, *"No man ever spoke like this Man"* (v. 46). This meant that the officers realized that Jesus was a most unusual individual and sensed that He was likely more than a mere man. Their response infuriated the religious leaders who asked the officers if they had been deceived by Jesus and become His followers (v. 47). Surely, if Jesus of Nazareth was the Christ, the Jewish rulers and religious leaders would be following Him, but they implied that none were (v. 48). These haughty leaders thought that they were too highly educated to be duped by Jesus, who they believed was deceiving the people. However, we find out later that Nicodemus and Joseph, members of the Sanhedrin, were secret followers of Christ (19:38-39).

The Pharisees then accused those in the crowd that believed that Jesus was the Christ of being ignorant of the Law, and thus accursed (v. 49). Nicodemus, who had secretly met with Jesus previously (John 3) and was now a secret follower of Christ, challenged the decree that all following Christ, the supposed deceiver, were accursed (v. 50). Nicodemus asserted that the Law does not condemn someone before hearing all the evidence – true justice is not afraid of the truth, but seeks after it (v. 51).

Because Nicodemus had challenged their presumptuous assessment of Jesus, they demeaned his assertion by stating that, like Jesus, Nicodemus must be from Galilee also, for no true prophet of God came out of Galilee (v. 52). In other words, Nicodemus was in error, just like others who thought Christ could come from Galilee. But their prejudice and hatred of Christ had clearly clouded their reasoning, for the prophet Jonah was from Galilee. However, because Jonah had been sent by God to preach to Gentiles (the Ninevites) instead of the Jews, he was not esteemed by the Jewish leaders. Because of racial pride, Jonah was considered to be an inferior prophet. Consequently, the religious elite did not see the possibility of anything good coming out of Galilee, and especially Nazareth a city associated with shame. Hence, everyone went to his own house with a divided opinion concerning Christ (v. 53).

John Chapter 8

The Woman Caught in Adultery (vv. 1-11)

While everyone else departed to his own home after the final day of the feast, the Lord went to the Mount of Olives, as He had no house to return to (v. 1). Early the next morning, the Lord returned to the temple (apparently by Himself) and taught the people (v. 2). As He was teaching, a group of scribes and Pharisees approached Him with a woman, who they said had been caught in the act of adultery (v. 3).

John is the only Gospel writer that records Christ's encounter with this group of self-righteous, religious zealots who were demanding the death of an adulteress according to the Law of God delivered by Moses (vv. 4-5). Their demands were hypocritical; the fact that the guilty man had not also been arrested demonstrated their lack of reverence for God's Law (Deut. 22:22-24). But this was a devised test, to hopefully entrap the Lord in what seemed to be a no-win scenario (v. 6). If He did not uphold the condemnation of the Law demanding the woman's death, then all Israel would see Him in rebellion against the Law of Moses. However, if He said the woman should be stoned for her sin, that would put Him at odds with Roman authorities, as the Jews could not condemn someone to death without Roman approval.

The Lord ignored their challenge and acted as if He had not heard them. He stooped down and wrote something in the dust with His finger. But the Pharisees continued to badger the Lord with their question. "They continued" is derived from an imperfect tense verb, while "asking" is a present tense verb. This means that the Pharisees repeatedly posed their question until the Lord answered them. Finally, the Lord responded to their inquiry, *"He who is without sin among you, let him throw a stone at her first"* (v. 7). He then stooped down again to write on the ground (v. 8).

The Lord's statement is in the singular which reflected the Law's edict that those who had directly witnessed the offense demanding death were to cast the first stone, and then others would follow suit (Deut. 17:7). Notice that He said that those *"among you"* without sin may cast the first stone. He was sinless and could have thrown the first stone at the woman if inclined to do so. But He had not come into the world to judge people for their sins, but to give Himself, God's Lamb, for a sin offering so that the condemned could be saved.

Like the moralizer of Romans 2:1, the Pharisees were "rejoicing in iniquity," that is, they had eased their own guilty consciences by judging others who they reckoned were worse sinners than themselves. But Paul reminded the moralizer that God does not judge sin on a curve and that no one from Adam is sinless or will escape His judgment (Rom. 2:2-3).

The Lord's statement successfully appealed to the consciences of the Pharisees. The oldest to the youngest, in turn, became self-condemned before the Lord and departed without casting one stone at the guilty woman (v. 9). Afterwards, the Lord stood up and asked the woman if there was anyone else that wanted to condemn her (v. 10). She responded, *"No one, Lord."* Then Jesus said to her, *"Neither do I condemn you; go and sin no more"* (v. 11). As it is unbiblical to declare forgiveness to someone without repentance, the Lord did not forgive the woman's sins, as she did not ask to be forgiven. But neither did He condemn her, as His ministry during His first advent was to seek and to save the lost. At His second advent to the earth, He will judge the wicked.

Although the Lord did not forgive the woman or condemn her, He did warn her, *"Go and sin no more."* Being the Son of God, He could not condone sin, for, ultimately, He would judge all those in sin. Hence, He did not say to her, "Go and sin as little as possible." If she continued in sin without repentance and receiving Him for salvation, then she would be judged by Him in a coming day. The Lord could not condone her sin; she was guilty and deserved death, but He extended her mercy – she received more time to find salvation in Him. As John earlier noted, the Lord Jesus was full of grace and truth (1:14). He showed grace by not immediately judging the woman's sin and He declared the truth by warning her of the consequences of continuing in sin.

Pharisees Oppose the Light of the World (vv. 12-59)

During the Feast of Tabernacles, huge lamps were lit above the women's court of the temple at night. This was also the location of the temple treasury and was where the Lord was speaking presently (v. 20). This sight was to remind the people of the pillar of fire that guided the Israelites through the wilderness (i.e., God was in the pillar and present with His people). The wicks of the lamps were made from the priests' worn-out garments.[82] Hanging the lamps over the women's court at the temple ensured that *all* would be able to see the spectacular sight.

Christ utilized this traditional ceremony to declare to the whole congregation that He was God's light shining forth to mankind; its illumination had no prejudice to gender, ethnic origin, or social status. Christ came into the world, and He died for all those in the world (Heb. 2:9; 1 Jn. 2:2), that "whosoever will" may step into the light and have fellowship with God through Him.

At the conclusion of the Feast of Tabernacles, the Lord Jesus said, *"I am the light of the world. He who follows Me shall not walk in darkness, but have the light of life"* (v. 12). The Lord Jesus was God's abiding presence in the world and through Him God would guide blind sinners into life-transforming truth. Light is a visible evidence or testimony that a lamp's wick is burning. The Pharisees understood the Lord's meaning and confronted His statement, *"You bear witness of Yourself; Your witness is not true"* (v. 13). They were referring to the Law that required a minimum of two witnesses to confirm that someone's testimony was true (v. 17). By applying the phrase "your law," the Lord was saying that the Pharisees understood that Moses taught the necessity of obtaining a legitimate testimony before rendering a judicial verdict (Deut. 19:15).

In a human court of law, the testimony of plural witnesses was necessary to verify the truth; however, since God always spoke the truth, His words did not need human validation. Hence, the Lord could say, *"Even if I bear witness of Myself, My witness is true"* (v. 14). The Pharisees were judging according to the flesh and were therefore fallible and even multiple human witnesses did not necessarily validate the truth (v. 15; 1 Kgs. 21:13). But Christ had come into the world to seek and to save the lost, thus, He was not passing judgment on anyone at this time; that task would come later at His second advent to the earth. However, even if He was moved to judge now, His judgment would be true and just because He and His Father were together and unified in all that they accomplished (v. 16). In fact, the Son and the Father were two infallible witnesses of the truth (v. 18).

Having spoken of His Father several times in this dialogue, the Jews asked the Lord, *"Where is Your Father?"* (v. 19). The Lord responded that they did not know His Father, for they had to trust in Him first before they could know Him. Previously, the Lord had affirmed through the expression "My Father" that He had a unique relationship with God that they did not have. The Jews had been enraged by this notion and wanted to put the supposed blasphemer to death because He was claiming equality with God (5:17-18). The Lord's words had the same effect in the treasury (associated with the women's court at the temple), but they could not lay hands on the Lord Jesus, because it was not yet "His hour" appointed by God for suffering (v. 20).

The Lord then told His contrary audience what was going to happen to them in the future. They would continue waiting for the Messiah to come, and then die in their sins condemned, which meant they would never be with Him, their true Messiah (v. 21). The Jews focused in on the latter part of the Lord's statement, *"Where I go you cannot come."* They wondered if the reason that they would not be able to find Him in the future was that He was going to kill Himself to hide in a grave. But their thinking was limited by earthly reasoning because they were of the world, but He came from above and was not of the world (v. 23). Because they were of the world and thought of worldly things, rather than trusting in Him, God's message from heaven, they would die in their sins (v. 24).

Because the Lord had employed the "I am" statement with His authoritative decree in verse 24, the Jews abruptly asked Him, essentially, "Who do you think you are?" in verse 25. The Lord responded to their forthright inquiry by affirming two matters: First, He could say many additional things to expose their sin, guilt, and ungodly motives but that was not His primary reason for addressing them. Second, and the more crucial point, was that His teaching about Himself and why He had been sent to earth had not changed, for it had been received from heaven (v. 26). John notes at this juncture that the Jews did not understand that the Lord was speaking of God the Father as the One who had sent Him (v. 27).

The Light of the World then told the Pharisees exactly what they were going to do to Him because they were determined to walk in darkness instead of the light of His truth: *"When you lift up the Son of Man, then you will know that I am He, and that I do nothing of Myself; but as My Father taught Me, I speak these things. And He who sent Me is with Me"* (vv. 28-29). Israel's leaders were plotting to crucify the Son of Man because He was doing His Father's will. The Lord could only do what pleased the Father, even if it meant His death! After speaking these words, many believed that His message was true and from God (v. 30).

The Lord provided a test for those who said that they believed in Him: *"If you abide in My word, you are My disciples indeed"* (v. 31).

John

Many claim to be followers of Christ, but who are "disciples indeed"? Previously, He told His audience not to call Him Lord unless they were going to do what He said (Luke 6:46). Later, the Lord would say, *"If you love Me, keep My commandments"* (14:15). Sixty years later John would write, *"We know that we know Him, if we keep His commandments"* (1 Jn. 2:3). Obedience to God demonstrates the reality of someone's profession of Faith. *"Blessed are those who hear the word of God and keep it!"* (Luke 11:28). Good works cannot save anyone, but true faith never stands alone; it is accompanied by good works (Jas. 2:17). No one is forced into God's light, but those who come to God's truth in Christ find freedom and serve Him freely (v. 32; 1 Jn. 1:5-7).

The Jews took issue with the latter part of Christ's statement in verse 32, that through Him they could be set free. They pompously declared that, as Abraham's descendants, they had always been free and not in bondage to anyone (v. 33). Obviously, they had forgotten about centuries of Gentile oppression in Egypt, by foreign invaders during the era of the Judges, then by the Assyrian, Babylonian, Medo-Persian, Greek, and Roman Empires. The Romans controlled them at that time. But they were missing the point; He was speaking of spiritual deliverance from sin and death. Those continuing in sin, as they were, were slaves to sin (v. 34).

A household slave abides in a home until he or she is no longer needed, but those sons of the master have a family inheritance forever (v. 35). Without Christ, the Jews were slaves to sin with no future hope. But through Christ, they would be liberated from the condemnation and slavery of sin and its condemnation – they would be "free indeed" (v. 36). Thus, the unregenerate man will not abide in the house of sin forever. If converted, he will be liberated from the house of sin and receive spiritual life; if unconverted, he will be liberated from sin by physical death, but then will suffer eternal death.

Although his audience were descendants of Abraham, they were not acting like Father Abraham (Rom. 4:16). Rather than exercising faith in God's Word and being justified by God as Abraham was (Rom. 4:3), they were rejecting God's message and desiring to kill His Messenger (v. 37). Christ completely lived out what He had seen of His Father, and the Jews were doing the same of their father (v. 38). The Pharisees quickly responded, *"Abraham is our father"* (v. 39). The Lord rejected this statement; if they were the spiritual children of Abraham, they would have followed His example of trusting in God's Word and obeying God's commands (v. 40). True descendants of Abraham do what Abraham did!

The Man and Your God

Basically, the Lord was admonishing His audience, "You really do not know who your father is, but it is not Abraham." "You act like your father, but not like Abraham" (v. 41).

The dialogue had now become intense, and the Jews levied the first of four slurs against the Lord: *"We are not born of fornication; we have one Father – God"* (v. 41). The Jews inferred that Mary, the mother of Jesus, was a loose woman who had become pregnant during the time of purity while betrothed to Joseph. They were implying that Jesus could not know who His real father was. The Lord completely ignores the insult to His mother and Himself to counter their statement that if God was really their Father, then they would love Him, for He came forth from God (v. 42).

But they could not understand what He was saying or from where He came, because their father was the devil, and they could only do what he lusted for (desired; v. 43). The devil deceived Adam and the woman in Eden to rebel against God, resulting in sin and death for humanity; thus, he was *"a murderer from the beginning"* (v. 44). There is no truth in the devil; he only speaks from his evil essence and therefore is "the father of lies." Children of the devil, like their father, loath the truth, which is why they were rejecting Christ's words (vv. 45, 47). In contrast, the Lord could only tell the truth and do what pleased His Father. Hence, He could challenge the Jews to look at His sinless life as evidence that He was from God and told the truth – no one could convict Him of sin (v. 46)!

The Jews had no reasonable argument against Christ's challenge, so they resorted to name calling and slurs to defend themselves (v. 48). They called the Lord a Samaritan, a people of mixed pedigree that the Judean Jews especially despised. The Lord said that their father was the devil, so they quipped that He was demon-possessed and under Satan's control. The Lord said that He was not being controlled by a demon because His utmost ambition in life was to honor His Father. A demon-possessed person would not care about honoring God. However, they were disdaining God because they had dishonored Him (v. 49). In retrospect, they were the ones acting as a demon-possessed person would. He did not seek glory for Himself, but to be honored by the One who knows and judges all things, speaking of His Father (v. 50).

The Lord reiterates the message He received from His father – eternal life is in the Son and one must believe in Him to receive it (v. 51). The Pharisees again claimed that Jesus was demon-possessed and speaking out of His mind, because He spoke of never dying, but faithful Abraham and the holy prophets were already dead (v. 52). The Lord was speaking of eternal, spiritual life, which was in Him, not of physical death, a consequence of sin (Rom. 5:12).

The Pharisees were repulsed by the idea that those believing in Jesus of Nazareth's message would never die when the patriarchs and the prophets had all died. Did Jesus think He was greater than Abraham and the prophets (v. 54)? Their rejection culminated with the charge, "Who do you think you are?" The Lord responded by saying that He was not promoting Himself; all that mattered was that the Father, who they claimed was their God, was honoring Him (v. 55). But, in fact, their true father, the devil, would never seek to honor Him.

Additionally, the Lord said that Abraham, the father of the Jewish nation, by faith foresaw Messiah's coming to Israel to fulfill God's covenant with him. Therefore, the Lord Jesus said, *"Abraham rejoiced to see My day"* (v. 56). A theophany or Christophany is an Old Testament appearance of the second person of the Godhead to convey God's word to individuals and sometimes to the Jewish nation. Often this divine Messenger is referred to as "the Angel of the Lord" (angel means "messenger"). As God incarnate, Christ continues this role in the New Testament as God's living Word to humanity. The Lord personally spoke to Abraham on several occasions (e.g., Gen. 15:1, 17:12, 22:11) and appeared to Him at least three times (Acts 7:2, Gen. 12:7, 18:1). From what was revealed to Abraham, the patriarch knew Christ would be his seed (Gal. 3:16), that that Son of promise would experience resurrection (Heb. 11:19) and that Christ would reign over a heavenly city filled with the redeemed in a heavenly country (Heb. 11:10, 16). Indeed, "Abraham rejoiced to see Christ's day."

The Jews quickly rejected this idea, for Jesus was not even fifty years old, so how could Abraham have known Him (v. 57)? The Lord responded, *"Most assuredly, I say to you, before Abraham was, I AM"* (v. 58). All the harsh rhetoric had its apex with this statement: the One speaking to them was God incarnate. The Jews understood Jesus' statement and immediately picked up stones to strike Him down for His apparent blasphemy (v. 59). But it was not yet His hour, so He ducked out of sight and passed through the crowd unharmed. Ironically, the religious leaders at that moment had driven the Son of God from the temple, which was supposed to be the house of God.

John Chapter 9

The Lord was walking along the streets of Jerusalem with His disciples when He saw a man that was born blind (v. 1). The man was probably begging for alms. The disciples assumed that the man's blindness was the result of divine chastening for sin, so they asked the Lord whether it was the blind man's parents who sinned or the blind man himself (v. 2). The latter option seems unreasonable as the man was born blind before he had the opportunity to sin, but perhaps the disciples were thinking that God, foreknowing the man's sin, chose to punish him while he was in his mother's womb. But would not the man's blindness then have prevented him from engaging in much of the wickedness presupposed? In any case, the disciples associated the man's blindness with sin in the family.

The Lord graciously responded to their bizarre question by saying that the man's blindness did not result from personal sin or the sin of his parents. Rather, his blindness had been permitted for the glory of God to be displayed, for the Lord knew that He was about to heal the man (v. 3). The context of verse 3 is explained by the Lord's statement in verses 4-5. While He was in the world, those living in spiritual darkness could gain spiritual sight through receiving the light of the world – Himself.

Next, the Lord spat on the ground and made clay with His saliva, then anointed the man's eyes with the clay (v. 6). Afterwards, He told the man to *"Go wash in the pool of Siloam"* (v. 7). Ironically, Siloam means "sent" and that is exactly what the Lord did; He sent the man to the pool of Siloam. We do not know how long it took the blind man to stumble through the streets of Jerusalem to get to the pool on the southeast side of the city, but He obeyed the Lord's command and gained His sight after washing there (v. 8). The prophet Isaiah foretold that when Messiah came to Israel, He would open the eyes of the blind (Isa. 42:7). Matthew records five separate instances in which Christ fulfilled this prophecy (Matt. 9:27-31, 12:22-23, 15:30, 20:29-34, 21:14).

We pause here to consider a historical event that happened near this pool about six centuries earlier. According to Nehemiah, there was a

John

man-made pool called the "king's pool" (Neh. 2:14) near the king's garden by the fountain gate (Neh. 3:16). The prophet Isaiah spoke of a "lower pool" at this location two centuries earlier (Isa. 22:9). This is likely the location of the Pool of Siloam. This was the pool where the blind man was sent by the Lord to wash and to be healed; the journey served as a test of his faith. It was also from here that King Zedekiah unsuccessfully attempted to escape Jerusalem during the last days of the Babylonian siege (Jer. 39:4). He had rebelled against God's command to surrender to the Babylonians, and they killed his sons in front of him and then put out his eyes to seal the agonizing memory (Jer. 39:7). These two references in Scripture to this pool provide a valuable lesson: those faithful to God gain greater insight into the things of God, and those who are not, lose sight of what is important.

Returning to the text, those who knew the man, especially his neighbors, were perplexed by the sight of the healed blind man. Because some thought the man's condition was hopeless, they could not believe that it was the same man, but the healed blind man emphatically stated to his inquirers, *"I am he"* (v. 9). When asked how he received his sight, the man reported all that he knew (v. 10). A Man called Jesus made clay and anointed my eyes and told me to wash in the pool of Siloam. I did and that is how I received my sight (v. 11). When the people asked where this Jesus was, the blind man did not know (v. 12). This is the first of three times that the blind man will be asked by others to explain "how" he obtained his sight.

Perhaps, because it was the Sabbath, some Jews thought it appropriate to bring the former blind man to the Pharisees for questioning (vv. 13-14). The healed man recounted the story of his healing again to the Pharisees (v. 15). Some Pharisees concluded that the man who healed the blind man could not be from God, because he performed the miracle on the Sabbath. However, more level-headed Pharisees recognized that such an incredible feat could only be accomplished by God, meaning that the man who performed it had to be from God (v. 16).

The Pharisees then asked the former blind man what He thought about his healer; he responded to their question by saying, *"He is a prophet"* (v. 17). But rather than believing the evidence before them, the Pharisees took the position that the whole thing was a hoax and that the man before them had never been blind (v. 18). They summoned the man's parents to testify as to whether he was born blind, and, if so, how

The Man and Your God

did he receive his sight (v. 19)? The man's parents confirmed that the man they were questioning was their son and that indeed he had been born blind, but they did not know how he gained his sight (vv. 20-21).

The healed man's parents feared the Jewish leaders, for they knew anyone identifying with Jesus Christ would be put out of the synagogue, so they deferred questioning to their adult son, who was of age (vv. 22-23). Therefore, the Pharisees summoned the healed man a second time for further questioning. Using intimidation tactics, the Pharisees attempted to lead the man into confessing that Jesus was a sinner and not from God (v. 24). The former blind man did not know anything about Jesus (i.e., whether He was a sinner or not), but he did testify *"that though I was blind, now I see"* (v. 25). The Pharisees again asked the man how he was healed by Jesus, but the blind man refused to answer, saying he had already told them the truth and they were refusing to accept his testimony (vv. 26-27). Then the man wondered if the reason they wanted to hear more about Jesus was to become His disciples.

The Pharisees reviled the man for this comment. They indicted the man as a disciple of Jesus, though the man knew nothing about Him. They proudly proclaimed that they were Moses' disciples and, therefore, they did not know where Jesus was from (vv. 28-29).

The healed man seized on this statement with a sarcastic observation: *"Why, this is a marvelous thing, that you do not know where He is from; yet, He has opened my eyes!"* (v. 30). The blind man then uttered the most spiritual statement of this entire dialogue: *"Now we know that God does not hear sinners; but if anyone is a worshiper of God and does His will, He hears him"* (v. 31). He continued by saying that no one born blind in Israel had ever been healed before; hence, the One who gave him sight must be from God; otherwise, He could do nothing (vv. 32-33).

Although an accurate assessment, the Pharisees were enraged by the man's conclusions. They said that he was completely in his sins and yet dared to teach them, Israel's religious leaders (v. 34). Although the healed man told the truth, the Pharisees hated Jesus; thus the man was put out of the synagogue.

After hearing that the healed man had been excommunicated from Judaism, the Lord Jesus sought him. Until this moment, the man had only heard the Lord's voice; he did not know what the Lord looked like. So, when the Lord approached him, the man did not know who it was until the Lord spoke the words, *"Do you believe in the Son of God?"* (v. 35). The healed man said, *"Who is He, Lord, that I may believe in Him?"* (v.

36). The Lord Jesus then confirmed that it was Him, the One the man both saw and was speaking with (v. 37). The man immediately confessed that he believed Him to be the Son of God and worshiped Him (v. 38).

The man's understanding of his Healer progressively increased throughout the chapter: a man named Jesus (v. 11), a prophet (v. 17), a man from God (v. 33), and the Son of God, his Lord (vv. 35-38). While it is true that the Lord Jesus is a man and a prophet from God, He is so much more – He is God incarnate and deserves our worship.

Worship focuses on who God is inherently, His "worth-ship." Praise acknowledges God's blessings to us. The blind man of John 9 was thankful that Jesus healed his blindness, but it was only when he realized that he was in the presence of the Son of God that he fell before Him in worship. This realization came after more exposure to the truth. The healed blind man worshiped the Lord Jesus, not for what He had done for him, but for who the Lord was – the Son of God. Praise has its place, but if worshipers focus only on the gifts God bestows and not upon why God has given them, our worship will become shallow and selfish. Worship focuses on the Giver, not the gift itself, and thus requires believers to examine Scripture to determine why God does what He does.

John 6 demonstrates that the unrighteous long to see a "sign or a wonder" in order to believe (6:30), while the righteous believe in order to see and understand (6:68-69). "Light," symbolizing divine truth, and "believing," an action of faith not based on sight, are paramount topics throughout John's Gospel. The antitype of each of these is strongly tied together in the behavior of the spiritually blind Pharisees. They were blind because they chose to ignore the truth and continued in the darkness of self-righteousness.

> *And Jesus said, "For judgment I have come into this world, that those who do not see may see, and that those who see may be made blind." Then some of the Pharisees who were with Him heard these words, and said to Him, "Are we blind also?" Jesus said to them, "If you were blind, you would have no sin; but now you say, 'We see.' Therefore your sin remains"* (vv. 39-41).

Spiritual blindness ignores the true reality of things and instead embraces what is often an obvious perversion of the truth. By posing the rhetorical question, "Are we blind?" they were implying that they had absolute spiritual insight into the truth. But religious pride and sin blind

The Man and Your God

people from seeing the truth clearly and reasoning as they should. For example, mark the utter stupidity of the Pharisees' statements while speaking with the Lord Jesus:

> These strict, self-righteous, Law-keepers had to be reminded by Christ that their plans to murder Him would, in fact, break the Mosaic Law (7:19, 8:59).
>
> Speaking to the Lord Jesus, the Pharisees said, *"Are You also from Galilee? Search and look, for no prophet has arisen out of Galilee"* (7:52). But they had forgotten that Jonah was of Galilee.
>
> The Pharisees brought a woman caught in the act of adultery before the Lord to be judged, but where was the man? The Law was no respecter of persons – adultery demanded the death of both parties (8:1-11; Lev. 20:10).
>
> The Pharisees proclaimed to Christ, *"We are Abraham's descendants, and have never been in bondage to anyone. How can You say, 'You will be made free'?"* (8:33). But, in fact, they had been ruled relentlessly by four world empires over the last 600 years.

God has offered mankind a choice – to hide in the calamity of darkness and suffer eternal death, or by faith venture into divine light (i.e., believe the truth) and receive eternal life in Christ.

Spiritual blindness clouds human reasoning and distorts our perception of reality. Therefore, in spiritual matters, man must ignore sight-based faith, our mutable feelings, and simply trust God at His word – this is true faith. God rewards true faith by opening our understanding of spiritual truth; naturally speaking, we cannot understand the things of God (1 Cor. 2:9-13).

> Darkness is my point of view, my right to myself; light is God's point of view.
>
> — Oswald Chambers

> Where, except in uncreated light, can the darkness be drowned?
>
> — C. S. Lewis

John Chapter 10

The shepherd imagery conveyed in this chapter is only a portion of a New Testament trilogy pertaining to Christ. First, John presents Christ as the "Good Shepherd" who lays His life down for the sheep. Then the writer of Hebrews highlights the sanctifying work of the Lord Jesus as the "Great Shepherd" (Heb. 13:20-21). Finally, Peter proclaims Christ as the "Chief Shepherd" who will return and gather His sheep to Himself (1 Pet. 5:4). The latter reference speaks of Christ's return to the air to "snatch away" from the earth those who have truly believed on Him.

This same shepherding imagery is also prophetically declared to us in Psalms 22-24: In Psalm 22, the Good Shepherd gives His life for His sheep on Mount Calvary. In Psalm 23, the Great Shepherd leads His sheep through the valley of shadows. Lastly, in Psalm 24, the Chief Shepherd (the King of Glory) appears and takes His sheep to Mount Zion in glory. Thus, the valley of shadows in Psalm 23 lies between the two mountains of Psalms 22 and 24.

The Good Shepherd (vv. 1-21)

Christ's sacrificial love for His sheep in this chapter stands in sharp contrast to the hireling shepherds of Israel down through the centuries. These false shepherds of Israel led God's sheep astray, neglected their care, and deserted them in times of danger (e.g., Ezek. 34). How would the promised Messiah, the true Shepherd of Israel, be recognized? It is on this point the Lord commences His teaching about the Good Shepherd with two distinct allegories (vv. 1-5 and vv. 7-18).

John speaks of a sheepfold which was a walled enclosure with a single door. Shepherds would bring their flocks to the fold to be kept safe during nighttime hours by a doorkeeper who guarded the sheep from harm. In the morning, the shepherds would come and call their sheep out of the fold and then would lead them out to pasture. The first allegory pertains to legitimacy of the shepherd and identification of his sheep. The second allegory addresses the behavior of the Good Shepherd and how He blesses His flock.

Only the legitimate shepherd of the sheep enters the sheepfold by the door, while thieves and robbers attempt to climb over the wall to enter in (vv. 1-2). This means that God's Shepherd will be recognized by the sheep after walking through the door of fulfilled Old Testament prophecy. Anyone claiming to be God's true Shepherd but does not fulfill all previous prophecies concerning the Messiah is a fake shepherd and a robber of the sheep.

The doorkeeper recognizes the true Shepherd and permits Him to enter the sheepfold through the doorway (v. 3). It is possible that the doorkeeper is John the baptizer, the forerunner of Christ, who pointed others to God's Messiah (1:29, 36, 3:28). However, the Holy Spirit, who inspired the Old Testament prophecies concerning Christ, would be able to perfectly endorse Jesus Christ as having fulfilled all of them. Later, the Lord told His disciples that when the Holy Spirit came to dwell with them, *"He will guide you into all truth"* and *"He will glorify Me"* (16:14-15). So here it would be fitting for the Holy Spirit to introduce God's true Shepherd to the lost sheep of Israel.

The sheep constrained and protected by the fold are the lost sheep of Israel. Those who believe the Spirit's testimony through Old Testament Scripture will trust the message of the Messiah when He calls them out of Judaism, and they will become His sheep. These will obey the voice of the Good Shepherd and be led out of the sheepfold by Him into green pastures (v. 3). The sheepfold had walls which protected the sheep from outside threats at night, but the fold was not meant to be a permanent enclosure for the sheep during the day. For the sheep to live, they must be led out by the Good Shepherd to obtain good pasture and water.

Likewise, the Law conveyed God's standard of righteousness for Israel to live by and its legal constraints hemmed in the Jewish people, so to speak. Although the Law protected Israel from Gentile spiritual corruption beyond the fold, it also could not offer life to those within its walls. August Van Ryn further describes the meaning of the sheepfold:

> The true shepherd enters by the first door (v. 2). The sheepfold speaks of Israel's place in the Old Testament. They were God's sheep, as is repeatedly asserted. The walls of law restrained them. All through the long night of the law dispensation, they were shut up without the liberty of grace which God has now brought to us. Of course, they jumped the bars – all have gone astray – and turned everyone to his own way.

Dispensationally, however, we see law in the Old Testament, shutting the sheep in.[83]

The purpose of the Law was to show sin (Rom. 3:20) and to point the Jews to the Good Shepherd (Gal. 3:24). The Good Shepherd does not force Himself on anyone; those who understand who He is will obey His voice and be gladly led by Him (v. 4). True sheep (speaking of the Lord's disciples at that time) knew God's true Shepherd; hence, they will not follow or listen to strangers – their allegiance is to Christ (v. 5). Examples of true sheep from the Jewish fold would be Simon (1:42), Lazarus, Mary, and Martha (11:1-5), Philip (14:9), Joseph of Arimathea and Nicodemus (20:38-39), Mary (20:16), Thomas (20:27), the other disciples excluding Judas, and many others who traveled with the Lord and served Him during His earthly ministry.

Regrettably, many Jews at Christ's first advent preferred the walls of the sheepfold (the rigidity of the Law) rather than the liberty of God's grace that the Good Shepherd desired to lead them into. In verse 6, the Lord told the Pharisees that they were not God's sheep because they had not listened to the voice of God's Shepherd. This was the reason that they did not understand the meaning of the Lord's illustration. Sadly, many today still seek to live within the walls of religious legalism, rather than answering the call of God's Good Shepherd. Those who choose to follow and be near to Christ will experience His love, His life, and His care. Those remaining in the fold will not.

John repeatedly affirms the deity of Christ in his account and, therefore, repeatedly connects Christ to the completion of the Old Testament "types." Interestingly, the English word "parable" is rendered thirty-two times in the four Gospels. In the KJV of the Bible, the word "parable" is found only once in John's Gospel, verse 6. However, this is not the same Greek word translated "parable" in the other Gospels, which is why it is rendered "illustration" in the NKJV.

The Greek word in verse 6 is *paroimia*, literally meaning "a proverb" or a "figure of speech." J. H. Thayer defines it this way: "a saying out of the usual course or deviating from the usual manner of speaking … any dark saying which shadows forth some didactic truth, especially a symbolic or figurative saying."[84] The normal Greek word used thirty-one times in the synoptic Gospels is *parabole*, meaning "a similitude implied by a fictitious narrative."[85] The Lord articulated the importance of Himself as the Good Shepherd in this chapter, but this was not an

The Man and Your God

application-enriched story to prompt the listener to action. Technically, then, there are no parables within the Gospel of John.

Continuing His address, the Lord Jesus said that He was the legitimate fulfillment of Old Testament prophecy and that He could lead those who obeyed His voice out of the Law's condemnation and into abundant life (green pastures, so to speak). The second allegory, beginning in verse 7, describes what happens after the Good Shepherd leads His disciples out of Judaism.

The Lord Jesus Christ declares of Himself, *"I am the door of the sheep"* (v. 7). There were those claiming to be God's true shepherd previously, but they had not been validated by Old Testament prophecy; therefore, God's sheep (the true remnant in Israel) did not listen to them (v. 8). In verses 7-10, the true sheep of Israel will be protected by the true Shepherd until He leads them out to pasture through Himself, as the doorway to divine blessing. Because Jesus Christ is God's door into eternal life, those approaching God through Him will enter the unfathomable blessings of being led and protected by the Good Shepherd forever.

The thief (the devil) and those who are his (the Jewish leaders), however, do not care about the sheep (God's covenant people). The "thieves and robbers" (v. 8) were on the outside of the fold, spiritually speaking, and the doorkeeper would not permit them entrance through the doorway and the Good Shepherd would protect the sheep if intruders tried to come over the walls of the fold. A thief will steal, kill, and destroy what is not his, but in contrast, the Good Shepherd gives His life for the sheep, so that the sheep can enjoy an abundant life (vv. 9-10).

The Greek words rendered "life" in verses 10 and 11 are different. The word *psuche* (normally rendered "soul" in the New Testament) is used to speak of the whole life of a person; this is what Christ sacrificed at Calvary on behalf of the sheep (v. 11). How did the sheep benefit from the Shepherd's sacrifice? They received a *zoe*, an abundant life worth living (v. 10). The Greek word translated "good" to modify Shepherd is *kalos*, which means magnificent, worthy, and beautiful. It is used to describe the beautiful stones of the temple (Luke 21:5). The Good Shepherd is altogether lovely and worthy!

Verses 11-18 address conditions outside the Jewish fold in connection with the Good Shepherd. Hirelings care for the sheep to earn a wage, but when the sheep are threatened by a wolf, the hireling runs to safety and permits the wolf to devour and scatter the sheep (speaking of

Satan's wicked and pernicious activities; 2 Cor. 11:14; 1 Pet. 5:8). This is what Israel's carnal shepherds had done for centuries; they did not have a heart for God's people as David did (e.g., Ezek. 34). A hireling does not know or care about the sheep, but the Good Shepherd does (v. 13). His sheep are intimately known by Him, and they intimately know Him also (v. 14).

This intimacy shared between the Good Shepherd and His sheep is a manifestation on earth of the love and communion shared between God the Father and the Son (v. 15). This type of divine love is sacrificial. The Father demonstrated His love for the world by giving His only begotten Son for sacrifice (3:16) and the Son was willing to lay down His life to please the Father (v. 15). The Lord then alluded to "other sheep" that were His besides those in Israel (speaking of the Gentiles). The Greek word for "other" is *allos*, which means "others of the same kind." These latter sheep (also true sheep) would be added to His one flock (speaking of the Church which would be composed of both Jewish and Gentile believers; Eph. 2:11-22), which He alone would shepherd (v. 16).

The Lord then affirms the love of the Father for the Son and that the Son will lay down His own life and raise it up again (v. 17). Because the Father commanded it, Christ, in Himself, would give up His life at Calvary when the judgment of sin was complete, and He would also affect His own resurrection three days later (v. 18). How could a dead shepherd, one who gave his life for the sheep, promise continuing care of his sheep unless that shepherd was resurrected from the grave?

Previously, speaking of His own body, the Lord had said, *"Destroy this temple, and in three days I will raise it up"* (2:19). He demonstrated His sovereign authority and power over creation by walking upon water, calming storms, feeding multitudes, healing disabilities and diseases, and raising the dead. Only three resurrections were recorded in the Old Testament; Elijah and Elisha are associated with these. The Lord raised three people from the dead during His earthly ministry, then would instigate His own resurrection. The number *seven* is used in the Bible to convey the idea of completion and perfection. The Lord Jesus was the seventh person raised from the dead in Scripture; He was the perfect resurrection.

In the Garden of Gethsemane, the Lord commanded the very soldiers that were arresting Him to take only Him and let His disciples go – this after Peter tried to kill a man (18:8-12). They complied because the Lord Jesus was in complete control of every detail that night. While He would die on the cross, He did not die by the cross; He laid down His own life. Then, three days later He would raise Himself up from the grave as commanded by the Father. How could Jesus Christ cause His own resurrection unless He had the essence of life in Himself (1:4)?

Concerning the Triune nature of God, we cannot constrain what is mysterious and beyond our comprehension into some formulated understanding. Yet, Scripture does portray the Trinity in a consistent way and with distinct roles. For what we do not understand, let us simply remove our shoes and not trespass upon holy ground. Scripture reveals a Triune God working together in unity to complete the plan of salvation for humanity: The Father purposed to save souls through His Son's sacrifice (3:16; 1 Pet. 1:2). Christ gave Himself freely to achieve the will of the Father (vv. 17-18). The Holy Spirit makes effectual the work of the Son by convicting mankind of sin and wooing sinners to the Savior (16:8).

John initially identified Jesus Christ as the Good Shepherd and the door into the sheepfold (vv. 1-2). The door represents Christ's legitimacy to be Israel's Shepherd as affirmed by Old Testament prophecies. Then John identifies seven things that the Good Shepherd does:

The Good Shepherd calls to His Sheep, and they obey Him (v. 3).

The Good Shepherd leads His Sheep, and they follow Him (v. 4).

The Good Shepherd comes to give abundant life to His sheep (v. 10).

The Good Shepherd gives His life for the sheep (vv. 11, 15).

The Good Shepherd knows and cares for His sheep (vv. 12-14).

The Good Shepherd brings other sheep (Gentiles) into His fold (v. 16).

The Good Shepherd raises Himself from the dead (vv. 17-18).

There was much division among the Jews after Christ finished speaking (v. 19). Some thought He was possessed by a demon and charged others not to listen to a deranged man (v. 20). However, others agreed that His words were of a spiritual nature and not the ravings of a demon-possessed person, for how could a demon heal a man born blind? (v. 21).

Christ Affirms His Deity (vv. 22-39)

The ministry in Decapolis concluded with the Lord's return to Jerusalem for the Feast of Tabernacles in the Fall of 29 A.D. (7:1-8:11).

For the next two-plus months, the Lord and His disciples traveled throughout Judea spreading the Kingdom Gospel message (Luke 10:1-17). This ministry concluded with the Feast of Dedication in Jerusalem (called *Hanukkah* today) in mid-December of that year (v. 22). This eight-day feast commemorated the reconsecration of the temple by Judas Maccabeus in 165 B.C. after being desecrated by Antiochus Epiphanes in 168 B.C.

The Lord was at Solomon's porch in the temple when He was surrounded by Jews who asked Him to tell them plainly if He was the Christ or not (vv. 23-24). The Lord said that He had already told them the truth, but they did not believe it. He had performed many miracles and wonders in the Father's name, but they had not believed the legitimacy of these signs either (v. 25). The problem of their not knowing was not the lack of information on His part, but of faith on their part.

About two months earlier, the Lord had said, *"I know My sheep, and am known by My own"* (v. 14) and that His sheep follow Him because *"they know My voice"* (v. 4). Now, He declared, *"But you do not believe, because you are not My sheep"* (v. 26). They were not His sheep because, though He had called to them, they had not responded to His voice (v. 3). Speaking to the same people, the Lord implored them to believe on Him because of the works that He was performing, then they would know that He and the Father were one (v. 38).

Obviously, the Lord knows who His sheep are (those who would believe on Him), so when He called out to the sheepfold of Israel, those who were known to Him obeyed His voice in faith and followed Him (v. 27). Yet, the Lord was still imploring others in the same fold to believe on Him. Anyone thirsting in his or her soul for God is invited to *"take the water of life freely"* (Rev. 22:17). The Lord already knew who would believe on Him and who would not, but He continued pleading with the entire Jewish fold regardless. The opportunity to choose the Good Shepherd was still available to those who had not yet believed on Him.

Those sheep who obey the Lord's voice received eternal life in Him (v. 28). These souls can never be lost from the Lord's grip and therefore will never suffer God's condemnation of the wicked. The souls entrusted to the Son by the Father can never be snatched from the Father's hand either. Paul tells us that believers are also sealed by the power of the Holy Spirit (Eph. 1:13). The believer's salvation is held secure by the power of a Triune God. No one is going to snatch a soul out of the Father's hands or the Son's hands, nor break the seal of the Holy Spirit!

In this dialogue the Lord Jesus clearly asserts His deity, *"I and My Father are one"* (v. 30). Again, the Jews perfectly understood the Lord's claim: *"Then the Jews took up stones again to stone Him"* (v. 31). Albert Barnes comments as to the vast weight of the Lord's statement in John 10:30 – His affirmation of deity:

> The word translated "one" is not in the *masculine*, but in the *neuter* gender. It expresses *union*, but not the precise nature of the union. It may express any union, and the particular kind intended is to be inferred from the connection. In the previous verse He had said that He and His Father were united in the same object – that is, in redeeming and preserving His people. It was this that gave occasion for this remark. Most of the Christian fathers understood [this verse] ... as referring to the oneness or unity of nature between the Father and the Son; and that this was the design of Christ appears probable from the following considerations: *First.* The question in debate was not about His being united with the Father in plan and counsel, but in power. He affirmed that he was able to rescue and keep His people from all enemies, or that He had power superior to men and devils – that is, that He had supreme power over all creation. He affirmed the same of His Father. In this, therefore, they were united. *Second.* The Jews understood Him as affirming His equality with God, for they took up stones to punish Him for blasphemy (John 10:31, 33), and they said to Him that they understood Him as affirming that He was God. *Third.* Jesus did not deny that it was His intention to be so understood. *Fourth.* He immediately made another declaration implying the same thing, leaving the same impression, and which they attempted to punish in the same manner (John 10:37-39). If Jesus had not intended so to be understood, it cannot be easily reconciled with moral honesty that He did not distinctly disavow that such was His intention. The Jews were well acquainted with their own language. They understood Him in this manner, and He left this impression on their minds.[86]

The Lord Jesus was claiming to be God and that He was one with His Father. When the Jews began picking up stones, the Lord asked them for which of the miraculous works that He performed were they desiring to stone Him (v. 32). The Jews answered that it was not for His works that they wanted to stone Him, but for His blasphemous words. They then accused Him of committing the sin of blasphemy: *"because You, being a Man, make Yourself God"* (v. 33). Instead of believing the truth and obeying His voice, they wanted to put the Good Shepherd to death, which God would permit in His timing.

After hearing their charge of blasphemy, the Lord reminded them that the judges of Israel were referred to as "gods" by God Himself (v. 34; Ps. 82:6). This referred to the era when God sent judges to deliver His people from oppression. When acting righteously and doing the will of God, these judges were little gods representing the one true God in Israel, thus God says, *"You are gods"* (v. 35; Ex. 21:6, 22:8). The Lord's point was that He, as the Son of God, had been sent by God to deliver His people and was perfectly reflecting the character of God while performing that work, so how could they call Him a blasphemer (v. 36)?

Lastly, the Lord implored His audience that if they could not believe their ears (His words), they should believe their eyes: they had witnessed powerful signs worked by the Son, which proved that He and the Father were one (vv. 37-38). But the Jews rejected this line of reasoning and they sought to seize Him, but the Lord escaped out of their hands, for it was not yet His appointed hour to be bound and to suffer at their hands (v. 39).

Christ Withdraws From Jerusalem (vv. 40-42)

The Lord and His disciples now largely withdraw from public ministry. They will spend the next four months in Perea, where John had previously foretold of Messiah's coming and baptized those repenting of their sins (v. 40). The specific location was Bethabara (1:28). John did not perform any miraculous signs but foretold that the true Messiah would when He arrived; thus, many remembered John's word and believed on Christ as the Messiah (vv. 41-42).

It is during the Judean and Perean ministries that the Lord told most of His parables, that is, during the last six months of His earthly sojourn. Luke is the only writer to record the events that transpired during the Lord's Perean ministry (Luke 13:23-18:30). In the next chapter, Christ and His disciples will depart Perea and travel through Jericho to Bethany (a village near Jerusalem). This journey occurred just prior to the Passover feast in 30 A.D. It is at this time that the Lord raises His friend Lazarus from the dead and the Lord enters the final days of His heavenly mission on earth.

John Chapter 11

While the Lord Jesus was dwelling in Perea with His disciples, Mary and Martha from Bethany sent word to the Lord that their brother Lazarus, whom He loved, was seriously ill (vv. 1-3). The Lord loved Mary, Martha, and Lazarus and had frequently visited their home in Bethany (v. 5). There are six different Marys mentioned in Scripture, so John adds that this was the Mary who anointed the Lord's feet with spikenard and then wiped them with her hair (v. 2; 12:1-11).

After being aware of Lazarus' sickness, the Lord told His disciples that his sickness was not unto death, but for the glory of God (v. 4). Indeed, the Son of God would be glorified through Lazarus' situation. It would have taken a messenger a full day to travel from Bethany to Bethabara near the Jordan River. (This was about a twenty-mile journey.) The Lord then waited two more days before telling His disciples that it was time to return to Judea (vv. 6-7). This declaration closed the Lord's Perean ministry, which began four months previous.

The disciples were not excited about returning to Jerusalem and reminded the Lord that there were Jews there that wanted to stone Him (v. 8). Certainly, the Lord Jesus had not forgotten this fact, but He was not concerned and offered an illustration to clarify why. There were normally twelve hours of daylight each day that laborers could work safely without stumbling in darkness (vv. 9-10). Indeed, the dark day of Calvary was coming, but until then it was daytime, so the Lord would continue laboring for God without harm to Himself. This is true for all believers today also. If believers are walking with the Lord and doing what He requests, we are invincible while serving Him, that is, until He determines that our work is done! Then we will ever be with the Lord (2 Cor. 5:8).

The Lord then told His disciples that their friend Lazarus was "asleep" (v. 11). The Greek verb *koimaomai* in the perfect tense is used in verse 11 to convey the idea that Lazarus was in a forever sleep. Accordingly, this verb is widely used in the New Testament to speak of death (e.g., 1 Cor. 15:18-20; 1 Thess. 4:13-15). The verb *katheudo* in the present tense is used to convey the idea of a temporary or physical sleep (e.g., Mark 5:39, 13:36, 14:37). The Lord's usage of *koimaomai* indicated that Lazarus was dead.

The disciples misinterpreted the metaphor (i.e., the Lord was speaking of physical death). They thought the Lord's statement was good news, *"If he sleeps, he will get well"* (v. 12). Perhaps they were suggesting this outcome to deter the Lord from journeying to Jerusalem. To eliminate any confusion, the Lord plainly told His disciples that Lazarus had died (vv. 13-14). The Lord knew that He would raise Lazarus from the dead, so He told His disciples that it would be beneficial for them that He had not been with Lazarus earlier to heal him (v. 15). Although Lazarus was dead, the Lord said that it was necessary that they go to him. The disciples did not understand why, but they obeyed the Lord's command and departed with their Master. It was at this moment that Thomas, also called "Didymus" (or "the Twin"), sarcastically rallied his brethren, *"Let us also go, that we may die with Him!"* (v. 16). John Heading observes that only John records Thomas's words and that each time his negative comment was transformed by Christ into a positive outcome: "He manifested fatalism (11:16), ignorance (14:5), doubt (20:24-29), and worldly occupation (21:2-3). All these weaknesses were transformed by the Lord on each occasion."[87]

It would have taken at least one full day to journey from Bethabara to Bethany. Apparently, Lazarus had died shortly after the messenger had been sent four to six days previously, as Lazarus had already been dead four days when the Lord arrived in Bethany (v. 17). Bethany was situated on the southeast side of Mount Olivet about two miles east of Jerusalem (v. 18). It was customary for the Jews to mourn with grieving family members for many days after the death of a loved one. Because Jerusalem was near to Bethany there were many people visiting Mary and Martha in their home. This cultural dynamic provided an opportunity for many to witness the miracle that Christ was about to do.

As the Lord Jesus and His disciples neared Bethany, many Jews were gathered at the home of Mary and Martha to mourn the death of Lazarus. When Martha heard that the Lord was nearby, she immediately went out to speak to Him, but Mary remained in the house (v. 20). We are not told why Mary remained in the house. It seems likely that she was aware of the Lord's approach, but for whatever reason she chose to remain with their many guests. She, no doubt, knew that the Lord would soon be entering their home, for He had often resided there previously.

The Man and Your God

After finding the Lord Jesus, Martha said to Him: *"Lord, if You had been here, my brother would not have died. But even now I know that whatever You ask of God, God will give You"* (vv. 21-22). Martha knew that the Lord could have healed her brother if He had been bodily present before he died, but her understanding of who Jesus really was, was imperfect, and thus her faith was deficient. Surely the Son of God could have healed Lazarus from Bethabara as easily as if He were in Bethany. Martha also knew that Jesus had the ear of God and would work something good out of the tragedy, but her response to the Lord's next statement indicated that the resurrection of her brother was not in her contemplation.

The Lord responded to Martha's statement: *"Your brother will rise again"* (v. 23). Martha believed that the Lord was speaking of the resurrection of the dead associated with Israel's future restoration to God and the judgment of the wicked (5:28-29; Isa. 26:19-20). She referred to these events occurring "at the last day." But the Lord was not speaking of raising up many souls in a future day; rather, He was referring to raising up one beloved friend from the dead on that very day.

Her brother's death provided the Lord a perfect platform to expand Martha's understanding of Himself as the One who was the source of life and had power over death: *"I am the resurrection and the life. He who believes in Me, though he may die, he shall live. And whoever lives and believes in Me shall never die. Do you believe this?"* (vv. 25-26). Martha responded to the Lord's question with a wonderful statement of faith: *"Yes, Lord, I believe that You are the Christ, the Son of God, who is to come into the world"* (v. 27). Later, John would pose this declaration as the telltale sign of a true believer in Christ (1 Jn. 4:2-3). Martha then departed to her home to secretly tell her sister Mary that the Teacher sought her (v. 28).

In the previous chapter we learned that Christ's sheep know and respond to His voice, and Mary immediately went to the Lord after learning that He was calling for her (v. 29). John then informs us that Martha had met the Lord at a location just outside of Bethany and He remained there for Mary to arrive (v. 30). Those grieving with Mary thought that she was going to the tomb, so they also departed to accompany her (v. 31).

Mary immediately came to the Lord and fell at His feet weeping. She repeated the same confidence in Him that Martha had already declared (v. 32). The Lord's care for both sisters in grace is quite different. He tested Martha's understanding by speaking good words that revealed Himself as the Resurrection and the Life. But Mary's weeping caused Him to attend to her with good works instead of good words.

The Lord groaned in His spirit after hearing Mary's words and witnessing her brokenness and those weeping with her (v. 33). The Greek verb *embrimaomai* is rendered "He groaned" in verse 33 and has the meaning of "expressing indignation, blame, sternness, or anger." Additionally, the Lord was "troubled" (or agitated) in His spirit. The context of the passage would indicate that He had no indignation towards those who had an imperfect understanding of Him as "the resurrection and the life." Rather, His disgust in His spirit was for the one who had brought sin, suffering, and death into the world, Satan (Heb. 2:14-15).

The Lord then asked where Lazarus was buried, and they showed Him the place (v. 34). It was at this moment that John records that Jesus wept with those who were grieving for Lazarus (v. 35). The Jews interpreted the Lord's tears as being for His deceased friend Lazarus, but that was not the case. He did not mourn for the one He was about to raise from the dead, but He was mourning with those who mourn (v. 36). The Lord Jesus said, *"Blessed are those who mourn, for they shall be comforted"* (Matt. 5:4). The psalmist writes, *"He* [God] *heals the brokenhearted and binds up their wounds"* (Ps. 147:3). After witnessing the Lord's grief, the Jews wondered why someone who had performed so many miracles for others could not have prevented His friend's death by healing him (v. 37).

When the Lord came to Lazarus's tomb (a cave with a stone blocking the entrance), He again groaned in His spirit (v. 38). The Lord then requested that the tomb's covering stone be rolled away, but Martha objected to this request, noting that her brother had been dead for four days and the stench of his decomposing body would be strong (v. 39). This meant that there had been a same day burial and that Lazarus's body had not been embalmed. Additionally, the Jews believed that the soul of a deceased person remained near its corpse for three days before departing to Sheol (the place that disembodied spirits await resurrection). After this there would be no hope of reviving the person. It seems likely that these circumstances at least partially explain why the Lord waited to come to Bethany, to better magnify the miracle He was about to perform.

The Lord told Martha that if she would believe in Him as the resurrection and the life, as He had told her previously, she would see the glory of God (v. 40). The objection was quelled, and the stone

The Man and Your God

removed (v. 41). The Lord then prayed out loud to His heavenly Father, which was not necessary, but He did so that those observing would know that He had been sent by His Father and that He was under the Father's authority and thus could perform the miracle they were about to witness (v. 42). The Lord cried out with a loud voice, *"Lazarus, come forth!"* (v. 43). Then Lazarus, wrapped with grave clothes from head to toe, came staggering out of the tomb (v. 44). The Lord said to those observing the sight to loosen him from his burial attire.

Many Jewish Converts (vv. 45-57)

The scene was astounding; not only could Jesus bring a dead person back to life, but He had the power to reverse days of decomposing damage done to Lazarus's body also. Many Jews that witnessed the miracle trusted in Christ afterwards (v. 45). But others, denying the spectacular nature of the sign, went to and told the Pharisees what Jesus of Nazareth had done (v. 46). Afterwards the chief priests and Pharisees gathered in council to determine what could be done about this Man who works such powerful signs among the people (v. 47).

The Sanhedrin worried that if they did nothing, Jesus would convert the nation and thus force the Romans to retaliate by removing what autonomy Israel still retained (v. 48). The discussion was then interrupted by a prophetic word from God through Caiaphas, the high priest: *"It is expedient for us that one man should die for the people, and not that the whole nation should perish"* (vv. 49-50). Apparently, as John explains, Caiaphas further stated that Jesus would die not just for Israel, but also for God's children that were scattered abroad to make all people one (vv. 51-52). Hence, from that day forward Israel's religious leaders had a new fervency in plotting Jesus' death.

Of course, the Lord Jesus knew all about their evil plotting, so He departed with His disciples briefly to the wilderness near the city of Ephraim (v. 54). Ephraim was located about fifteen miles north of Bethany. He would remain there until about a week before the Passover, then return to Bethany and Jerusalem for His passion. Many came to Jerusalem before the Passover to ceremonially purify themselves (v. 55). There was much discussion among the people as to whether Jesus of Nazareth would come to the feast or not (v. 56). The Sanhedrin had commanded the people to report to them if they saw Jesus so that they might arrest Him (v. 57).

John Chapter 12

Christ Anointed for His Burial (vv. 1-11)

The Lord was in Bethany at the home of a cleansed leper named Simon (Matt. 26:6). Matthew and Mark state that this incident occurred on Wednesday, two days before the Passover. The circumstances which John describes in this chapter are similar, but he places the anointing just prior to Christ's triumphant entry into Jerusalem on Sunday, six days before the Passover (vv. 1, 12). John names the woman who anointed the Lord, Mary (Lazarus's and Martha's sister), but Matthew and Mark do not identify the woman. Matthew and Mark state that the woman anointed the Lord's head (Matt. 26:7; Mark 14:3), while John indicates that Mary anointed the Lord's feet (v. 3). It is therefore likely that there were two separate anointings by two different women in the final week of the Lord's ministry. However, to simplify the discussion, we will consider both accounts as one incident, as most commentators do.

Lazarus, who had been raised from the dead, was sitting with the Lord at a table, while Martha was serving (v. 2). Their sister Mary arrived with a flask of costly fragrant oil (Matt. 26:7). John tells us that it was a pound of spikenard oil (v. 3). Matthew and Mark state that the unnamed woman anointed the Lord's head, while John indicates that Mary anointed Christ's feet with the ointment. This scene indicates how believers should be enjoying the Lord's presence, namely, by engaging in fellowship (Lazarus at the table), service (Martha in the kitchen), and worship (Mary at the Lord's feet).

Judas, the betrayer, condemned Mary for her wastefulness (v. 4), as did some of the other disciples, saying that the oil could have been sold for 300 denarii and the proceeds used to assist the poor (vv. 5-6). But the Lord defended Mary and acknowledged her good work towards Him, *"Let her alone; she has kept this for the day of My burial"* (v. 7). The Lord reminded His disciples that the poor would always be with them, but He was about to depart from them (v. 8). As F. B. Hole surmises, Judas's attitude represents the carnal estimation of Christ which humanized religion will always affirm:

The Man and Your God

The world is incapable of appreciating true worship, and in spite of his fair exterior Judas was wholly of the world. Ruled by covetousness, Judas had become a thief; and not only a thief but a hypocrite, masking his self-seeking by the profession of care for the poor. He posed as an eminently practical man, fully alive to the value of solid, material benefits for the poor, whilst Mary was, in his view, squandering valuable substance, moved by silly sentiment. The world is exactly of that opinion today. The religion which suits its taste is one which lays all the emphasis upon material and earthly benefits for mankind. And today, as much as then, carnally minded believers are very prone to be in agreement with the world and echo its opinions.[88]

Mary apparently possessed a deeper understanding of what was coming than that of the disciples and she wanted to show her utmost appreciation. She gave her best to the Lord and kept none of the oil for herself. It would be inappropriate to speak of personal cost or limiting gratitude for the One possessing all things and yet was willing to give His life for her to live. On this point, William Kelly adds:

Mary had not at all misread the position of the Lord. The crisis was at hand. Perfectly did He understand to what point every current was flowing; He knew what was in man, in Satan, and in God, and that as the malice of the creature would thus push to the uttermost in rebellious hatred, God would go farther still in redeeming love, but withal in His most solemn judgment of sin. Of this moral glory how little as yet could any heart conceive! Yet Mary's affection was led of God to divine the enmity growing up rapidly and ruthlessly against the One who more than ever possessed her heart's homage and love.[89]

John notes that the house was filled with the sweet fragrance of Mary's worship (v. 3). Genuine, selfless worship will refresh the hearts of all those who love the Lord Jesus. At the Lord's feet, Mary learned (Luke 10:39), she prayed (11:32), and she worshiped (v. 3) – her example is a superb one to follow. Let us remember that *"Christ came, who is over all, the eternally blessed God"* (Rom. 9:5) and He deserves our best.

Matthew notes that because of her sincere and selfless act towards the Lord, wherever the gospel was preached, this woman (or perhaps two women) would be remembered as someone who truly loved the Lord Jesus (Matt. 26:13). True devotion for Christ is not impeded by any ideas of self-sacrifice, but is prompted by genuine appreciation of Him.

Apparently, it did not take long for the word to get out where Jesus was, for many Jews came to Simon's house seeking Him and to see Lazarus, whom the Lord Jesus raised from the dead (v. 9). Because many Jews were now following Jesus, because of Lazarus's resurrection, the Jewish leaders were also plotting the murder of Lazarus (vv. 10-11). These Jewish leaders had forgotten that the sixth of the Ten Commandments prohibited murder, but when the flesh is governing human behavior, any sin or offense can be justified for what seems by human reasoning to be a greater good.

The King's Triumphant Entry Into Jerusalem (vv. 12-19)

The next day, Sunday, after hearing that Jesus was coming into Jerusalem, the multitudes, gathered in Jerusalem for the feast, took palm branches and went out to greet Him (v. 12). When the people saw the Lord Jesus, they cried out, *"Hosanna! Blessed is He who comes in the name of the Lord! The King of Israel!"* (v. 13). The Lord then descended the Mount of Olives on the colt of a donkey before the cheering crowd that was placing articles of clothing and palm branches before Him (v. 14; Matt. 21:7-8). John refers to the prophecy of Zechariah four centuries earlier that was being fulfilled at that moment:

Fear not, daughter of Zion, "Behold, your King is coming, sitting on a donkey's colt" (v. 15; Zech. 9:9).

Here the idea of "daughter" means an "inhabitant," that is, those dwelling in Jerusalem, Israel's capital. John's quotation of Zechariah's prophecy reveals the general disposition of Israel towards the One riding on the foal of a donkey. Zechariah says for Israel to "rejoice greatly," but John says "fear not" to the nation, which underscores the lack of joy and anticipation for the One who was entering Jerusalem. In fact, many did not know who Jesus was, or thought Him to be merely a prophet from Nazareth (Matt. 21:10-12).

Notice that when John refers to the prophecy of Zechariah 9:9, that he omits "just, having salvation, and lowly." John is upholding the vantagepoint of Christ's deity in his Gospel and for this reason he does not fully quote Zechariah.

Christendom often refers to this event as *Palm Sunday*, but this scene has little to do with the palm branches being placed on the road ahead of the Lord. This was the triumphant entry of Christ into His kingdom's capital. Kings usually mounted horses in time of war (Rev. 19:11) but rode donkeys in time of peace. At this juncture, the Lord Jesus was offering genuine peace to the nation of Israel, but they must receive it on His terms through repentance and submission to His Father's will.

What did the freshly cut palm branches being laid before the Lord symbolize? Palm branches were tokens of victory and peace (Rev. 7:9) and of righteousness (Ps. 92:12). The multitude, referring to Psalm 118:25-26, shouted, *"Hosanna! Blessed is He who comes in the name of the Lord! The King of Israel!"* (v. 13). In this brief moment, the Lord was rightfully declared to be the long-awaited Jewish Messiah.

Psalm 118:25 reads, *"Save now, I pray, O Lord; O Lord, I pray send now prosperity."* The Greek form of the Hebrew *yasha na* (meaning "save now") is "Hosanna." In John's account of this event, he notes that the people called the Lord Jesus, "the King of Israel." This is also how Zechariah identified the one riding on the foal of a donkey. Mark states that the people said, *"Blessed is the kingdom of our father David that comes in the name of the Lord"* (Mark 11:10). All this highlights the intense desire of the Jewish people to be freed from Gentile oppression. They clearly wanted to be immediately liberated from Rome, but not to be saved from their sins. Many shouting "Hosanna" were merely curious seekers who got caught up in the fanfare of the moment without truly believing in Christ (v. 18). Even the disciples did not understand the significance of this event until after Christ's resurrection (v. 16).

Matthew states that the entire city was moved with wonder and curiosity concerning the One who rode on the colt of the donkey. *"Who is this?"* (Matt. 21:10). Could this be the One prophesied by Zechariah four centuries earlier? But the far majority believed that Jesus was merely a prophet from Nazareth of Galilee, thus implying that He was not the expected Messiah (Matt. 21:11). Yet, in all the confusion of this spectacular event, there were Jews present who had witnessed Lazarus's resurrection and their testimony had caused many to want to meet the Lord Jesus (vv. 17-18).

The Pharisees were greatly agitated by the immense crowd that were shouting "Hosanna," to the One they believed was threatening Judaism (v. 19). Given the many pilgrims from faraway lands in Jerusalem at that time, they said to themselves, *"Look, the world has gone after Him!"* Luke tells us that the Pharisees demanded that Jesus should rebuke His disciples for making such a declaration. But the Lord said to them, *"I tell you that if these should keep silent, the stones would immediately cry out"* (Luke 19:40). For three years Jesus' identity as Israel's Messiah had been kept secret, but now, five days before His crucifixion, His dignity was to be emphatically publicized. What had been considered dangerous to state earlier was now necessary to boldly publish. Ironically, however, only the Lord Jesus fully understood the significance of the incident, the fulfillment of the prophecy in Psalm 118 foretelling His death (v. 16).

Greeks Seek to Speak to Jesus (vv. 20-22)

Certain Greek proselytes (i.e., Greeks that embraced the Jewish religion) had come to Jerusalem for the Passover and wanted to speak with Jesus (v. 20). Because of the great multitude of people in Jerusalem for the feast the disciples were apparently screening who would be able to speak with the Lord. The Greeks made their request to "see Jesus" to Philip (perhaps because he had a Greek name). Philip then asked Andrew about the matter (v. 21). Philip was not sure if the Lord would want to speak with the Greeks, because earlier the disciples had been instructed by the Lord to only preach the kingdom message to the lost sheep of Israel (Matt. 10:5). Additionally, Jews would be ceremonially unclean if they had close contact with Gentiles, meaning that they could not participate in the Passover (e.g., 18:28).

After conferring with Andrew, both Philip and Andrew brought their request to the Lord (v. 22). Why did the Greeks want to speak with the Lord? One possible reason is that they wanted more than mere Jewish ritual; they wanted to intimately know God's Passover Lamb. Another reason is that the Greeks respected the Lord's wisdom and demeanor and wanted to warn Him of an imminent and dangerous clash with Jewish leaders.

Christ's response to their request indicates that the latter reason was likely. The Lord stated that His hour, speaking of suffering and death for human sin, had come (vv. 23-25). The Lord spoke of this "hour" seven times in John, but this is the first time that He states that His hour had come. Ironically, in verse 24, the Lord affirms the prophecy the Holy Spirit spoke through Caiaphas previously, that it was needful for one man to die in place of an entire nation (11:50). Just as a grain of wheat must fall in the ground and die (germinate) to produce much grain, the Son of Man must also die and be raised up to yield a harvest of souls unto God.

Although the Lord Jesus did not directly speak to the Greeks, He did subtly include them in His message after hearing their request to speak with Him. Saved Gentiles in the Church Age would be included in the "much grain" result of His death and resurrection (v. 24). Thus, Christ's redemptive work at Calvary could benefit "all men" (v. 32), that is, "anyone" in the entire "world" that would believe on Him (v. 47).

Believers are to live out the same paradox Christ spoke of, that is, choosing death to experience life. Self-sacrifice and submission are how we experience the resurrection power of Christ's life today! The test of love for Christ is that we love Him and yield to His plan for our lives rather than living for ourselves (v. 25). If we truly possess eternal life in Christ, we will loath living for earthly things and for ourselves. When our only ambition in this life is to please our Savior, we will also please the Father and have praise (v. 26).

> He is no fool who gives what he cannot keep, to gain what he cannot lose.
>
> – Jim Elliot

Jesus Christ fully understood why He had been sent into the world and His human soul was troubled as He now knew His "hour" of suffering had arrived (v. 27). Regardless, the Lord wanted to glorify His Father through obedience unto death, for this was the reason that He had come into the world (v. 28). A voice from heaven responded to Christ's request for the Father to glorify His name: *"I have both glorified it and will glorify it again."* This was the third time during His Son's earthly ministry that God the Father audibly affirmed His love and approval for His Son.

Although the voice from heaven was audible, the message was only discerned by Christ. However, the event did benefit others, who heard the voice and thought it was thunder or an angel speaking to Jesus (vv. 29-30). Heaven had declared that the One before them was approved by God and belonged in His presence, yet there was a work to be accomplished first.

At Calvary, Christ would take on Himself the judgment of human sin, which would release Satan's death hold on the world (Heb. 2:14-15). A triune God opposes evil and corruption, but it is Christ who triumphs over the devil to gain back what was lost in Eden. Hence, the Holy Spirit confronts the flesh (Gal. 5:17), the Father opposes worldliness (Jas. 4:4), and the Son at Calvary destroyed the works of the devil (v. 31).

John

On three occasions in the final days of His earthly ministry, the Lord Jesus said that Satan is *"the ruler of this world"* (12:31, 14:30, 16:11). Through Adam's sin the kingdom of God was lost, and the world became Satan's domain of control, but he must function within divine boundaries. God is holy, and He cannot tempt anyone to sin (Jas. 1:13), but Satan is allowed to test man's resolve to obey God's expressed will. Therefore, Paul refers to Satan as *"the god of this age"* (2 Cor. 4:4) and *"the prince of the power of the air"* (Eph. 2:2).

Because Christ was "lifted up" on a cross between heaven and earth, He became a beacon of life to everyone; those trusting in Him alone would be saved (v. 32). The Lord clarified how He would die in verse 33. He would not be stoned by the Jews, but rather He would be crucified by the Romans. This would fulfill David's prophecy that foretold that Messiah would be surrounded by dogs (representing Gentiles) and be nailed to a tree having His hands and feet pierced by nails (Ps. 22:16). Nailing a condemned criminal to a tree was a public sign of guilt and shame, which meant that such a person was cursed by God in Israel (Deut. 21:23). God cursing His Son in the place of the guilty was His plan of salvation before the foundations of the world were laid (Isa. 53:2-5; 1 Pet. 1:18-20). The people understood what Jesus was saying about Christ remaining forever, but they could not understand why He, "the Son of Man," had to die by crucifixion (v. 34). Was not Messiah coming to deliver Israel from Gentile oppression, fulfill God's promises to the patriarchs, and establish an everlasting kingdom (v. 35)?

In expressing their confusion, they asked the Lord, "Who is the Son of Man?" This title related to the Lord's condescending journey to earth for the sole purpose of suffering death, that mankind might have an opportunity to be restored to a holy God. Consequently, the Lord Jesus referred to Himself more often by the title "Son of Man" than by the title "Son of God." In so doing, He was not calling attention to His divine essence but to His lowly position and ministry on earth. For this reason, no man ever addressed Him personally by this title.

The Lord referred to Himself by this title before the Sanhedrin, and later Stephen, speaking to the Sanhedrin, said that he saw the Son of Man standing at the right hand of God in heaven. They stoned Stephen for that declaration; they did not want to hear that the Man they sentenced to death was now alive and at the highest place of honor in heaven.

In each of the four Gospels, there is a transition point in which the Lord ceases to offer Himself to only the lost sheep of Israel but conveys a "whosoever will" invitation to the Gentiles also. In the Synoptic Gospels this occurs shortly after the transfiguration of Christ. However, since John largely passes over Christ's ministry in Decapolis and Perea, the transition is apparent much later in His ministry. In John, this transition occurs in verses 35-50. (These were Christ's last public words to the Jewish people.)

The Lord answers the question posed to Him in verse 34, "Who is the Son of Man?" The Son of Man is God's light to the world, not just Israel. By believing in Him, individuals would become "sons of light" (v. 36). As soon as the Lord said these words, He departed and was hidden from them. There was nothing else to be said and there were no more signs to be performed – the Jewish nation had rejected Him and His message! Regrettably, those who choose not to believe in Christ will at some point not be able to choose Him. For example, those who reject the gospel message in the Church Age will not be permitted to believe the truth to obtain salvation during the Tribulation Period (2 Thess. 2:10-12).

Because of Israel's ongoing rejection of God's revelation, which culminated in her rejection of His living Word, Israel would be given over to *judicial blindness* (vv. 37-41; Rom. 11:7; 2 Cor. 3:14-16). John quotes the prophecy of Isaiah pertaining to Israel's disbelief and resulting blindness to show that God foreknew Israel's rejection of Christ (vv. 38-40). Since the Jewish nation would not believe (v. 37), God's justice ensured that they could not believe (v. 39), that is, until the Church Age has concluded (Rom. 11:25).

John writes something in verse 41 that is vitally important to observe: *"These things Isaiah said when he saw His glory and spoke of Him."* This is a reference to Isaiah's vision of God on His holy throne at the time He was called to be a prophet to Israel (Isa. 6).

There are about two dozen separate visitations of "the Angel of the Lord" in the Old Testament. When God appeared to someone in the Old Testament, the event is referred to as a *theophany,* which means "God appearance." At such times, the Lord usually appeared as a normal-looking man, but on certain occasions He took other forms to accentuate His message. For example, the Lord spoke to Moses from a bush that appeared to be burning (Ex. 3), and to the Israelites from within a pillar of cloud (Ex. 13). The Israelites watched Mount Sinai visibly burn and quake at God's presence, though He Himself was concealed by thick, ominous clouds.

John

Specifically, a theophany is a pre-incarnate visit of the second Person of the Godhead to the earth as God's messenger. The Lord Jesus stated that no one had ever personally seen God the Father (6:46). The Lord also said, *"He who has seen Me has seen the Father"* (14:9). This means that God the Father did not appear to anyone previously, but rather the only One who could perfectly represent Him did, the Lord Jesus pre-incarnate. Hence, some refer to these appearances as *Christophanies*, or literally, "Christ appearances."

Angel means "messenger" in both the Hebrew and Greek texts. In the Old Testament, the Son of God brought the message of God to those who needed to hear it. In the New Testament, the Messenger was God's Message – *"the Word became flesh and dwelt among us, and we beheld His glory"* (1:14). In most Old Testament occurrences, the Angel of the Lord identifies Himself as God by title, or the covenants He makes, or the worship He receives (e.g., Gen. 31:11-13; Ex. 3:2-6).

In verses 39-41, John refers to an Old Testament appearance of God that Isaiah witnessed in such a way as to verify that the Person of Christ was the one that was present: *"In the year that King Uzziah died, I saw the Lord sitting on a throne, high and lifted up, and the train of His robe filled the temple"* (Isa. 6:1). John confirms that the Lord Jesus, as the Son of God, was the prominent One speaking to Isaiah from heaven's throne and was also the One (now in flesh) that His word given to Isaiah as a prophecy refer to.

Although the nation of Israel would not receive the blessings of Christ at this juncture, many individuals did believe on Him and were personally blessed. For example, some Jewish leaders did believe the truth, but chose not to openly identify with Christ as they did not want to be put out of Judaism (vv. 42-43; Rom. 10:10). John addresses their convictions (v. 42a), their cowardice (v. 42b), and their compromise (v. 43). It seems doubtful that these individuals were saved, as they were not willing to confess Christ publicly, which is an indication of what someone really believes in his or her heart (Rom. 10:10). But there were other Jews, such as Nicodemus and Joseph of Arimathea, who believed that Jesus was the Christ and did not compromise. Later these two men obtained Christ's body from the Romans, wrapped it with myrrh and aloes in grave clothes, and placed it in a new tomb (Joseph's own tomb; 19:38-42).

The Lord Jesus only spoke the words of His Father. He did His Father's will in all things. Therefore, those trusting in Him also received the Father and His life (vv. 44-45, 49-50). Those who step into the light (truth) must leave the darkness to do so (v. 46). Verse 47 speaks of Christ's first advent to the earth to seek and to save lost sinners. He refrained from judging others at this time, because He first needed to be judged for human sin. Verse 48 refers to Christ's second advent when He will return to the earth to judge wickedness and all that have rejected Him (Rev. 20).

As previously mentioned, we now come to a distinct transition in the narrative; the Lord Jesus no longer seeks the lost sheep of Israel, but rather spends His final days on earth preparing His disciples for the sorrows to come. William MacDonald summarizes how the Lord has presented Himself to Israel up to this point by performing seven specific signs (miracles) as recorded by John:

> Seven distinct signs or miracles are recorded, each one illustrating an experience which will result when a sinner puts his faith in Christ. The signs are:
>
> 1. Changing the water into wine at the wedding in Cana of Galilee (2:1–12). This pictures the sinner who is a stranger to divine joy being transformed by the power of Christ.
> 2. Healing the nobleman's son (4:46–54). This pictures the sinner as being sick and in need of spiritual health.
> 3. Healing the cripple at the pool of Bethesda (chap. 5). The poor sinner is without strength, helpless, and unable to do a thing to remedy his own condition. Jesus cures him of his infirmity.
> 4. Feeding the five thousand (chap. 6). The sinner is without food, hungry, and in need of that which imparts strength. The Lord provides food for his soul so that he never needs to hunger.
> 5. Calming the Sea of Galilee (6:16–21). The sinner is seen in a place of danger. The Lord rescues him from the storm.
> 6. Healing a man blind from birth (chap. 9). This man pictures the blindness of the human heart until it is touched by the power of Christ. Man cannot see his own sinfulness, or the beauties of the Savior, until enlightened by the Holy Spirit.
> 7. Raising Lazarus from the dead (chap. 11). This, of course, reminds us that the sinner is dead in trespasses and in sins and needs life from above.
>
> All these signs are intended to prove that Jesus is the Christ, the Son of God.[90]

John Chapter 13

John does not address any of the Lord's ministry in Jerusalem on "Super Tuesday." Christ told several parables, delivered His "Woe" message to the Pharisees, and baffled the Herodians, the Sadducees, and the Pharisees by answering their questions, and then by asking His own questions on Tuesday. That evening, the Lord Jesus took His disciples to the Mount of Olives and taught them about things to come.

The Last Passover – Christ Washes Dirty Feet (vv. 1-20)

The events of John chapters 13 and 14 occurred in the upper room, where the Lord had gathered with His disciples to eat the Passover meal. John chapters 15 to 17 record the Lord's dialogue with His disciples while venturing from the upper room of a house in Jerusalem eastward to the Garden of Gethsemane on Mount Olivet.

Before the Lord gathered with His disciples in the upper room, John notes that the Lord knew that "His hour" (His passion) had come and that He would be departing from the world soon. This is the sixth of seven times that John speaks of this specific "hour" of suffering, concluding with the Lord's death at Calvary. Throughout His earthly ministry, the Lord had demonstrated the love of God to His disciples – *"He loved them to the end"* (v. 1).

The Lord knew that He was God's Passover Lamb for sacrifice (1:29) and that the work of redemption and restoring fallen humanity to God had been entrusted to Him (v. 3). He also knew that Judas Iscariot had already agreed to betray Him to the Pharisees for thirty pieces of silver (v. 2). Judas had often stolen from the money box used to store ministry contributions (12:6). The devil knew about this greedy bent and put a thought into Judas' mind to betray the Lord for money. Judas yielded to this solicitation. Later, we are informed that the devil did more than just obsess Judas' mind with an ill suggestion; he entered into Judas after Judas received the sop from the Lord's hand (v. 27).

Around sundown on Nissan the fourteenth, the Lord gathered with His disciples to keep the Passover in a large, furnished, upper room

(Mark 14:17; Luke 22:12). After the Passover feast was finished but before the Lord's Supper was instituted (Matt. 26:25-26), the Lord girded Himself as a slave, poured water in a basin, picked up a towel, and began washing the dirty feet of His disciples (vv. 4-5). After arriving at someone's home, foot washing was a necessary and courteous routine for sandal-clad travelers, who had been walking on dry and dusty roads. Normally, this was the task of a household servant to refresh visitors, but since the Lord was the host of the Passover feast and the disciples were His guests, He humbled Himself to serve them.

The Lord Jesus poured water into a basin, which typified the precise and sufficient quantity of God's Word, as empowered by the Holy Spirit, to accomplish the present need (Eph. 5:26). The water was not to bathe them or to overwhelm them in any way, but for the specific operation of cleaning the filth away from their feet.

Peter did not appreciate the Lord's act of kindness and refused to have his feet washed (v. 6). Without rebuking Peter, the Lord told him that in a future day he would understand what He was doing (v. 7). Commenting on the Lord's response to Peter, L. M. Grant writes:

> Verse 7 is proof that the Lord was not intending by His example a mere literal washing of feet to be thereafter carried on by the disciples, but something more important, of which feet-washing is typical. For this speaks of the application of the Word of God to the details of our walk through a defiling world (Eph. 5:26). Contact with defilement requires contact with the Word, if the defilement is to be removed, and who is more gentle and thorough than the Lord Jesus in applying that Word?[91]

After Peter informed the Lord that he would never permit Him to wash his feet, the Lord replied, *"If I do not wash you, you have no part with Me"* (v. 8). This statement caused Peter, who was suffering in ignorance, to reverse his position, *"Lord, not my feet only, but also my hands and my head!"* (v. 9). The Lord's answer is remarkable: *"'He who is bathed needs only to wash his feet, but is completely clean; and you are clean, but not all of you.' For He knew who would betray Him; therefore He said, 'You are not all clean'"* (vv. 10-11). Besides setting an example of service that He expected His disciples to follow, the Lord was revealing important doctrinal truth about regeneration.

The symbolic meaning of the scene before us was first typified during the consecration process of the first high priest. Moses bathed

Aaron once at the Bronze Laver (Lev. 8:6), but afterwards Aaron would have to stop at the Laver and wash his hands and feet before entering the tabernacle (i.e., into God's presence; Ex. 30:17-21). The full bath pictures spiritual regeneration of a true believer, which would never be repeated. Therefore, the Lord told Peter (a true believer) that he was already clean (positionally saved in Himself and regeneration by the Holy Spirit was assured). Those who have been regenerated do not need to be spiritually bathed again. Judas was a phony. He had identified with Christ, but had not trusted in Him; therefore, he was not clean and would never experience the washing of regeneration (v. 11).

Paul writes: *"Not by works of righteousness which we have done, but according to His mercy He saved us, through the washing of regeneration and renewing of the Holy Spirit"* (Tit. 3:5). The Holy Spirit works to convict the lost of their sinful state, their need of righteousness, and that God must judge their sin (16:8-10). At conversion, the Holy Spirit implants a desire for holiness and works to cleanse the new believer from polluted things. The act of regeneration occurs at conversion and implants new life and a new order of living within the believer; what was dead becomes spiritually alive (Eph. 2:1-3)! Regeneration of the disciples occurred at Pentecost when the Holy Spirit created the Church and took up eternal residence in all true believers (Acts 2).

So, those once "bathed" (*louo*) only need to wash (*nipto*) their feet afterwards. The believer's feet connect with the earth while walking. Just as the soles of our shoes pick up dirt from what we walk on, the believer's soul picks up secular defilement while being in the world. When this occurs, we are commanded to confess our sin to Christ, who responds by cleansing us of the defilement and restoring us back into full fellowship with God (1 Jn. 1:9). Believers are to represent Christ in the world, but not be of the world. After washing the feet of His disciples, the Lord put His garments back on, sat down again, and posed a question to His disciples, *"Do you know what I have done to you?"* (v. 12). "Have done" is derived from a perfect tense verb meaning that there was an enduring truth associated with His action. Then the Lord proceeded to answer His own question with an explanation:

> *You call Me **Teacher and Lord**, and you say well, for so I am. If I then, your **Lord and Teacher**, have washed your feet, you also ought to wash one another's feet. For I have given you an example, that you should*

do as I have done to you. Most assuredly, I say to you, a servant is not greater than his master; nor is he who is sent greater than he who sent him (vv. 13-16).

The Lord was the perfect *Teacher* (or "Master" in KJV) because He was first a selfless servant of others. The disciples rightly referred to Jesus Christ as their "Teacher and Lord," but notice Christ switched the order of these titles to "Lord and Teacher" to declare the right priority in which His disciples should relate to Him. True authority serves others instead of being served. If the disciples did not relate to Him as Lord above all else, they would fail to represent Him properly in ministry.

Because He was Lord, He willingly served those He loved. He was their Lord and Teacher. Just a few days earlier the Lord had taught His disciples: *"But you, do not be called 'Rabbi'; for one is your Teacher, the Christ, and you are all brethren. ... But he who is greatest among you shall be your servant. And whoever exalts himself will be humbled, and he who humbles himself will be exalted"* (Matt. 23:8-12). This was Christ's example; although He was Lord, He was willing to humble Himself to serve others. We are to follow His example also, and if we do, we will have His blessing: *"If you know these things, blessed are you if you do them"* (v. 17). Instead of arguing about their kingdom status (Luke 22:24), the disciples should exhibit the King's humility by serving each other. True humility is a quiet heart that expects nothing, gives its best, and is not offended when others expect what is not deserved.

True disciples obey the Lord and are blessed by Him, but Judas was not a true disciple (v. 18). There is no record in Scripture that he ever referred to Jesus as "Lord." Previously, the Lord chose all His disciples, including Judas, even though He foreknew that Judas would never trust in Him as his Lord and Savior, but would rather betray Him. *Choosing* in Scripture has the idea of a sovereign God accomplishing His purposes in time. And one of the many prophecies that would assist Israel in identifying the true Messiah when He came was that He would be betrayed by a friend (Ps. 41:9). The Lord reminded His disciples of this prediction so that, when it came time for His suffering and death, they would remember His words and believe that he is I AM (v. 19).

Christ Predicts His Betrayal (vv. 21-35)

After explaining that His example of lowly service was one that they should follow in serving others, the Lord, troubled in His spirit, informed

His disciples that one of them would betray Him (v. 21). On the previous night, Judas had agreed to betray Christ to the chief priests for thirty pieces of silver (Matt. 26:15). Judas had obviously covered his tracks well, so to speak, as the other disciples had no clue of his devilish plan.

The perplexed disciples became sorrowful after hearing this news and began asking Jesus, *"Lord, is it I?"* (v. 22; Mark 14:19). Although Judas shunned Christ's authority over him, the other disciples willfully acknowledge Jesus as their Lord. Acknowledging Christ's lordship before others is a tell-tale sign of true conversion and devotion. Those merely referring to Christ, as "Jesus" or "sweet Jesus" are relating to Him in a sphere of familiarity that is demeaning to His divine station.

John records that while leaning on the Lord's breast, Peter prompted John to ask the Lord about the matter (vv. 23-24). Although John was already resting on the Lord's bosom, the beloved disciple leaned back further (i.e., tilting his head further back to make direct eye contact) to asked Him who the betrayer was (v. 25). John teaches us that our desire to be near to the Lord is reciprocated by the Lord in blessed communion. The Lord does not choose favorites, per se, but He does have intimates!

The Lord responded to His question by referring to Psalm 41:9 and saying, *"It is he to whom I shall give a piece of bread when I have dipped it"* (v. 26). The Lord added that the betrayer would suffer God's wrath for his evil deed, and it would have been better if he had never been born (Mark 14:21). It was customary for the host to dip a piece of bread in gravy or vinegar and give it to the honored guest (sitting to his left) during the feast. It is likely, given Christ's private charge to Judas, that he occupied this place of honor (vv. 27, 30). Christ gave Judas the sop and thus identified him as the betrayer (v. 26). John says that Satan entered Judas after he received the sop. Judas then asked the Lord, deceitfully, *"Rabbi, is it I?"* (Mark 14:25). The Lord confirmed that it was and told Judas, *"What you do, do quickly"* (v. 27). Judas then immediately departed the upper room; the other disciples did not discern what Christ meant by these words at that time. They assumed that Judas, having the ministry purse, was taking care of feast-related matters or giving a gift to the poor (vv. 28-29).

The statement *"when he had gone out"* indicates Judas chose to depart from the light of divine truth and to venture into satanic darkness, for *"it was night"* (vv. 30-31). The Greek verb in this phrase is in the active voice, meaning that Judas was not forced to depart from the Lord, but he willingly chose to leave the Lord's presence and be incorporated into the devil's hideous agenda. From that moment on, Judas would remain in spiritual darkness forever. Jude later informs us that *Hell*, "the Lake of Fire," is *"the blackness of darkness forever"* (v. 13).

Christ was determined to glorify His Father through obedience unto death. The Son was equally confident that His Father would respond to His faithfulness by glorifying the Son (vv. 31-32). God's love and righteousness were revealed in His Son's willful condescension and death; thus, the Father was glorified by His Son at Calvary and the Father did immediately glorify the Son after His resurrection (Heb. 1:4).

Christ refers to His disciples by the affectionate term "little children" to highlight their vulnerability and weakness and also His concern and care for them. The Lord then informed them that He was leaving them, and that they could not follow Him at that time (v. 33). This is the only time in the Gospels that the Lord applies this tender term to His disciples, although He does address them simply as "children" after His resurrection (21:5). An elderly John will later refer to his audience in his first epistle as "little children" seven times.

Death was not defeat, but a high example of God's love in action (v. 34). To have sacrificial love for one another was not only a new command but would show the world that they had experienced Christ's love and indeed were His disciples (v. 35). The Law taught self-sacrifice but gave no power to accomplish it.

God's love is the binding agent that marks Christians as a peculiar people in the world. Through the power of the Holy Spirit, Christ's love draws those who previously had nothing in common into intimate communion with each other. This is why Paul exhorts believers to behave *"with all lowliness and gentleness, with longsuffering, bearing with one another in love, endeavoring to keep the unity of the Spirit in the bond of peace"* (Eph. 4:2-3). Of course, the unity that the Holy Spirit labors to maintain within the Body of Christ is not divorced from the Truth. The Lord Jesus referred to the Holy Spirit as the Spirit of Truth and stated that He would soon indwell them (14:17). Therefore, the type of love and unity God desires to be displayed in the Church will always have His truth as a basis. Genuine love cannot benefit others unless it is centered in God's will as demonstrated by God-honoring conduct.

How is the world to see Christ? The Lord Jesus told His disciples: *"By this all will know that you are My disciples, if you have love for one another."* Christ would be known when the disciples exhibited the same love for each other that Christ had already demonstrated to them.

Christian love is a powerful weapon against the enemy, for it practically conveys the gospel message to the lost. If we are not displaying the love of Christ in what we do, we are wasting our time (1 Cor. 13:2). The love of the saints is a rich heritage; may we always value each other above temporal things.

Christ Foretells Peter's Denial (vv. 36-38)

After the Lord Jesus instituted His remembrance feast, the Lord informed His disciples that He would soon be leaving them (v. 33). Matthew, who referred his Jewish audience to the Old Testament prophecies concerning the Messiah throughout his gospel account, states that the Lord quoted Zechariah 13:7 to inform His disciples that they would all scatter from Him that night. God was about to strike His Shepherd with a sword at Calvary and all the disciples would stumble before the Lord because of it. But the Lord then promised that after His resurrection He would see them again in Galilee (Matt. 26:32).

Peter specifically asked where the Lord was going (v. 36). The Lord answered his question by saying where He was going Peter could not follow Him then, but implied that he would later. Christ was going to the cross and then on to heaven. Peter would do the same in about thirty-five years.

Peter then declared his allegiance to the Lord and that he would lay down his life for the Lord even if all others stumbled at Him (v. 37; Matt. 26:33). But the Lord informed Peter that before the early morning watch was over (known by the cock's crowing), he would have denied him three times (v. 34; John 13:38). Matthew informs us that the other disciples also affirmed the same allegiance to the Lord.

The Lord then warned Peter with a question, *"Will you lay down your life for My sake?"* (v. 38). In a few hours, Peter would learn just how impossible it was to serve Christ in the strength of the flesh. Before the rooster was heard crowing that very morning, Peter would forsake the Lord Jesus. The Lord was conveying a specific idea to Peter: before dawn, Peter would deny Him three times, and the rooster's crowing would remind Peter of the Lord's prediction.

> Wherever the flesh appears, there is something that Satan can touch, and unless we judge ourselves, can turn to grief of heart in us and dishonor to God.
>
> – G. V. Wigram

John Chapter 14

Be Comforted – Christ Is Coming Again (vv. 1-6)

While still in the upper room, the Lord commenced a lengthy discourse intended to prepare His disciples for His forthcoming absence. His message was briefly interrupted by questions or comments from Thomas (v. 5), Philip (v. 8), and Judas (not Iscariot; v. 22).

The Lord began by speaking of a new peace (v. 1), a new place (v. 2) and a new pledge (v. 3). Although the Lord had been speaking directly to Peter in the previous verse (13:38), the Greek words rendered "your" and "you" in verse 1 are plural in number. Thus, the Lord was telling all of His disciples that the solution to a troubled heart was to believe in Him (i.e., His character, abilities and promises). The verb associated with "be troubled" in the statement, *"Let not your heart be troubled"* (v. 1), is a present imperative in the passive voice. The Lord was charging His disciples not to permit any outside influence to trouble their hearts. This could only be accomplished if they trusted in Him as they had before trusted in God. He, being the Son of God, had been entrusted with all things by His Father. Hence, faith in Him would repel worry and anxiety.

There was no need for them to be terrified by death, for He was going to the cross to open the way for them to heaven and then He would be preparing a new home for them in heaven! Following the Jewish betrothal custom, the groom returned to his father's home to prepare a place for his bride after a marriage covenant had been sealed (v. 2). When all was ready, the father of the groom would tell his son to go and receive his bride. Likewise, Christ will return from heaven for His bride on earth, and then she will be where He is (v. 3; 1 Thess. 4:13-18). The Greek word *monai* translated "mansions" in verse 2 is plural and thus refers to "abodes." Christ is preparing a special heavenly abode for every believer. The same root word is found in verse 23 but is singular to speak of God the Father and God the Son making Their "home" or "abode" within every genuine believer.

The Lord then told His disciples that they already knew where He was going and how to come to Him (v. 4). Although this place of many

John

mansions sounded wonderful to the disciples, they did not know where it was or how they would get there. Thomas voiced the concern that all the disciples had, *"Lord, we do not know where You are going, so how can we know the way?"* (v. 5). But they were thinking in earthly terms of location and travel and Christ was speaking of spiritual certainties. He, Himself, was God's only means of finding and entering the Father's heavenly abode (v. 6). After passing from this world (by death or glorification), those trusting in Christ alone for salvation would have a special dwelling place in His Father's house.

Jesus Christ and the Father Are One (vv. 7-11)

The Lord then said, *"If you had known Me, you would have known My Father also; and from now on you know Him and have seen Him"* (v. 7). It is possible that this statement may have been meant as a promise, that those who really know Christ will ultimately know His Father also (1 Cor. 2:11-13). However, the context of the surrounding statements does convey the idea that the Lord was reproving their ignorance. They were not to be like the Pharisees who did not know His Father (8:19), for they had been witnessing the goodness of the Father in the Son for some time.

Philip then requested that the Lord show them the Father (v. 8). While on the earth, the Lord's life had fully shown the character of His loving, merciful, gracious, faithful, holy, jealous, just, and wise Father. All of God's characteristics are holy and none are compromised in any of His actions. A. W. Tozer puts the matter this way: "All of God's acts are consistent with all of His attributes. No attribute contradicts any other, but all harmonize and blend into each other in the infinite abyss of the Godhead. All that God does agrees with all that God is, and being and doing are one in Him."[92] Thus, the Lord Jesus was saying that everything God is, is what God does as He had demonstrated by all of His doings while on earth. The statement, *"from now on you know Him* (the Father) *and have seen Him"* refers to the glorious union of the Father and the Son that the disciples would witness after the Son's resurrection.

The goodness of God causes Him to be kind, cordial, generous, and to have goodwill toward all men, as shown in the giving of His Son on our behalf (Luke 2:14). When the Lord Jesus walked upon the earth, He personally exhibited God's character for everyone to see. Although Philip had been with Him longer than most of the disciples (1:43), yet he still did not comprehend Christ's deity and unique union with the Father. This prompted the Lord to gently reprove Philip, *"He who has seen Me has seen the Father"* (v. 9). The sweet aroma of Christ's divine nature permeates every page of the gospel accounts. All His speech, gestures, and actions perfectly represented the character of God (v. 10, 5:19, 8:29, 17:6).

If some could not trust His declaration that He and the Father are completely one, then the Lord referred them to His works, which clearly only God could accomplish, such as the resurrection of the dead (v. 11). The Lord Jesus said the same thing to the Pharisees in John 10: He and the Father are one (10:30) and if they would not believe His declaration to be true, then they were to believe because of the miraculous works (signs) that He had accomplished (10:38).

The Privilege of Prayer (vv. 12-14)

The Lord foretold that after Pentecost, the disciples, through faith in Him, would be able to do the works that He had performed while on the earth (v. 12). In fact, because God would accomplish what seemed to be impossible through mere men, their feats would be considered even greater than what the Son of God had performed while on the earth. The Lord then told His disciples how this would be possible – by prayers of faith centered in God's will.

John's Gospel presents a strong connection between prayer and knowing and doing the will of God. In fact, the Lord Jesus refers to His Father's "will" *seven* times, speaking only His Father's words *seven* times, and that His disciples should pray only in His name on *seven* different instances. Hence, perfect praying centers in the will and the Word of God; it is not selfish. When we petition the Father in prayer, we are asking Him to grant our requests to honor His Son's name. Likewise, the Son wants to honor God-honoring prayers for the glory of His Father (vv. 13-14). This should be the ultimate objective of all our prayers!

The only way to ensure that this will occur is for the Holy Spirit to lead us into prayer after we have properly discerned God's will from studying His Word. Then with confidence we can close our prayer with a hearty "amen," which literally means "so be it." *"Now this is the confidence that we have in Him, that if we ask anything according to His will, He hears us"* (1 Jn. 5:14). We must know God's Word to know how to pray in a way that would honor Christ's name. Obedience to God's

Word demonstrates our love for the Lord (v. 15). Hence, love for the Lord, confidence in His character and abilities, and knowing and obeying His Word are necessary prerequisites for effectual prayers (Jas. 5:16).

Prayer is not a "name it and claim it" – "blab it and grab it" – formula for success. Righteous praying centers in God's will and is motivated by love for the Savior's name. Prayer shows faith and dependence in a loving God to initiate, direct, and complete each matter of our lives according to His sovereign will.

> Prayer is reaching out after the unseen; fasting is letting go of all that is seen and temporal. Fasting helps express, deepen, confirm the resolution that we are ready to sacrifice anything, even ourselves to attain what we seek for the kingdom of God. ... The great thing in prayer is to feel that we are putting our supplications into the bosom of omnipotent love.
> — Andrew Murray

Indeed, the believer's access to the throne of grace through Christ provides a wonderful opportunity to experience God's mercy and grace through prayer (Heb. 4:15-16). Yet, believers also have a responsibility to honor Christ in their praying; His name should not be associated with anything that is polluted or of the flesh. The 19th century evangelist Charles Finney summarizes what it means to pray in Christ's name:

> To use this name acceptably implies a realizing sense of our character and relations, and of His character and relations; God's character and governmental position – our character and governmental position. Now, unless the mind has a realizing sense, so as really to mean what it ought to mean in using Christ's name, it does not do so acceptably. ... To pray in His name, we must ask the thing not for ourselves, because we are not our own; we do not own ourselves, and of course, therefore, we can own nothing else. The fact is, we are Christ's, and when we seek anything in Christ's name, we seek it for Him. We are Christ's servants, and as children we belong to Christ.[93]

Prayer transforms our hearts by conforming our thinking to the mind of Christ. As guided by God's Word and His Spirit, we learn to want only what Christ wants – nothing else matters. For those who love the name of Jesus Christ and His will, prayer is a great blessing which moves the hand of God!

The Helper Is Coming (vv. 16-26)

The matter of preparing His disciples for the arduous task ahead was very much on the mind of the Lord Jesus the night before He died. Much of the Lord's discourse with His disciples, as recorded in John 14 through 16, centers on this topic. After telling the disciples in John 13 that one of them was a betrayer, that Peter was going to deny Him, and that He was leaving them, the Lord provides a message of comfort in John 14. He informed them that after His departure another Helper or Comforter, speaking of the Holy Spirit, would be coming to them.

It is through the Gospel of John that we obtain the fuller revelation of the Holy Spirit's work concerning believers. He is the Comforter (literally, the legal advocate) of the believer. He is the Helper, the Teacher, the Convicter, and the Guide into deeper truth.

The Lord was returning to heaven and leaving His disciples, but He would not leave them as helpless orphans (v. 18). He was sending them *"another Helper"* and promised to be with them again, but in a different manner than before (v. 20). The Greek word *allos* rendered "another" means "another of the same kind," thus the Holy Spirit would continue the ministry Christ had begun in the disciples and ensure its completion (v. 16). Those in the world do not know the Holy Spirit, nor would they receive Him when He comes into the world, but He would take up residence in all true believers.

Because the Holy Spirit had anointed the Lord Jesus after His baptism, He had already *been with* the disciples for some time (v. 17). However, after His ascension, the Lord would send the Holy Spirit to them; He would *reside in them* forever. This union would also ensure that Christ would be with them forever. Although the Lord may have been speaking of His resurrection, it seems most likely that this is what He meant by His promise "I will come to you," as the statement is tied with the coming of the Holy Spirit. At Pentecost, the disciples would then receive eternal life and resurrection power in Christ (v. 19). Their eternal oneness with the Son, which also meant experiencing oneness with the Father would occur on a particular future day (v. 20). "At that day," speaking of Pentecost, the Holy Spirit would baptize all believers into Christ to create a spiritual temple called the "Church" (v. 20).

After His resurrection, the Lord commissioned His disciples and opened their understanding of Scripture. He then instructed them to wait in Jerusalem for the coming of the Holy Spirit (Luke 24:49). He, the

Comforter, would infuse them with divine power to enable their ministry. Knowledge of their divine calling and their new understanding of Scripture would be of no avail without God's facilitating power.

The Holy Spirit is not the "force" or "influence" of God as some cults teach but is the third person of the Godhead. The deity of the Holy Spirit is expressed in various ways in Scripture, but one of the most obvious is through His direct association with the other Persons of the Godhead. This association with other members of the Trinity is expressed sixteen times in the New Testament. For example, He is called "the Spirit of God" (1 Cor. 6:11), and "the Spirit of Jesus" (Acts 16:7). Clearly, the Spirit of God has full association with the other members of the Godhead (Matt. 28:19; 2 Cor. 13:14). While forgiven sinners can obtain a position of holiness in Christ through justification, individual believers are never called "Holy" by name. However, "Holy" is a personal name for God, speaking of His uniqueness (Ps. 111:9; Isa. 57:15). There are about eighty references to "the Holy Spirit" or "Spirit Holy" in Scripture. God does not attribute His name to others, so it is evident that His Spirit is a Person within the Godhead.

The Holy Spirit has divine attributes clearly consistent with each member of the Godhead:

- Omniscience: the Holy Spirit knows the things of God (1 Cor. 2:11-12).
- Omnipresence: we cannot flee from the Spirit's presence (Ps. 139:7).
- Eternal Existence: He is the "Eternal Spirit" (Heb. 9:14).
- Omnipotence: the Holy Spirit was involved in creation (Job 33:4; Ps. 104:30).
- Without error: the Holy Spirit is "the Spirit of Truth" (1 Jn. 5:6).
- Divine Wisdom: no one can counsel God's Spirit (Isa. 40:13).
- Immutable: The Holy Spirit does not change (Isa. 11:2).

The Holy Spirit is divine; in essence He has the same attributes and character qualities as the other members of the Godhead. As God, the Holy Spirit is a Person who unmistakably disapproves of sin, is deeply grieved by it, and works to save sinners from its deadly influence. The Holy Spirit's ministry is essential to the revelation of God's Son to the world!

Five times the night before the Lord was crucified (while still in the upper room), He told His disciples of the inseparable tie between their love for Him and practical obedience to His commands: *"If you love Me, keep My commandments"* (v. 15). He was going to demonstrate this truth the next day: *"But that the world may know that I love the Father, and as the Father gave Me commandment, so I do"* (v. 31). There was no question of the love of the Father for the Son, or of the Son for the Father, but the Son was going to show the world how much He loved the Father through obedience.

Verse 21 contains a promise for all those who will likewise demonstrate love for God by simply obeying His Word: The Lord said that He would manifest himself to him. John was the beloved disciple and, apparently, the least inhibited in expressing his love for the Lord – it was to him, the disciple who loved much, that a fuller manifestation of Christ was granted. It was John, and only John, who was an eyewitness to the Apocalypse, *"The Revelation of Jesus Christ"* (Rev. 1:1). The divine disclosure of Christ's glory to John is a direct testimony of the immensity of John's love for the Lord Jesus. Those who have been forgiven much love Christ more, those who love much obey Christ more, and those who obey Christ much comprehend Him more. We must obey Him to know Him more!

Judas, not Iscariot (also called Thaddaeus and Lebbaeus), did not understand how the Lord could manifest Himself to them in a way that the world would not perceive (v. 22). Clearly, Judas was thinking of the physical realm and not about experiencing oneness with the Lord after His resurrection. The Lord answered his quandary by affirming the spiritual nature of His statement. By obeying Christ's commands, true believers demonstrate their love for and commitment to the Savior (v. 23). Such saints will enjoy the presence of God and experience the communion of the Son and the Father. The word translated "home" in verse 23 means "abode." God is at home in humble, obedient believers who love the Savior.

Humility before God and reverence for His Word result in blessing and further understanding of God's will. Willful ignorance, rebellion, or compromise should be unheard of responses to Scripture for those who truly long to know and experience God (v. 24). The irresistible love of God can only be experienced by answering His invitation to know Him. Our understanding of God's plan and our commitment to live it out will be directly proportionate to the extent that we have known and experienced Him. Continued submission to divine truth is the pathway to intimately experiencing and knowing God in deepening degrees. It is this consistent contact with God's nature that results in our comprehension of His wondrous design for our lives.

The Lord Jesus understood that in their present situation they would not be able to understand all that He wanted them to know and remember (v. 25). However, He was confident that when the Father sent the Holy Spirit to them in His name, He would teach them all that they should know and bring into remembrance what He had already taught them (v. 26). This blessing was evident at Pentecost, when Peter, after receiving the Holy Spirit, connected many Old Testament passages while speaking to a large Jewish audience about Jesus Christ (Acts 2). Hence, it was the Father's will to send the Holy Spirit to thoroughly equip those trusting in His Son to be believer-priests (vv. 16, 26). Likewise, the Son would send the Holy Spirit to connect believers to His Father forever (15:26, 16:7).

Christ's Peace (vv. 27-31)

The Lord then repeated the exhortation in verse 1, *"Let not your heart be troubled"* (v. 27). Although the Lord was departing His disciples, He was leaving something of Himself behind, His peace. The Lord not only made *peace with God* on our behalf at Calvary (Rom. 5:1), but now offers us the *peace of God*:

> *Be anxious for nothing, but in everything by prayer and supplication, with thanksgiving, let your requests be made known to God; and the peace of God, which surpasses all understanding, will guard your hearts and minds through Christ Jesus* (Phil. 4:6-7).

He not only offers salvation of the soul, but of the mind also. The Greek word for "peace" in verse 27 is *eirene*. It is derived from a verb meaning "to bond together," or "to be made at one again." The applied meaning of *eirene* in Romans 5:1 is that an individual is made "one again" with God in relationship after trusting the gospel; this is the saving of the soul. Yet, Philippians 4:7 refers to the saving of the mind – this is achieved when we are "one again" with Christ in thinking.

It is difficult to serve the Lord fully and faithfully if we are anxious over arduous situations or are harboring guilt over past mistakes. The word *worry* means "to strangle something," while the word *anxiety* conveys the thought of "being pulled in different directions at the same time." Worry and anxiety rob us of our peace and in doing so prevent us from being a good testimony of Christ to the world. The world cannot offer the believer true peace, that is, a peace that pacifies doubts and fears and puts our spirit in a state of tranquility. Only when a believer knows the peace of God in this way can he or she effectively share God's message of peace with others.

Christ again mentions that He is going to His Father (who was greater than He), but that He would also be returning for them (v. 28). The Son was not less than His Father in essence, but the Son had assumed a lower position while in the world. So, when the Lord stated that His Father was greater than Himself, He was not speaking of personal greatness, but of positional greatness (v. 28). The Father was in glory above, while He had assumed the humiliating role as God's sin-bearer for humanity below (Phil. 2:5-8).

The Lord wanted to strengthen His disciples' faith by foretelling the events of Calvary (v. 29). Then, after His death, they would know that He was in full control of all that transpired concerning His sufferings and crucifixion. In the same way, the prophet Isaiah told his countrymen how God was going to use the Babylonians to specifically chastise them for their idolatry a century before it happened so that they would know that Jehovah was the one true God afterwards (Isa. 48:5).

The Lord Jesus was God's perfect, sinless Lamb for sacrifice, thus Satan, "the ruler of this world," had "nothing" against Him. Consequently, Satan would be defeated at Calvary, because the One without sin willingly took the place in judgment for those in sin (v. 30). The main reason that Christ gave up His life at Calvary was to demonstrate His love for the Father through obeying His command (v. 31). The Lord's submission to His Father's will, even unto death, would show the entire world how much He loved His Father. Likewise, our submission to Christ, regardless of the cost, demonstrates our love for Him to the world (v. 15).

After these statements, the Lord and His disciples departed the upper room. The dialog of the Lord with His disciples while walking through the streets of Jerusalem en route to the Garden of Gethsemane is recorded in John chapters 15, 16, and 17.

> Nothing of spiritual significance comes without sacrifice. Your spirituality will always be measured by the size of your sacrifice.
>
> – Jerry Falwell

John Chapter 15

The Vine and the Branches (vv. 1-6)

The Lord continues to speak to His disciples while leading them from the upper room location in Jerusalem to the Garden of Gethsemane on the Mount of Olives. Unlike the previous chapter, where the Lord was interrupted three times by His disciples, there were no interruptions to His teaching in John 15. Through the vine and the branch analogy, the Lord taught His disciples the necessity of abiding in Him to experience God's love and to be fruitful for Him (vv. 1-17). In verses 18-27, the Lord will speak of the world's hatred of Himself and of those who identify with Him.

Historically speaking, God had planted the Jewish people in Israel as His choice vine (vineyard) to bear Him good fruit, but instead they produced the wild grapes of rebellion (Isa. 5:1-4). Having disregarded the warnings of His prophets, God was prompted to destroy His vineyard, the northern kingdom (Israel) in 8th century B.C. by the Assyrians and then the southern kingdom (Judah) in 6th century B.C. by the Babylonians.

Now, God was again passing judgment on Israel. Despite the pleas of John the baptizer and the Lord Jesus Christ, His covenant people had again rejected what was necessary to make them fruitful. Consequently, the Jewish nation (corporately speaking) would suffer spiritual blindness until the Church Age concluded (Rom. 11:7, 25). Shortly before His crucifixion, the Lord warned Israel's religious leaders, *"The kingdom of God will be taken from you and given to a nation bearing the fruits of it"* (Matt. 21:43). God, the Vinedresser, was now going to establish a new Vine, Christ, that would enable Gentiles to bear good fruit to Him (v. 1).

Besides the vine referring to a man's wife (Ps. 128:3; SOS 7:8), the only other time that the vine is used in an allegorical representation in Scripture is to indicate the judicially ripened state of the Gentile nations at Christ's second coming to the earth (Rev. 14:14-20).

Properly interpreting allegorical teaching requires the careful study of Scripture to ensure that an erroneous meaning is not being assumed.

Scripture must interpret Scripture. Regrettably, some have made this passage say what it does not – the analogy does not teach that true believers can lose their salvation. In fact, the word "salvation" does not appear in the entire chapter. The subject matter is fruit-bearing. Christ wants believers to bear "fruit" (v. 2), "more fruit" (v. 2), and "much fruit" (vv. 5, 8). Those who do not choose to abide in the goodness of Christ will be incapable of bearing spiritual fruit (v. 4).

Having just departed the upper room, the Lord is speaking only to His disciples (i.e., true believers, as Judas has already departed the group). The fact that Christ refers to "a man" and not "them" in verse 6 affirms that Christ knew the eleven were branches in the Vine (i.e., true believers in Him). The key words in this text are: "love" (ten occurrences), "abide" (nine times mentioned), and fruit (found eight times). The Lord's desire for all believers is that they would abide in Him, experience the love and joy of God, and yield spiritual fruit.

Through the Vine illustration, the Lord taught His true disciples several important applications concerning fruit-bearing.

First, those who are fruitful to God can expect God to further prune them such that they can bear even more fruit (v. 2). Just as pruning fruit trees stimulates fruit production, the Lord uses a variety of experiences to further refine and practically sanctify believers. Faith-building trials, learning and applying God's Word, and experiencing God's faithfulness, including His chastening for sin, are just some of His pruning methods. As less of the flesh and more of Christ is apparent in the believer's life, the Holy Spirit further enables fruit-bearing to God. Christ promised, *"He who abides in Me, and I in him, bears much fruit"* (v. 5).

Second, some may say that they are true branches, but their mimicked fruit-bearing will be proven to be counterfeit in time. True faith has a lasting reality (Jas. 2:17). Some can fake real life for a while, but not without zapping themselves dry, as only Christ's resources can prompt true fruit-bearing in believers. The Lord reminded His disciples, *"Without Me you can do nothing"* (v. 5). Yet, Paul experientially knew what was possible through abiding in Christ: *"I can do all things through Christ who strengthens me"* (Phil. 4:13).

Third, the Greek verb *airo*, translated "takes away" in verse 2, is better rendered as "lifts up." *Airo* has vast implications depending upon the context of the passage. In the New Testament, *airo* is rendered as some form of "taking away" twenty-two times or of "lifting up" thirty-six times (e.g., Matt. 9:6; Luke 9:17, 17:13; Acts 4:24; Rev. 10:5). So what does our kind Lord do when true believers (branches in Him) are not bearing fruit? He cleans the sinful muck off them through His Word (v. 3) and "lifts" them up out of it to obtain better conditions for bearing fruit (v. 2). The Lord does not cast away believers the moment they become unfruitful because of sin; rather, He works to restore them to a state of fruitfulness.

The ongoing washing of the Word enables believers to identify and repudiate thoughts, motives, and behavior which do not have the Lord's approval (Eph. 5:25-27). Paul tells us that *"to be carnally minded is death ... the carnal mind is enmity against God. ... So then, those who are in the flesh cannot please God"* (Rom. 8:6-8). What exposes the depravity of our carnal thinking? The answer is the conviction of the Holy Spirit through exposure to God's Word and we all need this ministry daily. Thus, branches, believers, need divine light and divine nourishment from the Vine to be fruitful to God. Without abiding in Christ, believers can do absolutely nothing to please God (v. 5), for there is nothing in the flesh that God wants. Therefore, the Lord invoked the imperative verb *meinate* to charge His disciples to abide in Him; otherwise, they would not be fruitful (v. 4).

Fourth, we observe that those in the world are ready to burn up a believer's testimony when failure occurs for not abiding in Christ (v. 6). Notice that it is not the Lord or His angels, but men who gather and burn the fruitless branches. Whenever angels gather up men for the fire in Scripture, this always speaks of the eternal judgment of the wicked (e.g., Gen. 19:13; Matt. 13:41-42, 49-50; Rev. 14:17-19). But this is not the case in this scenario.

Commentators who say that the branches are believers in verse 2 but then are not believers in verse 6 are not being consistent with the text; the Lord is speaking of branches in Him throughout. Those in the world cannot remove believers who have suffered failure from Christ. But branches in Him must choose to abide in Him to be fruitful and Christ is ever working to ensure all believers are fruitful. Hence, it seems out of character with the text to assume that the incinerated branches in verse 6 represent God's parental judgment to end a rebellious believer's life (i.e., for "sins unto death"; 1 Jn. 5:16). Rather, the human activity of burning branches in verse 6 pertains to the *practice* of the believer and not his or her *position* in Christ. On this point, William MacDonald writes:

We believe that this person is a true believer because it is with true Christians that this section is concerned. The subject is not salvation but abiding and *fruitbearing.* But through carelessness and prayerlessness this believer gets out of touch with the Lord. As a result, he commits some sin, and his testimony is ruined. Through failure to abide in Christ, he is thrown out as a branch – not by Christ, but by other people. The branches are gathered and thrown into the fire, and they are burned. It is not God who does it, but people. What does this mean? It means that people scoff at this backslidden Christian. They drag his name in the mud. They throw his testimony as a Christian into the fire.[94]

In verses 1-6, the Lord is speaking of two kinds of believers, two methods of promoting fruitfulness in believers, and two possible outcomes depending on how believers respond to His care. John Heading summarizes Christ's teaching:

1. Those branches that have become earthbound, He lifts up, for contact with the world interferes with effective service. Thus in 1 Corinthians 3:3, there were those in Corinth who walked "as men," with but little to distinguish them from unbelievers. In Galatians 3:1, there were many who had been "bewitched" by religionists around. There may be an unsanctified preoccupation with the literature and sport of this world. Such believers need to be lifted up by exhortation, that they should mortify their members upon the earth so as to rise to spiritual heights (Col. 3:1–4), that they should separate themselves from degrading moral and religious influences (2 Cor. 6:14–16).

2. Those branches producing fruit are purged so as to produce more. Here is pruning so as to render believers even more spiritual, separated, and practically holy. In v. 3, these are already "clean," referring to the apostles who were with Him. This cannot refer to the original cleansing from sin upon one's conversion; rather to the daily cleansing by the Word, as in 13:10. This would lead to further hearing the Word, understanding it, and to the production of fruit.[95]

Clearly, the Lord's desire is for all believers to be fruitful to God. His ministry as the Vine and Caretaker of His branches is to achieve this goal. Those yielding to His care will be fruitful, and those who are not will have a damaging testimony of Christ to the world.

Blessings of Abiding in Christ (vv. 7-17)

The Lord Jesus has implored His eleven true branches to choose to abide in Him, their spiritual Vine. He has told them that without Him they can do nothing; branches must draw their life from the vine in order to bear fruit. Fruit-bearing honors the Father and is one of six benefits that the Lord identifies for those branches abiding in Him (v. 8). Fruit-bearing speaks of all that the Holy Spirit desires to do through us to honor Christ and bestow glory to God (e.g., giving to and serving others, using our spiritual gifts and resources to encourage others, praising God, etc.).

The second benefit of abiding in Christ is that we get to enjoy a powerful prayer-life (v. 7). If we are praying in the will of God, the Lord wants us to ask His Father for anything and He will do it (v. 16). This gives every believer the opportunity to see the good hand of God in his or her life and to witness the grace of God.

The third benefit of abiding in Christ is that we get to experience the love of God (vv. 9-10). In Christ, the Father lavishes us with the same love He conveys to His Son. Catesby Paget puts the matter this way:

> So near, so very near to God, I cannot nearer be;
> For in the person of His Son, I am as near as He.
> So dear, so very dear to God, more dear I cannot be;
> The love wherewith He loves the Son: such is His love to me!

The fourth benefit of abiding in the Vine is to experience real, tangible joy that can only be sourced from God (v. 11). Nehemiah tells us that *"the joy of the Lord is our strength"* in all of life's challenges. The Lord did not promise His disciples a happy life during their earthly sojourn, but He did leave them His joy and no one could take that from them!

The fifth benefit of abiding in Christ is the ability to love others as only God can. Before spiritual rebirth in Christ, we could only love others in the flesh. In our unregenerate state, even our best sacrificial gestures were tainted by selfish ideals and insincere motives. However, after experiencing God's love in Christ (3:16), the Holy Spirit enables believers to mortify the impulses of the flesh to sacrificially share with others as God would. John puts the matter this way: *"We love ... because He* [Christ] *first loved us"* (1 Jn. 4:19). Christ proved the greatest possible display of love, the willful laying down of one's life for others (v. 13). This is the cause and effect of God's love, and the flesh has no desire or capacity to exhibit it. However, Christ commands believers to follow His example of selfless love in loving each other (v. 12).

The sixth benefit of abiding in Christ is that believers can enjoy spiritual intimacy with Him. The Lord told His disciples, *"You are My friends if you do whatever I command you"* (v. 14). Their obedience would be rewarded with His intimacy. In fact, He would no longer refer to them as servants, but as His friends (v. 15). The idea being that it was not appropriate for a master to disclose personal thoughts and information to his servants. However, as His friends, He would not withhold anything from them that His Father desired them to know.

It is noteworthy that Scripture always conveys the thought of believers being the Lord's friends, rather than Christ being the friend of believers. The Holy Spirit was consistent in this association for a reason. Abraham was called "a friend of God" (2 Chron. 20:7; Isa. 41:8; Jas. 2:23). In Exodus 33:11 we read, *"So the Lord spoke to Moses face to face, as a man speaks to his friend"* (Ex. 33:11). John the baptizer spoke of *"the friend of the Bridegroom"* (3:29) or "the Bridegroom's friend." Speaking to His disciples, the Lord Jesus referred to Lazarus as *"our friend"* (11:11). Friendship involves selfless ministry, and Christ demonstrated at Calvary His sacrificial love for His friends (13:1, 15:13). As far as distorting the proper focus, it was the Pharisees, not believers, which said of the Lord, *"Behold a man gluttonous, and a winebibber, a friend of publicans and sinners"* (Matt. 11:19).

It is Christ's connection with us that ensures fellowship, not our expressions of familiarity with Him. The receipt of His love consequently prompts our allegiance, reverence, and sacrificial love to Him. We prove we are His friends through these media, which means that each of us is as near to the Lord as we desire to be. Peter claimed to love the Lord and would even die to protect Him (13:37), but when the test came, Peter was not as close to Christ as He thought – He denied knowing Him (18:26-27). Peter was the Lord's friend, but the opposite was not affirmed by Peter's failure. Thankfully, Christ never fails His friends, though we often fail Him.

Positionally speaking, all believers are co-seated with Christ on His Father's throne (Eph. 2:6; Heb. 8:1; Rev 3:21). As His friend, a believer relates to Christ in His position of authority, whereas referring to Christ as "my friend" lowers Him (though likely unintentionally) to our lowly, earthly station. Proverbs 18:24 pictures the kind of Friend the Lord is to His own: *"But there is a friend who sticks closer than a brother."*

Certainly, the Lord has proven Himself friendly, but let us be careful not to lower Him from His exalted position by earthly expressions of familiarity. This is especially true when we are not proving our friendship with Him.

The World's Hatred of Christ (vv. 18-27)

The Lord had just told His disciples that He was leaving them but would also come again for them. In His absence, they were to abide in Him and be fruitful. Yet, those who abide in Him must expect trouble. This chapter has the highest concentration of the word *hate* in the Bible (seven occurrences). The hate of the *world* ("world" is found six times) is contrasted with God's *love* (spoken of ten times). The synopsis is that God's love trumps the hate of the world. Believers living for Christ cannot escape the world's hate, but they can experience the goodness of God now, in ways not possible in heaven. Worldliness is any sphere in which Christ is excluded. The world, under satanic control, values what Christ does not:

- *The world* wants to be served, but Christ says humble yourself and serve others.
- *The world* says save your life, but the Lord says lose your life to gain a life worth living.
- *The world* exclaims "live for the moment," but Christians are to live for eternity.
- *The world* says live for self, but the Lord says lose your life for Him.
- *The world* is into power, but the Lord uses weak things to confound the mighty.
- *The world* permits greed to rule distribution, but Christians are to give according to need.
- *The world* says acquire wealth, but God teaches us not to seek to be rich.
- *The world* uses money and power to rule, but Christians are to pray and to use Scripture in love to serve others.
- *The world* says retaliate and get even, but the Lord teaches us to repay evil with good and be forgiving.

- *The world* uses violence, but Christians are to turn the other cheek.

Worldliness is the love of passing things, and things have no eternal value, except in how they are used to please God (Luke 16:9).

The Lord wanted His disciples to understand that because the world hated Him, it would also hate them for associating with Him (vv. 18-19). Furthermore, because the world persecuted Him, they should expect the same hostile treatment (v. 20). Those who kept Christ's teachings would agree with what the disciples taught, but those who would not heed His teachings would also reject the preaching of the disciples (v. 21). This behavior would prove that they did not know God, who sent His Son as a Messenger and message to the world. Hatred of the Son demonstrates hatred for the Father also (v. 23).

Later, Paul stated that suffering persecution in the world was unavoidable if one chooses to *"live godly in Christ Jesus"* (2 Tim. 3:12). Clearly, the world does not love followers of Christ, so let us not invest into something that offers us nothing of tangible value and is under God's judgment.

Additionally, those of this world hate their sin being exposed (vv. 22-24). Hence, the Lord realized and noted that mankind's hatred towards Him was an exact fulfillment of the prophecy in Psalm 69:4: *"They hated Me without a cause"* (v. 25). In contrast to the world's hatred of Christ for exposing human wickedness, citizens of heaven want their sin revealed and dealt with. Whether sins of omission, sins of wrong thinking, or sins of behavior, we must desire to be brought under the conviction of God's Word through the illumination of the Holy Spirit.

As in the last chapter, the Lord again affirms that He will send the Helper, the Spirit of truth, from the Father to them (v. 26). He, the Comforter, would infuse them with divine power to enable their ministry. Knowledge of their divine calling and their understanding of Scripture would be of no avail without God's facilitating power.

The English word "advocate" is only translated once from the Greek word *parakletos* in the New Testament (1 Jn 2:1). This word is usually translated "comforter," as in the four references to the Holy Spirit in John's Gospel. The role of an "advocate" or "comforter" is to legally plead one's case or to speak on the behalf of another in a court of law – a legal intercessor. Although in different aspects, both the Lord Jesus and the Holy Spirit take up this role on behalf of believers.

Thayer's Greek Dictionary describes the application of *parakletos* as pertaining to the Lord: "Christ's pleading for pardon of our sins before the Father." But when does Christ plead our case? Is it when we acknowledge and confess our sins? First John 2:1 states that Christ *is* our advocate when we sin, not when we confess our sins, though we should (1 Jn. 1:9). This ensures that each time the devil accuses us of wrongdoing before God's throne in heaven, Christ can point to His wounds sustained at Calvary and declare that though our sin is offensive, it has already been righteously judged. This upholds God's righteous displeasure over our sin, but also that it has been properly dealt with.

While on earth the Holy Spirit is our "Comforter." He was sent by the Lord Jesus to literally be "the One called alongside" to speak of Christ and accompany the Church along the perilous journey homeward. He is the Comforter, the Helper, the Teacher, the Convicter, and the One who guides us into deeper truth and enables us to share it effectively and accurately with others.

When the Comforter did come to indwell the disciples (after Christ's departure), He would testify of Christ to the world through them. The "you" in verse 27 is plural and speaks of those disciples that had been with Christ throughout His earthly ministry.

In the next chapter, the Lord again tells His disciples that after His departure, the Holy Spirit would come to actively convict those in the world of their sin, their need of a righteous standing before God, and to confirm the judgment of all those not receiving salvation in Christ (16:7-10). What was the purpose of all this information? That in Christ, the disciples would experience peace and joy despite suffering tribulations in the world, for He has *"overcome the world"* (16:33).

> It comes to my having the mind of God: Do I want to be like Christ in everything? If born of God, I have power to overcome all that is not of God, and to walk according to God.
>
> – G. V. Wigram

> A person who wholly follows the Lord is one who believes that the promises of God are trustworthy, that He is with His people, and that they are well able to overcome.
>
> – Watchman Nee

John Chapter 16

Christ Forewarns of Persecution (vv. 1-6)

The disciples should not be surprised by future Jewish persecution (v. 1). Some Jews, like Saul (later called Paul), would think they were serving God by persecuting Christians (v. 2). But these people were fools; they did not know the Father, nor His Son, Jesus Christ (v. 3). The grammar of verse 3 indicates that Jewish leaders would reject the deity of Christ, that is, that the Father and Jesus Christ were one entity.

John began His gospel account by stating that Jesus Christ first presented the Kingdom Gospel to His own (speaking of the Jews) but that they rejected Him (1:11). The main conflict in John's account is between Christ and the Jewish leaders, not the common people. John uses the phrase "the Jews" about fifty times, whereas the other three synoptic writers apply the phrase a mere sixteen times. While Matthew, Mark, and Luke refer specifically to "the scribes," "the Pharisees," "the Sadducees," or "the chief priests," John speaks of "the Jews" to identify Israel's leaders who were the determined enemies and haters of Christ.

Ten or more men could form a Jewish Synagogue at any location; thus, the Lord was implying that wherever in the world that Jews were gathered there would be opposition to the true gospel (v. 2). Those Jews following Christ should expect to be excommunicated from Judaism and be persecuted for their faith. To be put out of Jewish society was one of the worst things that could happen to a Jew.

At that present time, the disciples did not have the spiritual maturity to grasp the full meaning of Christ's words (v. 4). While He was with them, there was no need to inform them of the opposition that they would face in the world as they proclaimed the gospel message. But now that He was leaving, the Lord wanted them to understand and be prepared for the hardships ahead. Later, when they received the Holy Spirit, He would recall to their minds what Christ had taught them (14:26).

The Lord said that He was going to the Father, and that none of them would ask Him where He was going (v. 5). Peter did ask initially, but his inquiry was like that of a child lacking spiritual discernment (13:3). The

Lord had now informed them where He was going and what He expected of them after He departed. Their silence must have disappointed the Lord, for the disciples were more sorrowful over their own forthcoming troubles than His imminent suffering for them at Calvary (v. 6).

Christ to Send the Helper (vv. 7-11)

John continued to reveal Christ's teaching on what types of work the Holy Spirit will engage in after His resurrection and ascension. The Holy Spirit will be actively *reminding* (14:26, 15:26-27), *reproving* (16:7-11), and *revealing* (16:13-15) things to the disciples.

The Helper, the Holy Spirit, would be a great benefit to the disciples in gospel work (v. 7). He would convict the lost of "sin, righteousness, and judgment" (v. 8). His very presence would be a reproof to the Jewish nation who had rejected Christ. If they would have received Jesus as their Messiah, then the Holy Spirit would not have been sent into the world to cause them to feel the guilt of rejecting Christ.

The three activities of the Holy Spirit that Christ mentions, which would ensure that Israel would come under conviction for rejecting Him, are also effective today in drawing lost sinners to Christ.

First, the Holy Spirit convicts the unregenerate of their sin, to bring awareness of their guilt before God. All born of Adam enter the world judged by God (3:18) and will remain spiritually dead in their trespasses and sin unless they trust in Christ for salvation (v. 9; Rom. 5:12).

Second, the Holy Spirit affirms an individual's need of righteousness to be accepted by God (v. 10). The world rejected Christ's claim of being righteous and their need to be made right with God through Him. Through the Spirit's work of justification, a repentant sinner receives a position of righteousness in Christ, which permits him or her to be received by God (Rom. 3:26, 4:5). The Holy Spirit's presence in believers during the Church Age would affirm that Christ told the truth, that is, Christ's resurrection proved that the Father was satisfied with His Son's propitiation (Rom. 1:4). The presence of the Holy Spirit and absence of Christ in His rightful rulership on earth is what is meant by His statement, *"you see Me no more"* (v. 10). Although He was about to depart from His disciples, they would see Him again before He ascended into heaven. Therefore, the "you" in verse 10 is not likely speaking of the disciples but of worldlings who had rejected Him.

Third, the Holy Spirit convicts the unregenerate that they are under inescapable divine judgment for their sin. Christ defeated Satan at the cross and overcame death at the tomb. Hence, He is the only means of escaping spiritual death and obtaining eternal life. God's salvation for the condemned can only be found in Christ (v. 11). The Holy Spirit's presence in the world would remind condemned sinners in Israel initially and then throughout the world of this truth.

The Helper Will Reveal More Truth (vv. 12-15)

There was much for the disciples to learn as they progressed to spiritual maturity (v. 12). When the Holy Spirit arrived to indwell the disciples, He would guide them into all truth (v. 13). He would teach them what originated jointly with the Father and with Christ and reveal to the disciples things to come. The Holy Spirit would glorify Christ by revealing that which is from Him and pertains to Him (v. 14). This highlights the test of sound preaching – does the message glorify Christ? The Helper would declare truth from Christ to the apostles, just as Christ had done from the Father. The Holy Spirit would reveal all the divine attributes of the Father and of the Son to the apostles.

During the Apostolic Age, the Holy Spirit will have a reminding, reproving, and revealing ministry. The beneficial aspects of this agency are then recorded for us in New Testament Scripture, which the Holy Spirit inspired the Apostles to write: The Gospels (14:26), Acts (15:26-27), the Epistles (16:12-13), and the Revelation (16:13-14).

You Will Not See Me for a While, Then You Will (vv. 16-22)

The phrase "a little while" appears seven times in John 16. The disciples could not reconcile Christ's words *"you see Me no more"* (v. 10), and, *"[in] a little while you will see Me."* We also are left wondering as to the exact meaning of the Lord's words to His disciples. Was He speaking of His separation from them while His body was in the grave, but then they would see Him after His resurrection, but before His ascension to heaven? Or did the Lord have a more eschatological focus, that is, He would not be with them during the Church Age, but would return to the earth afterwards, which might occur in their lifetimes? Or was the Lord inferring that He would not be with them daily as before until after Pentecost, then He would be with them in Spirit forever?

Knowing that His disciples desired to understand, the Lord provided more information, which affirmed all three of these possible meanings (v. 19). From the events of Calvary until His second advent back to the earth, the world would rejoice, while believers suffered (v. 20). Despite this sorrow, the disciples would rejoice in Christ's resurrection, receive joy at Pentecost in becoming spiritually one with Him, and joyfully yearn for His future vindication in the world at His second advent.

At Christ's second coming, the previous toiling and suffering would be forgotten and replaced by joy, just as a new mother soon forgets her birthing travail (v. 21). Paul puts the matter this way: *"For I consider that the sufferings of this present time are not worthy to be compared with the glory which shall be revealed in us"* (Rom. 8:18). Suffering must precede glory! Both the Lord and Paul assure their audiences that their sufferings at this present time are not even comparable to the glory that will be realized in them later. The Lord is presently caring for us and watching over us. He knows the quality of our work and will reward it appropriately and abundantly in a coming day (Heb. 6:10-12).

Indeed, the disciples would rejoice after seeing Him resurrected from the grave, have the joy of His presence after Pentecost, but all their forthcoming sorrows would not turn into lasting joy until Christ came from heaven to them (v. 22).

Ask the Father and I Will Give It to You (vv. 23-27).

"In that day" in verse 23 speaks of the Church Age, which would begin fifty days after Christ's resurrection and ten days after His ascension back to heaven. Christ would not be physically present with His disciples on earth, but the indwelling Holy Spirit would be, and He would guide their praying according to the will of God (v. 23). The disciples did not have this open access to the Father previously, but now their joy could be full, as they observed how He granted their requests in Christ's name (v. 24).

The Lord had mainly spoken in allegory and in parables (to test the hearts of those listening to Him; Matt. 13:11-15), but in the future the disciples would receive the truth plainly (this is the revelation received and written in the Epistles; v. 25). In the Church Age, believers are in the Son. Since the Father loves the Son, the Father also loves those in His Son, and longs to answer their prayers (vv. 26-27). Through Christ the disciples had access to the Father and were not to be anxious about addressing Him directly in prayer. Furthermore, Christ continually intercedes for all believers before His Father, but not in the sense that He must urge His Father to answer the prayers of His children. The Father enjoys answering our prayers that will bring honor to His Son's name, so let us always pray with that yearning desire also.

Suffering in a World That Christ Has Overcome (vv. 28-33).

Christ said that He had departed Heaven to come into the world, but now that He was finishing His mission, He would be returning to heaven (vv. 28-29). The spirit of antichrist is to deny the incarnation of the Son of God, that is, that the second person of the Godhead did not leave heaven to be conceived in the womb of a virgin on earth. To deny this truth is a rejection of Christ's deity (1 Jn. 4:2-3). The Lord Jesus is fully God and fully man; He is and always will be holy humanity. Although they could not fully understand this truth, the disciples believed that Christ was God manifest in flesh (v. 30).

The Lord then asked, *"Do you really believe this?"* because in a few hours He knew that they would all depart from Him (v. 31). His question was acknowledging beforehand the fact that their limited faith without the assistance of the Holy Spirit would be futile in representing Him. Although He knew that His disciples would depart from Him, the Lord knew that the Father would be with Him and support Him in His "hour" of distress (excluding His suffering for human sin while hanging on a cross in darkness at Calvary).

Regardless of their shallow faith, all that Christ had spoken to His disciples in John chapters 14-16 was to enable them to have abiding joy after His departure. Verse 33 is a good summary of this section: *"In the world you will have tribulation, but be of good cheer, I have overcome the world."* Indeed, the Lord was leaving His disciples, but He was also leaving them His peace (vv. 1, 27). The Lord's message to all believers today is the same one He delivered to His disciples long ago: believe in Me and enjoy My peace!

> The labor of self-love is a heavy one indeed. Think whether much of your sorrow has not arisen from someone speaking slightingly of you. As long as you set yourself up as a little god to which you must be loyal, how can you hope to find inward peace?
>
> – A. W. Tozer

John Chapter 17

Luke portrays the Lord as a "man of prayer." Though He prayed often, Christ is only recorded as having prayed fifteen specific times in the Gospels. Luke records more of these incidents than any other writer – ten times in all. The Lord often sought the face of His Father early each day. Humanly speaking, the Lord was dependent on His Father. He received daily instruction and strength from heaven.

Although the Lord Jesus spent much time in prayer, precious few details of His prayers are recorded. He presented a model prayer to His disciples to teach them how to pray; this was done at their request. He prayed before certain miracles, that the people might know of His Father in heaven. He prayed before eating, as shown in the miracles of feeding the 5,000 and the 4,000, and later while instituting the Lord's Supper.

What is the "Lord's Prayer"? Sadly, it is not what is often quoted in churches today, a behavior that ignores Christ's command to exclude vain repetitions in our prayers (Matt. 6:7). The Lord's Prayer better refers to what is recorded in this chapter where Christ, in intimate communion with His Father, articulates His most inner thoughts just hours before His crucifixion. This is one of the longest prayers in the entire Bible, yet it only takes two or three minutes to read. In this tender petition of heaven, the Lord prays for Himself (vv. 1-5), for His disciples (vv. 6-19), and for all those who would believe on Him after them (vv. 20-26). How wonderful it is to know that long ago the Lord Jesus prayed for us.

As mentioned in the introduction section, John does not record Christ "praying" as a subordinate, but rather "asking" of His Father as an equal. The most common Greek word associated with "praying" in the Gospels is *proseuchomai*, which means "to pray to God either in supplication or worship." It is found forty-seven times in Matthew, Mark, and Luke but not once in John. The root word *proseuche,* also translated "prayer," occurs eight times in the synoptic Gospels but not at all in John. Another Greek word *deomai*, translated "beseech," "pray," or "make request," is found nine times in the synoptic accounts, but again not in John. One more Greek word that is translated as "prayer," *erotao,* when added with the preceding three Greek words, accounts for nearly all references to prayer in the Gospels. *Erotao*, a verb that denotes "to ask from an equal," is translated "pray" or "prayed" only four times in Matthew, Mark, and Luke and is used to show equality in human speech, not to petition the throne of heaven for help. If we were enjoying a meal together at our dining room table, I might ask you to "please pass the salt." I am speaking to you as an equal (*erotao*); it would be unbefitting for me to drop to my knees and beg you for the salt.

Erotao is associated with prayer seven times in John. Once it is used to illustrate the literal meaning of "asking" in John 4:31: *"In the meantime His disciples urged* ["prayed" in KJV] *Him, saying, 'Rabbi, eat.'"* This was clearly not a petition to God for something, but an expression of their concern for their leader. The remaining six occurrences are related to Christ "praying" to His Father or, literally, "talking to His Father as an equal." In all, *erotao* is translated "pray" six times in John (seven in the KJV). Why is this significant?

The Lord Jesus explained the answer publicly, *"I and My Father are one"* (10:30). The response of the Jews in the next verse showed that they understood that He was asserting divine equality: *"Then the Jews took up stones **again** to stone Him"* (10:31). Christ, being self-existing Himself, "spoke with" the Father as an equal, not as a subordinate. John employs *erotao* to show the Lord's equality with His Father in normal speech. In essence, they are equal and speak as equals. In the other Gospels, the Lord prays to His Father as a subordinate, because as the Son of Man, He took on the form of a servant and, thus, lowered Himself in "position," but not in essence.

Christ's Prayer of Intercession (vv. 1-26)

This entire chapter is a record of a prayer uttered by the Lord Jesus while in the presence of His disciples as they ventured towards the Garden of Gethsemane. Given that the prayer concluded just prior to them crossing over the Brook Kidron (18:1), it seems likely that the prayer occurred on the eastern slope of Mount Zion while facing the Mount of Olives to the northeast. The word "give" (in various forms) occurs seventeen times and the word "glory" (in various forms as derived from Greek *doxa*) is found eight times in this prayer. Clearly then it is an intercessory prayer that is affixed on the glory of God.

With the idea of glory on His heart, the Lord assumed a prayer posture fitting for that theme: He *"lifted up His eyes to heaven"* (v. 1). In contrast, a short while later in Gethsemane, the Lord *"fell on His face, and prayed"* (Matt. 26:39) and *"being in agony, He prayed more earnestly"* (Luke 22:44). He was anticipating glory, while sorrowing over the suffering that must come first. The writer of Hebrews puts the matter this way: *"For the joy that was set before Him endured the cross, despising the shame, and has sat down at the right hand of the throne of God"* (Heb. 12:2). Why could Christ lift His eyes heavenward? Because, as F. B. Hole explains, He, as God's Victor, had overcome the world and was returning to Heaven:

> We need to have in our minds the five words that close the previous chapter as we read the opening words of this chapter. He who had overcome the world "lifted up His eyes to heaven, and said, Father." In the knowledge of the Father and in the light of heaven, what is the world worth? And what are its threats or persecutions? Here was the Son of God Himself in the absolute fullness of both, and hence the world was, so to speak, beneath His feet. He is now going to present Himself before the Father, and to present His disciples also; so that they, begotten of God, and knowing Himself as the Son of God, and the Father revealed in Him, might be kept from the world through which they were to pass. When Bunyan in his allegory pictured a man with a crown of glory "before his eyes," he very rightly placed the world "behind his back."[96]

In verse 1, the Lord acknowledges that "the hour" (the time) of His suffering had come. This is the seventh and last time the Lord will speak of His hour. The Lord begins His prayer with an imperative request of the Father, *"Glorify Your Son, that Your Son also may glorify You."* The Greek verb *doxason* rendered "glorify" initiates this request and means "to praise, to magnify, to honor, or to celebrate." This verb is in the imperative mood, so the Lord is insisting on what He is requesting. As "glory" is a key component of His prayer, we pause to contemplate what the Lord is speaking of while addressing the Father.

The glories of the Lord Jesus are threefold: Intrinsic, Official, and Moral. His intrinsic glory is that which is essential to Him as the Son of God – He is fully divine and an equal to the Father: *"And now, O Father, glorify Me together with Yourself, with the glory which I had with You before the world was"* (v. 5). Christ's official glory is that which pertains to Him as the Mediator of the New Covenant – He is the Great High Priest. The Lord acquired His official glory – His reward and promotion for finishing the immeasurable work of redemption assigned to Him: *"Father, I desire that they also whom You gave Me may be with Me where I am, that they may behold My glory which You have given Me; for You loved Me before the foundation of the world"* (v. 24).

The Lord's moral glory consists of the perfections which characterize His earthly life and ministry: *"And the Word became flesh and dwelt among us, and we beheld His glory, the glory as of the only begotten of the Father, full of grace and truth"* (1:14). He was perfect in all His doings, in every circumstance, in each word spoken, and in every thought mentally conceived.

During His earthly sojourn, His intrinsic glory was veiled and His official glory not yet received. Yet, His moral glory could not be hidden; His character shined forth the integrity and perfections of His divine essence. Of this glory A. W. Tozer wrote, "Christ is God acting like God in the lowly raiments of human flesh."[97] William G. Moorehead speaks to the moral glory evident in the Lord's humanity:

> The moral glory of Jesus appears in His development as Son of Man. The nature which He assumed was our nature, sin and sinful propensities only excepted. His was a real and a true humanity, one which must pass through the various stages of growth like any other member of the race. From infancy to youth, from youth to manhood, there was steady increase both of His bodily powers and mental faculties, but the progress was orderly. "No unhealthy precocity marked the holiest of infancies." He was first a child, and afterwards a man, not a man in child's years. … At every stage of His development, in every relation of life, in every part of His service, He is absolutely perfect.[98]

It is His moral glory which was witnessed by man and illuminates every page of the gospel accounts.

While performing the mission on earth that His Father had assigned Him, the Lord's intrinsic glory was veiled by flesh. The Son now calls on the Father to honor His word and to return to Him the outshining brilliance of His divine essence, that He in turn may honor His Father by giving eternal life to those who receive His word. This was possible because the Father had given His Son authority *"over all flesh"* (v. 2). Seeing His Son's life and character manifested in converted souls honors the Father. Although all redeemed souls are gifts of the Father to the Son (6:37), it seems likely, given the context through verse 19, that the Lord is specifically speaking of the disciples that are with Him at that moment.

John

What is eternal life? Eternal life is knowing the only true God by receiving the One He sent, Jesus Christ (v. 3). Christ spoke as if He had already finished all that the Father had sent Him to do in declaring His message of life to the world (v. 4); He would glorify the Father. *Doxason* again occurs in verse 5 as the Son again calls on His Father to return to Him the manifestation of the glory intrinsic to His divine person. This was the outshining of His glory that He laid aside at His incarnation. In other words, "Glorify Me in Your presence again."

Next, the Lord Jesus told His Father: *"I have manifested Your name to the men"* (v. 6). What does it mean to manifest God's name? Attributes of *name* and *person* are inseparable; the Lord Jesus, in living flesh, had put God on display. God entered the realm of space and time in human form to declare His moral excellence, the power of His greatness, and the rich essence of His life. Consequently, man has been summoned to appreciate the goodness of God and thankfully many have responded to the drawing effect of God's love and have received and experienced eternal life in Christ (1 Jn. 1:1-2).

Christ had perfectly declared His Father's name. Christ had shown the nature of God to those He had been sent to declare God's message to. The Lord Jesus could only do what He saw His Father do (5:19) and that which would please His Father (8:29). The Lord could only speak His Father's words (12:48) and only do His will (John 5:30). Because the nature of God had been declared in every word and deed of the Lord Jesus, the name of God and Word of God was declared to the lost. Christ states that those trusting in the Father's Word kept His Word and therefore had been carved out of a lost world to live beyond it (v. 6).

Christ was given both the truth to share and the souls that responded to His message (v. 7). The "they" in verse 7 refers to the Lord's true disciples at the time. Christ shows us the importance of manifesting the character of the One whom we are proclaiming to others, if we want them to trust in His name. Furthermore, this can only happen when believers are living out their heavenly citizenship in Christ and not the behavior of the condemned world below that is under satanic control (2 Cor. 5:20; Phil. 3:20).

Christ perfectly delivered the words of life (not just commands) from His Father. Those responding to the Father's message had believed that He sent His Son to them (v. 8). Christ joyfully intercedes in grace for those who are His, but He does not intercede for those rejecting the truth (v. 9). From the cross, the Lord Jesus did ask His Father not to punish the wicked who were oppressing Him at that time (Luke 23:34), but that request was to extend mercy for a time, not grace for eternity.

Believers belong to both the Father and the Son. The mutual possession of believers proclaims the equality of the Father and the Son (vv. 9-10). Thankfully believers now and forever will bring glory to the Son (v. 10). The Greek verb rendered "glorified" (v. 10) is *dedoxasmai* and is in the perfect tense. Positionally speaking, all believers are eternally secure in Christ and will be an eternal blessing to Him.

Christ was coming to the Father, so in verse 11 He asked that all those given to Him would be kept safe during the persecutions to come. While He was with His disciples, they did not suffer, but all that was about to change. Additionally, the Lord requested that His disciples *"be one as We are"* (v. 11). The Lord desired that His disciples be unified in objective and in moral character, just as the Father and the Son always were. The Lord is not requesting that His disciples become one with God in His divinity; this would be an impossibility for God, for He is immutable and eternal.

By addressing His "Holy Father," Christ was affirming the benefits of speaking to the One who was infinitely high (holy) and infinitely nigh (His Father). The Lord speaks of keeping His disciples safe twice in verse 12. The first verb, *tereo*, is in the imperfect tense and therefore speaks of Christ keeping His disciples safe while He was physically with them during His earthly sojourn. The second verb, *phuylasso* in the aorist tense, conveys the idea that Christ had guarded all those entrusted to Him by the Father from falling prey to the devil's schemes and from regressing back into his domain of humanized religion. Judas only was lost, as he chose to betray the Lord as foreknown by God and foretold in Scripture. Judas was never saved, so he was always lost and would remain lost to God.

In verse 13, Christ transitions to making intercession for those whom He was leaving behind in the world, His disciples. He desired that these might have His joy (v. 13). The Lord knew that the world would hate those who were His, for the world only loves its own (vv. 14, 16). Hence, the Lord requested that they might be kept safe from the evil one (v. 15). By this petition, the Lord was not requesting that the disciples be removed out of the world to be with Him in heaven, but rather, that they would be kept strong in grace in the world as they live to represent Him.

Verse 16 describes the positional truth, that the disciples were no longer of the world; they were Christ's, so He desired them not to behave as worldlings; this was the practical request of His prayer (v. 17). Because the Lord was sending His disciples into the world to be His witnesses (v. 18), He desired that they would be further sanctified by the words of truth (vv. 17, 19). This was necessary, because they would be leading others to Christ through the words of truth (v. 20). The Lord's request indicates the necessity of both knowing and rightly applying Scripture to be effective in evangelistic ministry. Human arguments, fanciful apologetics, emotional pleas, and affixing guilt will never result in the conversion of souls to Christ. However, when Scripture is accurately declared by believers, the Holy Spirit works to save sinners.

In verse 20, the Lord shifts the focus of His prayer in two ways. First, He prays not only for His disciples, but also for those who would believe their testimony of Himself (i.e., other believers in the Church Age). Second, the Lord prayed that those who would believe on His message would be one, just as He and the Father were one (vv. 21-22). The unity of God's people displays God's glory – the unity of the Godhead. *Unity* is spiritual and reflects God's essence, but *uniformity* is carnal and ultimately divides the Church (1 Cor. 3:1-4). Christ desires that there be no divisions in the Church, but rather that all believers enjoy fellowship to the fullest degree possible in reference to their understanding of scriptural truth – unity rests on this foundation.

When the Church is unified, the glory of a triune God, who is always in unity, is displayed for all to witness. Peaceful unity and lovingkindness among men is not a naturally occurring phenomenon, so when it does transpire the world takes notice (13:35). The lost are prompted to consider what they see and by the grace of God some will be won to Christ (v. 23)! It is absolutely necessary for a local assembly to be of one accord before they can properly exhibit Christ to their neighborhood.

For this reason, the idea of "made perfect" in verse 23 is not speaking of the glorification of the Church when taken to heaven, but when heaven is seen in the Church while on earth. Although the verb *teleioo* is in the perfect tense, it is being used as a verbal noun to describe how the Church should behave on earth in its heavenly perfection.

> If we have got the true love of God shed abroad in our hearts, we will show it in our lives. We will not have to go up and down the earth proclaiming it. We will show it in everything we say or do.
>
> – D. L. Moody

The Man and Your God

If there is disunity in the local church, the work of the Holy Spirit is concentrated within the house of God to remove the rubbish of pride, hypocrisy, willful sin, and doctrinal error. When the flesh-controlled operations are removed from the local assembly, then Spirit-controlled saints will rise up together and be more than conquerors for the glory of God. Let us all remember that *"it is honorable for a man to stop striving, since any fool can start a quarrel"* (Prov. 20:3).

James ties strife and division with the work of the devil: *"For where envying and strife is, there is confusion and every evil work"* (Jas. 3:16; KJV). On the other hand, the unity of God's people is precious to Him: *"Behold, how good and how pleasant it is for brethren to dwell together in unity!"* (Ps. 133:1). Unity within the Church is something that the Holy Spirit is constantly working to achieve; sadly, our proud behavior opposes His efforts (Eph. 4:3). The consequence of grieving Him is powerless ministry and spiritual dryness. May we all strive for unity to show God's character and glory instead of striving with each other.

In verse 11, the Lord addressed His Father as "Holy Father" to speak of His unique perfection and righteousness. However, in verse 25, the Lord calls upon His "righteous Father." Here the Son is relating to the Father's high authority in tasking Him to come into the world (see verse 5). Indeed, the Son came into the world that we might know the words of the Father, the character of the Father (His name), and the love of the Father (vv. 25-26). The "these" in verse 25 indicates a transition of focus from future believers back to the eleven disciples with the Lord – they knew that the Father had sent the Son into the world and therefore would receive the same love of the Father that the Son enjoyed.

One of the encouraging aspects of this prayer is that Christ reveals His earnest desire for us to be with Him once our earthly work has been completed. Although as God the Lord Jesus is self-sufficient, from a relationship standpoint, He does not enjoy completeness until His beloved Bride is with Him (Eph. 1:23). Hence, we can have confidence that our Beloved, our Great Shepherd and Great High Priest, is still praying for us until we all are home in His presence (Heb. 4:14-16, 13:20-21)! Just as the Father has glorified His Son for finishing His propitiatory work on the earth, the Son will also glorify His saints after their assigned ministries have been completed.

John Chapter 18

Jesus Christ Betrayed and Arrested in Gethsemane (vv. 1-11)

After finishing His prayer recorded in John 17, the Lord with His disciples crossed over the Brook Kidron which separated Mount Zion from the Mount of Olives. Kidron means "dark or murky" and depending where they crossed the stream, the water may have been tainted with the blood of the thousands of Passover lambs slain on the temple mount above them earlier that day. John informs us that the Lord and His disciples trekked up the western slope of Olivet to a garden where they often resided (vv. 1-2). This was a location familiar to Judas.

Matthew and Mark inform us that the place was the Garden of Gethsemane. Gethsemane means "olive press," an appropriate name for a mountain known for its olive groves. Both the Kidron Brook and Gethsemane would have reminded the Lord that as God's Passover Lamb, He was about to be pressed at Calvary and shed His own blood.

In comparing Luke's and John's accounts of the events in the Garden of Gethsemane the night Christ was arrested, you might think the writers were speaking of two different instances. John describes a detachment of Roman troops, with Jewish officers, priests and Pharisees approaching the garden with *"lanterns and torches and weapons"* to seek out and arrest Jesus (v. 3). In verse 12, we learn that a Roman captain commanded the detachment. Matthew describes this arresting force as "a great multitude" (Matt. 26:47).

Why were so many soldiers and officials needed to arrest Jesus? Was He a violent man? Was He leading a political rebellion? The answer to both latter questions is "No." In response to the first question, apparently Christ's arresters thought that a large number would be needed to search out and find a "hiding" Jesus on the Mount of Olives at night. But it was the Pascal Feast and, thus, a full moon and to their surprise, they did not have to find a hiding Jesus. Rather, already knowing what must happen to Him, the Lord came to them and asked, *"Whom are you seeking?"* (v. 4).

The Man and Your God

The soldiers responded, *"Jesus of Nazareth"* (v. 5.) Judas was with the arresting soldiers and the Lord said to them all, *"I am [He]."* After Christ said this, *"they drew back and fell to the ground"* (v. 6). The Lord asked them a second time, *"Whom are you seeking?"* (v. 7). The soldiers responded, *"Jesus of Nazareth."* Jesus answered them, *"I have told you that I am [He]. Therefore, if you seek Me, let these go their way, that the saying might be fulfilled which He spoke, 'Of those whom You gave Me I have lost none'"* (vv. 8-9). The "He" in the above brackets is not within the Greek text; by the phrase *ego eimi*, the Lord proclaimed that He was I AM. The manifestation of power associated with His declaration of deity was not necessary the second time, as He had made His point and it was now the time of His arrest.

None of the other Gospel writers record this interchange in the Garden of Gethsemane, but John, who is presenting the incarnate Son of God to the world, does. John ensures that his audience sees the Lord Jesus as the great I AM (the self-existing One speaking to Moses in Exodus 3:14). The Lord employs the name three times in His response to His arresters' statements.

Peter, attempting to protect the Lord, struck a man's head and cut off his ear with a sword, yet the soldiers did not arrest him (v. 10). Why? First, because the Lord told them to let His disciples go (v. 8), and that is exactly what they did. Second, He must fulfill what He had previously stated (see 6:39 and 17:12), that is, that He would lose none of His true disciples and it was not yet time for Peter to die for Him. Peter needed to learn that the Lord did not want him to die once to serve Him, but to die daily to self to live for Him. It is easy to swing a sword when one is ignorant of God's will and make a mess of things. It is entirely another matter to fully rest in the Lord to witness God accomplish what only He can.

Hence, the Lord told Peter to sheath his sword and said, *"Shall I not drink the cup which My Father has given Me?"* (v. 11). There was to be only one smiting sword at Calvary, God's own sword against His own Shepherd (Zech. 13:7). John shows us that the Savior is God in flesh, the Great I AM, who is in full control of the events occurring in Gethsemane and all that would transpire afterwards at Calvary. The Son was controlling every detail of His arrest, trial, and crucifixion to ensure that He accomplished the redemptive work that had been assigned to Him by His Father.

John

Conversely, Luke upholds the Lord's humanity in Gethsemane. In Luke alone do we read of the Lord's anguish in prayer; *"His sweat was, as it were, great drops of blood falling"* (Luke 22:44). Only in Luke do we read of angels ministering to Christ in the garden and that the Lord healed Malchus' ear after Peter severed it. The same situation told from two perspectives!

Christ's Before Annas and Caiaphas (vv. 12-14)

John then states that Jesus was arrested, bound, and led away to Annas first, and then Caiaphas, the high priest that year (vv. 12-13). Although John does not mention the matter, it was at this juncture that all His disciples forsook the Lord and fled, just as He had foretold shortly after they had departed from the upper room (Matt. 26:31).

Why did the Jewish leaders want to arrest Jesus in the middle of the night and in a private place, like Gethsemane? The Roman historian Tacitus stated that Jerusalem's population was 600,000 when Rome assaulted the city in 70 A.D. Yet, this number seems high as compared with archeological information relating to that timeframe. Examining this evidence, Geva offers a minimal estimate of the city's population to be 20,000 at this time.[99] Others, such as Wikinson[100] and Broshi,[101] put the population of Jerusalem in 70 A.D. to be between 70,000 and 80,000 persons. Though estimates vary, it seems likely that Jerusalem's population at the time of Christ's crucifixion was likely between 50,000 and 80,000 people. However, during religious festivals this number often increased three- to fourfold.

The Jewish leaders knew the possibility of social unrest was high at such times and even a riot was a distinct possibility. Because the Pharisees feared the people (for many had high thoughts of Jesus), and of Roman repercussions for a riot, they chose to arrest Jesus of Nazareth in a private place, which the betrayal of Judas made possible.

The Lord would endure three religious trials and three civil trials in less than nine hours. Quirinius, the governor of Syria, appointed Annas as the Jewish high priest in 6 A.D. However, the Romans did not want a long-standing high priest. Limiting the high priest's tenure would reduce the priest's sway among the people. So Annas had been replaced in 15 A.D. by Valerius Gratus, procurator of Judea, and then each of his five sons were appointed the high priest and then Caiaphas, his son-in-law.[102] Luke confirms that both Annas and Caiaphas were high priests currently

(Luke 3:2). From the Jewish perspective, Annas was the true high priest, though Caiaphas was the acknowledged leader to pacify Roman rule.

John states that Christ first appeared before Annas and then was interrogated by a larger gathering of Jewish leaders with Caiaphas present (v. 13; Matt. 26:57). Interestingly, night gatherings of the Sanhedrin for a capital trial were illegal.[103] The introduction of false witnesses at the trial (Matt. 26:60) and the declaring of a verdict before the trial commenced (7:51) were also forbidden Sanhedrin activities.

Moreover, the Defendant was not permitted any time to prepare His case. This was a sham trial from start to finish, and one that violated Sanhedrin protocol on several points. At first light, the Lord would be brought before the full Sanhedrin to determine how He should be put to death. It was at this juncture that John recalls the earlier words of Caiaphas who had advised his Jewish constituents, *"it was expedient that one man should die for the people"* (v. 14, 11:49-50). Although Caiaphas did not understand the spiritual ramifications of what he had declared, the Spirit of God had spoken the truth through him.

In God's plan, Christ must die for the Jewish people to establish a new covenant with them that would righteously permit God to honor His covenant with Abraham and in a future day refine and restore a Jewish remnant to Himself (Heb. 8:8). Therefore, the wrath of the Jewish leaders was used to accomplish God's sovereign purposes, just as the psalmist declared centuries earlier, *"Surely the wrath of man shall praise You!"* (Ps. 76:10).

Peter Denies the Lord (vv. 15-27)

Peter followed the Lord at a distance, but after arriving at the high priest's courtyard, he sat down to see what would happen and warmed himself by a fire with Annas's servants (Matt. 26:58). John, who was known by the high priest, tells us that he spoke to the doorkeeper on Peter's behalf so that he would be permitted into the courtyard (vv. 15-16). It was cold, so Peter stood with Jewish servants and officers by a fire of coals to warm himself (v. 18). The doorkeeper was a servant girl who then recognized Peter and said to him, *"You are not also one of the Man's disciples, are you?"* (v. 17). But Peter said, *"I am not."* Strike one. Whether or not Peter heard or recognized the warning at this moment we do not know, but Mark states that a rooster crowed after his first denial (Mark 14:68).

John

Inside the hall, Annas was interrogating Jesus about His doctrine and His disciples (v. 19). The Lord answered that He had taught the people openly in the synagogues and in the temple and since nothing had been spoken in secret, Annas should be asking the people what He had taught them (vv. 20-21). According to the Law, two or more witnesses must confirm the facts in establishing a defendant's guilt or innocence; thus, His testimony was inconsequential. Clearly, the Jews were having difficulty obtaining two witnesses with a consistent condemning testimony, so the high priest was hoping Jesus would say something while in their presence that would condemn Him (Matt. 26:60).

After hearing the Lord's bold response, one of the officers slapped Jesus with the palm of his hand and said, *"Do You answer the high priest like that?"* (v. 22). Although Caiaphas was the recognized high priest by Rome, the Jews still considered his father-in-law Annas to be the high priest. The Lord then challenged the officer who had struck him to follow the Law: *"If I have spoken evil, bear witness of the evil; but if well, why do you strike Me?"* (v. 23). Commenting to this verse, William MacDonald writes: "With perfect poise and unanswerable logic, the Savior showed the unfairness of their position. They could not accuse Him of speaking evil; yet they struck Him for telling the truth."[104] If He had spoken evil, then an honorable court would prove it before punishment was pursued, and if He had spoken truthfully, an honorable court should explain the inappropriateness of smiting Him without judicial cause.

Although the Lord did not defend Himself during any of His trials, He does show us the value of reasoning with those who are oppressing the truth. In matters of sin, speaking to a person's conscience, rather than his or her intellect, is more effective in establishing guilt that will result in a change of heart.

Matthew informs us that the Lord was beaten at this juncture. The soldiers mocked His testimony by saying, *"Prophesy to us, Christ! Who is the one who struck You?"* (Matt. 26:68). Considering that He could have quickly ended all their lives, the Lord demonstrated incredible restraint in not swiftly judging His oppressors. Furthermore, the Lord Jesus maintained the molecular integrity of the very human fists that were battering His face! Paul writes, *"In Him all things consist"* (Col. 1:17) and thus He was able to demonstrate the "fullness of the Godhead bodily" (Col. 2:9) in all that He did. Afterwards Annas sent Jesus to Caiaphas, the high priest (v. 24).

Meanwhile Peter, who was still warming himself by a fire with worldlings, is challenged a second time by those standing with him, *"You are not also one of His disciples, are you?"* Again, Peter said, *"I am not"* (v. 25). Strike two. A little while later Peter was challenged by a relative of Malchus, whose ear Peter had severed in Gethsemane, *"Did I not see you in the garden with Him?"* (v. 26). Peter again denied the Lord. Matthew informs us that Peter did so while cursing and swearing, and adamantly declaring, *"I do not know the Man!"* (Matt. 26:74). Strike three.

No sooner had the despicable words departed from Peter's lips, when he heard the rooster crow (all four Gospel writers record this detail). It was normal for roosters to crow in the fourth watch (3 a.m. to 6 a.m.). Mark notes that the rooster had sounded his warning previously, but only now did Peter recognize it and remember the Lord's prediction, *"Before the rooster crows, you will deny Me three times"* (Mark 14:72). Luke states that at this moment Peter's eyes and the Lord's eyes briefly met (Luke 22:61). It was a sorrowful look that Peter would never forget. The defeated fisherman immediately went out of the courtyard and wept bitterly. F. B. Hole suggests that there is a practical lesson for all believers to glean from Peter's failure:

> That this [Peter's failure] should be one of the few episodes recorded by all four Evangelists is worthy of note. God does not take pleasure in recording the sins of His saints, so we may be sure that there is in it warning and instruction much needed by all saints in all ages, for self-confidence is one of the commonest and most deep-seated tendencies of the flesh: a tendency which, if not judged and refused, invariably leads to disaster.[105]

Jesus Christ Before Pilate (vv. 28-38)

John does not record the interchange between the Lord and Caiaphas or His trial before the full Jewish Sanhedrin at dawn. Matthew tells us that Christ was found guilty during His first meeting with Caiaphas, and the Sanhedrin hurriedly gathered at first light to determine *how* they should put Jesus to death (Matt. 27:1). He had already been found guilty and deemed worthy of execution by the high priest and some of the Sanhedrin (Matt. 26:66). In humanized religion, overzealous ritual will always undervalue morality eventually.

Because the Romans did not permit the Jews to execute anyone according to their laws and tradition, if Christ was to be executed, He must be taken to the Roman governor of the region, Pontius Pilate (vv. 28-29). The Jewish leaders did so immediately after concluding their bogus trial (Matt. 27:2).

The Lord Jesus was brought before the Roman Governor of Judea, Pilate, to be questioned. It did not take the Sanhedrin long to decide Jesus' fate, for when He arrived at the Praetorium, it was still early morning (v. 28). It is unknown if this was the Antonia Fortress on the north side of the temple mount or one of Herod's palaces on the west side of Jerusalem. To maintain ceremonial cleanliness, the Jewish leaders would not enter the governor's palace, so they remained in the courtyard. Their hypocrisy is self-evident; they were more concerned about ceremonial defilement than putting an innocent man to death.

Pilate yielded to their Jewish customs by going out to the courtyard to speak to the Jewish leaders. He asked, *"What accusation do you bring against this Man?"* (v. 29). Their ludicrous response to Pilate's question showed the foolish nature of their case against Jesus, *"If He were not an evildoer, we would not have delivered Him up to you"* (v. 30). In other words, "Pilate, you must sentence this man to death because we have found Him guilty of doing evil." Pilate was not impressed by their irrational ploy and told the Jews to judge Jesus according to their own laws (v. 31). However, the Jews reminded Pilate that only Rome had the authority to execute a condemned criminal in Israel. John also affirms that Jesus must be sentenced to death by Rome, rather than by the Jewish Sanhedrin, for the prophecy of Christ's crucifixion in Psalm 22 to be fulfilled. The Jewish means of capital punishment was stoning.

Luke records that the chief priests and elders then informed Pilate that Jesus was subverting the nation by denying that the Jews should pay Caesar tribute and by claiming Himself to be King instead of Caesar (Luke 23:2). Pontius Pilate then interrogated the Lord to discern if these charges of sedition were legitimate. Pilate asked Jesus if He was *"the King of the Jews"* (v. 33)? Before answering Pilate's question, the Lord asked him, if he had heard previous reports of Him doing this or was he responding to Jewish hearsay (v. 34). The Lord Jesus then affirmed that what Pilate had asked was correct. Pilate replied that He was not a Jew and therefore was not familiar with the charge His own countrymen had levied against Him (v. 35). As a Roman governor, he was only concerned about matters pertaining to civil order, and was obviously irritated to be forced into a situation involving Jewish customs.

The Lord then told Pilate that He was a king, but that His kingdom was not of this world; if it were, His servants would have fought for Him, and the Jews would not have arrested Him (v. 36). Pilate wanted to ensure that he had understood Jesus correctly, so he asked Him again, *"Are You a king then?"* (v. 37). The Lord again confirmed that He was a king and had been born to convey God's truth to the world. He then added that *"everyone who is of the truth hears My voice"* (v. 37). Having considered the Jewish charge and the lack of evidence pertaining to Jesus' case, Pilate asked Him, *"What is truth?"* (v. 38).

Normally we speak of truth as that which conforms to fact or reality; some use *truth* to refer to a sincere statement. However, the words of the Jewish leaders, though candidly spoken, were not truthful. We must realize that reality exists independent of our natural understanding of it. Because man is neither omniscient nor omnipresent, he cannot completely understand reality through natural means, nor through the wonderfully spoken words of intellectuals and philosophers.

Whatever is naturally developed will tend to be imperfect, meaning we need supernatural help from the Lord to understand what truth really is and who He is. Truth is truth; it is not relative. Absolute truth cannot contradict itself. God's Word wonderfully withstands the test of time and is proven trustworthy. Let us be very careful what we accept as truth when it originates in human reasoning, for as often is the case, time proves the fallibility of such things.

After the Lord said these words to Pilate, he departed the Praetorium and addressed a now larger Jewish crowd waiting for his verdict. Pilate said to them, *"I find no fault in Him at all"* (v. 38). However, this decree did not pacify the chief priests and Jewish elders who continued accusing Jesus of many things (Matt. 27:12-14). Matthew tells us that Pilate marveled greatly at the Lord Jesus' restraint, as He did not attempt to defend Himself against the Jewish charges.

Seeing Pilate's passive disposition, the Jewish elders became fiercer in their accusations against Jesus, saying that He was a Galilean and had incited trouble from Galilee to Judea (Luke 23:5). After hearing this, Pilate sent Jesus to Herod to be examined (Luke 23:6). John does not record this detail. Galilee was Herod's jurisdiction as a tetrarch, and he was in Jerusalem at that time for the feast (Luke 23:7). This was Christ's second civil trial. Although Herod asked Jesus many questions, the Lord answered him nothing. After Herod's soldiers had mocked and abused the Lord Jesus, Herod sent Him back to Pilate (Luke 23:13).

Barabbas or Jesus of Nazareth? (vv. 39-40)

As explained earlier in this chapter, there were likely between 150,000 to 300,000 people in Jerusalem for the Passover Feast. The potential for a riot was high and Pilate wanted to avoid that scenario, lest he be called to Rome and questioned by Caesar for the uprising. To encourage a peaceful situation, it was Pilate's custom to pardon a Jewish prisoner of the people's choosing during the feast (v. 39). As an attempt to release Jesus, Pilate offered the Jewish assembly a choice of whom he would pardon. They could choose to free Jesus of Nazareth or a notorious prisoner, Barabbas, who had been found guilty of inciting rebellion in Jerusalem and of murder (Matt. 27:16-17; Luke 23:19-25).

The Roman governor chose to contrast the worst convicted criminal available to him with an accused Man that, in his judgment, was completely innocent, to expose the envy of the Jewish leaders in indicting Jesus (Matt. 27:18). But Pilate was unable to persuade the Jews to turn from their bloodthirsty intentions. They wanted Barabbas released and Christ crucified (v. 40). Pilate again asserted that Jesus had done nothing worthy of death, but the crowd cried out the more, *"Let Him be crucified"* (Matt. 27:23).

Fearing a riot, Pilate washed his hands in a basin and proclaimed, *"I am innocent of the blood of this just Person. You see to it"* (Matt. 27:24). The Jewish crowd answered, *"His blood be on us and on our children"* (v. 25). In effect, they had put themselves under a blood curse for condemning a righteous man to death (Acts 2:23, 3:14-15, 5:28). The Jewish nation had no idea the centuries of pain and sorrow that would result from this proclamation. But the consequences of cutting off their Messiah were foretold by the prophet Daniel long ago: War and desolations would be determined against them until the end of the Tribulation Period, when, by grace, the blood of expiation will erase the blood of the curse (Dan. 9:24-27). Although the Jews crucified God's Son and their Messiah, His blood was on their hands, not their souls.

> There is either of two things we must do. One is to send back the message to heaven that we don't want the blood of Christ to cleanse us of our sin, or else accept it.
>
> – D. L. Moody

John Chapter 19

While there is some debate as to whether Christ was crucified on Thursday or Friday, the Scripture clearly informs us that He experienced resurrection early on Sunday morning. Traditionally speaking, Christ was crucified on Friday as indicated by the combined weight of the gospel accounts. The argument for a Thursday crucifixion arises from John's account in which the Pharisees were before Pilate prior to the Passover (18:28) and the reference to the forthcoming Sabbath as "a high day" (v. 31). This may indicate that at the time of Christ's passion, two Sabbath days followed each other (i.e., on Friday and Saturday). As the Feast of Unleavened Bread began on the fifteenth day of the first month, that day was a special Sabbath day no matter what day of the week it fell on (Lev. 23:5-7).

Those who hold to a Thursday crucifixion position take the Lord's statement to the Pharisees of the sign of Jonah literally, that is, Christ's body would be in the grave "three days and nights." However, the Lord spoke more often that He would rise on the third day (Matt. 17:23, 20:19; Luke 9:22, 18:33) or in the third day (2:19-22). However, while speaking to the Pharisees, the Lord referred to the sign of Jonah to foretell His death and resurrection: *"For as Jonah was three days and three nights in the belly of the great fish, so will the Son of Man be three days and three nights in the heart of the earth"* (12:40). The Pharisees later repeated Christ's statement to Pilate, *"after three days I will rise"* (Matt. 27:63), but then they only asked for a guard *"until the third day"* (Matt. 27:64). If the term, "after three days," was not interchangeable with "the third day," then the Pharisees would have asked that the tomb be guarded for four days. The term "one day and one night" was a Jewish idiom indicating a day, even when only a part of a day was indicated (e.g., Gen. 42:74; 1 Sam. 30:12). In summary, the terms "three days and nights" and "three days" were terms the Jews used interchangeably.

Because the Passover and the feast of Unleavened Bread were connected, the terminology referring to these feasts was often used interchangeably. Hence, since the first day of Unleavened Bread was a holy day, this may explain why the Pharisees did not want to defile themselves at Passover by coming inside the Gentile judgment hall (18:28). Luke quoted the Lord who plainly said that He was eating the Passover meal with His disciples the evening directly before His arrest and crucifixion, not a preparation meal (Luke 22:15).

It is likely, that this meal was eaten at sundown that ended the 14th of Nisan, rather than the sundown that began the 14th of Nisan. However, the Torah's requirement of eating the Passover at sundown on the 14th of Nisan is ambiguous, as it may refer to the sundown that begins or ends that specific day. It would be like us saying, "I will visit you tomorrow at midnight." There are two possible meanings of that expression. Traditionally speaking, the lambs were slaughtered on the afternoon of Nisan the 14th and the Passover was largely eaten that evening after sundown, which technically was the 15th. This mealtime was viewed as an extension of the 14th of Nisan. Overall, the scriptural evidence best affirms a Friday crucifixion date, but a Thursday date is possible.

Christ Stripped, Mocked, Beaten, and Rejected (vv. 1-3)

Being unable to dissuade the enraged Jewish mob, Pilate then released the notable murderer Barabbas and had Christ scourged (v. 1). Perhaps Pilate thought that by having Christ severely whipped, the hostile crowd might then show Him sympathy and His life would be spared. But the Jewish leaders, especially, had no sympathy for Jesus Christ. To prevent a riot in a city likely having four times its normal population for the feast, Pilate sentenced Christ to death by crucifixion.

A common punishment under the Law and practiced in both the Old and New Testaments by the Jews was that of scourging (Lev. 19:20). Up to forty stripes could be administered, but to ensure compliance with the Law, the Jews limited themselves to "forty stripes minus one" or *thirty-nine* stripes (Deut. 25:1-4; 2 Cor. 11:24). However, there were no such limitations of abuse during a Roman scourging, which typically preceded public executions to speed up the dying process of crucifixion.

The Roman whip did much more than put stripes on the condemned; it was designed to rip the flesh wide open. A Roman flogging resulted in deep lacerations which exposed muscles and caused excessive bleeding. Church historian Eusebius of Caesarea recounts the horror of a Roman scourging: "For they say that the bystanders were struck with amazement when they saw them lacerated with scourges even to the innermost veins and arteries, so that the hidden inward parts of the body, both their bowels and their members, were exposed to view."[106] The term "half-dead" was commonly associated with a Roman scourging, as many who endured its wrath died afterwards. Yet, the idea of scourging was to stop the beating before death resulted to ensure that the victim was still able to undergo the humiliation of a public crucifixion.

Isaiah foretold that the Messiah, God's Servant, would be faithful to live out what He was asked to do no matter the personal cost to Himself. In the prophecy, the Servant conveys His determination to expend Himself on Israel's behalf (and on ours too) despite the human brutality and divine judgment He knew He would suffer:

I gave My back to those who struck Me, and My cheeks to those who plucked out the beard; I did not hide My face from shame and spitting. For the Lord God will help Me; therefore, I will not be disgraced; therefore, I have set My face like a flint, and I know that I will not be ashamed (Isa. 50:6-7).

This prophecy tells us that Christ knew beforehand that He would be scourged, beaten in the face, and spat on. Matthew records the direct fulfillment of these prophecies in his gospel account (26:67, 27:26, 30). Thankfully, two thousand years ago, the Lord Jesus did not enter into His rest until He had secured ours, through the shedding of His own blood. We worship a brave, tenacious, and sacrificial Savior!

In the previous hours, the Lord Jesus had been abused by the servants of the chief priests and by Herod's men. He has already received many blows from human fists. After being scourged, Matthew informs us that the Lord was taken into the Roman Praetorium, and an entire garrison of soldiers (likely comprised of 200 to 300 men) gathered to have sport with Him (Matt. 27:27-31). They stripped Him of His clothes and put a scarlet robe or cloak on Him, which likely revealed His nakedness (v. 2). Scarlet and purple were colors of royalty. They also twisted a crown of thorns and placed it on His head and put a hollow reed in his right hand (Matt. 27:29). Thorns resulted after God cursed the ground (i.e., the earth; Rom. 8:20-22) because of Adam's sin (Gen. 3:17-18). Now the Creator was bearing on His brow the curse He levied on humanity in Eden.

Being adorned with a mock robe, crown, and scepter, the Roman soldiers then bowed the knee to Jesus in mock worship, *"Hail, king of the Jews!"* (v. 3). The Lord had been rejected and abused by the Jewish authorities; now the Gentiles also were guilty of disdaining the Savior. They spat on Him and took the reed out of His hand and beat the crown of thorns into His brow with it (Matt. 27:30). John states that the Roman soldiers also *"struck Him with their hands"* (v. 3).

Pilate's Final Attempt to Release Jesus (vv. 4-15)

Afterwards, Christ, still wearing the crown of thorns and the purple robe and having been severely whipped and beaten, was presented to the Jewish mob by Pilate (v. 4). Having examined Jesus by scourging, the governor again stated Jesus' innocence and then said to the multitude, "Behold the Man" (v. 5)! The chief priests and officers were not satisfied with Pilate's severe judgment of Jesus; they wanted Him dead (v. 6).

After hearing their chant "crucify, crucify," Pilate told the Jewish leaders to take Jesus and crucify Him, if that is what they desired to do, but he found no fault in Him. However, the Jews declared to Pilate that because Jesus of Nazareth had claimed to be the Son of God, He must be put to death for His blasphemy (v. 7). When Pilate heard this statement, he was more afraid of sentencing Jesus to death (v. 8). According to the Mosaic Law (e.g., Ex. 21:28), the Jews were to execute the condemned by stoning and not by crucifixion. However, Psalm 22:16 foretells that the true Messiah would be crucified by a wicked congregation; therefore, Christ must not be condemned and executed by the Jews, but by Rome. God used the hatred of the Jewish people to accomplish His will, for it was not enough to merely put Jesus to death; they wanted Him to be hung on a tree as a public testimony that He had been cursed by God for being a condemned malefactor (Deut. 21:22-23). This was God's plan; His innocent, sinless Son would be cursed by Him to satisfy His judicial wrath over human sin (Rom. 3:25; Heb. 2:9; 1 Jn. 2:2).

Pilate again withdrew to the Praetorium to further question Jesus. He asked the Lord, *"Where are you from?"* but Jesus did not answer Pilate (v. 9). Pilate then admonished the Lord for not speaking to him, and then reminded Him that He had the authority to end His life or to release Him (v. 10). The Lord answered Pilate's charge, *"You could have no power at all against Me unless it had been given you from above. Therefore the one who delivered Me to you has the greater sin"* (v. 11). One must be under authority to have authority. True, Pilate had Roman authority from Caesar, but the Lord Jesus was under His Father's authority and the only

The Man and Your God

way Pilate could put Him to death was if His Father permitted it. Judas had acted under Satan's authority; thus, committing a greater offense.

Pilate again sought to release Jesus, but the Jews sternly confronted him, *"If you let this Man go, you are not Caesar's friend. Whoever makes himself a king speaks against Caesar"* (v. 12). Unable to subdue the escalating situation and wanting to avoid a riot that would likely cause him to be questioned by Caesar, Pilate sat on the judgment seat (called *the Pavement*, but in Hebrew *Gabbatha*) and ordered Jesus' crucifixion (v. 13). This occurred at 6 a.m. *"on the Preparation Day of the Passover"* (v. 14; 18:28), which is likely referring specifically to the Feast of Unleavened Bread, as the Passover lambs had been slaughtered the previous afternoon. Although this was to be a high day, a holy convocation to the Lord (Lev. 23:5-8), the Sanhedrin was not following the Law or their developed traditions in their condemnation of Christ.

With Pilate sitting on the judgment seat and Jesus before the hostile Jewish crowd, Pilate said to them, *"Behold your King"* (v. 14). This statement further riled the Jews, who cried out, *"Crucify Him!"* Pilate knew that because of envy they wanted to put Jesus to death, so he further infuriated them by saying, *"Shall I crucify your King?"* (v. 15). The Jews' response to this question indicated their total rejection of God's Messiah, and their acceptance of a Gentile ruler who would oppress them, *"We have no king but Caesar!"* Until *the Times of the Gentiles* be fulfilled at the end of the Tribulation Period, such will be the adverse condition of the Jewish people (Luke 21:24).

We pause to consider the two "behold" statements uttered by Pilate in this chapter that wonderfully fulfill the Messianic Old Testament declarations. There are four unique "behold" statements found within the Old Testament that prepare the way for Christ's first earthly advent as each one emphasizes a distinct gospel theme. Each "behold" declaration is a unique invitation by God the Father for all humanity to gaze upon and admire His dear Son.

Behold your King (Zech. 9:9) – the Gospel of Matthew
Behold My Servant (Isa. 42:1) – the Gospel of Mark
Behold the Man (Zech. 6:12) – the Gospel of Luke
Behold your God (Isa. 40:9) – the Gospel of John

What is additionally fascinating is that the same Old Testament declarations are repeated in the New Testament as explicit confirmation that Jesus Christ was the direct fulfillment: "Behold your King" (v. 14), "Behold My Servant" (Matt. 12:18), "Behold the Man" (v. 5), "Behold ... God with us" or "Behold your God" (Matt. 1:23).

The New Testament validation of Christ is completely homogeneous with the pronoun coupling found in the Old Testament announcements. When the Lord is presented in a position of authority (as King and as God), the possessive pronoun "your" precedes the title, but when the position of a lowly servant is stated, the pronoun "My" appears. When the Lord is introduced in the intermediate stature, as a man, the neutral "the" is applied. This arrangement demonstrates the various facets and positional glories of the Lord's ministry and how He would relate to mankind.

Jesus Christ Is Crucified (vv. 16-30)

Pilate's soldiers put His own clothes on the Lord and led Him away to be crucified (v. 16). In His physically weakened state, the Lord was not able to bear His own cross (bar or beam) on His shoulder. Such a beam typically weighed between 75 and 125 pounds. The Romans compelled Simon from Cyrene (a city in northern Africa with a significant Jewish population) to bear Christ's cross to the place of public execution (Matt. 27:32). John does not record this detail, but merely states that Jesus Christ was brought to Golgotha, the "Place of the Skull," to be crucified (v. 17). John Heading describes the meaning of Golgotha and what it symbolized:

> Golgotha and the corresponding Roman name Calvary (Luke 23:33) both mean "skull" – hence Matthew's interpretation "a place of a skull." Various reasons have been suggested why the place had this name – for example, because the shape of the place resembled a skull. Typically, however, the name speaks of the apex of human wisdom, for those who crucified the Lord of glory possessed this wisdom, the opposite to the wisdom of God (1 Cor. 2:6–8). It speaks of the unsanctified intelligence of men who still reject Christ in unbelief.[107]

The Roman soldiers then stripped the Lord of His clothes and crucified Him. They cast lots for His outer garment that was woven without seam and tore His inner garment into four pieces, so that each soldier would receive a portion (vv. 23-24). John notes that the soldiers' actions concerning Jesus' clothing precisely fulfilled the Psalm 22:18 Messianic prophecy.

The Man and Your God

After the soldiers had crucified two condemned men on either side of the Lord, they placed a placard written by Pilate in Hebrew, Greek, and Latin over the Lord's head that read, *"Jesus of Nazareth, The King of the Jews"* (vv. 19-20). Luke also states that the superscription hanging above the Lord's head was written in Hebrew, Greek, and Latin. As Luke is an appeal to humanity and John is writing to the whole world, it makes sense that the use of all three languages was recorded by these two evangelists. If Matthew had written concerning this detail, perhaps he would have only focused on the Hebrew language. Likewise, Mark would have likely referred to the language of the Roman Empire, Latin.

The Jewish leaders were insulted by Pilate's placard and asked him to rewrite it as, *"He said, 'I am the King of the Jews'"* (v. 21). But Pilate refused to do so, saying, *"What I have written, I have written"* (v. 22).

Mark informs us that Christ was crucified at the third hour (9 a.m.; Mark 15:25). Matthew does not record any of the Lord's statements or intercession during His first three hours on the cross. He states that at the sixth hour (noon in Roman time) until the ninth hour (3 p.m.) there was an intense darkness "over all the land" (Matt. 27:45). The judgment of human sin was a private matter between the Son and the Father; nothing would be permitted to intrude into the work of eternal propitiation.

Before the intense darkness veiled the Savior, several women were standing nearby. These were Mary (the mother of Jesus), her unnamed sister, Mary (the wife of Clopas, also called Salome, the mother of James and John; Mark 15:40), and Mary Magdalene (v. 25). The Lord, seeing both His mother, and the beloved disciple (John) near to Him, said to His mother, *"Woman, behold your son!"* (v. 26). To John, the Lord said, *"Behold your mother"* and from that moment onward, John took care of Mary, the mother of the Lord (v. 27). Church tradition records that John took Mary to Ephesus and cared for her there until the time of her death.

Matthew tells us that before the nails were driven through the Lord's wrists to the cross bar, He was offered wine mingled with gall (a narcotic to numb the senses to reduce pain), but after tasting the mixture, He would not drink it (Matt. 27:34). This partially fulfilled the Messianic prophecy of Psalm 69:21. However, the second portion of this prophecy had not yet been fulfilled, *"For my thirst they gave me vinegar to drink."* Having completed the propitiatory suffering for human sin, the Lord said, *"I thirst"* (v. 28). According to Matthew's account this statement must have occurred directly after the Lord cried out with a loud voice, saying, *"Eli, Eli, lama, sabachthani?"* meaning, *"My God, My God, why have You forsaken Me?"* (Matt. 27:46). This quotation of Psalm 22:1 was declared just prior to His death at 3:00 p.m. The Lord affirmed that while He was being our Sin-bearer, fellowship with His Father was severed. The Lord also wanted to ensure that Psalm 22 would be associated with His redemptive work. While the Lord Jesus was hanging from a cross, He was fully aware and in complete control of His situation. He astutely fulfilled every Old Testament prophecy so there would be no question that He was Israel's promised Messiah.

Some standing by thought that Jesus was calling for Elijah to assist Him (Matt. 27:47). One of them immediately got up and filled a sponge with sour wine and placed it on a reed and lifted it up to the Lord to drink from it (v. 29; Matt. 27:48).

After finishing the required suffering for all human sin, the Lord Jesus *"cried out again with a loud voice, and yielded up His spirit"* (Matt. 27:50). "Loud voice" is derived from the Greek phrase *megas phone*. The Greek verb rendered "cried out again" is *krazo*, which means "to scream." This was the kind of loud shrill scream that one would not soon forget. John tells us what the Lord said, before commending His spirit into His Father's care: *"It is finished!"* (v. 30). John uses the perfect tense verb *teleo* to declare that what Christ had just accomplished at Calvary could never be undone – it was an eternal propitiatory and redemptive work. Afterwards, there would never be another offering for the offence or damages of human sin (Heb. 9:28, 10:12-14).

Before the sin offering was killed in Levitical days, the offerer placed his hands on the head of the animal and confessed his sins to symbolize the transfer of the offense to the animal. The sacrifice was then killed and completely burned to show that the sin had been fully atoned for and forgiven. The picture of the sin offering is clear; Christ identified with us by becoming a man, took our sin upon Himself at Calvary as God's Lamb, and was judged by God in our place: *"For Christ also suffered once for sins, the just for the unjust, that He might bring us to God, being put to death in the flesh but made alive by the Spirit"* (1 Pet. 3:18-19).

The sin offering was completely consumed by fire and the Lord Jesus was completely consumed in the judgment for our sin. David prophesied that the billows and waves of God's wrath would break upon the Sin-bearer, the Messiah (Ps. 42:7). During those three hours of darkness, while hanging between heaven and earth nailed to a cross, the Lord Jesus was forsaken by God the Father (Matt. 27:45-46). He was stripped of His clothing and His dignity – as a public spectacle He endured the persistent insults, the demeaning jeers, and the blatant blasphemy. Having completed His task as the sin offering, the Lord declared with a loud voice, *"It is finished!"* (v. 30). He then offered up His spirit to the Father which fulfilled His prophetic words, *"I lay down My life that I may take it again. No one takes it from Me, but I lay it down of Myself"* (10:17).

The Lord Jesus was both the Mediator of a New Covenant (Heb. 8:7-9) and the ransom that established it: *"For there is one God and one Mediator between God and men, the Man Christ Jesus, who gave Himself a ransom for all, to be testified in due time"* (1 Tim. 2:5-6). The priest who presided over the sin offering was innocent of the offerer's sin, yet became connected with it in order to apply the blood of the sacrifice to make atonement for the sinner – this pictures Christ's ministry as the Mediator between God and men.

Jesus Christ Is Buried (vv. 31-42)

Although the Jewish leaders had just leveraged Pilate to condemn an innocent man to death, they asked the governor to break the legs of the three crucified men, lest they remain on their crosses during the Sabbath, which was "a high day" (v. 31). Friday, the first day of the Feast of Unleavened Bread, was to be considered as a Sabbath (Lev. 23:5-7). The Jews told Pilate, *"that the bodies should not remain on the cross on the Sabbath"* (v. 31). If a Friday morning crucifixion, then the bodies were not to "remain" on their crosses during the high day. If a Thursday morning crucifixion of Christ, then the bodies were to be taken down prior to sunset on the 14th day of Nisan.

When the legs of a crucified person were broken, breathing became quite difficult, because the weight of the body pulled down on the arms and impeded exhalation. Given the weakened and exhausted condition of the victim, suffocation usually occurred within a few minutes. Pilate honored the Jewish request, and the Roman soldiers broke the legs of both the criminals hanging on either side of the Lord (v. 32). However, when they came to Jesus, they found that He was already dead; therefore they did not break His legs, but pierced His side with a spear to ensure that He was dead (v. 33). Blood and water immediate poured out of the wound imposed by the spear (v. 34).

John pauses to ensure that His audience understands that He was an eyewitness of the events that he is describing and is writing an accurate account of what he witnessed (v. 35). He also notes that in His death, Christ fulfilled two more Messianic prophecies. First, Psalm 34:20 states that God's Passover Lamb, Christ, would be perfect and that no bone would be broken in His body (Ex. 12:46). Second, Zechariah 12:10 foretold that Christ would be pierced, a fact that the restored Jewish remnant would see and weep over when Christ returns to the earth.

A rich man named Joseph, a secret disciple of Christ from Arimathea, went to Pilate and requested the body of Jesus (v. 38; Matt. 27:57). He was a just man, a member of the Sanhedrin, but had not consented to the Lord's death (Luke 23:51). Pilate was surprised that Jesus had already expired and asked the centurion in charge of His execution to confirm the matter (Mark 15:44). Learning that the claim was true, Pilate granted Joseph's request (Matt. 27:58). There was not much time to bury the body as the Sabbath was at hand. As the Lord's death was at 3:00 p.m. and the dialogue between Pilate, Joseph, and the centurion occurred afterwards, there was likely less than 90 minutes to take the body off the cross (Luke 23:53), transport it to the tomb, wrap it, and seal it in the tomb. Nicodemus, another Jewish ruler and secret disciple of Christ, joined Joseph in the task. He brought a hundred pounds of myrrh and aloes to the tomb (v. 39).

Joseph and Nicodemus quickly wrapped Jesus' body with the spices in strips of clean linen (v. 40). Then both men placed the Lord's body in Joseph's own tomb hewn out of rock (Matt. 27:59). This new tomb was in a garden near the crucifixion site (vv. 41-42). After the body was placed in the tomb, the men sealed it with a large rolling stone (Matt. 27:60). Because both men had touched a corpse, they were ceremonially unclean for seven days and would not be able to participate in the feasts or any public affairs during that time interval (Lev. 21:11).

Matthew informs us that Mary Magdalene and Mary the mother of James the less had observed where Christ's body was placed and then came to the tomb Sunday morning with other women to properly prepare the body after the Sabbath had concluded (Matt. 27:61).

The Pharisees were concerned that Jesus' disciples would steal the body of Jesus to fake His resurrection. So, they asked Pilate to secure the tomb to ensure that this would not happen. Pilate granted their request and gave them a guard (likely four soldiers) to make the tomb as secure as they could (Matt. 27:65). The Jewish leaders went to the tomb where Christ's body was laid and put a seal on the rolling stone and ensured that the Roman guard was placed before the stone (Matt. 27:66).

John Chapter 20

Matthew informs us that Mary Magdalene, Mary the mother of James the less, and Salome, the mother of James and John, observed where the body of Christ was entombed. Now that the Sabbath had passed, they and other women were going to the tomb at the earliest possible moment to properly prepare the Lord's body for burial (Matt. 28:1). How these women were going to get past the Roman guard, open a tomb that had been officially sealed, and move the large rolling stone to gain access to the tomb is unknown; regardless, they came to show their love and respect for the Savior.

Matthew states that the Marys were en route to the tomb at the starting of dawn. Mark's account has three women (Salome is included with the Marys) arriving at the tomb near sunrise (Mark 16:1). John states that Mary Magdalene came to the tomb when it was yet dark (v. 1). Luke mentions at least five women that came early to the tomb that morning (Luke 24:10). Putting the accounts together, we have various women coming from various locations and arriving at the tomb early Sunday morning at various times. Some arrived while it was still dark, while others arrived at sunrise.

We then learn what happened just prior to the women arriving at Christ's tomb; an angel descended from heaven and rolled away the stone that sealed the tomb and then sat on it (Matt. 28:2). This feat was accompanied by, but not caused by, an earthquake. A great earthquake had occurred at Christ's death and now another announced His resurrection. The countenance of the angel was like lightning and his clothing as white as snow (Matt. 28:3). The guards were terrified at the angel's presence and fell to the ground like dead men (Matt. 28:4).

When the women arrived at the tomb, the angel spoke to them, saying, *"Do not be afraid, for I know that you seek Jesus who was crucified. He is not here; for He is risen, as He said. Come, see the place where the Lord lay"* (Matt. 28:5-6). As the women were coming forward to peer into the tomb, the angel instructed the women to go and inform the disciples that Christ had risen and would meet them in Galilee, as He had previously stated (Matt. 28:7). Matthew and Mark describe one angel speaking to the women, while Luke and John state that two angels were in the tomb. We may conclude that, indeed, there were two angels at the tomb, but only one served as the spokesman.

It is important to realize that each Gospel writer presents Christ from a different perspective. If all the writers gave the same story, same order, same details, we would immediately become suspicious that the records were the copies of a single account. But because some events are recorded in some Gospels and not others, we have proof of multiple accounts and not one story repeated. For example, only Matthew records Christ's first appearance to the women, while only Luke records the events transpiring on the Emmaus Road. Luke does not record Mary Magdalene's visit to the tomb. Only John and Luke record Christ's appearance in the upper room on resurrection day. Given all the information recorded in the Gospels, there is a reasonable construction of all that took place on resurrection morning without contradiction.

New Testament Scripture confirms at least ten separate post-resurrection appearances of Christ prior to His ascension. Five of these incidents occurred on the day of Christ's resurrection. None of the Gospel writers mention all of these appearances. The following is the likely order of Christ's post-resurrection appearances:

First, to Mary Magdalene after telling Peter and John that Christ had arisen and having returned to the tomb (John 20:11-18).

Second, to women returning from the tomb after they had heard the angel's declaration and instructions (28:8-10). These women had apparently departed the tomb after Mary Magdalene had left.

Third, to Peter to deal with his sin of denial privately and to restore him (Luke 24:34; 1 Cor. 15:5). Peter's sin would be publicly dealt with later (John 21).

Fourth, to the two disciples on the Emmaus Road (Luke 24:13-32). The Lord became known to them in the breaking of the bread.

Fifth, to ten of His disciples, plus others, who were together behind locked doors listening to the men who had walked with Christ on the Emmaus Road (Luke 24:36-43). Thomas was not present.

Sixth, to the disciples, with Thomas present (John 20:26-31).

Seventh, to seven disciples who had fished all night on the Sea of Galilee (John 21). The Lord cooked them breakfast.

Eighth, to the apostles and above 500 brethren (1 Cor. 15:6). It seems likely that this event coincides with Matthew's account but may refer to a separate post-resurrection experience, such as Christ's ascension (vv. 16-20).

Ninth, to Christ's half-brother James, which led to his conversion as well as of His other half-siblings (1 Cor. 15:7; Acts 1:14). The timing of this resurrection appearance is unknown.

Tenth, to the disciples and many other followers on Mount Olivet before ascending into Heaven forty days after His resurrection.

I went to a psychologist friend and said if 500 people claimed to see Jesus after he died, it was just a hallucination. He said hallucinations are an individual event. If 500 people have the same hallucination, that's a bigger miracle than the resurrection.

– Lee Strobel

Christ's Resurrection and Appearance to Mary (vv. 1-18)

Early Sunday morning, Mary Magdalene arrived at the tomb where she had observed Christ's body being placed just before the Sabbath (v. 1). After noticing that the rolling stone had been removed from the tomb's entrance, Mary ran to tell Peter and John (the beloved disciple) that the Lord's body had been removed from the tomb. Mary also said, *"We do not know where they have laid Him"* (v. 2). The "we" indicates that there were likely other women who had arrived at the tomb, before Mary had departed to inform the disciples of the news.

After hearing Mary's observation, Peter and John ran to the tomb, but John arrived ahead of Peter to find that indeed the stone had been rolled away from the entrance and the tomb no longer contained a corpse (vv. 3-4). Looking through the doorway, John observed that the body of Christ was gone, but that the linens that had wrapped His body were still in the tomb (v. 5). After Peter arrived, he went directly into the tomb and discovered that the head wrap had been folded and was lying in a different location than the linens used to wrap the Lord's body (vv. 6-7). John then entered the tomb and seeing the scene "believed," meaning that he *understood* that both Christ and Scripture had foretold that *"He must rise again from the dead"* (vv. 8-9). Afterwards both men returned to where they were lodging during the feast (v. 10).

John

After informing Peter and John that the tomb was empty, Mary returned to the tomb after Peter and John had departed (the other women had also departed the garden area). While weeping she stooped down and looked into the tomb and saw two angels in white array sitting at either end of where Christ's body had been laid (vv. 11-12). Apparently, Mary had departed the tomb before the angels had appeared to a larger group of women at the tomb (Matt. 28:5).

The angels asked Mary why she was weeping, and she told them *"because they have taken away my Lord, and I do not know where they have laid Him"* (v. 13). F. B. Hole suggests that the conduct of Mary stands out in bright contrast to all the rest who had visited the tomb:

> The two disciples had left for their home convinced that the body of Jesus was not there. Mary was equally convinced but she left her home to linger at the sepulcher, weeping in her sense of utter desolation. They knew the Lord as One who had called them from boats and nets. She knew Him as One who had delivered her from the grip of seven demons. It had been a mighty deliverance and she loved much. To her two angels appeared and there is no record of her having been afraid of their presence. This is remarkable since in the other Gospels fear is mentioned in connection with each appearance. Her case evidently illustrates how an overpowering affection can drive out of the heart every other emotion.[108]

At that moment that Mary spoke to the angels, the Lord appeared behind her, but she did not recognize Him when she turned towards Him (v. 14). While her vision may have been impaired by swollen eyes full of tears and although she was not looking directly at the person speaking to her (v. 16), it seems most likely that she did not recognize the Lord because she was not expecting Him to be alive. In fact, she was still trying to locate His body.

The Lord spoke to Mary and asked her why she was weeping and for whom she was looking (v. 15). As the tomb was in a garden, she supposed that the man speaking to her was the gardener. She then pleaded with the supposed gardener that if he had removed the body from the tomb, to tell her where it had been placed and she would take it away. Instead of reproving her inadequate faith in what He had previously taught her about His resurrection, the Lord chose to speak to her heart as the Good Shepherd. The Lord called her by name, "Mary," and she immediately recognized His voice, for true sheep know and respond to the voice of the true Shepherd (John 10:3-4). Mary turned and greeted the Lord Jesus, "Rabboni" ("Teacher") and embraced Him (v. 16).

Why did the Lord appear to Mary Magdalene first, rather than His disciples? Scripture does not tell us, but the Lord said that those who have been forgiven much, love much (Luke 7:47). The Lord had driven seven demons from her (Luke 8:2). We are not informed of what wickedness Mary may have engaged in while demon-possessed, but regardless, Christ forgave her sins. Accordingly, Mary loved the Lord much and had served Him faithfully since her conversion. Mary is the only woman mentioned in all four Gospels that witnessed the crucifixion and the resurrection of Christ.

The Lord told Mary not to cling to Him as He must shortly ascend to His Father. He told her to tell *"My brethren"* (speaking of the disciples) that *"I am ascending to My Father and your Father, and to My God and your God"* (v. 17). The language here is precise and indicates that a new relationship between God and men had been secured by Christ's propitiation at Calvary.

First, He does not say, "go to My disciples," but rather, "go to My brethren." Hebrews 2:11 affirms how this intimate oneness was obtained, *"For both He who sanctifies* [Christ] *and those who are being sanctified* [believers in Christ] *are all of one, for which reason He is not ashamed to call them brethren."*

Second, both times the word "your" appears in verse 17 it is plural in number. The Lord did not say that He was going merely to His Father and His God, but that now all those who believed in Him were one with Him and could have intimate fellowship with God the Father also. Mary obeyed the Lord and immediately came to the disciples and informed them of what she had seen at the tomb: The Lord Jesus was alive (v. 18)!

Christ Appears to Disciples Minus Thomas (vv. 19-23)

On Sunday evening, the disciples, except Thomas, were together behind locked doors for fear of the Jews when the Lord Jesus suddenly stood before them (v. 19). Although they had heard Mary's testimony that the Lord was alive, there can be little doubt that they were startled by His abrupt appearance. They had witnessed His brutal death and burial and now He was standing before them alive. To ease their anxiety, the Lord said to them, *"Peace be with you."* After the Lord showed them the wounds in His hands and side (the wounds in His feet would have

John

been visible already), the disciples were filled with joy (v. 20). Truly their Master had risen from the tomb, just as He said that He would. Through His finished work at Calvary, the disciples could enjoy oneness with God, for God was now at peace with them.

But the Lord did not end the conversation with this realization. He again said to them, *"peace to you"* (v. 21). Why did the Lord tell His disciples *"peace be to you"* twice? What followed the Lord's second declaration answers this question. Just *"as the Father has sent Me, I also send you"* into the world so that more lost souls might be reconciled with God. The Lord was sending His disciples into the world with the same message of peace that He brought from Heaven. However, enjoying relational oneness with God through grace is not sufficient to convey this message to the world. His disciples would need a continuing work of grace in their hearts and minds to have God's peace while they conveyed His message of peace. The Lord knew that His apostles needed to have peace within before they could outwardly convey a message of peace.

The Lord then breathed on them, and they received the Holy Spirit (v. 22). This ministry of the Holy Spirit seems to have equipped the disciples with understanding of Scripture (Luke 24:45) and of their apostolic ministry. The disciples now had the authority to tell those who received their message of peace by faith that their sins were forgiven (v. 23). Likewise, those rejecting their message would remain dead in trespasses and sins (John 3:18). The disciples would experience spiritual regeneration, baptism, sealing, anointing, earnest, indwelling, and cleansing of the Holy Spirit fifty days later at the feast of Pentecost. They would receive spiritual gifts to enable them to fulfill their divine calling at that time also.

The disciples had gathered on resurrection day (Sunday) with the world shut out. Then the Lord Jesus had come into their gathering. It is the beautiful anticipative picture of *the local assembly* in the Church Age where the Lord promises to be in the midst whenever two or three believers are gathered in His name (Matt. 18:20). But Thomas was not present, and he missed out on the blessing that the Lord had for His people. Let it not happen to you, dear believer!

Christ Appears to Disciples Including Thomas (vv. 24-29)

Because Thomas, also called "the Twin," was not gathered with the disciples on the day of Christ's resurrection, he did not see or talk with

The Man and Your God

the Lord (v. 24). Thomas was reluctant to believe the testimony of his brethren; he wanted to see and feel the living Savior for himself (v. 25). Eight days later, the disciples with Thomas present were again gathered behind locked doors. The Lord suddenly appeared before them and again greeted them, *"Peace to you"* (v. 26). The Lord then afforded Thomas the opportunity to feel the nail prints in His hands and the wound in His side caused by the spear (v. 27). He also challenged Thomas, *"Do not be unbelieving, but believing."*

Thomas wasted no time in declaring what he then knew to be truth: *"My Lord and my God!"* (v. 28). It was a profound declaration, but the Lord responded to it by admonishing His disciple: *"Thomas, because you have seen Me, you have believed. Blessed are those who have not seen and yet have believed"* (v. 29). In other words, blessed are those who read God's Word and believe that Jesus Christ is Lord and God. The testimony of Scripture clearly declares this truth and we must believe it:

- Paul identified Jesus Christ as our Great God and Savior (Tit. 2:13).
- Paul and James stated that the Lord Jesus is the Lord of Glory (1 Cor. 2:8; Jas. 2:1).
- Referring to Christ, John and Paul said that God was made manifest in the flesh (John 1:14, 18; 1 Tim. 3:16).
- The Lord Jesus said that He was the divine Shepherd who was smitten of God (Zech. 13:7; Matt. 26:31).
- Isaiah proclaimed that the Savior to be born was the Almighty: the everlasting God (Isa. 9:6-7).
- The apostles preached that Jesus Christ was the Son of God (Acts 9:20).
- Paul taught that God was in Christ reconciling the world (2 Cor. 5:19).
- The Lord Jesus forgave sins and only God has the right to do that (Isa. 42:24; Mark 2:5-7; Luke 7:48-50, 5:18-26).
- God and the Lamb are one in divine glory and are worshiped by all (Rev. 7:17, 15:4, 21:23).
- The demons recognized Jesus as God and feared Him (Luke 4:24, 4:41, 8:28).
- The Lord Jesus is the wisdom of God (Matt. 23:24; Luke 11:49).
- The Lord Jesus knows the thoughts of men (John 6:64).
- Speaking of Christ, Paul states that *"in Him dwells the fullness of the Godhead bodily"* (Col. 2:9).

The Lord Jesus Christ is the eternal Son of God in whom all the fullness of God dwells bodily. His divinity is recognized throughout Scripture. Blessed are you if you believe He is Lord and God.

The Purpose of John's Gospel (vv. 30-31)

What is the main aspiration of the gospel message? John affords a vital summary: *"And truly Jesus did many other signs in the presence of His disciples, which are not written in this book; but these are written **that you may believe that Jesus is the Christ**, the Son of God, and **that believing you may have life in His name**"* (vv. 30-31). Did you notice the two "believes" in this passage? In the Greek language, the first verb "believe" is in the "aorist" tense, while the second verb is in the "present" tense. John wrote his record of Christ for two reasons. First, that we might believe, speaking of a unique action in the past, which has a continuing effect – this relates to trusting the gospel message for salvation and being regenerated. After receiving eternal life, the second "believe" becomes most important. This believing should be continuous and progressing in maturity such that the believer displays and enjoys the life of Christ more and more and, no less, learns to love the Lord more and more.

Many Christians today are retaining doctrinal purity, maintaining a blameless life, and serving the Church continuously, yet they lack a deep devotion to Christ. The Church today must heed the same warning that Christ issued to the church at Ephesus: *"Nevertheless I have this against you, that you have left your first love. Remember therefore from where you have fallen; repent and do the first works, or else I will come to you quickly and remove your lampstand from its place – unless you repent"* (Rev. 2:4-5). The Lord does not want just followers; He wants disciples that will die to self and live for Him. Orthodoxy and ministry are not enough; Christ demands the believer's heart, as well as his or her mind, hands, and feet. Those believers who deny Christ as their first love will ultimately lose their testimony for Him. Our deficient love for Him hinders us from experiencing His abundant life!

John could have written much more about the life of the Lord Jesus, but what the Spirit of God inspired John to write is sufficient to lead anyone to saving faith, which will be evidenced by a living faith. Faith, if it does not have good works, is not true faith (Jas. 2:17). But faith that expresses the life of Christ in deed will draw others to Him (13:35).

John Chapter 21

Christ Serves His Disciples at the Sea of Galilee (vv. 1-14)

The Bible records five eyewitness accounts of seeing Jesus Christ on resurrection day and then at least five more over the next forty days before His ascension back to Heaven (Acts 1). Paul states that at least 500 people saw Him on one of these occurrences, perhaps in Galilee (1 Cor. 15:6). John closes his gospel account by reporting a post-resurrection encounter of the Lord with seven of His disciples at the Sea of Galilee (also called the Sea of Tiberias; v. 1). The events recorded in this chapter are not mentioned by Matthew, Mark, or Luke.

Simon Peter, Thomas, Nathanael, brothers James and John, and two other disciples were together at the Sea of Galilee (v. 2). Peter said that he was going fishing and the other disciples decided to go with him (v. 3). They fished all night but caught nothing. As this situation had happened before (Luke 5:5), perhaps Peter was wondering if the Lord would appear and again remedy the shortfall. Peter had been fishing on this very shoreline over three years earlier when the Lord first called him to be a disciple (Matt. 4:18-19).

Ironically, the Lord Jesus was on the shore waiting for His disciples to return from their fishing excursion; yet, the disciples did not recognize Him when He asked them if they had anything to eat. They replied "no" (v. 5). This meant that they had not caught any fish. The Lord said to them, *"Cast the net on the right side of the boat, and you will find some"* (v. 6). Perhaps the disciples thought they had nothing to lose by casting once more, so they obeyed the counsel of the one speaking to them, and they caught so many fish that they could not pull the net into the boat.

Peter, James, and John had witnessed another spectacular catch of fish after the Lord had commanded Peter to put down his nets for a catch (Luke 5:5-10). John was first to reason out the correct conclusion, *"It is the Lord"* (v. 7). When Peter heard John's statement, he put on his outer garment (for he had removed it while laboring) and plunged into the sea to reach the shore quickly. As they were only about 100 yards from shore, the other disciples remained in the boat and dragged the net full of fish along the side of the boat to the shoreline (v. 8).

The Lord knew that His disciples would be hungry and weary, so He had bread and fish cooking on a fire of coals for them (v. 9). The Lord then instructed the disciples to bring some of the fish that they had caught to add to what He had already prepared (v. 10). Peter went back to the boat and dragged the net full of fish to land. He was amazed that although there were 153 large fish in the net, the net did not break (v. 11).

There has been much speculation as to what the number 153 might symbolize, but as the text states that the fish caught were large, it seems likely that the number and size of fish are mentioned to authenticate the miracle (as the net did not break despite the large catch). What the Lord gives to those He loves often confounds natural law and cannot be lost.

The Lord Jesus demonstrates several wonderful applications concerning how to properly serve and encourage others in this text. First, He anticipated the needs of others and chose to satisfy them. Second, He provided an ample supply of what was needed to ensure that everyone would be completely satisfied. Third, the Lord said to His disciples, *"bring some of the fish which you have just caught"* (v. 10), so that, although He had supplied the fish for their net, the disciples were made to think that they had also contributed to the communal breakfast. Saints working together and sharing and serving each other is a mutual blessing – this outcome is better than just receiving service from another. Fourth, although Peter's previous denials of Christ needed to be confronted publicly, the Lord cared for his physical needs before addressing his spiritual failure. Fifth, the Lord of glory humbled Himself to clean fish, cook breakfast, and then He served the disciples as they ate (v. 13). The Lord desires all believers to likewise serve each other (13:15-16, 35).

When they were in the boat, they did not recognize the Lord, but when He called them to eat breakfast, they all knew who He was (v. 12). This was the third time that the Lord had appeared to His disciples since His resurrection. The first occurrence was on resurrection day and the second was eight days later. On both occasions the disciples were covertly gathered behind locked doors for fear of the Jews.

Christ Speaks to Simon Peter (vv. 15-25)

Christ had met with Peter privately on resurrection day to restore him after he had denied Him (Luke 24:34). However, as Peter's denials were of a public nature, his sin must be publicly rebuked. This is a good pattern to follow in dealing with sinning believers in the local assembly also. First, seek confession of sin and repentance privately, then the offender should seek to repair the damage that his or her sin caused to those affected by it. It is noted that Matthew, Mark, and Luke mostly refer to Peter as "Simon" in their gospel accounts, while John normally refers to him as "Simon Peter" or just "Peter."

After breakfast was over, the Lord asked Peter, *"Simon, son of Jonah, do you love Me more than these?"* (v. 15). Peter responded, *"Yes, Lord; You know that I love You."* The Lord then said, *"Feed My lambs."* The Lord again asked Peter, *"Simon, son of Jonah, do you love Me?"* (v. 16). Peter again affirmed that he did, and the Lord then told him, *"Tend My sheep."* Then the Lord repeated the same question to Peter a third time, which grieved Peter's heart (v. 17). Afterwards Peter said, *"Lord, You know all things; You know that I love You."* The Lord Jesus then said to him, *"Feed My Sheep."*

Earlier, John presented Christ as the "Good Shepherd" who lays His life down for the sheep (10:7-18). His sacrificial love for the sheep stands in sharp contrast to the hireling shepherds of Israel, who led God's sheep astray, neglected their care, and then deserted them in times of danger; these would be judged accordingly (see Ezek. 34).

Those who have been charged with the care of God's sheep must attend to His flock. Peter is now called to be one of many shepherds (church elders) of God's sheep (1 Pet. 5:1-2), and although he could only be martyred once for the Lord, he would die a hundred times in caring for God's sheep. Three times, in one fashion or another, the Lord Jesus asked Peter, *"Do you love Me?"* Peter affirmed a friendship kind of love (*phileo*) for the Lord each time the Lord questioned him. However, the Lord had asked on the first two occasions if Peter had the deepest kind of affection for Him, that is, sacrificial love (*agapao*). For whatever reason, Peter did not affirm that he had that kind of love for Christ, so on the third question the Lord asked Peter if he had a friendship type of regard for Him. After affirming this kind of affection for the Lord, the Lord implied that Peter should prove his love by feeding the Lord's lambs, tending His sheep, and feeding His sheep. Likewise, let all those who have a portion of the Lord's flock to care for prove their love to the Lord Jesus by tending His sheep (1 Pet. 5:3).

Sheep stink, they wander, they kick, they bite, and they glare, but they are still the Lord's sheep. He loves His sheep and we should love all those that Christ has redeemed by His blood. It is quite problematic to care for the Lord's sheep unless you are in love with the Good Shepherd. Only love for Christ can make this arduous task bearable.

Next, the Lord informed Peter that though he had his freedom to serve Him presently, there would come a day that he would be bound (arrested; v. 18) and be lifted up and carried away against his will (speaking of his crucifixion; v. 19). The Lord was telling Peter that if he followed Him, he would be martyred for Him. At the end of his life, Peter recalled what the Lord had told him years earlier about his forthcoming martyrdom to "stir up" his audience to live for Christ now while there was an opportunity to do so (1 Pet. 1:13-14). Church history records that Peter was hung upside down on a cross in 66 or 67 A.D.; he was put to death by Emperor Nero.

A few days before their seashore breakfast, Peter had feared death and regrettably denied the Lord. The Lord was telling Peter to settle the death question now or he would not be able to properly follow or serve Him in the future. Previously, the Lord Jesus put the matter this way: *"If anyone desires to come after Me, let him deny himself, and take up his cross daily, and follow Me. For whoever desires to save his life will lose it, but whoever loses his life for My sake will save it"* (Luke 9:23-24).

Certainly, being told how he was going to die must have been a shock to Peter. But rather than saying, "Lord, Your will be done," Peter turned around and seeing John (i.e., the beloved disciple, who while leaning on the Lord's breast, asked Him about His betrayer) inquired how he was going to die (vv. 20-21). The Lord admonished Peter that John's future service to Him should be no concern of his: *"If I will that he remain till I come, what is that to you? You follow Me"* (v. 22). John was quick to clarify the Lord's statement as some had the notion that John would remain alive until Christ's second coming, but that was not what He said (v. 23). Rather, the Lord was exhorting Peter to live for Him now and not be distracted by how He had determined to use others to build His Church. True disciples follow Christ no matter what others do!

The Lord Jesus exhibited tremendous patience in calling His disciples. Initially, He invited two of John's disciples, including Andrew (Peter's brother), to His home to spend some time with Him, but at the end of the day they departed (1:39). Andrew then told Peter that he had found the Messiah, but Peter did not come to Christ on his own. The Lord had to repeatedly call Peter to follow Him, but after each time, Peter dedicated more of himself to Christ.

The Man and Your God

First, Peter forsook his fishing nets to follow Christ at His bidding in Mark 1:18. Later, Peter forsook all to pursue the Savior (Luke 5:11). After Christ's resurrection, the Lord again called Peter to follow Him with the understanding that it would cost Peter his life (vv. 15-19). A few days earlier Peter had vehemently denied the Lord to protect himself from harm, but it is at this juncture that Peter settled "the death question" once and for all. He had learned that it was harder to live daily for the Lord than to die for Him once. In Acts 2 we do not see a shrinking, denying Peter, but a fully restored, Spirit-filled apostle preaching Christ to the saving of 3,000 souls. The Lord's patience with Peter is an encouragement to all those who are involved in training others. Those who mentor younger believers must be patient and tender.

The apostle John posed a notable hyperbole at the conclusion of his gospel account. He could have written much more about the Lord's ministry but realized that all the books in the world could not adequately proclaim His teachings, feats, or moral excellence (vv. 24-25). John had wonderfully revealed the splendor of the Lord's deity throughout his record. In closing, it seemed only fitting to say that the One who was so much bigger than the world obviously had done and could do much more than the world could ever be aware of, let alone understand.

Paul expresses a similar truth in his epistle to the Ephesians: *"That in the ages to come He might show the exceeding riches of His grace in His kindness toward us in Christ Jesus"* (Eph. 2:7). The implication is that believers will need all of eternity to fully comprehend the grace of God shown to us in Christ! This means that there is so much more of the Savior to learn than what has been already revealed to us in God's Word about Him. Indeed, there is much more truth to come, but we simply cannot comprehend it now in our present situation; however, we are to learn what we can of Him now. This is possible by meditating on what God has revealed about Christ in Scripture and what the Holy Spirit reveals of Him to us through obedience and experience.

Moses said long ago: *"The secret things belong to the Lord our God, but those things which are revealed belong to us and to our children forever, that we may do all the words of this law"* (Deut. 29:29). There is much about the Lord that has not yet been revealed to us, but we are not responsible to understand such mysteries. We are, however, to value what God has and is showing us of Christ now. Our spiritual appetite should be to know more of Him and obey what we know to be true. For those who do, Christ promises to manifest Himself to them (14:21).

Endnotes

1. Andrew Jukes, *Four Views of Christ* (Kregel Publications, Grand Rapids, MI; 1966), p. 21
2. William Kelly, *Introductory Lectures NT Vol. The Gospels* (Believers Book Shelf, Sunbury PA; 1970 reprint), p. 143
3. David Gooding, *According to Luke* (Gospel Folio Press, Port Colborne, ON; 1987), p. 9
4. Alanna Nobbs, "What Do Ancient Historians Make of the New Testament" (*TB*, 57.2; 2006), p. 189
5. J. N. Darby, *The Holy Scriptures: A New Translation From the Original Languages* (Logos Research Systems, Oak Harbor; 1996), electronic copy – 1 Timothy 3:16
6. Edythe Draper, *Draper's Quotations From the Christian World* (Tyndale House Publishers Inc., Wheaton, IL – electronic copy), J. B. Phillips
7. William MacDonald, *Believer's Bible Commentary* (Thomas Nelson Publishers, Nashville, TN; 1989), p. 1370
8. Norman Crawford, *What the Bible Teaches: Luke* (John Ritchie Ltd., 2000), p 25
9. Ibid., pp. 30-31
10. Warren W. Wiersbe, *The Bible Exposition Commentary*, Vol. 1 (Victor Books, Wheaton, IL; 1996), p. 174
11. Ibid., p. 175
12. Josephus (*Antiquities* XVIII, 26 [ii.1])
13. Daryl E. Witmer, "When Did the Luke 2 Census Occur?" (Christiananswers.net; 2002): https://christiananswers.net/q-aiia/census-luke2.html
14. William M. Ramsay, *The Bearing of Recent Discovery on the Trustworthiness of the New Testament* (Hodder and Stoughton, London; 1915), pp. 292-300
15. Alexander Hislop, *The Two Babylons* (Loizeaux Brothers, Neptune, NJ; 2nd ed. - 1959), pp. 93-94
16. Edwin Blum, *The Bible Knowledge Commentary* by Dallas Seminary (Victor Books, Wheaton, IL; 1983), p. 335
17. William MacDonald, op. cit., p. 1377
18. C. H. Spurgeon, C. H.: *Morning and Evening: Daily Readings* (Logos Research Systems, Inc., Oak Harbor, WA; 1995), December 26 AM
19. F. B. Hole, *Matthew* (STEM Publishing); chp. 4: https://stempublishing.com/authors/hole/NT/MATTHEW.html
20. Arthur Pink, op. cit., pp. 109-110
21. A. C. Gaebelein, *The Gospel of Matthew* (Loizeaux Bros., NY; 1910), p. 420
22. Norman Crawford, op. cit., p. 119
23. William MacDonald, op. cit., p. 1394
24. William MacDonald, op. cit., p. 1233

25. Warren W. Wiersbe, *The Bible Exposition Commentary*, Vol. 1 (Victor Books, Wheaton, IL; 1996), p. 37
26. Josephus (*Antiquities* 17. 10. 10 [17. 295-298]; 20. 5. 2 [20. 100-104]; 13. 14. 2 [379-383])
27. Josephus (*Jewish Wars* 5.449–51)
28. William MacDonald, op. cit. p. 1403
29. F. B. Hole, *Luke*, (STEM Publishing); chp. 9: https://www.stempublishing.com/authors/hole/NT/LUKE.html#a9
30. F. B. Hole, op. cit., chp. 10
31. Edythe Draper, *Draper's Quotations From the Christian World* (Tyndale House Publishers Inc., Wheaton, IL – electronic copy)
32. William MacDonald, op. cit., p. 1252
33. F. B. Hole, op. cit., chp. 11
34. William MacDonald, op. cit. p. 1418
35. Warren Wiersbe, op. cit., p. 46
36. Warren Wiersbe, op. cit., p. 46
37. William MacDonald, op. cit., p. 1427
38. William Kelly, *Luke – Introductory Lectures*, (STEM Publishing); chp. 17: https://www.stempublishing.com/authors/kelly/2Newtest/LUKE_PT2.html#a17
39. William MacDonald, op. cit., p. 1434
40. Louis A. Barbieri, Jr., op. cit., p. 79
41. F. B. Hole, op. cit., chp. 18
42. Norman Crawford, op. cit., p. 289
43. Norman Crawford, op. cit., p. 316
44. F. B. Hole, op. cit., chp. 20
45. William Kelly, op. cit., chp. 22
46. F. B. Hole, op. cit., chp. 22
47. Talmud: Babba B. 97b (lines 11 and 12 from top)
48. Warren Wiersbe, op. cit., p. 269
49. William MacDonald, op. cit., p. 1451
50. Edwin Blum, *The Bible Knowledge Commentary* by Dallas Seminary (Victor Books, Wheaton, IL; 1983), p. 335
51. Mishnah (Sanhedrin 4.1)%
52. F. B. Hole, op. cit., Matt. 26
53. *Ecclesiastical History*, Book 4, chp. 15
54. John Heading, op. cit., p. 393
55. David W. Bercot, A Dictionary of Early Christians Beliefs (Hendrickson Pub., Peabody, MA; 1998), p. 381
56. Ibid.
57. Dr. Howard Taylor, *Spiritual Secret of Hudson Taylor* (Whitaker House, New Kensington, PA; 1996), p. 368
58. Samuel Ridout, *The Serious Christian* (Books for Christians, Charlotte, NC; no date), p. 171
59. August Van Ryn, *Meditations in John* (Walterick Pub., Kansas, City, KS; 1995), p. 67
60. Edythe Draper, op. cit., quoting Thomas A. Kempis

Endnotes

61 Albert Barnes, op. cit., pp. 273-274
62 Andrew Jukes, op. cit., p. 107
63 F. B. Hole, *John* (STEM Publishing); John 1
https://stempublishing.com/authors/hole/NT/JOHN.html
64 John Heading, *What the Bible Teaches: John* (John Ritchie Ltd., 2000), p. 18
65 Edwin A. Blum, op. cit., p. 273
66 Harold S. Paisley, *What the Bible Teaches: Matthew and Mark* (John Ritchie, 2000), p. 526
67 Edwin A. Blum, op. cit., p. 274
68 John Heading, op. cit., p. 56
69 L. M. Grant, John (STEM Publishing); John 3
https://stempublishing.com/authors/grantlm/JOHN.html
70 F. B. Hole, op. cit., John 3
71 C. A. Coates, *C. A. Coates Commentary – Numbers* (Kingston Bible Trust, West Sussex, UK), Num. 21
72 L. M. Grant, op. cit., John 5
73 John Heading, op. cit., p. 86
74 August Van Ryn, op. cit., p. 32
75 William Kelly, *An Exposition of the Gospel of John* (STEM Publishing); John 6
https://stempublishing.com/authors/kelly/2Newtest/John_pt1.html#a6
76 Warren Wiersbe, op cit., p. 312
77 John Phillips, *The John Phillips Commentary Series: John* (Kregel Pub., Grand Rapids, MI; 1989), p. 129
78 Oswald Chambers, message entitled *Gateway to Heaven*
79 F. B. Hole, op. cit., John 7
80 Edwin A. Blum, op. cit., p. 301
81 J. G. Bellett, *On the Gospel of John* (STEM Publishing); John 7
https://stempublishing.com/authors/bellett/evang1.html#a2
82 Edwin A. Blum, op. cit., p. 303
83 August Van Ryn, op. cit., p. 33
84 J. H. Thayer, *Thayer's Greek Lexicon* (Biblesoft; 2000), electronic database
85 James Strong, *New Exhaustive Strong's Numbers and Concordance With Expanded Greek-Hebrew Dictionary* (Biblesoft and International Bible Translators, Inc.; 1994)
86 Albert Barnes, *Barnes' Notes – The Gospels* (Baker Book House, Grand Rapids, MI; 1884 reprint), p. 293
87 John Heading, op. cit., p. 193
88 F. B. Hole, op. cit., John 12
89 William Kelly, op. cit., John 12
90 William MacDonald, op. cit., p. 1541
91 L. M. Grant, op. cit., John 13
92 A. W. Tozer, *Knowledge of the Holy* (Send the Light Trust; 1976), ch. 1
93 Charles Finney, *The Use and Prevalence of Christ's Name* (from *Lectures on the Conditions of Prevailing Prayer*) (Oberlin College; 1850 – copyright by Gospel Truth Ministries)
94 William MacDonald, op. cit., p. 1550

May We See Christ?

95 John Heading, op. cit., pp. 252-253
96 F. B. Hole, op. cit., John 17
97 A. W. Tozer, from Edythe Draper, *Draper's Quotations From the Christian World* (Tyndale House Publishers Inc., Wheaton, IL)
98 William G. Moorehead, *The Fundamentals of Christianity: The Moral Glory of Jesus Christ* (Biblesoft, Electronic Database, 1997)
99 Hillel Geva, *"Jerusalem's Population in Antiquity: A Minimalist View"* (Tel Aviv, 42:2; 2013), pp. 131-160
100 John Wilkinson, *"Ancient Jerusalem, Its Water Supply and Population"* (PEFQS 106; 1974), pp. 33–51
101 Magen Broshi, *"Estimating the Population of Ancient Jerusalem"* (BAR 4:02; June 1978)
102 Edwin Blum, op. cit., p. 335
103 Mishnah (Sanhedrin 4.1)%
104 William MacDonald, op. cit., p. 1561
105 F. B. Hole, op. cit., John 18
106 *Ecclesiastical History*, Book 4, chp. 15
107 John Heading, op. cit., p. 393
108 F. B. Hole, op. cit., John 20

www.ingramcontent.com/pod-product-compliance
Lightning Source LLC
Chambersburg PA
CBHW060103170426
43198CB00010B/753